KU-317-080

FRENCH REGIONAL COOKING

JEAN FERNIOT

FRENCH REGIONAL COOKING

Vineyards and Wines of France
by Jacques Puisais

CRESCENT BOOKS
New York

The publisher thanks Mrs Paule Meunier for her invaluable help

Translated by Sara Harris

Art Director: Giorgio Seppi
Production: Asterisco s.r.l., Milan

This 1991 edition published by CRESCENT BOOKS, distributed by Outlet Book Company, Inc., a Random House Company, 225 Park Avenue South, New York, New York 10003

ISBN 0-517-06145-7

8 7 6 5 4 3 2 1

Typeset in Great Britain by Tradespools Ltd, Frome, Somerset
Printed and bound in Spain
D.L.TO:1282-1991

Contents

*One of the main objectives of France's International Gastronomic Academy (*Académie Internationale de la Gastronomie*) is to safeguard the precious legacy of French national and regional culinary traditions and keep them alive at a time when there is a general tendency toward uniformity of taste, a trend which in time could threaten the country's gastronomic standards.*

Jean Ferniot has followed in the footsteps of his great predecessor, Curnonsky, visiting every region of France to sample its products, cooking, and wines. The regional recipes in this book have been collected from local cooks who share his lifelong fascination for the French regional culinary heritage and his delight in good food and gastronomic scholarship.

The author is well known in France both as a political journalist and as a literary figure. He is also a popular and enthusiastic writer on everything to do with good food. In common with a great many of France's amateur cooks, he sets out to achieve professional standards when preparing meals and is a fervent believer in the importance of taking a great deal of trouble when shopping for food to ensure that all the ingredients meet his exacting standards, particularly important when cooking these regional recipes. Most French cooks firmly believe that only the freshest, prime-quality products should be used if the end result is to fulfill all their expectations. As a token of the esteem in which Jean Ferniot is held in gastronomic circles, seventy of France's most famous chefs held a dinner in Paris to celebrate his seventieth birthday. Each chef chose a dish to prepare in front of the guests who then sampled the best that their celebrated confrères *could offer, a selection of the choicest items from their menus. On a more modest scale, the recipes in this collection have been kept as straightforward as possible, enabling the home cook to enjoy trying out dishes from the length and breadth of France.*

Many of these dishes can be further enhanced by choosing a suitable wine, beer or cider, depending on the region, that will complement the food to best advantage. The wine section of this book has been compiled by one of France's foremost wine experts, Jacques Puisais, President of the professional association of oenologists. He is also Vice-President of the French Academy of Wine. The different wine-producing regions are covered, their growing conditions and historical importance in the wine industry, with concise descriptions of the most outstanding wines, guidance as to the temperatures at which they should be drunk and some of the dishes with which they go particularly well.

You may be lucky enough to find a good many of the wines Jacques Puisais has selected; as he points out, a glass of wine embodies the countryside where the grape varietal is ideally suited to local conditions. Besides the general climate and the soil, it will mirror that year's weather and, of course, much skilled work and patient care. Many, though not all, of these wines are exported, but whether you track down the exact wine that the locals would drink with your chosen recipe, or prefer to be inspired by its description and substitute another with similar characteristics, you can have the satisfaction of knowing that you are enjoying your own interpretation of the best France has to offer.

Jean Ferniot points out in his introduction to the recipes that it is the home cooks who have created and developed the regional cooking of France. Over the centuries they learned how to exploit the local produce to its best possible advantage so that they could provide delicious and nourishing meals. France has been lucky in its widely varying soils, growing conditions and climate and it is hardly surprising that her regional cookery is so rich and diverse, changing constantly as the traveler heads south from the cool, moist apple orchards and rich dairy pastures of Normandy, growing gradually warmer (with the exception of such upland areas as the Massif Central and the mountainous regions of the Alps in the east and the Pyrenees in the west), toward the sun-baked Mediterranean hinterland where the olive trees grow in their thousands. Regional cuisines developed in very distinct ways during the days before transport was easy, when ordinary people seldom traveled far from their native province, causing customs, tastes and traditions to vary widely, so that the difference beween one part of France and another was equivalent to a visit to another continent.

What the local people chose to drink with their meals was also determined by the geography and climate of their region: in Brittany and Normandy, for example, this would often be cider; toward the Belgian and German borders in the east more beer was produced and drunk, while the great vineyards have historically been in the slightly warmer latitudes mainly in the center and west of the country, where soil conditions and rainfall are ideal for producing fine wines.

Anyone who enjoys good food and aims to eat a well balanced, healthy diet can enjoy keeping traditional French country cooking alive by trying out some of the recipes that have been handed down from one generation to another. The home cook is one of the staunchest and most valuable defenders of diversity and choice in what we eat, a valuable ally in resisting the bland, processed and sometimes harmful foods that some manufacturers seek to foist on the public. It is well worth fighting the good fight against the tyranny of the mass market, refusing to accept the dreadful sameness that threatens to engulf food retailing in the so-called developed countries of the world. Choice is being whittled away wherever and whenever the giants of the food and agriculture industries can get away with it: before World War II the French could choose between 20 different varieties of potatoes, some of which were uniquely well suited to the preparation of certain dishes; nowadays the big producers have ensured regular access to only a handful of different types. The same is true of pears and apples, and many other basic foodstuffs. Our "bank" or reserve of species is endangered in this, as in other areas. Admittedly the agronomists are doing their best to develop disease-resistant strains of plants and breeds of animals but this does not excuse neglect or suppression of the best of the old varieties and profit should not be the main criterion.

We shall be the poorer if we do not make sure that we preserve the almost infinite variety of tastes and aromas our forebears have handed down to us, even if this means we have to pay a little more for our food on occasion.

There is, however, no need to become too depressed at these threats to some of the world's best food. There has been an enormous growth in interest and knowledge when it comes to growing, marketing, preparing, and eating excellent, lovingly cooked raw materials. In France, as elsewhere in the world, the total number of cookery books sold is at an all time high, and magazines devoted to food and wine are increasing their circulation while the cooks' columns in the newspapers remain firm favorites. Cookery programs on T.V. attract huge and growing audiences who are inspired to take a real interest in what they eat and how they cook it.

Both Jean Ferniot and Jacques Puisais have each written several successful books on food and wine before this joint venture and while such enthusiastic and knowledgeable gourmets are willing to guide us through the landscapes of France's regional cuisine, traditional French cooking is in safe hands.

Michel Genin
President and Founder
Académie Internationale de la Gastronomie

Note
Preparation and cooking times given are approximate.
An asterisk after the recipe title indicates that the recipe is illustrated.

On pages 10–11: *The village of Santenay in Burgundy.*

INTRODUCTION

For many hundreds of years French cooking developed two parallel traditions: one was aristocratic, the cuisine of the court which was first inspired by Italian influence in the sixteenth century during the reigns of the Valois monarchs. The other can be called the native, rural tradition.

This rural tradition is the one that mainly concerns us in this book, for it gave birth to most of the regional cooking of France. And it was created by the women of France, whereas at court the cooks were men, the *officiers de bouche* and chefs who served the kings and courtiers of the *Ancien Régime*. Although the 1789 Revolution supposedly swept away such elitism and magnificence for ever, court life was to return for a while under a different guise during the Napoleonic era and the Orleans monarchy and its culinary legacy has survived in a modified form, known as *haute cuisine*.

While the rich and noble were enjoying their rarefied existence, the country people lived off what they could grow, rear or barter. Throughout the vicissitudes of French history, away from the capital city, Frenchwomen sought to feed their families, and especially their children, as best they could by relying on their own inventiveness to set appetizing meals on the table. These women often had to resort to ingenious stratagems to turn scarce or inferior raw materials into palatable and satisfying dishes. This meant that some of the regions less blessed by nature developed a more original, sometimes tastier repertoire than regions where good raw materials needed less skill and painstaking preparation.

Most of these recipes therefore belong to a feminine tradition. Whenever there was something readily available, locally reared or grown, it found its way into traditional dishes. Often the ingredients were there for the taking, growing wild such as mushrooms, herbs, and wild plants, fruits, berries, freshwater crayfish, frogs, snails, and so on.

Countrywomen were traditionally responsible for looking after the farmyard chickens, ducks, geese, and rabbits, with additional duties in the milking sheds and cheesemaking. Indeed, cheesemaking was an exclusively female preserve; historically, women and monastic orders were famous for their cheeses. Religious orders owned flocks of sheep and goats and herds of cattle. They also owned vineyards, from which they produced their own wine, some for use in the Communion service, the rest for their own consumption.

But the role played by generations of frugal and imaginative French housewives down the ages is not the only reason as to why cooking assumed such importance and brilliance in France.

We are talking of a country with a land area 20 percent less than that of the State of Texas, yet which possesses a staggering variety of outstanding regional dishes, ranging from the *choucroute* of Alsace, with its Germanic flavor of sauerkraut, to Béarn's *garbure*, a rich pork stew with vegetables and *confit* (salted meat or poultry preserved in fat); Burgundy's beef casserole; the Dauphiné's gratin of baked potatoes with cream, onions, and cheese; the Provençal *bouillabaisse*, the famous fish soup-stew; Languedoc's *cassoulet*, made with white kidney beans, bacon, lamb and goose; Lorraine's *quiches*, savory flans; the beef and beer casserole of Flanders; Normandy's tripe with onions and cider; Brittany's *crêpes*; *aligot* (potato and cheese purée) from the Auvergne and countless others.

France is a jigsaw of provinces, assembled and sometimes lost after many bitterly fought foreign and civil wars, revolutions, annexations, and invasions. Many different races and cultures have left their mark on France throughout her history.

For many centuries northern France and parts of southern France spoke distinct dialects that almost amounted to different languages (the *langue d'oïl* for the former and the *langue d'oc*, from which the southwestern province, Languedoc takes its name). Despite all the French state's efforts to centralize and standardize so many aspects of French life, distinct ethnic communities still survive along her borders with other countries and cling to their cultural and social heritage. This is surprising when we consider how France has, until comparatively recently, always felt that her survival as a strong nation-state was under continual threat whether by hostile powers who sought to exploit such populations, as in Alsace-Lorraine, or by separatist movements, or even by the provinces' resentment of so much power and dominance being wielded by the capital.

Centralization did not, however, succeed in destroying regional characteristics. Anyone who loves good food can feel deeply grateful that Flemish, Alsatian, Savoyard, Provençal, Corsican, Catalan, Basque, and Breton cuisines have survived intact.

One of the best examples of French resourcefulness in transforming what might appear to be unpromising raw materials is provided by their preparation of variety meats. One has only to think of tripe and all the local styles of cooking it: à la mode de Caen; à La Ferté-Macé, Pau, Rouergate, Angoulême, Nice; Nivernais and Corsican style, reading like a tour of provincial France. The city of Lyons, the town of Albi, the province of the Dauphiné, and the Basque region also vaunt their recipes for this humble, nourishing, and digestible offal. Little was wasted in peasant cooking: the pig's feet would be prepared in the local style, that of Sainte-Menhould becoming famous; intestines and stomach stuffed with chopped variety meats were transformed into the *andouillettes* of Vouvray, Troyes, Arras; the *andouilles* of Vire and Guémenée and Rethel's white puddings. Just a few examples of how to make savory delicacies from the less attractive parts of a beast's anatomy.

In the realm of *charcuterie* the pig is obviously king. Each region, and often each province (now *département*) of each region, has its own special recipe for preparing ham, be it dried, smoked, cooked, rubbed with ashes, salted, peppered, boned or left whole. Sausage may be an important ingredient in both the northerners' *choucroute* and in the *cassoulet* beloved by the southerners in the Midi but that is where the resemblance ends.

Pork butchery products in France are amazing in their profusion, variety, and quality: sausages from Toulouse, Strasbourg, Montbéliard, Savoy, Morteau, Gascony are easily distinguishable and equally noteworthy; and then there are the all those different types of smaller sausages made in Forez, Lyons, Arles, Morlaàs, Brittany, and Cerdagne.

As you travel through France, the only constant is change. Fish soups (usually substantial enough to merit description as casseroles or stews) use the best seafood that the region's fisherman can catch in coastal waters and the local cooks turn them into mouthwatering specialties which are as unlike one another as their names: bouillabaisse, ttoro, chaudrée, cotriade, bouillinade, to name but a few.

The classic peasant all-in-one meals, or hotpots, easy to cook in the most rudimentary kitchens, are just as distinctive; one region's version cannot be confused with another's traditional fare.

Patisserie, largely developed by great pastry chefs for the delectation of those at court and the rich who afford the costly and often very refined ingredients, has long been one of France's glories. Country cakes, desserts, and confectionery was much less elaborate but out of such simple but good-quality ingredients as flour, sugar, eggs, milk, butter, with the addition, perhaps, of almonds and many other nuts and all sorts of fruits came creations that were both usually appealing and delectable. Brandy and liqueurs were often added to further enhance these delicacies. For the sweet-toothed Albi's *gimblettes* (almond and citrus ring cookies), Alsatian *kugelhupf* (yeast cake), *brioches* from Riom, *clafoutis* (cherry flan) from the Limousin, Mauriac's *croquants* (crunchy nut petit fours), Burgundy's *rigodon* (cinnamon and nut pudding), Angoulême's *casseron* (almond and curd cheese cookies); *pognes* (yeast buns filled with candied fruit or jam) from Romans, Lorraine's *tôt-fait* (lemon pound cake); *bugnes* (hot, sweet fritters) from Lyons, Norman *douillons* (apple dumplings) and *gâteau de Savoie* (Savoy sponge cake) sound like a litany of temptations.

Most of us know about the wide range of wines produced in France. Just as telling an illustration can be seen in the vast number of different cheeses produced all over the country, made with that simplest ingredient, milk, with the aid of nature and a good deal of skill and experience. Winston Churchill got to the heart of the matter, the sheer diversity of France and the French, when he wondered aloud to General de Gaulle, how anyone could hope to govern a country that has so many different cheeses. This individualism and refusal to conform may pose problems for politicians but not for gourmets, especially when they reflect that for every cheese there are several wines to choose from.

Obviously local growing conditions and climate help to account for this bewildering choice. In the past people chose to cook with whatever was plentiful in their part of France: so historically there was an olive oil region, and butter, goose fat, and lard regions.

Similarly, there are the wine, beer, and cider countries of France.

So no one should be surprised that very small regions such as the Basque country, the former county of Nice, and Flanders are as well off for different tastes and flavors as much larger regions like Normandy, Lorraine or Gascony.

When it comes to organizing a cookery book, simplicity is the best policy, and the country has been divided into culinary regions as follows:

North (Flanders, Hainaut, Avesnois, Artois, Boulonnais, Ponthieu, Picardy, and Cambrésis).

East (Champagne, Lorraine, Alsace, Burgundy, Franche-Comté, and the Nivernais).

West (Berry, Orléanais, Touraine, Anjou,

Brittany, Maine, and Normandy).

Atlantic Coast (the Bordeaux country, Périgord).

Alpine East (Lyonnais, Bresse, Bugey, Savoy, and the Dauphiné)

The Massif Central (Bourbonnais, Auvergne, Velay, Vivarais, Gévaudan, Rouergue, Limousin, and Marche)

South: the Midi (Mediterranean coast) (Provence, the county of Nice, Corsica, the Mediterranean coastal region of Languedoc and Roussillon).

The Southwest and the Pyrenees (Gascony, part of Languedoc around Toulouse, Béarn, the Basque country, the county of Foix, and the area around Albi).

No introduction to a book of French regional cookery would be complete without acknowledging our debt to all those who have already made their journeys of discovery, researching and documenting the origins of our provincial cuisine: the "prince of gastronomes," Curnonsky (whose real name was Maurice Sailland), his friend Marcel Rouff, and Robert Courtine. There have been many others: Florence Arzel, Monique Gruénais-Vanverts, Marie Ceccaldi, Irène Karsenty, Jeanne Léveillé, Simone Morand, Doris and Anne Walther, Monique Esquerré-Ancieux, Christiane Schapira, Céline Vence, Jacques Médecin, Joseph Koscher, Christian Délu, Jean-Pierre Poulain, Jean-Luc Rouyer, Roger Lallemand, La Mazille, M. Barberousse, Simin Palay, Henri Philippon, Pierre Gaertner, Louis Le Cunff, Philippe Guéroult, the Vincenot family, Christian Bernadac, *Amicale des cuisiniers auvergnats de Paris* (Society of Auvergnat cooks in Paris), Jean-Marie Cuny, François Decuq, and many others . . . And not forgetting all those chefs who take pride in reintroducing old regional recipes into their menus.

Lastly I hope that you, the reader and cook, will derive great enjoyment from preparing and eating these dishes in which our ancestors took so much pride and pleasure.

J.F.

North

Flanders
Hainaut
Avesnois
Artois
Boulonnais
Ponthieu
Picardy
Cambrésis

North of Paris, between the sea and Belgium, are the old provinces of Flanders, Hainaut, Avesnois, Artois, Boulonnais, Ponthieu, Picardy, and Cambrésis. Geography and history have made them vulnerable to invasion and they have been repeatedly devastated by protracted battles. These flat lands where only the sparse trees, clocktowers, and church spires rise above the fertile plains, are ideal for the swift movement of invading armies and for the staging of set-piece battles.

On the previous pages: *windmills are a typical feature of the Flanders plain.* Below: *a network of canals marks out productive vegetable plots, called "hortillonages" when reclaimed from marshland, where abundant produce is grown and put to good use in Picard cooking.*

The climate tends to be cool and wet and there is often a misty, melancholy atmosphere to the countryside. Flemish, Artésian, and Picard men and women are hard workers who greatly enjoy public entertainments, celebrations, and feast days, which are seized upon as a chance to take some well earned relaxation and enjoy the best local food and drink. The cooking of these provinces tends to be substantial, based on prime raw materials; the dish that typifies it is the *hochepot* or hotpot, a rich casserole made with plenty of good beef or pork and a variety of vegetables.

It is hardly surprising that in a region where the fire or stove would have been kept almost constantly alight to keep the damp and cold at bay during all but the warmest summer months, many of the most typical main course recipes call for long, slow simmering. For much the same reasons, soup plays a large part in the northern repertoire, based on ingredients such as pumpkin, leek, beetroot, tripe, beer, and frog's legs.

Beer replaces wine in these parts. Since vines do not take kindly to these cold, exposed conditions hops and barley are planted instead. The locals enjoy their good beer and in Germanic style, include it in many of their recipes.

Vegetables are grown in abundance here, especially onions, which are used in countless different ways. These northern kitchens are full of appetizing aromas of beer, onions, and frying. French fried potatoes cooked in good vegetable oil until crisp outside and melting inside are a passion the inhabitants share with their Belgian neighbors. On both sides of the border the plump mussels gathered from the shores of the North Sea, succulent and flavorsome, are used in tempting soups and stews.

Because the local raw materials are of prime quality, preparation tends to be simple and straightforward. Herrings caught in coastal waters (prized as 'king herring' by the English and by the Dutch) are another staple food beloved by the inhabitants of Flanders, Artois, and Picardy, a taste shared by their fellow countrymen to the southwest, in Normandy. During the Middle Ages the plentiful and cheap supply of these nutritious fish must have saved the lives of many of the poorest northern French who would otherwise have starved. Herrings are served in many delicious ways: marinated in white wine, often flavored with juniper berries, onions, and peppercorns, or fried in oil; turned a richer, darker color when pickled or smoked, or broiled.

Boulogne is the most important port in the

French fishing industry: besides herring, very large landings of all sorts of excellent cold-water fish and crustaceans command high prices. Such delicacies as lobster and the superb flatfish, Dover sole and turbot, are, curiously, not as popular with these northerners as the herring which, together with freshwater fish such as carp and eel, remains the firm favorite.

This taste for robust, satisfying food is echoed by the regional cheeses, many of which are very strong; some, like Maroilles, one of the oldest French cheeses, is almost too overpowering for delicate palates. Its scent and taste, however, pale into insignificance when compared with other northern cheeses such as *boulette d'Avesnes* or Lille's *gris*, which is also called "*puant*" or "stinky"!

Right: *an old farmhouse in Picardy with a steeply sloping thatched roof, nestling in green and sparsely wooded countryside in the middle of a gently rolling plain, never more than 650 ft above sea level.* Below: *a fisherman sets up his nets on a long, level, sandy beach beside the North Sea.*

The Picard are by tradition talented and enthusiastic pastry cooks, priding themselves on their leek flans and apple tarts. They also excel at various types of pâté: some of these are quite light, cooked in molds and then unmolded and served hot; some are firm, substantial and always served cold, while others, such as the renowned Amiens duck paté, are served, hot or cold, in a pastry case. The main ingredient of these different varieties of pâté can be seafood, meat, game, poultry, cheese or fruit.

There is a marked tendency to mix sweet and savory in many ways: one is by adding very sweet fruit such as prunes to meat dishes, especially rabbit or pork. As we have seen, these northerners like the occasional strong flavor and not just when it comes to cheese: the excellent gin distilled in Wambrechies is a very popular *digestif* (a drink taken at the end of a meal, thought to aid digestion) after rich, rather heavy meals. Though distilled from grain like the dry gin used for gin cocktail mixtures, it has a very different taste and deserves to be better known.

Opposite above: *the local café and bar, meeting place for the fortunate locals with its brightly painted shutters and sign so typical of this region.* Opposite below: *the low, gently rolling pastures of Flanders provide good grazing for a large livestock industry.* Above: *Formerly a fortress facing north over the English Channel, Dunkirk was later to provide the backdrop for the dramatic events of May and June 1940 when British and French forces retreated in front of the invading German army and escaped by sea. Destroyed during World War II, the port was completely rebuilt, to become France's third largest trading port, situated where four large canals reach the coast.*

SOUPS

SOUPE DES HORTILLONAGES*

Market gardener's soup

Picardy

Preparation: 40 minutes
Cooking: 1 hour
Easy

Serves 6:
1 large cabbage heart
6 large leeks, white part only
½ lb new potatoes, peeled
1 lb fresh peas in the pod (or 1 small packet frozen peas or petit pois*)*
5 tbsp butter
¼ lb sorrel or spinach
1 large lettuce heart
1 small bunch fresh chervil
salt and pepper
6 slices French bread

Shred the cabbage heart and slice the leeks into very thin rings. Dice the potatoes. Shuck the peas if fresh.

Heat 2 tbsp of the butter gently in a very large, heavy-bottomed saucepan and sweat the cabbage and leeks over low heat.

Add 2 quarts water, the potatoes, and the peas and bring to a boil (if using frozen peas, add when the water boils). Season with plenty of freshly ground pepper and salt to taste; cover and simmer gently for 45 minutes. Trim off the stalks from the sorrel, wash the leaves well and pat dry; wash and shred the lettuce. Sweat both in the remaining butter with the chopped chervil until wilted and tender and add to the soup ten minutes before it is done.

To serve, place a piece of toasted French bread in each soup bowl and ladle the soup on top.

SOUPE À LA BIÈRE

Beer and onion soup

Flanders

Preparation: 30 minutes
Cooking: 35 minutes
Very easy

Serves 6:
5 tbsp butter
1 large onion, peeled
½ cup all-purpose flour
1½ quarts beer
1 tsp sugar
pinch ground cinnamon
2 egg yolks
½ cup heavy cream
salt and pepper
6 slices French bread

Cook the very finely sliced onion in the butter until tender and pale golden brown. Add the flour and stir for 2–3 minutes to make a roux. Add the beer a little at a time, stirring continually to prevent lumps forming. Bring to a boil, season with salt and pepper, then stir in the sugar and cinnamon. Reduce the heat and simmer very gently for 30 minutes. Shortly before serving, beat the egg yolks lightly into the cream in a small bowl. When the soup is ready, draw aside from the heat, beat in the thickening liaison of cream and eggs and serve at once, poured over thick, crisply toasted slices of French bread.

SOUPE DE GRENOUILLES*

Frog's legs soup

Picardy

Preparation: 30 minutes
Cooking: 35 minutes
Easy

Serves 4:
3 medium-sized onions, peeled
24 pairs prepared frog's legs
¼ cup butter
1 cup dry white wine
1 bouquet garni (thyme, bay leaf, and parsley)
1 clove
1 clove garlic, peeled
3 tbsp stale breadcrumbs
2 eggs
1 cup heavy cream
2 tbsp chopped chives
salt and pepper

Slice two onions thinly and sweat in the butter in a large saucepan for 15 minutes, stirring frequently, until very soft but not at all browned. Add the frog's legs, wine, 2¼ cups water, the bouquet garni, the third onion (studded with the clove), the garlic, salt, and pepper. Allow to return to a very gentle simmer and cook for a further 15 minutes.

Remove and discard the bouquet garni, the clove-studded onion, and the garlic. Take out the frog's legs, take the meat off the bone and keep two thirds of it hot. Place the bread and one third of the frog's leg meat in a food processor, blend briefly, then stir into the soup and simmer for 5 minutes.

Just before the soup is ready, beat the egg yolks lightly into the cream; strain ¼ cup of the hot soup and beat in to the eggs and cream. Do not strain the rest of the soup. Turn the heat down to very low under the soup and add the cream and egg mixture slowly, stirring all the time with a wooden spoon. The soup must not boil or the liaison will curdle. Put the remaining pieces of frog's leg meat in a heated soup tureen and add the hot soup.

Place crisped bread slices (oven-baked or toasted) in each bowl and ladle in the soup. Sprinkle with chives.

FLAMICHE AUX POIREAUX
Leek Pie

Picardy

Preparation: 35 minutes + 15 minutes resting time for pastry
Cooking: 30 minutes
Easy

Serves 6:
3 cups all-purpose flour
1 cup butter
2¼–2½ large leeks, white part only
2¼ cups milk
1 egg yolk
salt and pepper
pinch nutmeg

Measure out ½ cup of the flour and ¼ cup butter and set these aside. Make the pie dough with the remaining, larger quantities of butter and flour, a pinch of salt, and sufficient cold water to make a firm, homogenous dough (see glossary for method). Shape into a ball. Leave to rest for 15 minutes. Slice the leeks into very thin rings, and sweat gently in the reserved butter in a covered saucepan until soft and transparent, stirring with a wooden spoon at intervals to ensure that they cook evenly and do not stick or brown at all.

Sprinkle the reserved flour over the leeks and stir over low heat until smoothly blended. Reserve 2½ tbsp of the milk for later use; gradually add all the rest to the leeks, stirring continuously over low heat until the mixture has reached a very gentle boil. Continue cooking and stirring for another 3–4 minutes. Season to taste with salt, pepper, and a pinch of ground nutmeg. Draw aside from the heat.

Using two thirds of the pastry, roll out into a circle ⅛ in thick. Lightly grease a fairly deep tart pan with a little butter and line with the pastry, overlapping the rim by about ⅜ in. Fill this pie shell with the leek mixture. Roll out the remaining pastry to form a circular lid matching the diameter of the tart pan and place on top of the leeks. Fold the overlapping edge over the lid and pinch at regular intervals with fingers dipped in cold water to seal.

Pierce the pie lid here and there with the tip of a sharp pointed knife. Beat the egg yolk into the remaining milk and brush all over the surface.

Place in the oven, preheated to 400°F; after 15 minutes, lower the heat to 350°F and bake for a further 15 minutes.

GOYÈRE
Cheese flan

Hainaut and Flanders

Preparation: 30 minutes + 1 hour resting time for pastry
Cooking time: 30 minutes
Easy

Serves 6:
1 Maroilles cheese
¼ oz fresh yeast
1 cup milk
2¼ cups all-purpose flour
½ cup butter
1 egg
¼ cup crème fraîche *or heavy cream*
salt and pepper

The dough must be made 2 hours in advance. Crumble the yeast into the lukewarm milk and stir gently to dissolve. (If using dried yeast, halve the weight used and sprinkle into milk; leave to reactivate until it froths.) Melt the butter gently; remove from the heat. Sift the flour into a mixing bowl; make a well in the center and pour in the milk and yeast and the melted butter. Stir these ingredients, gradually incorporating all the flour. Add a pinch of salt and work in the egg.

Knead the dough for 5 or 6 minutes, then roll out on a lightly floured board and use to line a pie plate greased with butter and lightly dusted with flour. Leave to stand in a warm place for 1 hour for the dough to rise. Cut the rind off the cheese and slice thinly; arrange these slices in the pie shell in one or more layers. Mix the *crème fraîche* with plenty of freshly ground pepper and spread all over the cheese. Place in the oven, preheated to 400°F. After 30 minutes, remove from the oven and immediately dot the surface with very thin flakes of butter.

TARTE AUX OIGNONS*
Onion flan

Picardy

Preparation: 30 minutes + resting time for the pastry
Cooking: 20 minutes
Easy

Serves 6:
1¾ cups all-purpose flour
½ cup + 2 tbsp sweet butter
2¼ lb Bermuda onions, peeled
1½ tbsp oil
1 cup heavy cream
3 eggs
salt and pepper

Sift the flour into a mixing bowl. Reserve ¼ cup of the butter for later use and rub all the rest into the flour and a pinch of salt; gradually stir in enough cold water (approx. 6 tbsp) to form a firm, smooth pie dough that comes cleanly away from the sides of the bowl (see glossary for method). Shape into a ball and leave to rest for 30 minutes while you prepare the onions: peel these and slice into wafer-thin rings, sweat them in half the reserved butter and all the oil over low heat until very tender; do not allow to brown. Season with salt and pepper. Grease a 9–10 in pie plate with the remaining butter; roll out the pie dough and line the pan. Spread the onions out evenly in the pie shell. Beat the cream and eggs together, adding salt and pepper, and pour all over the onions. Place in a preheated oven (400°F) and cook for 20 minutes.

FISCELLES PICARDES
Mushroom, cheese, and ham pancake rolls

Picardy

Preparation (start 1 hour in advance): 1 hour
Cooking: 10 minutes
Easy

Serves 6:
3 cups all-purpose flour
3 tbsp peanut oil
3 eggs
1 quart rich milk
½ lb button mushrooms
½ cup butter
pinch nutmeg
6 tbsp grated Gruyère cheese
¼ cup fresh pork fat or shortening
6 thin slices cooked lean ham
salt and pepper
½ cup crème fraîche *or heavy cream*

An hour before you intend starting your main preparations, make the pancake batter. Reserve ¾ cup of the flour for later use. Sift the rest into a mixing bowl with a pinch of salt, make a well in the center, pour in the oil, and break the eggs into the well. Stir the oil and eggs gently and pour in half the milk (2¼ cups); continue stirring, gradually incorporating all the flour. Beat the batter well to eliminate any lumps. Leave to stand. Trim, rinse, and dry the mushrooms then cut into small dice. Cook gently in 2½ tbsp of the butter until they have released most of their moisture content.

Make a white sauce with the remaining

butter, flour, and milk; season with salt, pepper, and nutmeg. Continue cooking the sauce over low heat for a few minutes after it has thickened. Stir in the drained mushrooms. Draw aside from the heat and stir in half the grated cheese. Keep warm.

Grease a large skillet with the pork fat or shortening. Pour in about ½ cup of the batter when the skillet is very hot and immediately tilt the pan this way and that so that the batter spreads out evenly to give a thin pancake. Turn once when the underside is lightly browned. Stack the cooked pancakes on a plate and keep warm until all the batter has been used. Grease the skillet again whenever necessary.

Cut the ham slices into thin strips. Spread a few strips of ham and some of the sauce over the surface of each pancake, leaving a clear border uncovered all round the edge. Roll up and place in a single layer in a butter-greased shallow gratin dish. Heat the *crème fraîche* over very low heat, season with salt and freshly ground pepper, and pour over the pancakes, coating them lightly. Sprinkle the remaining grated cheese over the surface and bake in a preheated oven at 425°F for 10 minutes.

FISH

HARENGS À LA BOULONNAISE*

Stuffed herrings

Boulonnais

Preparation: 20 minutes
Cooking: 15 minutes
Easy

Serves 4:
4 fresh whole herrings, about ½ lb each, preferably with roes
2 shallots, peeled
4 medium-sized white, closed cap mushrooms
1 small bunch parsley
¼ cup butter, softened
1½ tbsp peanut oil
salt and pepper

Remove the scales from the herrings by running the back of a kitchen knife along them from tail to head. Cut off their heads and fins, slit them open along the backbone, and remove the backbone (the small bones will come away with it). Discard all the entrails but keep the soft or hard roes. Rinse the fish thoroughly and dry. Place the shallots, the mushrooms, parsley, roes, and the butter in a food processor and reduce to a coarse paste, adding a little salt and pepper. Fill each fish with some of this stuffing, place on a fairly large piece of foil, sprinkle with a little more salt, pepper, and oil then fold up into loose but well-sealed parcels leaving plenty of air space inside.

Bake in a preheated oven at 500°F for 10 minutes.

HARENGS AU GRATIN

Baked herrings

Boulonnais

Preparation: 10 minutes
Cooking: 40 minutes
Very easy

Serves 6:
6 fresh herrings, filleted
2 medium-sized onions, peeled
3 tbsp peanut oil
3 tbsp chopped parsley
2 bay leaves
1 sprig thyme
½ cup dry red wine
¼ cup red wine vinegar
salt and pepper

See previous recipe for filleting method. If soft roes are present, they can be used in this recipe but not hard roes. Slice the onions into wafer-thin rings. Use a little of the oil to coat the inside of a shallow, ovenproof dish lightly. Cover the bottom of the dish with the onion rings and the parsley.

Arrange the fish fillets in a single layer on top, overlapping them slightly. Sprinkle with freshly ground pepper and a little salt, place the bay leaf and thyme on top. Bake, uncovered, in a preheated oven at 325°F for 10 minutes.

Take the dish out of the oven. Increase the heat to 375°F. Sprinkle the wine, vinegar, and remaining oil all over the herrings. If you have reserved the roes, slot these lengthwise between the fish. Return the dish to the oven and cook for a further 30 minutes.

ANGUILLES AU VERT*

Baked eel with herbs

Flanders

Preparation: 30 minutes
Cooking: 20 minutes
Easy

Serves 4:
3–3½ lb small eels
1¾ cup all-purpose flour
½ lb sorrel or watercress
5 oz spinach
1 large bunch parsley
1 large bunch chervil
2 or 3 leaves fresh sage, 1 small sprig each fresh savory, French tarragon, and thyme
6 tbsp butter
2¼ cups dry white wine
4 eggs
1 cup crème fraîche *or heavy cream*
1 lemon
salt and pepper

Have your fishmonger skin the eels and cut off their heads. Cut them into 2-in sections and coat them with flour, shaking off excess. If sorrel is unavailable, substitute Swiss chard (leaves only) or make up the weight with more spinach. Remove the stalks from the sorrel. Wash and dry the leaves thoroughly. Coarsely chop the tarragon, sage, parsley, and chervil.

Brown the eel pieces all over in half the butter (3 tbsp). Add the wine and season with salt and pepper. Reduce the heat and simmer very gently for 10 minutes.

Heat the remaining butter over very low heat in another saucepan and add the sorrel, spinach, and herbs together with the savory and thyme leaves. Cook gently for a few minutes, turning once or twice, until the leaves are wilted and tender. Drain the cooking liquid from the eels and reserve. Transfer the eels to a heated serving dish. Beat the eggs with the *crème fraîche* in the top of a double boiler or in a heatproof bowl over gently simmering water; gradually beat in 1 tbsp lemon juice.

Combine the reserved liquid with the thickened creamy sauce, adding a little at a time while beating continuously. Add the sorrel, spinach, and herbs and season with salt and pepper. Pour this sauce all over the eels.

This dish may be served hot or cold.

MAQUEREUX À LA BOULONNAISE*

Baked mackerel in mussel sauce

Boulonnais

Preparation: 40 minutes
Cooking: 1 hour
Easy

Serves 6:
6 small mackerel, cleaned and prepared
1 quart mussels
1/4 lb small button mushrooms
1 small bunch parsley
2 medium-sized onions
1 cup beer
1/4 cup all-purpose flour
1 egg
2 tbsp butter
salt, pepper, and peppercorns

Scrub the mussels, removing all beards and barnacles; wash thoroughly, and discard any that do not close when handled. Spread out in a very wide saucepan, cover, and place over high heat without any water. Remove from the heat as soon as the mussels have opened (this will take only minutes) and discard any that have failed to open. Remove the mollusks from their shells, saving all the juice (strain this through cheesecloth).

Bring a pan of lightly salted water to a boil with a few peppercorns. Finely slice the mushrooms, chop the parsley coarsely, and slice the onions into thin rings. Add all three to the boiling water together with a few peppercorns; simmer for 10 minutes. Remove the mushrooms and set aside with the mussels. (Discard the water, parsley, and onions). Stir the beer gradually into the flour, making sure there are no lumps; stir in the lightly beaten egg, followed by the mussels, mushrooms, and the strained mussel juice. Make shallow slanting incisions on both sides of the fish.

Grease an ovenproof dish with butter; spoon half the sauce mixture over the bottom of the dish and place the fish on top in a single layer. Spoon the rest of the sauce over the fish. Dot small flakes of the remaining butter over the fish and bake at 375°F for 1 hour.

CAUDIÈRE DE BERCK*

North Sea fish casserole

Boulonnais

Preparation: 45 minutes
Cooking: 30 minutes
Easy

Serves 4–6:
3–3 1/2 lb mixed prepared and cleaned fish

(e.g. turbot, sole, sea-robin, John Dory, conger eel)
4 medium-sized onions, peeled
3 cloves garlic, peeled
1 bouquet garni (thyme, bay leaf, parsley)
3–4 sprigs parsley
2¼ lb waxy or new potatoes
2 quarts mussels
4 egg yolks
1 cup crème fraîche *or heavy cream*
salt and pepper

Slice the onions into very thin rings. Chop the parsley and garlic coarsely and spread over the bottom of a large fireproof casserole dish: add the bouquet garni and the quartered potatoes. Add 3 quarts cold water. Season with salt and pepper and bring to a boil. Boil for 10 minutes.

Cut the fish into fairly large pieces and place on top of the potatoes. The cooking liquid should just cover the fish; add a little boiling water if needed. Bring to a gentle boil and simmer for 15 minutes.

Scrub the mussels thoroughly under running cold water; discard any that do not close when handled. Place in a very wide, covered saucepan over high heat for a few minutes to open. Discard any that fail to open. Remove the mollusks from their shells (strain and reserve their juices) and place in a warmed soup tureen; add all the solid ingredients from the casserole dish, using a slotted spoon.

Discard the bouquet garni. Cover and keep warm. Beat the egg yolks lightly with the *crème fraîche* in a bowl; gradually beat in 6 tbsp of the cooking liquid. Stir the strained mussel juice into the pan of cooking liquid, which should not be allowed to boil again as you stir or whisk in the egg and cream liaison in a very thin stream. The liquid will thicken very slightly. Pour into the tureen and serve.

MEAT

POTJEVLEISCH*

Potted meat in aspic

Flanders

Prepare 24 hours in advance
Preparation: 40 minutes
Cooking: 3 hours
Complicated

Serves 8:
1 large chicken (approx 5 1/2 lb)
1 large, young rabbit (approx. 4 1/2 lb)
3/4 lb boned veal shoulder
1/2 lb fresh pork belly or unsmoked bacon
1/2 lb shallots or mild onions, peeled
1 bottle dry white wine
1 large bunch parsley
2 sprigs thyme
1 bay leaf
1 large piece fresh pork skin
salt and pepper

For this recipe you need only the wing, leg, and thigh portions of the chicken and the fore and rear quarters of the rabbit (the rest of the chicken and rabbit can be used for other dishes). Do not take the meat off the bone at this stage. Cut the veal into 2-in cubes. Remove the skin and any tough pieces (cartilage) from the pork belly or bacon and cut into strips (lardons). Chop the shallots. Chop the parsley.

Pack the pieces of meat loosely into an earthenware casserole dish, filling the spaces with the fatty lardons; sprinkle each layer with the mixed shallots and parsley. Pour in the wine, which should only just cover the meat completely. Put the thyme and bay leaf on top, then cover with a "lid" of the fresh pork skin, cut to fit neatly inside the rim of the casserole dish, fatty side down, on top of the meat.

Cover with a tight-fitting lid; use a thick flour and water paste if necessary to give an airtight seal. Place in a roasting pan, pour sufficient hot water into the pan to come halfway up the sides and cook at 350°F for 3 hours; the contents should cook at a gentle but continuous simmer. Remove from the oven. When no longer too hot to handle, remove the pork skin, thyme, and bay leaf. Take the flesh off the chicken and rabbit bones, taking care not to waste any of the juices. Return all the meat to the casserole dish, packing neatly, with all the juices, replace the pork skin on top. When completely cold, chill. The juices will form a delicious savory jelly or aspic around the meat.

CARBONNADE*

Beef and beer stew

Flanders

Preparation: 40 minutes
Cooking: 3 hours
Easy

Serves 6:
2¾–3 lb lean braising beef cut into 2-in square pieces just under ½ in thick
¾ lb onions, peeled
½ lb smoked fat bacon
¼ cup butter
1 tbsp brown sugar
1 tbsp red wine vinegar
1 bouquet garni (thyme, bay leaf, parsley)
5 oz 2-day old French bread
1 tbsp strong mustard
2¼ cups beer
salt and pepper

Peel and chop the onions. Trim off the skin and any tough parts from the bacon and dice.

Heat the butter in a large fireproof casserole and brown the beef well over high heat, turning frequently. Remove the beef and set aside. Add the diced bacon and brown in the remaining butter and its own fat; set aside with the beef. Fry the finely sliced or chopped onions in the fat and butter left in the pan until pale golden brown and tender, stirring with a wooden spoon. Sprinkle the sugar all over the onions; reduce the heat and allow the sugar to melt and caramelize the onions. Remove from the heat and stir in the vinegar; return to a gentle heat and stir for 3 minutes.

Arrange the meat, bacon, and onions in layers, seasoning with a little salt and pepper; bury the bouquet garni in the center. Slice the bread thickly and bake in a gentle oven until very crisp and golden brown; spread some mustard on top of each slice. Pour in sufficient beer to cover the meat completely; arrange the bread slices on top in a single layer, cover, and continue to cook over gentle heat on top of the stove once the liquid has come to a boil or in the oven at about 350°F until very tender (about 3 hours).

Serve with French fries.

LAPIN AUX PRUNEAUX*

Rabbit with prunes

Artois, Flanders, Hainaut

Start preparation 24 hours in advance
Preparation: 30 minutes
Cooking: 1 hour 20 minutes
Complicated

Serves 6:
1 rabbit weighing approx. 3½ lb
1½ cups red wine vinegar
2 carrots, peeled
5 medium-sized onions, peeled
2 bottles dry red wine
1 small bunch parsley, 2 sprigs thyme, 1 bay leaf
2 lb prunes
¼ cup butter
¼ cup peanut oil
5 oz pork breast or belly
12 baby onions, peeled
6 tbsp all-purpose flour
2 cloves garlic, peeled
¼ cup redcurrant jelly
salt and black peppercorns

Ask your butcher to joint the rabbit into 6–8 portions and save the liver for you. Place the liver, if available, in a small, nonmetallic bowl with half the vinegar. Slice the carrots and onions and place in a large nonmetallic bowl with the rabbit pieces. Add the remaining vinegar, a few peppercorns, half the wine, the bay leaf, thyme, and parsley. Leave to marinate, stirring and turning occasionally, for about 24 hours. Place the prunes in another bowl, pour over the remaining bottle of wine, and leave to soak overnight. When you are about to start cooking the rabbit, drain off the marinade and reserve; pat the portions lightly with kitchen towels to remove excess moisture and brown all over in the hot butter and oil in a fireproof casserole dish over gentle heat. Take out the rabbit pieces and set aside.

Remove the skin and any tough pieces from the pork breast or belly, and dice; brown in the oil and butter in the casserole dish then remove and set aside. Add the whole, peeled baby onions to the fat in the casserole dish and brown lightly all over. Return the bacon and rabbit to the casserole; sprinkle in the flour, then stir the contents well over low heat for a few minutes until the flour has turned a pale golden brown.

Drain the prunes and set aside; add the wine used for soaking them to the casserole, together with the parsley, thyme, bay leaf, and garlic cloves. Strain the reserved marinade and pour into the casserole dish. Bring to a boil.

Reduce the heat, cover, and simmer gently, adding the prunes after 30 minutes. Continue simmering with the lid on for another 25

COQ A LA BIÈRE*

Chicken with beer

Flanders and Artois

Preparation: 15 minutes
Cooking: 2 hours 40 minutes
Easy

Serves 6:
1 7½–8-lb chicken
¼ cup peanut oil
½ cup butter
4 shallots, peeled
1½ quarts beer
1 bouquet garni (thyme, bay leaf, parsley)
¾–1 lb small button mushrooms
¾–1 cup crème fraîche *or heavy cream*
salt and pepper

Cut the chicken into 10–12 pieces. Heat all the oil and 1 tbsp of the butter in a large skillet and brown well all over; set aside. Drain off and discard all the fat. Heat 2 tbsp fresh butter and sweat the very finely chopped shallots for 5 minutes. Place the chicken pieces on the bed of onions and add the beer and bouquet garni. Season with salt and pepper. Cover and cook over very gentle heat for 2 hours, then add the very finely sliced mushrooms. Cook for a further 30 minutes. Transfer the chicken pieces to a heated serving dish; reduce the cooking liquid considerably over high heat until it has thickened and has a glossy appearance. Add the *crème fraîche* and boil for 3 minutes. Beat in the remaining butter with a balloon whisk, adding a small piece at a time. Add a little more salt and pepper if needed; pour all over the chicken portions. Sprinkle with finely chopped parsley if wished.

The inhabitants of Lille adore frites *(French fried potatoes) and the streets are full of their appetizing smell. In his book* Les Provinciaux *("The Provincials"), the journalist Henri Deligny wrote: "Toulouse smells of violets; Brest, of crêpes; Strasbourg, Sauerkraut; Bordeaux, wine casks. Lille smells of fried potatoes (...) Lille's fried potatoes are republican, socialist, plebeian. A visitor arriving by train at Lille station could be excused for thinking that the locomotives must run on* "frites" *in an era when electricity has long since replaced steam traction ..."*

minutes. Drain the liver, discarding the soaking vinegar, and pound to a thick paste. Add this to the pan and stir and cook for a final 5 minutes. Use a slotted spoon to transfer all the rabbit portions, bacon, and onions to a heated serving dish. Discard the parsley, thyme, bay leaf, and garlic cloves. Stir the redcurrant jelly quickly into the sauce in the pan and pour over the rabbit.

HOCHEPOT
Meat and vegetable stew

Flanders and Hainaut

Preparation: 30 minutes
Cooking: 3 hours
Easy

Serves 6:
1–$1\frac{1}{4}$ lb beef short ribs
2 pig's feet (optional)
1 lb semisalted pork breast or loin
1–$1\frac{1}{4}$ lb lamb shoulder, boned and rolled
1–$1\frac{1}{4}$ lb oxtail pieces (optional)
1 white cabbage
1 lb carrots, peeled
6 medium-sized waxy potatoes
6 medium-sized leeks, white part only
1 stick celery
1 medium-sized onion, peeled and studded with 1–2 cloves
1 bouquet garni
1 German Bratwurst (optional)
salt and pepper

The original version often calls for two semisalted pork cuts: pig's tail, and the pork loin or breast, which have to be blanched for 10 minutes, then rinsed. This is omitted for fresh pork. If you cannot buy pig's feet, substitute the oxtail for the necessary gelatinous consistency. Put all the meats except the sausage into a large, deep pot or heavy-bottomed saucepan; add sufficient cold water to cover, a generous pinch each of salt and pepper, and bring to a boil. Skim off any scum. Simmer gently for 2 hours.

While the meat is cooking, wash and quarter the cabbage and add to a large pan of boiling salted water to blanch for 5 minutes. Drain and refresh under running cold water; shred coarsely.

After the meats have cooked for 2 hours, add all the vegetables and the bouquet garni; simmer for a further 45 minutes, then add the sausage, if used. Continue cooking for a further 15 minutes.

Serve the liquid with some of the vegetables, (chopped as necessary), as a soup, then the meat, potatoes, cabbage, and remaining vegetables as a main course.

CAQHUSE*
Roast pork with onions

Picardie

Preparation: 10 minutes
Cooking: $1\frac{1}{2}$ hours
Very easy

Serves 6:
$2\frac{3}{4}$–3 lb pork arm shoulder
$1\frac{1}{2}$ lb onions, peeled
$\frac{1}{4}$ cup butter
1 tbsp wine or cider vinegar
salt and pepper

The lower, tapering section of the arm shoulder is usual for this dish, but any prime, fairly lean roasting cut is suitable. Place the meat in a roasting pan (do not remove the skin or any of the fat). Season with salt and freshly ground pepper. Slice the onions into rings and arrange all round the pork. Dot the butter in flakes over the onions.

Place in a preheated oven (350°F) and roast for $1\frac{1}{2}$ hours. Remove from the oven; pour the vinegar into the roasting pan and mix with the cooking juices and onions. Leave to cool. Serve cold.

ROGNONS AU GENIÈVRE*
Kidneys with gin

Flanders and Artois

Preparation: 20 minutes
Cooking: 25 minutes
Easy

Serves 4:
4 veal kidneys
$1\frac{1}{2}$–$1\frac{3}{4}$ lb waxy potatoes, peeled
$\frac{1}{4}$ cup olive oil
$\frac{1}{4}$ cup butter
$\frac{1}{2}$ cup gin
$\frac{1}{4}$ cup dry white wine
salt and pepper

Cut the kidneys lengthwise in half and remove any visible pieces of gristle or blood. Rinse and dry. Slice the potatoes very thinly. Wrap the slices in a clean cloth to absorb any moisture. Heat the oil in a large nonstick skillet and fry the potatoes until golden brown, turning once. Sprinkle with a little salt and pepper, cover, and continue cooking over lower heat until cooked through, turning once more (about 20 minutes).

Meanwhile, heat the butter in another pan until foaming; add the kidneys and cook for only 2–3 minutes on each side, to seal. Reduce the heat to very low, season lightly with salt and pepper, cover, and cook very gently for up 20 minutes. Take the kidneys out of the pan and slice quickly before they have time to cool (see illustration below); they should be pale pink inside. Save all the juices that run out as you slice them and mix with the hot butter and cooking juices.

Arrange a bed of the potatoes on a heated serving platter, place the kidneys on top; keep warm briefly as you pour the gin into the skillet and scrape any cooking deposits free over high heat. Add the wine; cook for 2 minutes over lower heat. Pour over the kidneys or hand round separately in a sauceboat.

WATERZOÏ DE POULARDE
Chicken waterzooï

Flanders

Start preparation 24 hours in advance
Preparation: 20 minutes
Cooking: 1 hour 20 minutes
Complicated

Serves 8:
1 4-lb chicken or capon
3 large leeks, white part only
2 onions, peeled, one studded with 2 cloves
2 heads celery
6 large sprigs parsley
1/2 cup butter
1/2 cup dry white wine
2 1/4 cups veal broth
3/4 cup crème fraîche *or heavy cream*
4 egg yolks
1 tbsp finely chopped parsley
salt and pepper

For the broth:
1 shin of veal
2 carrots
2 small turnips
2 leeks
1 onion, studded with 1 clove

Make the broth (see glossary) 24 hours in advance. Cut the chicken into 8–10 portions. Slit the leeks lengthwise. Slice one onion into strips; do likewise with the celery and leeks. Tie the parsley into bunches.

Heat half the butter gently in a deep, heavy saucepan or fireproof casserole dish; place the parsley bunches and the whole, clove-studded onion in the center and surround with the vegetables. Dot all but 1 1/2 tbsp of the remaining butter in flakes on top of the vegetables and add the white wine. Cover and cook slowly for 20 minutes, then lay the chicken pieces over the vegetables and pour in sufficient veal broth to cover.

Add salt and pepper to taste and scrape up any deposits which may have formed in the bottom of the casserole. Remove and discard the whole onion and the parsley bundles. Bring to a boil, then reduce the heat to very low, cover, and simmer gently for 1 hour.

Pour the cream into a bowl and add the egg yolks, chopped parsley, and the remaining 1 tbsp softened (not melted) butter; beat with a balloon whisk until very well blended. When the chicken flesh almost falls off the bones, transfer the portions to a hot soup tureen, leaving all the liquid behind. Draw aside from the heat and gradually add the cream and egg liaison to the liquid and vegetables, stirring constantly with a wooden spoon. Add more salt and pepper if necessary. Return to an extremely low heat for 1 minute, stirring constantly. Do not allow to boil. Pour over the chicken pieces and serve.

VEGETABLES

ASPERGES À LA FLAMANDE*
Asparagus with eggs and butter

Flanders

Preparation: 30 minutes
Cooking: 45 minutes
Very easy

Serves 6:
3–3 1/2 lb fresh white asparagus
6 eggs
1/2 lb sweet butter
1 large bunch parsley
salt and pepper

Peel the asparagus stalks, working away from the tips; cut off the tough, thicker ends making sure the pieces are of fairly even length. Tie firmly but not too tightly in bundles of 5–6 spears with kitchen string. Bring approx. 3 quarts salted water to a boil in a large pan; add the asparagus bundles and boil gently for 45 minutes.

Remove the bundles carefully and drain thoroughly on kitchen towels. Cut the string and remove; place the asparagus carefully on a clean, white folded cloth on a serving platter.

While the asparagus is cooking, hard boil the eggs (8–10 minutes), peel, and cut lengthwise into quarters. Melt the butter over hot water. Finely chop the parsley.

Each person takes a quartered egg and some parsley and uses a fork to mash these into some hot melted butter, adding salt and freshly ground pepper to taste; the asparagus spears are then dipped in this mixture and eaten.

The local vegetable flan or flamiche *(made with leeks, onions or pumpkin) is a favorite dish of the northern French. A visitor to the region in the nineteenth century, Alphonse Karr, a famous writer and humorist, did not take to it: "In Picardy I was served a leek tart which was a disgrace, and I was quite unable to eat it."*

ENDIVES À LA FLAMANDE*

Braised Belgian endives

Flanders

Preparation: 20 minutes
Cooking: 30 minutes
Very easy

Serves 4:
2–2½ lb Belgian endives
½ cup butter
1½ tbsp sugar
1 lemon
salt and pepper

Make a deep incision in the form of a cross in the base of the endives or remove a cone-shaped piece from each with a very sharp knife, leaving a hollow about ¾ in deep.

Rinse briefly and dry with kitchen towels. Blanch in 2 quarts boiling salted water in a large pan for 5 minutes. Drain and dry thoroughly.

Heat the butter until it starts to foam in a fireproof dish just large enough to take the endives in a single layer; remove from the heat and add the endives, season with salt and pepper, then add the sugar and lemon juice. Grease a piece of waxed paper generously with butter and place it, butter side down, over the endives. Cover and braise in the oven, preheated to 325°F, for 30 minutes or until tender.

The endives can be served just as they are, or briefly browned in fresh butter over high heat, or they can be covered with a béchamel sauce, sprinkled with grated cheese mixed with fine breadcrumbs and browned in a hot oven.

The vegetable growers of Picardy are very successful: half the peas canned in France come from this region. In the vast, efficiently run market gardens in the Somme valley, pumpkins, cucumbers, cabbages, fava and white navy beans, salsify, leeks, cauliflowers, green beans, and squashes are grown on a very large scale and all are of exceptionally good quality. Parmentier, who first promoted the potato in France and made it popular was born in the town of Montdidier, in the midst of this vegetarian's paradise.

DESSERTS

GÂTEAU FLAMAND

Orange and cinnamon cake

Flanders

Preparation: 10 minutes
Cooking: 45 minutes
Easy

Serves 6:
$2^1/_2$ cups cake flour or all-purpose flour
1 cup superfine sugar
$^1/_2$ cup peanut oil
$1^1/_2$ tsp baking soda
3 eggs
$^3/_4$ cup beer
2 tbsp butter
finely grated peel of 1 orange
pinch ground cinnamon
pinch salt

Whisk together the eggs, sugar, salt, oil, beer, orange peel, and cinnamon until smooth. Stop beating while you sift in the flour and baking powder together a little at a time, then beat in until smoothly blended.

Grease a 10-in deep cake pan with butter and lightly dust the base with flour. Transfer the cake batter to this pan, tap the bottom on the work surface several times to level and eliminate any air bubbles. Bake for 45 minutes in a preheated oven at 350°F. When done, turn out carefully on to a cake rack and leave to cool.

When cold, the cake can be cut horizontally in half and a filling of marmalade added.

TARTE À LA RHUBARBE*

Rhubarb tart

Artois and Picardy

Preparation: 20 minutes
Cooking: 45 minutes
Easy

Serves 4:
$1^1/_2$ tbsp butter
12 oz pie dough (see glossary)
$2^1/_4$-$2^1/_2$ lb thin, tender rhubarb stalks
1 large egg
1 cup superfine sugar

Grease a 10-in pie pan with the butter. Roll the pie dough out into a sheet $^1/_8$ in thick and line the pie pan. Trim off the edges with a sharp knife and prick the bottom lightly with a fork.

Peel the rhubarb stalks carefully, pulling off all the outer skin. Cut into $^3/_4$-in lengths. Sprinkle half the sugar in an even layer completely covering the bottom of the pie shell and spread the rhubarb pieces out evenly on top. Lightly beat the egg and pour all over the rhubarb. Sprinkle the remaining sugar evenly over the rhubarb. Bake for 45 minutes in a preheated oven at 350°F. Serve warm or cold.

East

Champagne
Lorraine
Alsace
Burgundy
Franche-Comté
Nivernais

The region of France that lies to the east of Paris and comprises the old provinces of Champagne, Lorraine, Alsace, Burgundy, Franche-Comté, and the Nivernais probably has the best claim of all French regions to gastronomic self-sufficiency.

Certainly this large area wants for nothing where its wines are concerned, both for variety and excellence.

The wine-growing territory known as true Champagne country covers just over 54,300 acres. The boundaries are strictly set by the authorities, who only allow wine producers to put more land down to viticulture if they can prove that vines have been grown there in the past.

Champagne is a wine that owes more to man's skill and ingenuity than to nature's gifts: it is the product of blending anything from 30 to 40 wines, taken from areas around towns and villages that merit the description of *grand crus* or *premier crus* (the very best and the merely excellent growths respectively). Since all champagne is the product of blending, vintages do not have the same significance as they do with other wines; it is perfectly legal for up to 20 percent of champagne from a specified vintage to be wines from other vintages.

Between 120 and 130 million bottles of champagne are produced each year and three quarters of them are consumed in France.

A little further south we come to a province of which Erasmus once said: "Burgundy can be called the mother of mankind, for she produces such incomparable milk!" He was, of course, referring to the province's wines, and in the area that stretches from Auxerre to Chagny they are indeed incomparable. It is amazing that so many world-famous wines come from the irregular escarpment known as the *Côte d'Or* made up by the *Côte de Nuits* and the *Côte de Beaune*: such illustrious names as Chambertin, Clos-de-Vougeot, Romanée Conti, Corton, Pommard, Meursault, and Montrachet, and all produced within a very narrow strip of country 30 miles long and varying in width from a mile and a half to just a few hundred yards.

Talleyrand wrote: "Were one of the princes or potentates of this world to render you twenty signal services, you have only to give him some fine old Burgundy to drink and he will be forever in your debt."

Traveling eastward from Burgundy, the vineyards of Alsace grow superb Riesling, Gewürztraminer, Muscat, and Pinot grapes. In vintages when weather conditions are particularly favorable, some outstanding wines are made from late-picked grapes; these have a remarkable fragrance and lusciousness and are stronger and sweeter than is usual in Alsace. Unlike other French wines which are called after a town or vineyard, the labels on Alsatian wine bottles bear the names of the grape and the shipper. This area's production accounts for one in three of all the bottles of white wine drunk in France. The exceptionally high quality of the good growths (*crus*) enjoyed by wine drinkers today is due to the producers' foresight after World War II when they embarked on a major improvement program covering all aspects of their wine making and introduced rigorous selection processes.

Alsace can also boast the oldest wine growers' promotional body in France, the Confrérie de Saint-Étienne in Ammerschwihr, which dates back to the fourteenth century.

Next comes the Franche-Comté, the only wine-producing area in the world to produce five types of wine: white, rosé, red, *vins jaunes* or "yellow wines" (the most widely renowned being Château-Châlon which is aged in the barrel for at least six years) and, lastly, the so-called *"vins de paille"*, (straw wines): sweet and with a high alcohol

On the previous pages: *surrounded by woods and pasture, a substantial farmhouse nestles in a sheltered spot on the sparsely populated slopes of the imposing Morvan granite outcrop.* Below left: *in Franche-Comté, as in Burgundy, an increasing acreage is used for growing corn. The ears are hung out in the sun to dry more quickly.* Below right: *on the side of a house an advertisement invites the passer-by to visit some of Burgundy's innumerable cellars. Together with Nuits-Saint-Georges, Beaune is one of the most famous French wine towns.*

Above: *over the last few centuries Lorraine's wine-growing acreage has shrunk; today the only wines of any note that remain are the* vins gris *from the Côtes de Toul, (not "gray," as the name might suggest but a very pale pink), and a red Vin de Moselle.* Right: *this Alsatian wine grower has good reason to be proud of his province, which boasts the oldest wine guild or producers' association in France, the Confrérie de Saint-Etienne, founded in Ammerschwihr, near Colmar, during the fifteenth century.*

content, made with grapes that are laid on straw mats or hung on racks to dry slightly until midwinter.

Happily, as if different tasks had been shared out by nature, each of these old provinces has earned a reputation for producing and cooking certain foods particularly well.

Champagne and the spur that links up with the Ardennes excels in turning variety meats into excellent sausages and other forms of *charcuterie*. Troyes is famous for its *andouillettes*, Rethel for its savory white pudding, while Sainte-Menehould's stuffed pig's feet are legendary.

Pork butchery is almost synonymous with Alsace. One of the many tasty examples of this is the local dish of *choucroute*, an Alsatian version of the German *Sauerkraut*.

Each town and village and perhaps each household has its own favorite version of *choucroute*, into which go various pork products: fresh pork fat, pork chops, various types of boiling sausage, liver dumplings, etc.

Pork products are far from being Alsace's only claim to fame. Other specialties include the ever popular *bäckeoffe*, a casseroled mixture of lamb, beef, pork, onions, and potatoes, while the crowning glory of the province's rich but not heavy cuisine is that most aristocratic and highly prized delicacy, *foie gras*, greatly enlarged goose or duck liver. The method of cramming or force-feeding geese and ducks to produce *foie gras* was devised in this area by a Normandy-born cook who worked for the Maréchal de Contades, military governor of Alsace from 1762 to 1788.

Next we come to Lorraine, with a reputation for fine patisserie and confectionery. This province saw many notable introductions to the French repertoire

Above: *eating and drinking in the open air in the cathedral square in the heart of Strasbourg. This bustling city brings a great deal of prosperity to Alsace; besides being an artistic, cultural, and gastronomic center, it is also the headquarters of the Council of Europe and the European Parliament.* Right: *eastern France is no exception to the general French rule that menus make compulsive reading for serious gourmets.*

of sweets, candies, and desserts: a Polish-born king invented the *baba au rhum* (a sweet yeast cake soaked in sugar syrup and rum) when he ruled the province; an artist introduced the French to the delights of puff pastry; two nuns developed their own, superb macaroons, and a confectioner started to use bergamot as a flavoring (the essential oil is used for a specialty of Nancy, barley sugar, and the zest is used in patisserie).

Bar-le-Duc produces memorable jams, jellies, and conserves: redcurrant jelly with all the seeds painstakingly removed with a pin; Épinal makes marzipan "pebbles"; Longwy, almond cakes; Lunéville, brioches; while Metz specializes in candied Mirabelle plums and stuffed quetsches (small, oval purple plums with very tender skins and aromatic flesh); cherries are preserved in kirsch in Nancy; Plombières prides itself on its barley sugar; Saint-Mihiel on its *croquets* (almond petits fours); Verdun is synonymous with *dragées* (sugared almonds); Flavigny with aniseed-flavored candy. And although the savory dishes and main courses of Lorraine may not send the most exacting French gourmets into raptures, the cooking of the province is very good, noted for such dishes as sucking pig in aspic and the savory flans known as quiche.

In this eastern region traditional fish dishes are for freshwater varieties since the sea is far away and seemed even more distant in the days when transport was difficult and slow. Franche-Comté, with its heavy rainfall and abundant rivers and streams, has plenty of excellent river and lake fish. The little town of Verdun-sur-le-Doubs has earned a reputation for being the place to enjoy *pauchouse* (or *pochouse*), a freshwater fish soup. The inhabitants of Franche-Comté can thank their damp climate for another culinary treat: all sorts of wild mushrooms abound in the woods and forests of the province.

In common with the rest of France, all sorts of cheeses are made throughout the whole of the eastern region. Bries from Meaux and Melun, Coulommiers, Chaource, and Langres cheeses all come from Champagne country; Époisses and Soumaintrain from Burgundy; Munster from Alsace; Gérome from Lorraine; Comté, and the blue cheeses from Gex and Septmoncel, as well as Morbier, and Metton are all from Franche-Comté. The Nivernais produces excellent goat's cheeses: Chevrotin, Pouilly, and Gien.

All these provinces make excellent brandies: the *marcs* of Burgundy, Champagne, Alsace, and Franche-Comté; fruit brandies (pear, raspberry), plum brandies (mirabelle, quetsche) and cherry brandy (kirsch) from Alsace and Lorraine.

The abundance of wine in this area and its variety explain the local fondness for using wine when cooking all sorts of foods.

One example out of many is chicken: there are recipes for dishes in which it is cooked with the yellow wine of Franche-Comté, with Riesling in Alsace, with full-bodied red wine in Burgundy and with champagne . . . in Champagne.

With such an abundance of good things, the cooks of the area have the ideal raw materials with which to work their magic.

*The wine harvest in Alsace. Unlike normal French practice, Alsatian wines, which are predominantly white, are not named after communes or growths (*crus*) but after the vine varietal from which they are made. The labels on the typical tall green bottles bear the name of the type of grape: Pinot noir, Pinot gris (known locally as Tokay), Pinot blanc, Sylvaner, Riesling, Gewürztraminer, and Muscat.*

SOUPS

SOUPE À LA BIÈRE*
Beer soup

Alsace

Preparation: 5 minutes
Cooking: 25 minutes
Easy

Serves 4:
$1\frac{1}{2}$ quarts beer
$\frac{1}{4}$ cup butter
$\frac{1}{2}$ cup all-purpose flour
1 tbsp superfine sugar
pinch cinnamon
6 slices bread, fried in butter
1 cup heavy cream
salt and pepper

Make a roux: heat the butter and stir in the flour; cook until golden.

Gradually stir in the beer; season with salt and pepper; add the sugar and the cinnamon. Bring to a boil stirring continously so that the mixture thickens slightly without forming any lumps. Simmer for 20 minutes. Fry fairly thick slices of white bread in butter and place in heated soup bowls or a tureen.

Stir the cream into the soup and immediately ladle on top of the bread; serve.

SOUPE AUX ABATS D'OIE
Goose giblet soup

Alsace

Preparation: 20 minutes
Cooking: 2 hours
Easy

Serves 6:
2 goose necks
4 wing tips (last 2 joints)
2 gizzards
3 carrots, peeled
1 stick celery
3 leeks, white part only
$\frac{1}{4}$ cup butter
1 bouquet garni
2 onions, peeled, each studded with 1 clove
$\frac{2}{3}$ cup rice
1 tbsp chopped parsley
generous pinch nutmeg
salt and pepper

Clean, trim, and rinse the giblets. Blanch briefly in boiling water, drain, refresh, and drain again. Dice the carrots and celery and slice the leeks (use the white part only). Sweat the vegetables in the butter for 5 minutes; do not brown. Add the giblets, the bouquet garni, and the clove-studded onions. Add 2 quarts water and a little salt and pepper. Bring to a boil then simmer for $1\frac{1}{2}$ hours.

Skim off any fat from the resulting broth and bring back to a boil. Add the rice and boil gently for 30 minutes, stirring now and then.

Remove the bouquet garni and the onions and cloves. Take all the meat off the bones, cut into small pieces, and add to the soup. Correct the seasoning. Sprinkle in the parsley and nutmeg, stir, and serve.

CONSOMME AUX QUENELLES DE MOELLE*

Clear soup with marrow dumplings

Alsace

Preparation: 10 minutes
Cooking: 10 minutes
Easy

Serves 6:
Make the beef broth by using the broth after cooking the classic dish of boiled beef and vegetables, or boil 4½ lb beef bones (e.g. short ribs) and lean ground beef with turnips, carrots, leeks, celery, and onions in 2 quarts water; once the water boils, skim off any scum and simmer for 3 hours.

For the dumplings:
10–11 oz cooked beef marrow
½ cup fine breadcrumbs
2½ tbsp semolina
3 egg yolks
small pinch ground nutmeg
salt and pepper

Extract the marrow from the marrow bones and push through a sieve into a mixing bowl. Mix in the breadcrumbs, semolina, and egg yolks. Season lightly with salt, pepper, and nutmeg. Work together until smooth, then break off small pieces about the size of filberts and roll into balls. Strain the beef broth, bring back to a gentle boil, and poach the dumplings in it, simmering gently for 10 minutes. Serve.

POTAGE AUX GRENOUILLES

Frog's leg soup

Alsace

Preparation: 30 minutes
Cooking: 45 minutes
Easy

Serves 6:
12 pairs prepared frog's legs
3 egg yolks
½ cup butter
4 shallots, peeled
1 bunch watercress
1 large sprig parsley
½ cup crème fraîche *or heavy cream*
½ cup rice flour
1 quart light broth (or fish fumet*) (see glossary)*
1 cup Alsatian Riesling wine
pinch nutmeg
salt and pepper

Defrost the frog's legs totally if frozen. Finely slice the shallots and cook until lightly browned with the chopped parsley in 3 tbsp of the butter. Add the frog's legs. Cook gently for 5 minutes. Add the white wine and the broth. Season with salt and pepper and bring to a boil, then simmer gently, uncovered, for 25 minutes. Take out the frog's legs, remove all the bones, cut the flesh into small pieces, and keep warm.

Melt the remaining butter in a saucepan; add the chopped watercress and 1 cup water. Mix the rice flour thoroughly with ¾ cup cold water or milk, then stir into the watercress mixture. Continue stirring until it boils, then simmer for 15 minutes.

Strain the hot, wine-flavored broth into a clean saucepan; gradually stir in the thickened watercress mixture and the frog's leg meat over moderate heat. Beat the egg yolks lightly into the *crème fraîche* and stir into the soup over very low heat. Season with salt and pepper. Serve immediately in heated bowls.

ENTRÉES

COU D'OIE FARCI AU FOIE GRAS*

Goose neck stuffed with foie gras

Alsace

Preparation: 30 minutes
Cooking: 45 minutes
Complicated

Serves 6:
1/2–3/4 lb pork (e.g. boned blade shoulder)
1/2–3/4 lb veal shoulder
2 oz fresh foie gras *or canned, semicooked, pasteurized* foie gras
1 medium-sized truffle, fresh or canned
1/4 cup cognac
pinch nutmeg
pinch quatre-épices *(see glossary) or pinch each ground allspice, cloves, and cinnamon*
salt and pepper
2 goose necks (not skinned)
1 quart chicken broth (see glossary)

Trim and finely chop (or use the food processor) the pork and veal (do not grind). Cut the *foie gras* into small cubes and add to the meats with the coarsely chopped truffle (and its juice if canned), the cognac, spices, salt and freshly ground pepper. Mix gently but thoroughly with the meat. Carefully peel off the skin from the goose necks without puncturing it; sew up the narrower end opening securely and pack the stuffing into the skin. Sew up the remaining end. Add to the gently simmering broth and barely simmer for 45 minutes.

Serve cold or warm, with a salad.

LEVERKNEPFLE

Liver dumplings

Alsace

Preparation: 15 minutes
Cooking: 5 minutes
Easy

Serves 6:
1 lb pig's liver
1/2 lb fresh pork belly
1 onion, peeled
1 small bunch parsley
3 eggs
1/2 lb fine breadcrumbs

Chop the liver and the pork very finely (do not grind). Chop the onion and parsley. Mix all these with the eggs and breadcrumbs and shape into small dumplings. Add to a large pan of boiling salted water. When the dumplings bob up to the surface, they are cooked. Remove with a slotted spoon; transfer to a heated plate. These are usually served with *choucroute*.

ZIEWELKUECHE

Souffléed egg, onion, and ham flan

Alsace

Preparation: 30 minutes
Cooking: 30 minutes
Easy

Serves 6:
1/2 lb pie dough (see glossary)
1 lb onions, peeled
1/4 cup butter
1/2 cup all-purpose flour
1 cup milk
3 eggs, separated
1/2 cup crème fraîche *or heavy cream*
pinch ground nutmeg
salt and pepper
1/4 lb smoked bacon

Roll out the pie dough to a thickness of 1/8 in and use to line a 9–10-in tart pan. Sweat the thinly sliced onions in the butter until tender; sprinkle with the flour and cook, stirring, for 5 minutes. Add the milk and beat with a balloon whisk.

Remove from the heat when the sauce boils. Beat the egg yolks and cream lightly with a small pinch each of salt, pepper, and nutmeg. Mix into the onion sauce.

Cut off the skin or rind and any tough bits from the bacon and slice across the streaks of fat and lean into strips or lardons; blanch, drain, and refresh in cold water. Drain well on kitchen towels. Beat the egg whites until stiff but not dry, fold gently but thoroughly into the mixture, and turn into the pie shell. Sprinkle the bacon pieces all over the top. Cook in a preheated oven at 400°F for 30 minutes.

FLAMMEKUECHE*

Cheese, onion, and bacon pizza

Alsace

Start preparation 2–4 hours in advance
Preparation: 45 minutes
Cooking: 15 minutes
Fairly easy

Serves 4:
10 oz ready-prepared bread dough or pizza dough
7oz soft cream cheese (e.g. Petit Suisse), drained
1 cup very heavy cream
3 tbsp all-purpose flour
salt
5 tbsp peanut oil
5 oz bacon
5 oz Bermuda onions, peeled

Roll the prepared bread dough into a thin sheet and use to line a jelly roll pan greased with butter. Mix the cheese, cream, flour, 1 tsp salt, and the oil very thoroughly. Spread this mixture over the dough base.

Cut the bacon into strips; blanch and drain; chop or slice the onions very finely; sprinkle both evenly onto the cream and cheese mixture and use the spatula to press some of this topping just below the surface of the creamy filling. Bake in a preheated oven (450°F) for 15 minutes.

SALADE DE CERVELAS

Sausage salad

Alsace

Preparation: 15 minutes
Very easy

Serves 6:
6 Cervelas or Saveloy sausages
6 lettuce leaves
3 hard-boiled eggs
2 tomatoes
1 Bermuda onion, peeled
3 tbsp coarsely chopped parsley
wine vinegar
peanut oil
strong mustard
salt and pepper

Remove the skin from the sausages, cut lengthwise in half, and make several parallel incisions on the rounded sides. Place flat side down on a serving platter. Arrange the lettuce leaves around the outside of the dish. Cut the eggs lengthwise in half and arrange between the sausages. Quarter and deseed the tomatoes and place between the eggs.

Chop the onion finely and sprinkle all over the sausages, tomatoes, and eggs. Make a vinaigrette dressing with the vinegar, oil, and mustard, adding salt and pepper to taste, and sprinkle all over the salad. Garnish with the chopped parsley.

QUICHE AU LARD*

Bacon and egg flan

Lorraine

Preparation: 25 minutes
Cooking: 45 minutes
Easy

Serves 6:
$^1/_2$ lb pie dough (see glossary)
5 oz bacon
2 tbsp butter
$^1/_4$ lb Gruyère cheese, thinly sliced
6 egg yolks
$1^3/_4$ cups heavy cream
pinch nutmeg
salt and pepper

Roll out the pie dough into a sheet $^1/_8$ in thick and use to line a 9–10-in pie dish, greased with 1 tbsp of the butter. Prick the surface lightly with a fork.

Blanch the bacon and drain; remove the skin and cut at right angles to the streaks of lean and fat, into strips. Cook the bacon gently in the remaining butter; do not color. Drain off all the fat. Spread out the bacon and the thinly sliced Gruyère in the pie shell.

Beat the egg yolks and the cream in a bowl, add the nutmeg, a very small pinch of salt and some freshly ground pepper, and the nutmeg; pour all over the bacon and cheese. The mixture will rise as it cooks, so do not overfill the pie shell.

Place in the oven, preheated to 400°F and bake for 20 minutes, then reduce the heat to 350°F and cook for a further 25 minutes or until done.

TOURTE DE LA VALLÉE DE MUNSTER
Veal and pork pie

Alsace

Start preparation 12–24 hours in advance
Preparation: 20 minutes
Cooking: 1 hour
Complicated

Serves 8:
2 thick slices white bread, crusts removed
1 cup milk
10 oz veal noix *taken from round (leg)*
10 oz pork tenderloin
1 large bunch parsley
2 onions, peeled
2 tbsp butter
1½ cups Alsatian Riesling or Sylvaner wine
salt and pepper
14 oz pie dough
10 oz puff pastry
1 egg yolk

Soak the bread in the milk. Squeeze out excess moisture and place in the food processor with pork and veal (trimmed and cut into pieces). Process until evenly and finely chopped; do not grind. Transfer to a large mixing bowl. Chop the parsley. Slice the onions very finely and sweat until tender in the butter (5 minutes). Stir the parsley, onions, wine, and salt and pepper to taste into the meat mixture. Cover and refrigerate overnight.

Take the pork and veal mixture out of the refrigerator. Roll out the pie dough and use to line a pie plate or deep tart pan. Fill with the meat mixture. Roll out the puff pastry just under ⅛ in thick to make a lid for the pie, trimming the edges to size and sealing them by moistening with a little cold water and pinching together. Make a small, neat hole in the center to allow steam to escape. Brush the surface with egg yolk. Bake at 350°F for 1 hour.

PÂTÉ DE FOIE GRAS EN CROÛTE
Goose liver in a pastry case

Alsace

Start preparation 2 days in advance
Preparation: 40 minutes
Cooking: 45 minutes
Complicated

Serves 8:
2 raw foies gras, *weighing 1 lb each or canned, semicooked, pasteurized* foie gras
1 tbsp salt mixed with pinch quatre-épices *(see glossary) or allspice*
¼ cup cognac or brandy
¼ cup kirsch
½ lb pork tenderloin
½ lb veal tenderloin
salt and pepper
¼ cup butter
¼ lb truffles, fresh or canned
1¼ lb pie dough (see glossary)
1 egg yolk
1 cup chicken aspic jelly flavored with Madeira

If using fresh *foie gras*, make an incision between the two lobes of the liver and separate them to enable you to remove any clots of blood and gristle; carefully remove the very thin outer membrane. Keeping the 2 lobes intact, rub the salt and allspice mixture gently into the surface. Marinate the *foie gras* overnight in the mixed cognac and kirsch with a pinch each of allspice and salt.

Chop the trimmed pork and veal very finely (do not grind). Mix thoroughly, adding salt, pepper, and the softened butter.

Roll out the pastry into a thin sheet; use three quarters of it to line a large, deep, straight-sided paté dish or deep rectangular springform mold. Place half the meat mixture in the dish or mold; stud or spike the *foie gras* with small pieces of truffle (use all of them) and place flat on the meat mixture; cover with the remaining meat mixture, packing it neatly but not too tightly all around them.

Use the remaining pastry to make a lid, moistening the edges and sealing tightly. Make two small, neat holes in the lid and place a cylinder of foil in each. Brush the surface of the pastry with egg yolk. Preheat the oven to 375°F and cook for 45 minutes, reducing the heat slightly if the pastry colors too deeply. Test by inserting a skewer deep into the center of the pie; if the pointed end is warm when drawn out the pie is done.

Leave to cool and when nearly cold, pour the melted (liquid) aspic carefully into the foil chimneys, using a jug and funnel. Leave to cool and set overnight in a cold larder or refrigerator. Serve the following day.

TOURTE ALSACIENNE
Veal, ham, and egg pie

Alsace

Start preparation 24 hours in advance
Preparation: 30 minutes
Cooking: 40 minutes
Easy

Serves 6:
1 lb puff pastry (see glossary)
1½ lb pork tenderloin
1 lb veal tenderloin
1¾ cups Alsatian Riesling or Sylvaner wine
1 clove garlic, peeled
1 bouquet garni (thyme, bay leaf, parsley)
3 eggs + 1 extra yolk
1 cup crème fraîche *or heavy cream*
salt and pepper

The day before you plan to make and serve the pie, cut the pork and veal into short, thin strips about ¾ in wide and marinate for 24 hours in a bowl in the wine with the clove of garlic, bouquet garni, salt, and freshly ground pepper.

The following day preheat the oven to 375°F. Drain the meat and dry on kitchen towels. Reserve the marinade.

Roll out 10 oz of the pastry into a thin sheet and use to line a pie plate or deep tart pan; if using the latter, the pastry should overlap the edges by just over 1 in. Prick the base with a fork and cover with an even layer of all the meat strips.

Beat the three whole eggs into the cream, seasoning with salt and plenty of pepper. Pour over the meat. Roll out the remaining pastry to form a lid, place on top of the pie, fold the spare surround of pastry over the lid, pinching securely with your fingertips. Beat the egg yolk with 1 tbsp water and brush all over the surface. Cook in the oven for 40 minutes. Serve very hot.

FARCE CHAMPENOISE
Special sausage stuffing

Champagne

Preparation: 30 minutes
Easy

Serves 6:
1 lb good pork sausage meat
1 onion, peeled
1 shallot, peeled
1 clove garlic, peeled
¼ cup oz butter
½ cup still champagne
1 chicken liver
1 small bunch parsley
salt and pepper

Chop the onion, shallot, and garlic very finely; sweat in the butter until tender and very pale golden brown. Add the wine (if you cannot buy nonsparkling *champagne nature*, use a good dry white wine) and boil, uncovered, until reduced by half.

Trim off any discoloration from the chicken liver before chopping it, chop the parsley and mix both with the sausage meat; blend in the wine mixture. Season with salt and pepper. Pound this mixture with a pestle and mortar, or process in the blender, until very smooth. Use for *paupiettes* (veal parcels) or to stuff a boned, rolled lamb shoulder.

ESCARGOTS À LA BOURGUIGNONNE*

Snails with garlic and parsley butter

Burgundy

Preparation: 40 minutes for canned snails, 7½ hours longer for live snails
Cooking: 10 minutes
Easy, if snails are canned. Complicated, if live: for the latter use 1 cup coarse salt and ¾ cup wine vinegar and the court-bouillon

Serves 6:
3 dozen snails

For the *court-bouillon*:
1 quart dry white Burgundy wine (Aligoté)
1 cup water
6 shallots, peeled
6 cloves garlic, peeled
1 carrot, peeled and sliced into rounds
1 onion, peeled and studded with 2 cloves
1 bouquet garni (thyme, bay leaf, parsley)

For the garlic and parsley butter:
1¼ cups butter, softened
1 bunch parsley
2 cloves garlic, peeled
2 shallots, peeled
salt and pepper

If using live snails, buy from a reputable supplier. Wash the shells and the operculum very thoroughly. Drain and place in a large bowl with the salt and vinegar, stir well, and place a heavy lid on top. Leave for 3–4 hours, stirring now and then. The snails will release all their

slime and will die. Wash very thoroughly under running cold water. Dry. Place in a large saucepan with sufficient cold water to cover; bring to a boil, skim; boil for 3 minutes. Drain and rinse in cold water.

For the *court-bouillon* bring all the ingredients to a boil (reserve 1 shallot and 1 clove garlic for cooking the snails); simmer for 10 minutes. Cool. Place the snails in the cold liquid, bring to a boil, skim, and simmer gently for $3\frac{1}{2}$ hours. Drain. Remove the snails from their shells with a long needle, and remove the black section.

If using canned snails, join the recipe here. Finely chop the reserved garlic and shallot, cook gently in 1 tbsp of the butter until tender, add the snails and season with salt and pepper. Cook for a further 3 minutes. Set aside.

Make the garlic butter. Chop the parsley, garlic, and shallot very finely, mix well, season with salt and pepper, then work in the butter with a fork. Chill in the refrigerator for 5 minutes. Make sure the shells are dry: place about $\frac{1}{2}$ tsp of the garlic butter in each shell, place the snail on top, then cover completely with more butter, firmly pushed in. Place in snail plates, openings uppermost, and cook in a preheated oven at 475°F for 10 minutes. Serve at once. If the canned snails do not have a packet of shells with them, put the snails in ramekins, cover with the butter, and cook in the same way.

OEUFS EN MEURETTE*

Poached eggs with red wine sauce

Burgundy

Preparation: 10 minutes
Cooking: 35 minutes
Fairly easy

Serves 4:
8 very fresh eggs
$2\frac{1}{4}$ cups good red Burgundy or Beaujolais
1 tsp sugar
1 bouquet garni (thyme, bay leaf, parsley)
salt and pepper
1 large Bermuda onion, peeled
1 clove garlic, peeled
6 tbsp butter
1 clove
$\frac{1}{4}$ cup all-purpose flour
4 large slices coarse white bread
2 sprigs parsley

Bring the wine to a boil in a saucepan with the sugar, bouquet garni, and a little salt and pepper. Hold a match or taper close to the liquid and flame briefly; simmer for 10 minutes, uncovered.

Slice the onion thinly; mince the garlic with the flat of a knife blade. Fry the onion and garlic very gently in $1\frac{1}{2}$ tbsp of the butter for 5 minutes until golden in a wide saucepan; add the hot wine mixture and the clove. Boil gently for 15 minutes, uncovered, then remove the bouquet garni and clove.

Meanwhile, work the remaining butter, softened, with the flour to make a *beurre manié*; set aside in the refrigerator. Use extra butter to fry the bread slices until browned on both sides; keep warm on a hot serving platter. Poach the eggs two at a time for 2 minutes in the wine mixture; remove with a slotted spoon, trim off any ragged edges, and place on the bread slices. Keep warm.

Strain the wine; return to a clean saucepan on a very low heat; stir in the *beurre manié* to thicken the liquid. After a few minutes' cooking, pour the sauce over the eggs. Sprinkle with chopped parsley.

JAMBON PERSILLÉ*

Parsleyed ham in aspic

Burgundy

Soaking time for the ham: 12 hours
Preparation: 1 hour
Cooking: 4 hours
Complicated

Serves 15:
1 9-lb raw cured, salted ham (leg or picnic shoulder)
2 calf's feet, blanched
2¼ lb shin of veal
¼ lb carrots
1 onion, studded with 1 clove
1 large bouquet garni (thyme, bay leaf, parsley, tarragon)
1 bottle white Burgundy (Aligoté) or similar dry white wine
1½ tbsp peppercorns
3 cloves garlic, peeled
¼ lb shallots, peeled
10 large sprigs parsley

Remove excess salt from the ham by soaking in several changes of cold water for 12 hours. Drain and place the ham in a very large cooking pot, add sufficient cold water to cover, and bring slowly to a very gentle boil. Leave to simmer very slowly for 30 minutes. If the calf's feet are not already blanched, simmer with the ham.

Drain the ham and calf's feet. Remove the skin from the ham and take the flesh off the bone. Return all the ham pieces (skin, bone, flesh) to the cleaned cooking receptacle and pour in sufficient fresh, boiling water to cover. Add the calf's feet (split lengthwise in half), the bouquet garni, veal, peppercorns, peeled studded onion, and the wine. Simmer extremely gently (the liquid should just "shiver") until the ham pieces disintegrate when crushed with a wooden spatula. Halfway through cooking, check and correct the seasoning.

Take the ham out of the pan and cut into 1½–2-in cubes. Take the meat off the bones and cartilage of the shin and calf's feet respectively.

Finely chop the garlic, shallots, and parsley. Strain the cooking liquid for the aspic. When cold enough, remove the fat from the surface; spoon a thin coating of this aspic over the entire inside surface of a large chilled terrine or mold. Chill very briefly. Line the base and sides of the terrine with pieces of calf's foot and veal, sticking these to the aspic coating.

Fill the terrine with layers of ham, chopped garlic, shallots, and parsley. Finish with a layer of calf's foot and veal pieces. Slowly ladle in the aspic (if too set, warm the liquid slightly; it should look like oil when ready to use).

Cover and chill in the refrigerator until set. Unmold and serve in slices.

GOUGÈRES

Cheese choux puffs

Burgundy

Preparation: 20 minutes
Cooking: 30 minutes
Fairly easy

Serves 4:
1 cup water
¼ cup butter
1 cup all-purpose flour
4 eggs
3 oz Comté or Gruyère cheese, finely diced
salt and pepper
pinch nutmeg

Cut the butter into small pieces and place in a saucepan with the water with a pinch each of salt, pepper, and nutmeg; bring slowly to a boil. When melted, draw aside from the heat and immediately add all the flour, mixing it into the liquid. Stir over low heat for 1–2 minutes; when the choux mixture comes cleanly away from the sides of the pan, remove from the heat.

Add the eggs one at a time, beating each in very thoroughly before adding the next. Add the cheese and stir well.

Grease a cookie sheet with butter and, using a tablespoon, place walnut-sized portions of the choux mixture on it (or use a piping bag and large nozzle), well spaced out.

Place in a preheated oven (400°F) and bake for 30 minutes; turn off the heat and leave for a few minutes with the oven door open.

FISH

BROCHET AU RIESLING*

Pike with Riesling

Alsace

Preparation: 20 minutes
Cooking: 30 minutes
Easy

Serves 6:
1 5½-lb pike or 2 medium-sized pike
1 cup butter
5 shallots, peeled
1 cup Riesling
2¼ cups crème fraîche *or heavy cream*
1 bunch parsley
1 sprig thyme
juice of 1 lemon
salt and pepper

Remove the pike's scales, then gut, wash, and dry the fish. Grease an ovenproof dish with some of the butter, place the pike in it with the chopped shallots and parsley and the thyme leaves. Season with salt and pepper. Pour in the wine and cook in the oven (preheated to 425°F) for approx. 30 minutes (a shorter time if two, smaller fish are used). Baste several times with the wine during cooking.

When it is done, transfer the cooked fish to a heated serving platter; keep hot. Strain the cooking liquid into a saucepan, add more salt or pepper if necessary, add the remaining butter, stir, then pour in the cream and the lemon juice. Stir while heating to just below boiling point; coat the fish with some of the sauce and serve the rest separately.

Accompany with steamed new potatoes tossed in butter.

MATELOTE DE BROCHET À LA TOULOISE

Pike with plum brandy and wine

Lorraine

Preparation: 20 minutes
Cooking: 30 minutes
Easy

Serves 4:
2 pike, each weighing 1 lb
¾ cup butter
¼ cup French mirabelle plum brandy
1 bottle dry white wine
2 shallots, peeled
6 tbsp all-purpose flour
1 cup crème fraîche *or heavy cream*
1 bouquet garni (parsley, thyme, bay leaf)
8 slices white bread, fried in butter
salt and pepper

Descale, gut, wash, and dry the pike; cut into thick steaks. Cook these for 5–6 minutes in ¼ cup of the butter and brown lightly on both sides; add the warmed plum brandy, heat briefly, and flame by setting alight with a match or taper.

Add the finely chopped shallots. Cook for 5 minutes, add the wine and the bouquet garni, a little salt and pepper. Simmer gently, uncovered, until done.

Melt the remaining butter in a smaller saucepan, stir in the flour, and cook, stirring, for a few minutes. Do not allow to color. Gradually stir in ½ cup of the cooking liquid, strained, into this roux. Take the pike steaks out of the cooking liquid and keep hot. Strain the liquid and stir in the thickened liquid; cook over gentle heat, stirring continuously, for 15 minutes until smooth and glossy. Draw aside from the heat and stir in the cream. Arrange the fried bread pieces around the pike steaks, and cover the fish with a thin coating of the sauce.

MATELOTE AU RIESLING

Fish stew with wine

Alsace

Preparation: 45 minutes
Cooking: 30 minutes
Easy

Serves 6:
1 lb pike
1 lb tench or perch
1 lb carp or trout
1 lb eel
1 onion, peeled
3 cloves garlic, peeled
1 carrot, peeled
1 leek
1 bouquet garni (tarragon, bay leaf, thyme, parsley)
1/2 cup butter
2 oz shallots, peeled
2 1/4 cups Alsatian Riesling
1/4 cup all-purpose flour
1 cup crème fraîche *or heavy cream*
4 egg yolks
salt and pepper
small pinch nutmeg

Remove the scales from the fish where present, gut, cut off heads, tails, fins, etc., wash and dry thoroughly. Skin the eel, cut off the head, and clean. Cut all the fish and the eel into steaks or sections 2 in thick. Reserve all the fish heads and tails (discard the eel's head) and place in a very large saucepan with the peeled and thinly sliced onion and the lightly minced garlic cloves. Slice the carrot and leek into thin rings; add to the pan. Add the bouquet garni, a pinch of salt and pepper, and a small pinch of nutmeg. Add 2 quarts cold water; bring slowly to a boil and simmer for 30 minutes to make the fish *fumet*.

Heat 1/4 cup of the butter in a very large saucepan and cook the finely chopped shallots with the fish pieces over a high heat for 2 minutes to brown lightly, turning the fish once. Add the wine and sufficient strained fish *fumet* to just cover the fish pieces. Heat to a gentle simmer and cook slowly for 10 minutes.

Melt 2 tbsp butter in another saucepan and stir in the flour; after cooking for 2–3 minutes, gradually stir in 1 1/2 pints of the cooking liquid from the fish. Cook, stirring continuously, for 15 minutes.

Mix the cream with the egg yolks in a bowl over hot water or in a double boiler; gradually add the slightly thickened cooking liquid stirring continuously over gently simmering water until very hot but not boiling. Taste for seasoning and draw aside from the heat. Stir in the remaining butter, adding a small piece at a time.

Transfer the fish pieces to a large heated dish and cover completely with the sauce.

BROCHET RÔTI AU CHABLIS

Roast pike with white wine sauce

Burgundy

Preparation: 40 minutes
Cooking: 30 minutes
Easy

Serves 6:
1 pike weighing 2-2 1/4 lb
4 shallots, peeled
3 tomatoes, blanched and skinned
1 bottle Chablis or other dry white wine
1/4 cup butter
salt and pepper

For the fish *fumet*:
1 carrot, peeled
1 onion, peeled

Make the fish *fumet* by simmering the pike's head with the sliced onion and carrot and 3/4 cup Chablis. Simmer for 30 minutes; strain. Grease a large ovenproof dish liberally with half the butter. Cover the bottom with the finely sliced shallots. Place the sliced and deseeded tomatoes on top. Add 1 3/4 cups of the wine and the *fumet*.

Remove the pike's scales, fins and tail, gut, wash and dry it. Make several parallel incisions across the fleshiest part of the pike's back and place the fish on the bed of shallots and tomatoes moistened with the fish *fumet*. Place in the oven, preheated to 400°F and cook uncovered for approx. 30 minutes, basting frequently with the liquid. The skin should only brown very lightly.

When the pike is done, transfer to a heated serving platter. Strain the cooking liquid into a saucepan; heat and then beat in the remaining butter in small pieces, using a balloon whisk. Pour over the pike.

PAUCHOUSE

Burgundian fish stew with white wine

Franche-Comté

Preparation: 30 minutes
Cooking: 35 minutes
Easy

Serves 6:
6 1/2 lb mixed freshwater fish (e.g. pike, carp, pike-perch, eel, tench, perch, salmon, etc.)
3 cloves garlic, peeled
1 onion, peeled
4 shallots, peeled
coarse sea salt and peppercorns
1 sprig thyme
1 quart dry white wine (Aligoté)
1/4 cup Burgundy marc *or brandy*
5 tbsp butter
1/4 cup all-purpose flour
6 slices coarse white bread

Trim and gut the fish, wash, dry, and cut into 3/4-in thick steaks. Skin the eel, if used, and cut into 2-in sections. Peel and lightly mince the garlic cloves with the blade of a knife and place in a saucepan with the peeled and chopped onion and the finely sliced shallots. Sprinkle in 1 tbsp of coarse sea salt, 10 roughly crushed peppercorns, and the thyme. Place the fish steaks on top in a single layer. Pour in the wine, cover, and heat; as soon as the liquid boils, uncover, add the heated *marc* or brandy, and flame. Remove from the heat.

Work the soft but still solid butter with the flour and add to the saucepan containing the fish, stirring carefully into the liquid to thicken it, without breaking up the fish. Simmer over very gentle heat for 20 minutes.

Rub the bread slices with cut cloves of garlic and bake in the oven or fry in butter until golden brown.

Strain the sauce and pour over the fish. Surround with the toasted or fried bread slices.

SAUMON AU CHAMPAGNE*

Salmon in champagne sauce

Champagne

Preparation: 30 minutes
Cooking: 20 minutes
Easy

Serves 6:
6 salmon steaks, each weighing 1/2 lb
6 shallots, peeled and finely chopped
15 medium-sized closed cap (button) mushrooms
1 cup butter
1 bottle very dry (Brut) still champagne or dry white wine
1 3/4 cups crème fraîche *or heavy cream*
salt and pepper

Grease an ovenproof dish liberally with 6 tbsp of the butter. Cover the bottom with the shallots and the rinsed, dried and chopped mushroom stalks. Place the salmon steaks on top in a single layer. Surround the salmon steaks with the rinsed, dried mushroom caps, left whole. Season with salt and freshly ground white pepper and add the still champagne. Cook in the oven, preheated to 375°F, for 15 minutes or until the fish is just cooked.

Carefully remove the skin from the steaks and transfer them to a serving plate, surround with the mushroom caps, cover, and keep hot.

Strain the cooking liquid into a saucepan; boil, uncovered, until reduced by two thirds. Reduce the heat to very low; beat in the remaining ½ cup butter one small piece at a time. Add the *crème fraîche* and continue stirring for 1–2 minutes. The sauce should have thickened slightly and look very smooth. Pour the sauce all over the salmon and mushrooms and serve.

ÉCREVISSES À LA CHABLISIENNE

Freshwater crayfish poached in Chablis

Burgundy

Preparation: 30 minutes
Cooking: 10 minutes
Easy

Serves 6:
36 freshwater crayfish

For the *court-bouillon:*
2 carrots, peeled
2 medium-sized onions, peeled
2 shallots, peeled
2 tbsp butter
1½ bottles Chablis
1 bouquet garni (thyme, bay leaf, tarragon)
¼ cup Burgundy marc *or brandy*
1½ tbsp finely chopped parsley
salt and pepper

For the sauce:
¼ cup all-purpose flour
2 tbsp butter
2½ tbsp crème fraîche *or heavy cream*
1 tsp tomato paste

Cut the carrots, onions, and shallots into thin slices; sweat in 2 tbsp butter for 5 minutes in a large, covered saucepan. Add the wine and the bouquet garni and bring to a boil. Boil, uncovered, until reduced by one third. While the *court-bouillon* is reducing, grasp the central flipper on each crayfish's tail, give it a half turn and pull: the bitter black intestinal tract or gut should come out as you pull. Add the live crayfish to the fast boiling *court-bouillon*, cover, and shake the pan over the heat to ensure they cook evenly. As soon as they have all turned scarlet, add the heated *marc* or brandy and flame. Do not overcook (maximum 10 minutes total cooking time).

Transfer the crayfish to a serving dish and keep hot. Strain the liquid into a clean pan and boil until reduced by half. Work the solid butter and the flour together to form the *beurre manié*, add to the liquid over a gentler heat, and stir continuously to thicken slightly. Stir in the cream and the concentrated tomato paste, followed by the chopped parsley. Pour all over the crayfish or serve in a sauceboat.

MEAT

CHOUCROUTE À L'ALSACIENNE*

Sauerkraut with pork and sausages

Alsace

Preparation: 30 minutes
Cooking: 1½ hours
Easy

Serves 8:
4½ lb uncooked sauerkraut
1 lightly smoked pork shoulder
1 semisalted pork shank or lower end of leg
1½–1¾ lb middle to fore cut of loin of semisalted pork, cut into chops
1 14-oz piece of smoked bacon
½ cup goose fat or lard
2 onions, peeled
2¼ cups Alsatian Riesling
2½ cups water
1 small cheesecloth bag containing 3 peeled cloves garlic, 2 cloves, 1 bay leaf, 2 sprigs thyme, 6 juniper berries, 10 peppercorns
8 Strasbourg sausages or Frankfurters
steamed or boiled potatoes (optional)
salt

Rinse the sauerkraut in a sieve under running cold water. Drain well, squeezing out excess moisture. Blanch the various cuts of pork; rinse in cold water and dry.

Cook the finely sliced onions in the goose fat or lard in a very large cooking pot until lightly browned. Add the wine and water. Arrange the cuts of pork in the pan and place the sauerkraut on top. Add little or no salt, cover very tightly, and cook over moderate heat for 1½ hours.

Ten minutes before the cooking time is up, immerse the Strasbourg sausages in very hot (not boiling) water.

Heap up the sauerkraut in the middle of a heated serving platter; slice the meats and arrange around the sauerkraut, together with the sausages and the potatoes (peel these now if boiled in their skins).

There is a large variety of Alsatian *choucroutes*, served with savory blood or white puddings, liver dumplings, and any number of different sausages. Frankfurters can be substituted if Strasbourg sausages are unavailable.

BÄCKEOFFE*

Mixed meat casserole

Alsace

Start preparation 24 hours in advance
Preparation: 40 minutes
Cooking: 5 hours
Easy

Serves 8:
1½–1¾ lb lean stewing beef
1½–1¾ lb boned lamb shoulder
1½–1¾ lb boned pork loin
3 lb waxy potatoes, peeled
6 tbsp goose fat or lard
14 oz onions, peeled
salt and pepper

For the marinade:
1 bottle Alsatian Sylvaner
3 onions, peeled, 1 studded with 2 cloves
3 leeks, white part only, sliced
1 celery root, peeled and grated
4 cloves garlic, peeled and minced
1 bouquet garni (parsley, thyme, bay leaf)
salt and pepper

Cut the meats into 2-in cubes and place in a very large nonmetallic bowl with all the marinade ingredients. Leave to marinate in a cool place for 12-24 hours, turning the meats 2 or 3 times.

Grease a large earthenware or enameled cast-iron casserole liberally with goose fat or lard. Cut the potatoes and onions into thin slices and arrange some of each in a layer over the bottom of the casserole dish. Strain, and reserve the marinade. Take up the beef cubes and place in a layer on top of the potatoes and onions. Season with salt and pepper. Cover with another layer of sliced onions and potatoes. Repeat this layering process with the lamb, more onions and potatoes, then the pork and a final, top layer of onion and potatoes, seasoning as you go. Pour in the strained marinade (discard the vegetables) and dot the top layer of onions and potatoes with small pieces of the remaining goose fat or lard. Make a thick flour and water paste and apply round the rim of the casserole dish and lid to achieve a perfect seal. Heat gently on top of the stove for 10 minutes, then place in the oven, preheated to 300°F, and cook for 5 hours without removing the lid.

A seventeenth-century Polish king, Stanislas Leszcsynski, was exiled to Lorraine. He thought of moistening the rather dry local Kougelhupf *with rum and named his creation Ali-Baba after the hero of his favorite* Thousand and One Nights. *The rum baba is now a classic.*

POTÉE LORRAINE

Pork, sausage, and vegetable stew

Lorraine

Preparation: 30 minutes
Cooking: 3 hours
Easy

Serves 6:
1 lb smoked pork shoulder or shank
1 boiling sausage (Cervelas type) weighing 14 oz
½ lb smoked slab bacon
2½ tbsp lard
2 onions, 1 studded with 2 cloves
4 leeks
2 small turnips, peeled
4 carrots, peeled
1 bouquet garni (thyme, bay leaf, parsley)
1 clove garlic, peeled
1 small Savoy cabbage
¼ lb dried white beans
¼ lb French green beans
¼ lb green peas
6 small waxy or new potatoes
salt and pepper

Peel both onions and slice one finely; trim, wash, dry, and slice the leeks; chop the turnips and carrots into small pieces. Sweat all these vegetables in the lard in a large, fireproof cooking pot or cast-iron casserole for 10 minutes. Place the pork on this bed of vegetables, pour in sufficient water to cover, add the bouquet garni, the clove-studded onion, and the garlic clove. Bring to a boil and simmer, covered, for 1 hour. Remove the outer leaves of the Savoy cabbage and discard; cut the cabbage in quarters, wash and add to the casserole, together with the white beans (soak the beans for 4 hours in cold water before using) and the bacon. Replace the lid and simmer for a further 1½ hours, after which add the sausage (pricked in several places to prevent it bursting) burying it well down among the vegetables; add the trimmed and washed green beans, the peas, and the peeled, thickly sliced potatoes, and salt and pepper. Simmer, uncovered, for a final 30 minutes, tasting for seasoning halfway through this time.

PIEDS DE COCHON À LA SAINTE-MENEHOULD
Broiled pig's feet

Champagne

Preparation: 20 minutes
Cooking: 2 hours 10 minutes
Easy

Serves 6:
4 pig's feet
$1^3/_4$ cups light broth (e.g. veal) (see glossary)
$^1/_2$ bottle still champagne or dry white wine
2 onions, each studded with 1 clove
1 bouquet garni (thyme, bay leaf, parsley)
salt and pepper
$^1/_2$ cup butter

Split the pig's feet lengthwise down the middle, then replace the cut surfaces together and tie up with kitchen string (this process allows the flavors to penetrate during cooking and makes for neater presentation).

Pour the broth into a large pan, add the wine, the clove-studded onions, bouquet garni, salt, and pepper, and bring to a boil. Add the pig's feet and simmer gently for 2 hours. Leave to cool.

Take the pig's feet out of the pan and leave to cool. When cold, untie, brush all over with melted butter and place under a preheated broiler for 10 minutes, turning once halfway through this time.

Once brushed with melted butter, the pig's feet can be coated in breadcrumbs before broiling.

CÔTE DE BOEUF BOURGUIGNONNE
Rib of beef with wine sauce and marrow

Burgundy

Start preparation 6 hours in advance
Preparation: 20 minutes
Cooking: 20–30 minutes
Fairly easy

Serves 4:
1 rib of beef weighing approx. $3^1/_2$ lb
2–3 marrow bones (to yield $^1/_4$ lb marrow)
$1^1/_2$ tbsp peanut oil
$^3/_4$ cup butter
4 shallots, peeled
1 cup Burgundy
salt and pepper
1 small bunch parsley

Choucroute was traditional Sunday lunch fare in Alsace, a very practical dish for the housewives who prepared all the ingredients, put them in the cooking pot and placed a piece of fat bacon on top as they hurried off to church, leaving the meal to simmer gently during Mass. The Sunday service usually lasted a good two hours so, by the time they returned home, everything was ready. A cautionary tale is often told of the scatterbrain who popped her missal into the pot and set off for church with a slab of bacon in her hand.

Make sure the marrow bones are sawn into short lengths; press down on the marrow to push it out of the bone (loosen if necessary by running a knife carefully round the inside of the central bone cavity). Make sure the marrow remains in neat pieces. Soak in cold water for 6 hours.

Grind plenty of black pepper over both sides of the beef. Heat the oil with $^1/_2$ tbsp of the butter in a large, heavy-bottomed casserole; add the beef, laying it flat in the pan, and cook over moderately fast heat for 10 minutes; turn the meat for another 10 minutes' cooking (allow more or less time depending on how well done you like your beef). Remove from the heat. Sprinkle both sides of the meat with a little salt. Wrap in foil and keep warm in the oven with the door ajar (preheat the oven, then turn it off just before the meat is ready).

Meanwhile, place the finely chopped shallots in a nonstick pan and cook with $1^1/_2$ tbsp butter. When they have released most of their moisture, add all but $^1/_2$ cup of the wine. Boil to reduce by half. Poach the drained marrow gently in lightly salted water for 3 minutes.

Use the reserved $^1/_2$ cup wine to deglaze the casserole dish, scraping the caramelized deposits free with a wooden spoon as the wine boils for 1 minute. Pour the resulting mixture into the saucepan containing the wine and shallots, bring to a gentle boil and then beat in the remaining butter with a balloon whisk, adding a small piece at a time.

Add more seasoning if needed. Drain the marrow pieces, slice into rounds $^3/_8$ in thick, and keep warm while carving the beef into slices; arrange on a heated serving dish, place 1 or 2 slices of marrow on top of each beef slice, cover with the sauce, and sprinkle with the parsley.

CÔTES DE PORC À L'ARDENNAISE
Pork chops with ham and cheese filling

Champagne

Preparation: 5 minutes
Cooking: 25 minutes
Very easy

Serves 6:
4 large pork chops, $^3/_4$ in thick
2 slices Ardennes ham (smoked raw ham)
7 oz Gruyère cheese
$^1/_4$ cup butter
1 cup crème fraîche *or heavy cream*
salt and pepper

Ask your butcher to cut the flesh of the chops horizontally in half, back to the rib and backbone. In the resulting pocket, place a slice of ham and a slice of cheese liberally sprinkled with freshly ground pepper. Press the edges of the "pocket" firmly shut and brown the filled chops in hot butter on both sides in a large skillet, then lower the heat a little and cook for 20 minutes, turning again halfway through this time. Transfer to a heated serving platter; stir the cream into the juices and deposits left in the pan, scraping and stirring over fairly high heat. Add more pepper but only a small pinch of salt. Pour over the chops and serve.

POULET AU VIN JAUNE*
Chicken with wine and wild mushrooms

Franche-Comté

Preparation: 15 minutes
Cooking: 50 minutes
Easy

Serves 6:
1 $3^1/_2$-lb farm chicken, jointed into 8 pieces
pinch nutmeg
$^1/_2$ cup butter
2 tbsp peanut oil
2 shallots
$^1/_2$ bottle dry white wine
$^1/_2$ lb fresh morel wild mushrooms (or 3 oz dried)
1 tbsp white wine vinegar
1 cup crème fraîche *or heavy cream*
salt and pepper

Sprinkle the chicken pieces with salt, pepper, and nutmeg. Heat the butter and oil in a fireproof casserole dish and brown the chicken pieces on all sides over high heat for 8 minutes. Add the chopped shallots and $^1/_2$ cup of the wine, reduce the heat, cover, and cook gently for 20 minutes, turning once or twice.

If fresh mushrooms are used, cut off the muddy stalk ends, cut the large mushrooms lengthwise in half and wash well in a bowl of water mixed with the vinegar. Rinse several times. (If dried mushrooms are used, rinse briefly in cold water then soak for 15 minutes in cold water.) Drain the mushrooms and spread out on kitchen towels to remove excess moisture. Heat the remaining wine until nearly boiling and add to the casserole. Add the mushrooms and stir gently. Simmer, uncovered, for 15 minutes.

Transfer the chicken pieces, when cooked, to a hot serving dish. Add the cream to the liquid in the casserole dish and stir. Leave to thicken for 5 minutes. Pour over the chicken pieces.

ANDOUILLE VIGNERONNE

Mixed pork and vegetable stew

Burgundy

Start preparation 24 hours in advance
Preparation: 2 hours
Cooking: 1½ hours
Easy

Serves 8:
3½ lb dried red kidney beans
1 2-lb salted andouille *(or full-flavored broiling, or boiling sausage)*
1 semisalted knuckle end of pork leg
2 lb semisalted spareribs
2 semisalted pig's tails
2 semisalted hog's jowls
½ lb fresh pork skin
3 onions, peeled
3 carrots, peeled
1 bouquet garni (thyme, bay leaf, parsley, and 1 stick celery)
2 cloves garlic, peeled
2 cloves
12 peppercorns
1 bottle dry red wine, preferably Burgundy
¼ cup butter
1 small bunch parsley
salt

The day before you plan to cook this dish, put the beans to soak in cold water. Place the *andouille* in a saucepan of cold water and heat very slowly to boiling point; cook with the water barely simmering for 2 hours. Leave the sausage to cool and stand in the cooking liquid overnight.

The next day, drain the beans and bring to a boil in plenty of fresh, unsalted water. Place all the meats except the sausage in a large fireproof cooking pot or casserole dish, cover with cold water, and bring slowly to a boil. Skim. Simmer very gently for 30 minutes.

As soon as the beans have reached a fast boil, add the diced onions and carrots. Add the bouquet garni, garlic, cloves, and peppercorns, all tied up in a cheesecloth bag. Add the wine; when the liquid has returned to the boil, lower the heat, and add the meats, drained and cut into fairly small pieces (cut the pig's skin into small, neat squares). Simmer for 30 minutes. Finally, add the drained sausage and continue cooking until the beans are very tender. To serve, take out the sausage, slice fairly thickly and arrange down the center of a very large heated serving platter; arrange the pieces of meat (but not the pig's skin) all around it. Transfer the beans, vegetables, and pig's skin to a heated vegetable dish; dot the surface with small pieces of butter and sprinkle with coarsely chopped parsley.

BOEUF BOURGUIGNON*

Beef and red wine casserole

Burgundy

Preparation: 25 minutes
Cooking: 3 hours
Easy

Serves 6:
3½ lb braising beef
¼ cup butter
¼ cup peanut oil
20 baby onions, peeled
2 shallots, peeled
½ lb fresh bacon
1 bottle Burgundy
2 carrots, peeled
2 baby turnips, peeled
1 large, floury potato, peeled
1 bouquet garni (thyme, bay leaf, parsley)
1 clove garlic, peeled
1 tsp tomato paste (optional)
10 oz very small button mushrooms
salt and pepper

Heat the butter and oil in a large, fireproof casserole dish, add the beef cut into 2-in cubes and brown all over for at least 5 minutes. Use a slotted spoon to transfer the beef to a plate and set aside.

Add the whole baby onions and the sliced shallots to the oil, butter, and juices left in the casserole. Remove the skin from the fresh bacon, trim off any hard or tough pieces and cut the flesh crosswise into small pieces; add these to the casserole. Brown lightly all over. Return the beef to the casserole dish and pour in sufficient wine, plus a little water if necessary, to cover it completely. Add the diced carrots, turnips, and potato, the bouquet garni, garlic, salt, pepper, and the tomato paste if used. Stir, bring slowly to a boil, then cover and simmer for 2¾ hours. Ten minutes before this time is up, rinse and dry the mushrooms and sauté in a little extra butter over high heat until lightly browned.

Use a slotted spoon to remove the pieces of beef and bacon and the onions and place in a heated serving dish; surround with the mushrooms or scatter these on top. Strain the remaining contents of the casserole and pour over the meat.

ANDOUILLETTES AU CHABLIS

Sausages in Chablis and mustard sauce

Burgundy

Preparation: 5 minutes
Cooking: 25 minutes
Easy

Serves 4:
4 andouillettes *or delicately flavored broiling or boiling sausages*
3 tbsp lard
1 shallot, peeled
1 cup Chablis
1 tbsp Dijon mustard
salt and pepper

Prick each sausage in 4 places with the sharp point of a knife. Heat the lard and fry the sausages in a wide, heavy-bottomed saucepan, turning frequently until well browned.

Keep hot; drain off all but about 1 tbsp of the lard and cook the finely chopped shallot gently in this until golden. Add the wine, bring to a boil and cook, uncovered, over high heat to reduce the liquid for 5 minutes. Turn down the heat. Return the sausages to the pan, cover, and simmer for 10 minutes. Draw aside from the heat and stir the mustard into the liquid, mixing well; cover and keep warm away from direct heat until you are ready to serve.

RÂBLE DE LIÈVRE À L'ARBOISIENNE

Saddle of hare in a rich wine sauce

Franche-Comté

Start preparation 48 hours in advance
Preparation: 30 minutes
Cooking: 25 minutes
Easy

Serves 4:
1 saddle of hare
1/4 lb fresh pork fat or fat bacon
5 oz shallots, peeled
1 clove garlic, peeled
2 tbsp oil
1 medium-sized onion, peeled
1 medium-sized carrot, peeled
1 bouquet garni (thyme, bay leaf, parsley)
1 bottle dry red wine
1/2 cup butter
1/4 cup Arbois marc *or brandy*
1/4 cup all-purpose flour
1/2 cup crème fraîche *or heavy cream*
salt and pepper

Cut the pork fat into strips (lardons) to fit a larding needle and lard the saddle of hare. Alternatively, make incisions at regular intervals in the saddle and insert strips of pork fat or fat bacon in these. Make the marinade by mixing half the finely sliced shallots and garlic and the oil in a nonmetallic bowl with the finely chopped or minced onions and the sliced carrots, the bouquet garni, and 1 cup of the wine. Marinate the saddle of hare in this for 48 hours, turning at intervals.

Take the hare out of the marinade, pat dry all over with kitchen towels and brown over high heat for 5 minutes in the butter in a fireproof casserole dish. Season with salt and pepper and place in the oven (preheated to 400°F) for 6 minutes.

Take the casserole out of the oven, pour the heated *marc* or brandy over the hare, and flame. Take the hare out of the casserole dish and keep hot.

Finely chop the remaining shallots and cook until lightly browned in the butter and juices in the casserole dish; stir in the flour and continue cooking and stirring for a few minutes, until deep brown in color. Gradually stir in the remaining wine. Leave to cook and reduce for 10 minutes over moderate heat. Meanwhile, carve the hare. Stir the cream into the sauce and as soon as it has neared boiling point, strain through a conical sieve and pour all over the hare.

Philip the Good, Duke of Burgundy, came across a young woman working in his vineyards:
"And how are the grapes, my girl?" he asked.
"If we don't lose any before harvest, Sire, it will be a good year."
"Have you ever tasted my wine, child?"
"Yes, Sire, I drink it whenever I get the chance."
"So it gives you pleasure?"
"Oh, yes, Sire! But I am even better pleasured when my husband has been drinking it."

QUEUE DE BOEUF À LA BOURGUIGNONNE

Oxtail stew

Burgundy

Start preparation 24 hours in advance
Preparation: 30 minutes
Cooking: 2 hours
Easy

Serves 6:
1 oxtail, cut into sections
1 bottle Burgundy
2 onions, peeled
2 carrots, peeled
3 cloves garlic, peeled
1 bouquet garni (thyme, bay leaf, parsley)
1/4 cup lard
2 tbsp all-purpose flour
1/4 lb pig's skin, blanched
2 tsp sugar
salt and pepper

Garnish:
1/2 lb baby onions, peeled
1 tsp superfine sugar
1/2 lb small button mushrooms
6 tbsp butter

The day before you plan to cook this dish marinate the oxtail pieces in the wine with the sliced onions and carrots, the minced garlic, bouquet garni, salt, and pepper. The following day, remove the meat and vegetables and drain well, reserving the marinade. Discard the bouquet garni.

Heat the lard in a large saucepan and brown the oxtail pieces all over with the vegetables. Sprinkle in the flour and stir it into the fat. Cook until the resulting roux has turned light brown, then stir in the reserved marinade, adding a little water if it does not cover the meat. Bring to a boil and add a little salt and pepper if needed. Cut the pig's skin into fairly short, thin strips and spread out in a casserole dish; sprinkle with sugar and cover with the contents of the saucepan. Cover and bring to a gentle boil, then cook for 2 hours in the oven, preheated to 325°F.

Meanwhile, glaze the onions by cooking in the sugar and a sprinkling of water in an uncovered pan over high heat. Sauté the mushrooms separately in the butter.

When the oxtail is done, transfer to a heated serving dish, with all the vegetables and strips of pig's skin. Strain the sauce and pour over the meat. Garnish with the onions and mushrooms.

SAUPIQUET DES AMOGNES

Ham with white wine and tarragon

Nivernais

Preparation: 20 minutes
Cooking: 30 minutes
Easy

Serves 8:
2 1/4–2 1/2 lb Morvan ham (unsmoked)
1/2 lb butter
1/2 cup all-purpose flour
1 1/2 cups dry white wine (e.g. Pouilly, Sancerre or Quincy)
1 cup veal or chicken broth (see glossary)
4–5 peppercorns

10 juniper berries
4 shallots, peeled
½ cup white wine vinegar
¼ cup heavy cream
1 sprig tarragon
salt

Cut the boned, pressed ham into 8 large, neat slices just under ¼ in thick. Heat 2 tbsp of the butter in a skillet and brown the ham slices on both sides for about 5 minutes. Remove and keep hot.

Melt ¼ cup of the remaining butter in a saucepan, stir in the flour, and cook, stirring, until light brown; gradually stir in the wine and broth.

If there are any offcuts from the ham, cut them into very small pieces and stir into the sauce. Add the finely minced or coarsely ground peppercorns; mince the juniper berries with the flat of a large knife blade and add them too. Cook over high heat, stirring, for 5 minutes; cover and keep warm.

Heat the remaining butter in a saucepan and sweat the finely chopped shallots until soft but not browned. Sprinkle with the vinegar and cook until it has completely evaporated. Add 3–4 tbsp of the sauce and stir over fairly high heat. Stir this mixture into the saucepan containing all the rest of the sauce. Bring to a boil then cook uncovered over moderate heat for 10 minutes to reduce. Strain the sauce, stir in the cream, and add the blanched tarragon leaves. Do not allow to boil again. Spoon the sauce all over the ham slices.

ROGNONS DE VEAU AU CHABLIS*

Calves' kidneys in wine and mustard sauce

Burgundy

Preparation: 20 minutes
Cooking: 25 minutes
Fairly easy

Serves 4:
4 calves' kidneys
½ cup butter
2 shallots, peeled
¼ lb button mushrooms
2¼ cups Chablis
2 tbsp Dijon mustard
juice of 1 lemon
1 tbsp finely chopped parsley
salt and pepper

Slice through the thickness of the kidneys and open them out, taking out as much of the fat and gristle that runs down the middle inside. Slice across into pieces. Heat all the butter except for 2 tbsp until foaming then brown the kidneys all over, turning frequently, for about 2–3 minutes: they should be sealed on the outside, pink inside. Season with salt and pepper and keep hot in a covered serving dish.

In the butter and juices left in the pan, sauté the thinly sliced shallots and the washed, dried, and sliced mushrooms. Add the wine, bring to a boil and continue boiling, uncovered, for 10 minutes over high heat to reduce, stirring now and then. Draw aside from the heat. Stir in the mustard, add the kidneys to this sauce, and stir gently over low heat for 2 minutes without allowing the sauce to boil again. Transfer the kidneys and mushrooms back to the heated serving dish. Stir the remaining butter into the sauce a little at a time, followed by the lemon juice. Pour this sauce over the kidneys and sprinkle with the parsley.

RÂBLE DE LIÈVRE À LA PIRON

Saddle of hare with grapes

Burgundy

Start preparation 48 hours in advance
Preparation: 30 minutes
Cooking: 40 minutes
Fairly easy

Serves 6:
2 saddles of hare
1 5-oz piece fresh pork fat or sliced fat bacon
1 bottle dry white wine (Aligoté or Chablis)
1/2 cup Burgundy marc *or brandy*
1 bouquet garni (thyme, bay leaf, parsley, rosemary, tarragon)
3 cloves garlic, peeled
6 medium-sized onions, peeled
1/2 cup butter
1 1/2 lb underripe grapes, half black, half white
1 cup crème fraîche *or heavy cream*
salt and pepper

Cut the fresh pork fat into larding strips (lardons) and use a larding needle to lard the saddles of hare. Alternatively, make incisions in the meat and push small pieces of the pork fat or fat bacon into these. In a nonmetallic bowl, marinate the hare for 48 hours in the wine, all but 3 tbsp of the *marc* or brandy, the bouquet garni, the garlic cloves sliced in half and the thinly sliced onions; stir occasionally.

Take the hare out of the marinade, pat dry all over with kitchen towels, and place in an ovenproof and fireproof casserole dish greased with all the butter. Strain the marinade, pressing down on the solid ingredients to express all the moisture. Sprinkle 3 tbsp of this liquid over the saddles of hare, season with salt and pepper, and roast at 400°F, for 30 minutes, moistening with 1–2 tbsp of the marinade every now and then to prevent the meat catching and to keep it moist.

Remove the seeds from the grapes; take the casserole out of the oven and quickly sprinkle the grapes all round the hare saddles. Moisten the hare and grapes with the warmed remaining brandy and flame; return to the oven for 10 minutes, then take out of the oven again and stir in the cream. Transfer the hare to a heated serving dish, surround with the grapes and tip the creamy sauce into a sauceboat to serve separately.

The traditional accompaniment to this dish is a chestnut purée.

SAUCISSE DE MORTEAU AU GRATIN*

Sausages in tomato and vegetable sauce

Franche-Comté

Preparation: 45 minutes
Cooking: 45 minutes
Easy

Serves 2:
2 Morteau sausages (Jésus type) weighing 1/2–3/4 lb
1 carrot, peeled
1 onion, peeled
1 shallot, peeled
1 clove garlic, peeled
1/2 cup butter
1/4 cup all-purpose flour
1/2 cup tomato paste or 3/4 cup sieved tomatoes (passato)
bouquet garni (thyme, bay leaf, parsley)
1 quart water
1/4 lb grated Comté cheese
1/2–3/4 cup fine, dry breadcrumbs

Slice the carrot, onion, shallot, and garlic thinly. Cook in all but 1 1/2 tbsp of the butter over low heat until lightly browned, stir in the flour, and cook for a few minutes. Add the

tomato paste, the bouquet garni, and a little salt and pepper. Stir in the water, bring to a gentle boil and simmer, uncovered, for 35 minutes to reduce and thicken.

Prick the sausage skins in several places with a needle; boil very gently in salted water for 35 minutes. Drain, allow to cool, then carefully remove their skins.

Slice the sausages into 3/8–1/2-in thick rounds and place in a fairly shallow ovenproof dish greased with the remaining butter. Pour the sauce all over the slices, sprinkle with the mixed grated cheese and breadcrumbs and place in a very hot oven for 10 minutes to brown the topping. Serve straight from the ovenproof dish.

COQ AU VIN*

Chicken and red wine casserole

Burgundy

Preparation: 25 minutes
Cooking: 2 hours
Easy

Serves 6:
1 oven-ready chicken weighing 5 1/2 lb
1/4 lb slab bacon
20 baby onions
5 oz button mushrooms
1/4 cup lard
1/4 cup Burgundy marc *or brandy*
1 bottle full-bodied dry red wine (Côte-de-Nuits)
2 1/2 tsp sugar
1 bouquet garni (thyme, bay leaf, parsley)
1 clove garlic, peeled
6 small carrots (optional)
salt and pepper
1/4 cup butter
1/2 cup all-purpose flour

Joint the chicken into 8–10 pieces; remove the skin and any tough pieces of cartilage from the bacon and cut into short, fairly thick strips (lardons). Peel the baby onions; wash and dry the mushrooms. Cook the lardons very gently in the lard for 10 minutes in a large fireproof casserole dish, turning now and then with a wooden spoon. Add the onions and sauté.

Take the lardons and onions out of the fat and set aside. Cook the chicken pieces in the fat over a fairly high heat for 10 minutes, turning to brown all over. Return the lardons and onions to the casserole. Add the brandy then heat and flame. Add the wine, sugar, salt, pepper, bouquet garni, the garlic (lightly minced with the flat of a knife blade), the quartered mushrooms, and the peeled carrots sliced into rounds. Bring slowly to a gentle boil, then reduce the heat and simmer for 1 1/2 hours.

Ten minutes before serving, remove and discard the bouquet garni; take the chicken pieces, onions, mushrooms, and lardons out of the casserole dish with a slotted spoon and transfer to a heated serving dish. Keep hot. Work the slightly softened butter with the flour, add this *beurre manié* to the liquid in the casserole and stir over low heat until thickened. Cook for a few minutes; taste for seasoning, then pour all over the chicken pieces. Garnish with fried triangles or decorative shapes of sliced white bread if wished.

DESSERTS

TARTE AUX QUETSCHES
Plum tart

Alsace

Preparation: 15 minutes
Cooking: 35 minutes
Easy

Serves 6:
½ lb pie dough (see glossary)
2 lb small, mauve or red thin-skinned plums (preferably Quetsches)
1 cup superfine sugar

Grease a 9–10-in tart pan with butter. Roll out the pastry to a thin sheet just under ⅛ in thick and line the tart pan. Cut the plums in half, remove the pit and arrange these halves in concentric circles, cut side uppermost. Dredge all over with the sugar. Bake at 400°F for 35 minutes; reduce the heat to 375°F after 15–20 minutes if the pastry threatens to brown too quickly.

TARTOUILLAT
Cherry and rum cake

Burgundy

Preparation: 10 minutes
Cooking: 25 minutes
Very easy

Serves 4:
2¼ cups all-purpose flour
1 cup superfine sugar
1 tsp vanilla extract
2 tsps salt
4 eggs
¼ cup rum
½ cup milk
½ cup butter
1 lb ripe black cherries, pitted
2 tbsp confectioner's sugar

Sift the flour and salt into a large mixing bowl; stir in the sugar, make a well in the center, and place the lightly beaten eggs in it with the rum and vanilla. Stir, gradually incorporating the flour and sugar to form a thick, almost dough-like consistency. Mix in the milk, adding a little at a time to give a cake batter consistency.

Grease a fairly deep pie dish liberally with butter and spread out the cherries in it. Cover the cherries with the cake mixture and smooth out. Have the oven ready heated to 375°F and bake for 25 minutes. Dust all over with the confectioner's sugar and serve warm.

OGEI
Fruit and nut yeast cake

Alsace

Start preparation 24 hours in advance
Preparation: 1 hour 40 minutes
Cooking: 25 minutes
Complicated

Serves 6:

For the sweet yeast dough:
4½ cups all-purpose flour
just over ½ cake compressed yeast or just over ½ package dried yeast
1 cup lukewarm milk
¼ cup superfine sugar
2 egg yolks
½ cup butter, softened

For the filling:
7 oz pitted prunes
7 oz dried figs
3½ oz currants
2½ oz walnuts
¼ cup French quetsch (plum) brandy
½ cup superfine sugar
½ tsp ground cinnamon
1 egg yolk
1½ tbsp confectioner's sugar

Bring a fairly large saucepan of water to a gentle boil, add the prunes, and simmer very gently for 1 hour; after 30 minutes add the figs. Simmer the currants in a smaller pan for 30 minutes. Drain all the fruit thoroughly. Chop the prunes and figs and mix with the currants. Chop the walnuts coarsely, stir into the fruit mixture with the plum brandy. Sprinkle with the sugar and cinnamon, stir thoroughly, and leave to stand overnight.

Make the sweet yeast dough: dissolve the yeast in the milk and leave to stand until it froths. Sift the flour into a large mixing bowl, make a well in the center and pour in the yeast mixture. Add the sugar and the 2 egg yolks. Stir, gradually working in the flour. When the dough is smooth and leaves the sides of the bowl easily, work the butter into the dough. Knead for 10 minutes. Cover with a clean cloth and leave to rise for 30 minutes in a warm place, then knock down and knead again. Take half the dough and roll out into a 12 × 16-in rectangle. Cover the surface with the mixed fruit mixture and roll up. Do likewise with the remaining dough and filling.

Place both these rolls on a large cookie sheet greased with butter, leaving space between them as they will rise and expand as they cook. Leave to rise in a warm place. Brush the exposed surfaces with egg yolk, sprinkle with confectioner's sugar, and place in a preheated oven at 375°F for 25 minutes.

Journalist Pierre Scize once came upon the following epitaph on a tombstone in a Côte de Nuits cemetery: "Here lies Captain Francis Gabriel Charavin, Knight of the Legion of Honour. Born in Gevrey on 9th February 1785. He served his country faithfully from 1809 until 1846. He fought wars under seven kingdoms. He took part in twenty battles, eleven attacks, one blockade, and three sieges, under Napoleon, Louis XVIII, Charles X and Louis Philippe. Died in battle, defending his vines, in the Côte de Nuits on 16th September 1870."

GÂTEAU MOLLET*
Sweet yeast cake

Champagne

Preparation: 25 minutes
Rising time for dough: 2½ hours
Cooking: 30 minutes
Fairly easy

Serves 4:
2¼ cups all-purpose flour
1 cake fresh yeast or 1 package dried yeast
1 tsp superfine sugar
1 tsp salt
3 eggs
1 cup butter, cut into small pieces

Mix the yeast with ¼ cup lukewarm water and the sugar in a mixing bowl. Leave to work or reactivate; it will produce a covering of foam. Sift in ½ cup of the flour with the salt and mix; leave to stand in a warm place until doubled in volume (15–20 minutes).

Sift the rest of the flour into a larger mixing bowl, make a well in the center, break the eggs into it one by one, then beat in the yeast mixture. Mix very thoroughly, using your hands, and then gather up the rather sticky dough and knock it against the sides of the bowl or on a work surface until very elastic and smooth.

Reserve 2 tbsp of the butter. Have the rest of the small pieces softened at room temperature and work a small quantity at a time into the dough until completely blended. Shape the dough into a ball, cover with a damp cloth, and leave in a warm place for 2 hours to rise. Grease a large brioche mold or a cake pan with the remaining butter. Working with lightly floured hands, shape the dough so that it will fit neatly inside the pan or mold and is of an even thickness. Cover with damp cloth and leave until it has risen to within $^{3}/_{4}$ in of the rim.

Preheat the oven to 400°F and bake for 30 minutes. Insert a thin knife deep into the center of the cake and if the blade comes out dry and clean, the cake is ready.

KOUGELHOPF*

Alsace

Preparation: 30 minutes
Rising time for dough: 3 hours
Cooking: 50 minutes
Easy

Serves 8:
1/4 lb seedless white raisins or currants
1/4 cup kirsch
2 1/4 cups milk
1 cake fresh yeast or 1 package dried yeast
1/2 cup butter
4 1/2 cups cake flour or all-purpose flour
1/2 cup superfine sugar
pinch salt
3 eggs
3/8 cup slivered or chopped almonds

Soak your chosen dried fruit in the kirsch. Heat the milk to scalding point, then set aside to cool to blood heat. When lukewarm, pour off 3/4 cup into a bowl and mix in the yeast; when it has completely dissolved, stir it into the pan of lukewarm milk. Melt the butter gently. Place the flour in a large mixing bowl with the sugar and salt. Gradually stir in the milk and yeast mixture with a wooden spoon, adding a little at a time, then beat in the eggs one at a time. Beat in the melted butter. Stir in the raisins or currants. Work the dough energetically with your hands, scraping it away from the sides of the bowl and knocking it against them: it will become very smooth, elastic, and much less sticky. Shape into a ball, cover with a damp cloth, and leave to rise in a warm place for 1 hour.

Grease the inside of a Kougelhopf mold or ring tube mold generously with butter; press the almonds on to the buttered surfaces. Take the dough out of the bowl, push your fingers into the center, push the dough away to form a larger hole and shape to fit into the Kougelhopf mold. Cover and leave to rise for 2 hours.

Preheat the oven to 400°F for 15 minutes. Place the mold on a cookie sheet and bake for 50 minutes. Turn out of the mold; serve when cold with fruit compote or jam.

STRUDEL AUX POMMES

Apple and currant roll

Alsace

Preparation: 30 minutes
Resting time for the pastry: 2 hours
Cooking: 40 minutes
Fairly easy

Serves 4:

For the strudel pastry:
1 1/4 cups all-purpose flour
3 tbsp butter, softened
1 egg
3/4 cup lukewarm water
juice of 1/2 lemon
salt

For the filling:
1 lb firm apples
2 oz slivered almonds
2 oz currants
1/4 cup superfine sugar
1/2 cup very heavy cream
1/4 cup butter
pinch ground cinnamon
1 egg yolk

Use strong, unbleached flour if possible. Mix the flour with the butter and the egg, preferably using your fingers; when well worked together, gradually add the cold water, a pinch of salt, and the lemon juice. Knead thoroughly until smooth and elastic. Shape into a ball, cover with a clean cloth, and leave to rest for 2 hours. Lay a large clean cloth on the working surface and lightly sprinkle with flour. Roll out the pastry into a very thin sheet. Spread the cream over the surface, sprinkle all over with almonds, the peeled and thinly sliced apples, currants, sugar, and cinnamon.

Roll up the pastry and place on a very large greased cookie sheet. Brush the exposed surface of the pastry all over with egg yolk and melted butter. Place in a preheated oven at 325°F and bake for 40 minutes.

RIGODON

Egg, rice, and walnut pudding

Burgundy

Preparation: 20 minutes
Cooking: 45 minutes
Very easy

Serves 6:
1 quart milk
1 1/4 cups sugar
pinch ground cinnamon
pinch salt
1/4 lb 2-day old brioche
10 walnuts
6 filberts
6 tbsp ground rice
8 eggs
2 tbsp butter

Bring the milk to boiling point, add the sugar, cinnamon, and salt and stir until the sugar has completely dissolved.

Cut the brioche into small cubes; place these in a bowl and sprinkle with a few spoonfuls of the sweetened milk to moisten. Chop the walnuts and filberts finely. Mix the lightly beaten eggs well with the ground rice in a bowl. Gradually stir in the hot milk, then the brioche cubes and the nuts.

Grease a shallow pie dish with butter and pour in the mixture. Dot the surface with flakes of butter and bake for 45 minutes in the oven, preheated to 350°F.

FLAMUSSE AUX POMMES

Apple flan

Burgundy

Preparation: 25 minutes
Cooking: 30 minutes
Very easy

Serves 4:
10 firm apples (e.g. Rennet, Granny Smith or Green)
1/2 cup butter
6 eggs
2 1/2 tbsp all-purpose flour
1 cup milk
1/4 cup granulated sugar
2 1/2 tbsp superfine sugar

Peel, core, and thinly slice the apples (choose a variety that will hold its shape during cooking) then sauté them in the butter over high heat until lightly browned on both sides. Beat the eggs in a bowl (or in a blender) with the flour, milk, and sugar until very well blended. Combine with the apples, stirring gently. Grease a deep pie dish with butter and pour in the mixture into it. Have the oven preheated to 350°F and bake for 30 minutes. Turn the flan out onto a serving plate, sprinkle with superfine sugar, and serve hot.

POIRES À LA VIGNERONNE*

Pears in red wine

Burgundy

Preparation: 10 minutes
Cooking: 30 minutes
Very easy

Serves 6:
2–2 1/2 lb William or Doyenné du Comice pears
1 bottle dry red wine (e.g. Burgundy or Beaujolais)
1 cup water
1 1/4 cup sugar
pinch ground cinnamon
1 or 2 vanilla beans

Mix the wine and water in a nonmetallic saucepan, add the sugar, cinnamon, and vanilla beans (use 2 1/2 tsps real vanilla extract if preferred). Heat the wine and simmer until the sugar has completely dissolved.

Peel the pears very neatly, keep them whole and do not remove their stalks. Place upright in a fireproof casserole dish that will just accommodate them all. Pour the wine mixture into the casserole dish containing the pears; add more cooking liquid (in the same proportions of wine to water) if they are not completely covered.

Simmer gently until the pears are very tender (usually about 30 minutes, but this will vary).

West

Berry
Orléanais
Touraine
Anjou
Brittany
Maine
Normandy

This large region of France stretches westward from Paris and the River Somme across the Loire valley provinces (Berry, Orléanais, Touraine, Anjou, and Maine) and from the River Loire further north and west, to Normandy and Brittany. Each of the provinces has its own, unmistakable character and landscape but all the northwestern and western coastal areas benefit from the rich Channel and Atlantic fishing grounds, while much of the hinterland, with its important river basins, offers a wide variety of freshwater fish. The abundant rainfall provides lush pastures for a flourishing butter and cheese industry, with market gardening in the sheltered valleys producing large quantities of superb fruit and vegetables.

The chickens, duck, guinea fowl, turkeys, and geese bred and reared in this region are excellent, and the neighborhood of Loué in Maine is synonymous with good poultry. The pork butchers in the area produce a wide range of delicious sausages and cured meats. Some of the world's best cider comes from Brittany and Normandy, while some very good wines come from the Loire vineyards; the foods and cooking of the various provinces drained by the River Loire have much in common, each laying claim to the invention of such specialties as the mouthwatering *beurre blanc*. This sauce, made with butter, shallots, dry white wine, and vinegar is served with freshwater fish around Nantes, as well as in Touraine (often described as the garden of France), and in Anjou, the province whose beautiful countryside and temperate climate inspired some of the sixteenth-century poet Joachim du Bellay's most haunting sonnets.

Curnonsky took a more prosaic view when he classified Maine as the principal pig and pork center of France. The enchanting countryside all along the winding River Loire has been blessed with this superabundance, sharing the same mild climate and generally productive soil, from the provinces of Berry and the Orléanais to where the river reaches the sea.

Each of the provinces has something special to contribute to the cause of good food. Berry is among the least rich in agricultural produce but is renowned for the quality of its goats' cheeses (Levroux, Pouligny, Valençay, Selles-sur-Cher, Crottins de Chavignol, and, straying just over the border into Touraine, Sainte-Maure).

Game of all kinds abounds in Sologne, a hunting, shooting and fishing paradise.

Touraine, Maine and Anjou have good reason to be proud of their sausages, blood puddings, and potted meats (*andouillettes, boudins, rillettes,* and *rillons* or *rillaux*), as well as their vegetables and fruits. The round, closed cap white or palest brown mushrooms known as *champignon de Paris* are cultivated on a very large scale in chalk caves in this area.

While the Loire valley cooks certainly know how to show good game and pork products off to their best advantage, there are plenty of less robust dishes, many of which entail the use of cream (as in the delicately flavored recipes for veal loin and chicken from Anjou, in *beuchelle*, a mixture of calf's kidneys and sweetbreads, and in *géline à la lochoise* (a

On the previous pages: *the famous landmark of Mont-Saint-Michel, visible for miles around the immense sandy bay where Normandy meets Brittany, is cut off from the mainland twice a day at high tide.*
Above: *Bayeux: this picturesque old market town, surrounded by lush dairying country, grew rich enough to build a magnificent gothic cathedral, miraculously unscathed by heavy bombardments during the World War II Allied liberation of France.*

Above: *at Etretat the land comes to an abrupt end with a sheer drop of nearly 330 feet over the cliffs to the beach below with its arch and needle carved out by the waves.* Left: *this old-fashioned restaurant sign commemorates the exploits of St. Malo's seventeenth- and eighteenth-century gentleman-privateers.*

very young hen cooked with wine produced near Tours). Wines from the Loire valley, such as Sancerre, Muscadet, Vouvray, Montlouis, Bourgueil, Chinon, Champigny, and the magnificent Bonnezeaux and Coulée-de-Serrant offer plenty of inspiration to drinkers, cooks, and famous writers alike; Rabelais sang their praises rumbustiously in his books. Through geography and choice, Brittany has historically tended to be cut off from mainstream developments in French cooking. Two types of cuisine developed in this province whose barren, inland areas restricted the country people to very simple fare: here one of the greatest treats used to be *graisse de Cournouailles*, literally "Cornwall fat," a form of bread and dripping: grated hog's fat spread on bread, with onions. Potatoes with onions, cabbage and turnip soup, *galettes* (savory buckwheat pancakes), *crêpes* (pancakes, usually sweet) and wheat or buckwheat *farz* (originally a sort of porridge, now a flan, usually containing prunes). Brittany's only claim to fame in the pork butchery line is a very tasty sausage, the *andouille de Guéménée*.

With the exception of the country around Nantes, Brittany produces no outstanding wine or cheeses but her butter and cider are both superb.

Over the last twenty years the Breton country people in the north of the Brittany peninsula have shown tremendous initiative and perseverence in launching a successful intensive market gardening industry, growing cauliflowers, beans, onions, and artichokes and transforming the rural economy.

Brittany's lack of fertile inland areas is more than compensated by the harvest her fishermen gather from the Channel and the Atlantic; the sea is full of excellent fish, mollusks, shellfish, and crustaceans (Breton blue lobsters are among the most flavorsome in the world).

All along the coast the cooking reflects the diversity and abundance of seafood: there are as many variations on the Breton *cotriade*, a cross between a fish soup and a stew, as there are for the Midi's *bouillabaisse*.

This coastline is a favorite destination for lovers of fine seafood; here they can choose between the equally delectable *palourdes* and *praires* (clams) cooked with savory toppings; casserole of abalone, scallops Breton style, crab soup, mackerel in cider and, of course, cod: deep-fried Guingamp style or in a cream sauce, à la Paimpol; conger eel soup from the Isle of Sein, oyster soup and shellfish pie or flan from Cancale, baked gilthead bream (from Quimper), sardines in a puff pastry case (Douarnez), fried langoustine choux buns or *beignets* (Concarneau), baked, stuffed mussels (Penthièvre), small-fry, smelt and silverside soup (Lorient); lobster with curry sauce or in a tomato and shrimp sauce (the origins of this last recipe's name are still disputed (*à l'armoricaine*, the old name for Brittany being Armorica, or *à l'américaine*).

The barren land of Brittany's inland Argoat area contrasts starkly with the Norman hinterland: Cotentin, Bocage, Pays d'Ouche, Perche, the Pays d'Auge, Pays de Caux, and Pays de Bray.

Cows grazing the rich pasturelands of Normandy produce creamy milk for abundant cream, the fragrant butter of Isigny and Sainte-Mère-Église, and such world-famous cheeses as Camembert, Pont-l'Evêque, Livarot, and Bondon.

Normandy's cooks excel at turning tripe into a variety of appetizing dishes: small, skewered bundles à La Ferté-Macé; rolled into small packets, with cream (Coutances); gently simmered in cider or white wine (Caen), or used in Vire's *andouilles* (smoked sausages made with tripe and intestines).

Some of the great French dishes that have become part of the international repertoire of *haute cuisine* originated in Normandy: such duck recipes as Rouen's *canard au sang*, roast duck à la Duclair; baked and broiled chicken from Andelys, chicken in the style of the Auge valley, Alençon's braised goose, pig's feet à l'Argentan, and rabbit baked in a paper case, a receipe which hails from the port of Le Havre.

Coastal Normandy is as favored as the Brittany shoreline in its own way: what we call English or Dover sole (*soles normands* to the French) have long been the basis for an enormously wide range of sumptuous dishes:

Opposite above: *a typical Norman half-timbered thatched cottage.* Opposite below: *famous since the seventeenth century, Cancale's oyster beds cover nearly 400 hectares; the seed oysters reared in the Gulf of Morbihan are fattened here for 4 years.* Above: *a fisherman carries out a little maintenance work on the keel of his boat at low tide.* Right: *traditional Normandy costume and headdress is still worn for local festivals by the women and young girls of Vierville-sur-Mer, Bessin.*

cooked with white wine, madeira, cognac, mussels, shrimp, oysters, smelts or silversides, mushrooms, truffles, shallots (gray shallots, which have a particularly fine flavor), leeks, carrots, butter, cream, eggs, and herbs, and many more staples of the menus of top Parisian restaurants.

Dieppe's fish stew mixes such wonderful fish as turbot, sole, and burbot wth shrimp, butter, cream, and various vegetables.

Herrings fresh from the sea are broiled and served with a mustard sauce. Fécamp's specialty is cod with white wine; Caux is renowned for its brill; Cherbourg for superb little lobsters in a creamy sauce (*à la nage*). Baby mackerel landed in Norman ports are cooked in white wine, while small pink shrimp are thrown live in the saucepan, full of the fresh, iodine tang of the sea, eaten with such accompaniments as Normandy cider and fresh bread spread with sweet butter.

With orchards all over the countryside, it is hardly surprising that many desserts are based on apples, as far afield as the Orléanais, where the famous caramelized apples of the classic Tarte Tatin originate.

SOUPS

COTRIADE DE BELLE-ISLE

Breton seafood soup

Brittany

Preparation: 30 minutes
Cooking: 1¼ hours
Easy

Serves 10:
4½ lb assorted fish: approx. ⅔–¾ of this weight white fish (e.g. flounder, bonefish, porgy, silversides), the remainder oily and/or firm-fleshed fish (e.g. conger eel, jack mackerel, red snapper, pollock)
2½ lb crustaceans and shellfish (e.g. small Dungeness crabs, lobsterettes, mussels, clams, shrimp, lobster, crawfish etc.)
3 onions, peeled
¼ cup butter
1 leek, white part only, sliced
3 tomatoes, peeled and deseeded
1 stick celery, cut in half
1 bouquet garni (thyme, bay leaf, parsley)
10 oz small carrots, peeled
10 oz baby turnips, peeled
4½ lb waxy potatoes, peeled
large pinch cayenne or chili pepper
large pinch real saffron stamens
10 thick slices 2-day old coarse white bread, rubbed with 3 peeled and sliced garlic cloves
salt and pepper

Trim, gut, wash, and prepare all the fish (remove scales where necessary, skin and fillet the flatfish, leave the small round fish whole, cut larger round fish into steaks, keeping the oily and white fish separate. Wash and scrub the shellfish to rid them of grit, etc. Keep the little crabs whole). Keep the heads, bones, and trimmings and tie up in a piece of cheesecloth.

Lightly brown the finely sliced onions in the butter in a very large saucepan; add the leek, tomatoes, celery, bouquet garni, and bag of fish trimmings. Pour in 5 quarts cold water; season with salt and pepper. Bring to a boil and simmer for 30 minutes.

Remove the bag of trimmings. Add the carrots and turnips; boil gently for 15 minutes. Add the potatoes and boil for a further 15 minutes.

Add the firmer, oilier fish and any large crustaceans. Cover and cook for 6 minutes. Add the remaining white fish, the shellfish, and smaller crustaceans. Boil for a further 6 minutes. Use a slotted ladle to transfer all the solid ingredients to a heated serving dish; serve with a vinaigrette or mayonnaise of your choice, with or after the soup. Stir the saffron and cayenne into the cooking liquid; strain and pour this soup onto the bread slices in individual heated soup bowls.

MARMITE CAUCHOISE*

Norman seafood soup

Normandy

Preparation: 25 minutes
Cooking: 15 minutes
Easy

Serves 8:
4 slices conger eel
1 sea-robin
1 blue whiting or silver hake
1 porgy
8 small crabs
2 onions, peeled
2 cloves garlic, peeled and chopped
2 ripe tomatoes
3 tbsp peanut oil
1 bouquet garni (thyme, bay leaf, parsley)
salt and pepper
croûtons (optional)

Clean and prepare all the fish (see previous recipe; the trimmings can be saved to make a fish *fumet* for another dish). Rinse the live or freshly killed crabs well. Blanch, peel, slice, and deseed the tomatoes.

Sweat the finely sliced onions and the garlic in the oil in a large saucepan until very pale golden brown. Add the tomatoes. Cook gently, stirring, until soft.

Pour 2½ quarts cold water into the saucepan, add the bouquet garni and a good pinch each of sea salt and freshly ground pepper.

Bring to a boil; add the crabs, followed by the conger eel (cut into short sections) and the sea-robin. Allow to return to a very gentle boil, cook for 5 minutes, then add the whiting or hake and the porgy. Simmer, covered for 10 minutes.

Carefully strain off the liquid and ladle into heated soup bowls containing crisp bread croûtons. Serve the fish and crabs at the same time or afterward as a main course.

SOUPE TOURANGELLE
Bacon and vegetable soup

Touraine

Preparation: 45 minutes
Cooking: 1½ hours
Easy

Serves 8:
1 lb semisalted pork belly, or unsmoked bacon
1 small white or green cabbage
¾ cup white wine vinegar
1 lb leeks
¾ lb baby turnips, peeled
20 baby onions
¼ cup butter
3 quarts chicken broth (see glossary)
14 oz frozen petits pois *or larger peas*
salt and pepper

Blanch the pork or bacon, drain, rinse in cold water, and dry; cut off the skin and pieces of tough cartilage. Cut into small, thin crosswise strips (lardons). Peel off and discard the outer leaves of the cabbage, cut it from top to

bottom into 8 sections, remove the large ribs, and rinse the leaves in cold water mixed with the vinegar; bring these rapidly to a boil in a large saucepan of water; drain quickly, refresh, and drain again.

Slice the leeks; use the white part and the beginning of the green section. Dice the turnips.

Rinse out the large saucepan and sweat the turnips, onions, and leeks in the butter over low heat for 10 minutes with the lid on.

Add the cabbage, pork belly or bacon, and the chicken broth. Cover, heat to a gentle boil, then reduce the heat and simmer very gently for just over 1 hour. Season with salt and pepper to taste, add the peas, and cook until tender.

Ladle the soup into bowls containing thin, crisp slices of bread.

SOUPE AU LAPIN DE GARENNE

Creamy rabbit and mushroom soup

Touraine

Preparation: 30 minutes
Cooking: 2 hours 20 minutes
Easy

Serves 6:
1 rabbit weighing approx. 3 lb
3 onions, peeled
2 cloves garlic, peeled and chopped
1 bouquet garni (thyme, bay leaf, parsley, tarragon)
3/4 cup dry white wine
2 quarts light broth
10 oz small wild or button mushrooms
3 egg yolks
1/2 cup crème fraîche *or heavy cream*
salt and pepper

Ask your butcher to saw the cleaned rabbit into portions for you to avoid bone splinters, or joint it yourself. Place the pieces in a large, heavy-bottomed saucepan with the onions and garlic, bouquet garni, white wine, and broth. Cover and bring to a boil; skim off any scum. Reduce the heat and simmer for 2 hours or until the flesh comes off the bones easily.

Strain the contents of the pan, pouring the liquid into a clean saucepan. Remove and discard the bouquet garni and all the rabbit bones. Purée the rabbit meat in the food processor (or use a food mill, or chop).

Peel and chop all the mushrooms very finely; mix all but 3 tbsp with the puréed rabbit meat. Bring the strained liquid to a boil and add the rabbit mixture. Season with salt and pepper. Simmer for 15 minutes. Reduce the heat to very low.

Beat the egg yolks into the cream in a bowl. Add the reserved mushrooms and a cupful of the hot soup. Stir this mixture into the saucepan of soup; heat for a few minutes but do not allow to boil again.

During the German occupation of France, the great gastronome Curnonsky was a guest of two sisters, Mélanie and Marie Rouart who owned a restaurant at Riec-sur-Belon. The last lines of his poetic tribute are often quoted:

"Of lilies and sweet roses make a prize
For sisters Melanie and Marie
Who show us all by what they do
That the best cooking skill lies
In making flavours taste fresh and true."

SOUPE D'ÉTRILLES

Crab soup

Brittany

Preparation: 20 minutes
Cooking: 30 minutes
Easy

Serves 4:
2–2 1/2 lb very small Dungeness crabs
1 carrot, peeled and sliced
2 onions, peeled
1 cup Muscadet
1 bouquet garni (thyme, bay leaf, parsley, chervil)
1/2 cup rice
cayenne pepper, salt, white peppercorns
8 slices lightly toasted French bread

Make a *court-bouillon*: put the carrot, sliced onions, wine, bouquet garni and 2 quarts cold water in a large nonmetallic saucepan and heat slowly to boiling point.

Set the rice to boil in a large pan of salted water; cook for 17 minutes from when it boils.

Scrub the crabs well under running cold water. (You can use fresh or frozen cooked crabmeat, half the above weight, from large crabs for this soup if very small crabs are not available; thaw thoroughly if frozen). Add the crabs to the *court-bouillon*, bring to a boil, and cook for 5 minutes.

Discard the bouquet garni. Remove the carrots, onions, and crabs with a slotted ladle and process in the blender (shells and all) together with the cooked, drained rice until thoroughly liquidized.

Strain through a fine sieve into a saucepan, pressing with a wooden spoon to express all the moisture. Stir in all the broth; season with salt, freshly ground pepper, and a pinch of cayenne pepper. Boil gently for 5 minutes. Place 2 slices of toasted bread in 4 soup bowls and ladle the soup on top.

COTRIADE DE MAQUEREAUX*

Mackerel soup

Brittany

Preparation: 20 minutes
Cooking: 45 minutes
Easy

Serves 4:
8 small mackerel
2 onions, peeled
1/4 cup butter
1 cup Muscadet
1 1/2 pints cold water
1 bouquet garni (thyme, bay leaf, parsley)
1 lb small potatoes, peeled
1 lb leeks, white parts only
2 egg yolks
8 slices French bread fried in extra butter
1 1/2 tbsp finely choppped fresh herbs (parsley, chervil, tarragon, chives)
salt and pepper

Chop the onions finely; sweat in the butter until very tender. Add the wine, water, bouquet garni, a generous pinch of salt, and freshly ground pepper. Bring to a boil; add the potatoes and the leeks, tied in a bundle with string. Boil for 30 minutes. Add the cleaned, prepared fish and simmer for 15 minutes.

Transfer the fish and vegetables from the pan to a heated serving dish and keep hot. Add more seasoning to the liquid if needed, strain, and keep hot in a saucepan; beat a cupful into the egg yolks; stir this mixture into the hot, not boiling, liquid. Ladle the soup over the bread slices in heated bowls, sprinkle with the herbs and serve. Make a vinaigrette or mayonnaise flavored with plenty of strong mustard to accompany the fish and vegetables.

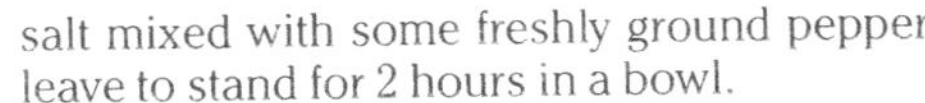

ENTRÉES

RILLETTES D'ANGERS*

Potted pork

Anjou

Preparation: 20 minutes
Cooking: 4½ hours
Easy

Serves 8 as a first course:
4½ lb assorted cuts fresh pork (blade, neck, breast, belly, leg)
1 lb flair or back pork fat, skin removed
salt and pepper

Cut the flair fat into small pieces and cook over very gentle heat for 30 minutes in a heavy enameled casserole dish. Cut the pork into fairly small cubes and mix with a generous pinch each of salt and freshly ground pepper; add to the fat in the casserole dish, together with ¾ cup water. Cover tightly and cook extremely slowly for 4 hours until the meat is meltingly tender. Stir occasionally.

After 4 hours, take the largest pieces of pork which are still solid out of the casserole dish: these are called "*rillaux*" and are eaten warm or cold.

Stir and break up the rest of the meat and fat with a fork and spoon into one or more preserving jars; make sure there is a layer of fat on the surface. This will keep, refrigerated, for up to 2 weeks. Serve at room temperature with crusty bread or toast.

RILLONS

Tender pork cubes

Touraine

Preparation: 10 minutes
Resting time: 2 hours
Cooking: 1–2 hours
Easy

Serves 8 as a first course or snack (yields about 2 lb):
2¼ lb fairly lean fresh pork breast or belly
1½–2 tbsp coarse sea salt
1¼ cups lard
salt and pepper

Cut the pork into 1½–2-in cubes (you do not have to remove the skin) and roll in the coarse salt mixed with some freshly ground pepper; leave to stand for 2 hours in a bowl.

Heat the lard slowly in a heavy-bottomed fireproof casserole dish; when it is very hot, add the cubed meat and cook until well browned all over; continue cooking, over much lower heat, for 1–2 hours or until the pork cubes are a rich brown color and very tender. Turn carefully once or twice while cooking without breaking up the meat.

Drain off the fat and serve hot or cold. Or transfer all the meat and fat to preserving jars, making sure that the meat pieces are covered by a layer of the liquid lard. Leave to cool. This will keep for 2 weeks if refrigerated.

OMELETTES AUX COQUES*

Shellfish omelet

Normandy

Preparation: 30 minutes
Cooking: 5–10 minutes
Fairly easy

Serves 6:
2–2½ lb small clams or quahogs
juice of 1 lemon
¼ cup heavy cream
8 eggs
chopped fresh parsley, chervil, tarragon, and chives
¼ cup butter
salt and pepper

Soak the shellfish in several changes of water and scrub well under running cold water; leave unshucked. Pour 1½ cups water into a very wide saucepan, add the lemon juice and the shellfish. Place over very high heat; as soon as the shells have opened, remove from the heat.

Take the mollusks out of their shells; reserve all their juice, strain this through a piece of cloth placed in a sieve, and mix with the cream and a little freshly ground pepper. Stir in the mollusks.

Beat the eggs for one very large omelet (or two or more smaller ones), adding salt, pepper and all or some of the herbs listed above (approx. 1–1½ tbsp). Stir in 1½–2 tbsp of the butter, in small flakes.

Heat the remaining butter in a large omelet pan until it froths, pour in the eggs and cook, stirring with the tines of a fork, until the omelet is set underneath but still creamy on top. Draw to one side, sprinkle the mollusks and creamy liquid all over the top then slide the omelet on to a heated plate and fold in half, enclosing the mollusks. Serve immediately.

RILLETTES DE TOURS*

Potted pork and wine

Touraine

Preparation: 20 minutes
Cooking: approx. 4 hours
Easy

Serves 12 as a first course or snack:
4½ lb pork hind loin with all its fat
3 tbsp coarse sea salt
1 bottle Vouvray or other dry white wine

Take the fat off the loin and cut into small cubes. Cut out the lean meat and slice lengthwise into strips, cutting with, not across, the grain of the meat and keep separate from the fat. Reserve the bones.

Spread the fat cubes over the bottom of an enameled cast iron casserole dish; cover with the bones, then spread the lean meat strips on top. Sprinkle with the salt and with ¾ cup cold water. Cover. Bring slowly to a boil and immediately reduce the heat to very low indeed; do not stir.

After 30 minutes, remove the bones, add the wine, and increase the heat a little. Stir at frequent intervals with a wooden spoon to mix the fat and lean meat thoroughly.

After about 4 hours the meat should have turned into a very soft, rather coarse purée. Transfer this to sterilized preserving jars, ensuring that there is a surface layer of fat. Seal tightly and refrigerate. Use within 2 weeks.

QUICHE TOURANGELLE

Potted pork flan

Touraine

Preparation: 20 minutes
Cooking: 45 minutes
Easy

Serves 8:
½ lb rillettes de Tours *(see above)*
1 lb rillons *(see page 78)*
5 eggs
1 pint milk
1 cup heavy cream
2½ tbsp finely chopped fresh parsley, chervil, tarragon, chives
salt and pepper
nutmeg

For the pie dough:
3 cups all-purpose flour
¾ cup softened butter, cubed
1 egg
pinch salt

Make the pie dough: place the flour in a large mixing bowl, make a well in the center, and fill with the butter cubes, egg, and salt; work these into the flour, adding only just enough cold water to make a firm dough which comes away cleanly from the sides of the bowl. Shape into a ball, flatten with your palms, and fold; shape into a ball once more and leave to rest in a cool place for 1 hour.

Remove any bones or tough bits from the *rillons* and dice. Roll out the pie dough and use to line a wide pie plate or deep flan dish; spread an even layer of the *rillettes* over the bottom of the pie shell and cover with the diced *rillons*.

Beat the eggs and mix thoroughly with the milk and cream. Add the herbs, a pinch each of salt and nutmeg, and a generous pinch of freshly ground pepper; pour all over the pork. Have the oven preheated to 400°F and cook for 30 minutes before reducing the heat to 350°F for a further 15 minutes. Serve warm.

FISH

MARMITE DIEPPOISE
Fish stew

Normandy

Preparation: 40 minutes
Cooking: 40 minutes
Complicated

Serves 6:
6 slices goosefish
1 flounder or sole (1½–1¾ lb)
6 ¼ lb slices turbot (or other fine, dense white fish)
6 scampi
1 quart mussels
30 peeled shrimp
2 leeks, white part only
1 stick celery
2 onions, peeled
¼ cup olive oil
2 blanched, peeled tomatoes
1 bouquet garni of parsley and fennel seeds
¼ cup butter
¼ cup all-purpose flour
¼ cup heavy cream
pinch each cayenne pepper and curry powder
salt and pepper

Have all the fish, crustaceans, and shellfish prepared and washed before you start. The sole should be skinned and filleted (your fishmonger can do this for you; have the other fish filleted if preferred). Having soaked the mussels in several changes of cold water, scrub them well under running cold water, discarding any that remain open or are damaged.

Slice the leeks, celery, and onions and sweat in the olive oil in a very large, fireproof casserole dish until tender. Add 6 cups cold water and the seeded and coarsely chopped tomatoes. Stir well, add salt, pepper, cayenne, and curry powder. Bring slowly to a boil and cook gently for 10 minutes. Pour 1 cup water into a wide saucepan, add salt and plenty of freshly ground pepper; add the mussels and place over very high heat for a few minutes. Take out the mussels as soon as they have opened, reserving all their juice; leave them on the half shell, removing and discarding the other half shell.

Strain all the juice and the water in the pan through a cloth placed in a sieve and reserve.

Add the fresh herbs, scampi, and any fish cut into slices or steaks to the casserole. Simmer very gently for 10 minutes, then add any filleted fish and the shrimp. Simmer for 5 minutes.

Take the fish out of the cooking liquid in the casserole and keep hot in a deep serving dish, surrounded by the crustaceans and mussels. Strain the liquid and mix with the reserved mussel liquid.

Melt the butter in a small saucepan, stir in the flour and heat until the mixture bubbles; gradually stir in the strained liquid and cook over low heat, stirring, for 5 minutes. Turn off the heat, stir in the cream, adjust the seasoning, and pour the sauce all over the fish.

BARBUE AU CIDRE
Brill cooked in cider

Normandy

Preparation: 20 minutes
Cooking: 30 minutes
Easy

Serves 6:
3–3½ lb flounder, brill or turbot
10 oz button mushrooms
3 shallots, peeled
¼ cup butter
¾ cup fine dry breadcrumbs
1½ cups still, dry cider
¼ cup crème fraîche *or heavy cream*
salt and pepper

Cut off the tail and the fins all round the fish. Gut, wash thoroughly, and dry. Do not remove the skin. Season on both sides with salt and pepper. Dice the mushrooms and add to a saucepan of boiling water; simmer gently for 10 minutes then drain and spread out on kitchen towels to dry. Slice the shallots thinly.

Use half the butter to grease a gratin dish or any fairly shallow ovenproof dish that will take the fish lying flat. Sprinkle half the mushrooms and shallots over the bottom and place the fish on top. Sprinkle the remaining mushrooms and shallots over the fish. Dot flakes of the remaining butter all over the top of the fish; sprinkle with the breadcrumbs. Add the cider, pouring it in to one side of the fish; if using *crème fraîche*, sprinkle around the edge of the fish. Cook in a preheated oven at 350°F for 30 minutes or until the fish is done. If heavy cream is used, add just before serving. Serve straight from the gratin dish.

Lobster à l'armoricaine (as in Armorica, the old name for Brittany) or à l'américaine (American style)? The name is disputed. According to one expert, a chef called Peters from Sète in the south of France who owned a restaurant in Paris a century ago invented the dish and called it homard à l'américaine.

The writer and Breton nationalist Gwenn-Aël, however, asserts that lobster à l'armoricaine hails from Brittany. The debate continues.

SOLE NORMANDE
Poached sole

Normandy

Preparation: 45 minutes
Cooking: 40 minutes
Easy

Serves 4:
2 soles or flounders, skinned, each weighing 1½–1¾ lb
¼ cup butter
6 tbsp very finely chopped shallots
1 cup dry white wine
1 quart mussels
½ lb peeled small shrimp
½ lb button mushrooms
6 tbsp lemon juice
1 cup crème fraîche *or heavy cream*
salt and pepper

Preheat the oven to 400°F. Grease liberally with butter a very large, shallow ovenproof dish (or two dishes) that will take the soles lying flat in a single layer. Sprinkle the shallots all over the bottom; season the soles on both sides with salt and pepper and place on the shallots. Add the wine; dot the surface of the fish with flakes of butter. Cover with aluminum foil and place in the oven to cook for 30 minutes.

Soak the mussels in several changes of cold water then scrub well. Discard any that are open. Place in a large saucepan with ½ cup water and place over high heat to make the mussels open.

Strain the mussel juice and liquid into a small saucepan through a fine cloth in a sieve. Take the mussels off the shell and keep warm in a covered dish with the shrimp.

Melt the butter in a small saucepan, stir in the lemon juice, add the mushrooms, and sauté briskly for a few minutes. Drain off the liquid into the mussel juices and add the mushrooms to the mussels and shrimp.

Take the cooked sole out of the oven; detach the fillets neatly and transfer to a heated serving platter. Keep hot. Strain the sole juices into the saucepan of liquid; boil hard, uncovered, until it acquires the consistency of a thin syrup; reduce the heat to very low and beat in the *crème fraîche*; the sauce should be smooth and velvety.

Arrange the mussels, shrimp, and mushrooms around the fish; coat the fish with the sauce.

ALOSE À L'ANGEVINE

Shad with sorrel and cream

Anjou

Preparation: 20 minutes
Cooking: 30 minutes
Easy

Serves 6:
1 3-lb shad
1 medium-sized onion, peeled
6 tbsp butter
1 lb sorrel or spinach
3/4 cup heavy cream
salt and pepper

Remove the stalk and central rib of each sorrel leaf. Wash, dry, and shred. Slice the onion wafer thin. Grease a large, rectangular, nonmetallic ovenproof dish liberally with butter; spread the onion and sorrel in it; sprinkle with the cream.

Remove the shad's fins and scales and gut, wash, and dry. Cut several parallel slashes down each side of the fish, season all over and inside with salt and pepper and place flat on the cream and vegetable bed. Dot the surface of the fish with flakes of butter and place in the oven, preheated to 400°F for 30 minutes or until done.

LISETTES DE DIEPPE AU CIDRE*

Baby mackerel with cider

Normandy

Start preparation 24 hours in advance:
Preparation: 40 minutes
Cooking: 10 minutes
Easy

Serves 4:
3–3 1/2 lb very small mackerel
2 carrots, peeled and sliced
2 onions, peeled
1 shallot, peeled
1 bouquet garni (thyme, bay leaf, parsley)
10 peppercorns
10 whole coriander
coarse sea salt
1 quart still, dry cider
1/2 lemon
few sprigs parsley

Cut off the fishes' fins, tails and heads, then gut, wash, and dry. Reserve the heads. Make the *court-bouillon*: place the heads, carrots, sliced onions and shallot, 2 tbsp sea salt, and the cider in a large, nonmetallic saucepan, bring to a boil and simmer very gently for 15 minutes.

Arrange the fish, alternating wider end to tail in an enameled casserole dish or a fish kettle; gently squeeze half the lemon over the fish, then cut it in 4 slices and place between the fish. Add the *court-bouillon* and heat until it is just beginning to boil; turn the fish, heat to boiling point again, and simmer gently for 2 minutes. Turn off the heat.

Chop the parsley leaves coarsely and slice the remaining half lemon into rounds. Take the fish out of the *court-bouillon* and arrange half of them in the bottom of a fairly deep, straight-sided dish. Cover with half the onion and carrot slices from the *court-bouillon*, two of the lemon slices and a sprinkling of parsley. Cover with another layer of fish and top this with the remaining vegetables, lemon, and parsley.

Boil the *court-bouillon* fast until it has reduced by one third. Draw aside from the heat, cool for 5 minutes, then pour through a fine sieve all over the fish. Leave to cool at room temperature, then cover with foil and refrigerate for 24 hours before serving.

CARRELETS AU CIDRE
Plaice with cider, cream, and chives

Normandy

Preparation: 10 minutes
Cooking: 20 minutes
Easy

Serves 4:
2 large, very fresh plaice or flounder
1/4 cup butter
few sprigs parsley and chives
1 pint still, dry cider
3/4 cup fine, dry breadcrumbs
salt and pepper
1/2 cup crème fraîche *or heavy cream*

Trim, gut, wash, and dry the flounder or plaice and arrange, lying flat beside each other in a large, well-buttered nonmetallic ovenproof gratin dish. Season with salt and pepper; sprinkle with finely chopped mixed parsley and chives. Pour in the cider; dot the fish with the butter, in small flakes, and sprinkle with a layer of the breadcrumbs. Bake, uncovered, in a preheated oven at 400°F for 20 minutes or until done.

Pour off the liquid from the dish carefully and strain into a small saucepan; stir in the cream and heat; do not allow to boil. Pour all over the fish.

GRATIN DE HARENGS À LA CRÈME*
Herrings with cream and Gruyère cheese

Normandy

Preparation: 25 minutes
Cooking: 25 minutes
Easy

Serves 6:
6 herrings
3 large waxy potatoes, peeled
1/4 cup butter
3 large mild onions, peeled
3/4 cup still, dry cider or dry white wine
3 large, ripe tomatoes
1 cup grated Gruyère cheese
1/2 cup crème fraîche *or heavy cream*
salt and pepper

Remove the scales, make an incision down the backbone of each fish, and work the flesh off the bones that are connected to it, giving two neat fillets per fish. Slice the potatoes thinly. Slice the onions into wafer thin rings. Grease an enameled casserole dish with butter and arrange the onions and potatoes in it. Add the cider and 1/2 cup cold water. Place the fillets in a layer on top of the bed of vegetables; peel the tomatoes and remove their seeds; slice or chop coarsely and arrange around the herring fillets. Season with salt and pepper.

Heat very slowly over very low heat until the liquid boils; simmer gently for 10 minutes. Dot the fillets with flakes of butter and bake in a preheated oven at 350°F until the potatoes are very tender (test with the tines of a fork). Remove from the oven, sprinkle the Gruyère cheese over the surface, followed by the cream and place under a preheated broiler for 5 minutes.

BOUILLETURE D'ANGUILLES
Eels with red wine and mushrooms

Anjou

Preparation: 30 minutes
Cooking: 2 hours
Easy

Serves 6:
2–2 1/2 lb fairly small eels
1 bouquet garni (thyme, bay leaf, parsley)
1 bottle dry red wine
1/4 cup Anjou marc or brandy
10 baby onions, peeled
1/2 lb button mushrooms
1/2 cup butter
1/2 cup all-purpose flour
6 slices French bread fried in extra butter
salt and pepper

Ask your fishmonger to skin the eels and cut off their heads. Cut them into 2-in sections and place these in a fireproof casserole dish with salt, pepper, and the bouquet garni. Add enough wine to cover, setting aside 1/2 cup for later use. Heat quickly to boiling point, add the warmed *marc* or brandy, flame, then reduce the heat to very low and barely simmer for 2 hours.

Cook the onions and mushrooms in 1/2 cup of the butter and the reserved wine in a covered saucepan for 20 minutes. Work the flour with the remaining, solid butter, stir this into the casserole containing the eels and liquid, and simmer for a few minutes as it thickens. Add the onions and mushrooms. Transfer to a heated serving dish and garnish with the fried bread croûtons.

BEURRE BLANC*

Sharp shallot butter

Anjou and Brittany (Nantes)

Preparation and cooking: approx. 25 minutes
Complicated

Serves 8:
1/4 lb shallots, peeled
1/2 cup dry white Anjou or Muscadet wine
1 cup white wine vinegar
1 1/4 sticks butter
salt and pepper

An agreeably sharp-tasting butter sauce served with fish poached in *court-bouillon* (especially pike and salmon). Keep the cooked fish hot on a serving dish while you make the *beurre blanc*: it separates and turns oily if kept waiting. Slice the shallots from top to bottom in half and remove the central shoot if it is discernible. Chop very finely indeed and place in a heavy-bottomed nonmetallic saucepan with the wine and vinegar. Simmer very gently, uncovered, for as long as it takes for the shallots to turn into a purée without browning at all; the liquid should evaporate completely. Cut the butter into small pieces.

Place the pan containing the shallots over a saucepan of very hot but not boiling water. Add the butter pieces one at a time, beating vigorously after each addition. Season with salt and freshly ground white pepper.

The finished sauce should be very pale, smooth, and creamy, yet light and frothy; it must be served at once. Keep barely warm, if you must, for a minute or two over tepid, not hot, water. Add 1 tbsp heavy cream to help stabilize the sauce if wished (*beurre Nantais*).

DEMOISELLES DE CHERBOURG À LA NAGE

Lobster in white wine

Normandy

Preparation: 25 minutes
Cooking: 10 minutes
Fairly easy

Serves 6:
3 lobsters, each weighing approx. 14 oz
2 1/2 quarts dry white wine (e.g. Muscadet)
1 carrot, peeled
1 onion, peeled
1 bouquet garni (thyme, bay leaf, parsley)
10 peppercorns
1/2 cup butter
salt

Norman cooks always use live lobsters for this recipe, tying their claws to the body with strong kitchen string.

Prepare the cooking liquid: pour the white wine into a large enameled fireproof casserole dish or saucepan; add the peeled carrot and onion, sliced into rings, the bouquet garni, the peppercorns tied in a piece of cheesecloth, and a generous pinch of salt. Heat very slowly until the liquid boils (20 minutes).

Add the lobsters, turning up the heat to keep the liquid boiling. Cook for 10 minutes by which time the lobsters will be scarlet.

Untie the string; detach the claws. Use a sharp, heavy knife to split the lobsters lengthwise in half; remove the stomach sac in the head and the black intestinal tract. Crack the shell of the claws with a nutcracker. Sprinkle each cut surface with a little of the cooking liquid and serve at once while very hot, each half topped with a rounded dessertspoon of solid butter.

HARENGS À LA MOUTARDE

Herrings with herb and mustard sauce

Normandy

Preparation: 10 minutes
Cooking: 20 minutes
Easy

Serves 6:
6 herrings
1 1/2 cups milk
approx. 6 tbsp all-purpose flour
1/4 cup butter
1/4 cup strong, pale French mustard
1/4 cup crème fraîche *or heavy cream*
fresh parsley, chervil, tarragon or marjoram, and chives
salt and pepper

Remove the scales from the herrings, cut off their heads, fins and tails, gut, wash, and dry them. Dip them in the milk, then roll in the flour, shaking off excess. Season inside and out with salt and pepper. Heat the butter in a large skillet and brown the herrings on both sides. Reduce the heat and cook for 10 minutes. Transfer them to a heated, butter-greased dish and keep warm in a slow oven. Save all the cooking juices to make the sauce: strain into a small saucepan and stir in the mustard, cream, and any extra seasoning over low heat. Stir in the finely chopped herbs and pour over the herrings.

MAQUEREAUX À LA QUIMPEROISE*

Mackerel with herb butter

Brittany

Preparation: 1 1/4 hours
Cooking: 10 minutes
Easy

Serves 4:
For the court-bouillon:
1 3/4 cups Muscadet or other dry white wine
1 bouquet garni (thyme, bay leaf, parsley)
1 onion, peeled
1 clove garlic, peeled
1 1/2 tbsp coarse sea salt
6 peppercorns

4 mackerel
2 egg yolks
1 tsp Dijon or English mustard
1 tsp wine vinegar
1 1/2 tbsp finely chopped fresh parsley, chervil, tarragon, and chives
1/4 cup butter
salt and pepper

Put all the ingredients for the *court-bouillon* in a large enameled saucepan or fish kettle, adding 2 quarts cold water. Bring slowly to a boil and simmer for 1 hour. Leave to cool.

Add the prepared and gutted mackerel to the cold *court-bouillon*; bring to a boil, then reduce the heat and leave to barely simmer for 10 minutes.

If wished, take the flesh off the bones in 4 neat fillets from each fish. Keep warm.

Melt the butter over hot water. Mix the egg yolks with the mustard and finely chopped herbs in a small bowl with a balloon whisk; beat in the melted butter a little at a time: the resulting sauce should resemble a thin mayonnaise. Sprinkle over the mackerel and serve at once.

A garnish of sautéed baby onions, mushrooms, and diced carrots can be added.

COQUILLES SAINT-JACQUES À LA BRETONNE

Scallops with breadcrumb topping

Brittany

Preparation: 2 1/4 hours
Cooking: 15 minutes
Easy

Serves 4:
8 large sea or bay scallops
2 medium-sized onions, peeled
1/4 cup butter
1 cup Muscadet or other dry white wine
fine, untoasted breadcrumbs
3–4 tbsp finely chopped parsley

If possible, buy fresh scallops in the shell. Take the mollusks off their flatter half shells; use the "beard" (the paleish frill or mantle), the white cushion of meat, and the attached coral for this recipe. Rinse well. Save the deep half shell and wash thoroughly. If using frozen

scallops, thaw well. Sweat the finely chopped onions in 2 tbsp of the butter until tender. Do not brown. Add the wine. Cover and simmer gently for 2 hours.

Slice the scallops horizontally into 3 disks; simmer these and the whole corals (if using fresh scallops) in the liquid for a maximum of 8 minutes.

Sprinkle a layer of breadcrumbs into 4 ramekin dishes, moisten with 1 tsp of the cooking liquid and arrange 6 scallop slices and 2 coral slices on top. Sprinkle with a little parsley, cover with breadcrumbs and dot the surface with flakes of butter.

Place under a hot broiler to heat through and brown lightly.

PALOURDES FARCIES

Clams with garlic and parsley butter

Brittany

Preparation: 40 minutes
Cooking: 10 minutes
Easy

Serves 6:
6 dozen small clams in the shell
4–5 tbsp finely chopped parsley
6 cloves garlic, peeled and finely chopped
2 sticks butter, softened
salt and pepper

Soak the clams in several changes of cold water and wash under running cold water, scrubbing the shells. Discard any that do not close when handled.

Place in a large, wide saucepan with approx. $^{3}/_{4}$ cup water. Cover and place over high heat; the clams should all have opened within 5 minutes; discard any that fail to open.

Take the mollusks off their half shells and discard the shell to which they were attached; keep the other half shell.

Work the parsley and garlic into the butter with a wooden spoon. Stir vigorously, seasoning with ground sea salt and freshly ground pepper and spread a very little in each half shell. Put the mollusk on top and smear it with more of the butter. Place in one large or 6 individual heatproof shallow dishes. Refrigerate until just before serving, then sprinkle with a thin covering of fine breadcrumbs if wished.

Preheat the oven to 400°F and bake the clams, with or without a breadcrumb topping, for 10 minutes.

HUÎTRES GRATINÉES*

Baked oysters

Brittany

Preparation: 40 minutes
Cooking: 5 minutes
Fairly easy

Serves 6:
2 dozen oysters
2 shallots, peeled
$^{1}/_{2}$ cup Muscadet or other dry white wine.
2 egg yolks
$^{1}/_{2}$ cup butter
3 tbsp flaked or chopped almonds
pepper
lemon juice

Open the oysters with a special oyster knife or strong, short-bladed knife and take them off the half shell. Keep the deeper half shell of each oyster, put the mollusks in these and place in oyster dishes or on a bed of coarse salt to prevent them tipping over. Save all the juice and strain through a cloth placed in a sieve into a small saucepan, add the finely chopped shallots and the wine, and boil until reduced to only 3 tbsp of liquid. Pour into a heatproof bowl set over a pan of very gently simmering water and beat in the egg yolks with a balloon whisk to give a light, velvety consistency. Gradually beat in the butter and the almonds, adding a little of each at a time. Season with freshly ground pepper; beat in a little lemon juice to taste.

Spoon a little sauce over each oyster and bake for 5 minutes in a preheated oven at 400°F. Serve immediately.

THON À LA CONCARNOISE

Fresh tuna casserole

Brittany

Preparation: 30 minutes
Cooking: 50 minutes
Easy

Serves 4:
1 large tuna steak weighing $1^{3}/_{4}$ lb
1 large, or 2 smaller pieces barding fat
$^{1}/_{2}$ cup butter
5 oz baby onions, peeled
1 cup Muscadet or other dry white wine
1 cup fish fumet *or vegetable broth*
1 bouquet garni
1 large round lettuce heart
3 carrots, peeled
3 baby turnips, peeled
1 lb frozen peas
salt and pepper

Remove the skin from the tuna and take out all the bones. Wrap in the barding fat (use pork flair or back fat, very thinly sliced, or several slices of bacon) and tie securely. Sauté the onions in the butter in a heavy-bottomed fireproof casserole dish until lightly browned; add the tuna and cook for a few minutes on each side over fairly high heat. Pour in the wine and the *fumet*. Add the bouquet garni. Season with salt and pepper. Once the liquid boils, reduce the heat, cover and simmer for 45 minutes.

Rinse the lettuce heart and quarter. Add the quarters to the casserole dish, arranging around the tuna; when they have wilted, add the carrots, cut into matchstick strips, and the quartered turnips. Barely simmer, covered, for 20 minutes. Add the peas, then cook for a further 30 minutes. Carefully remove and discard the barding fat and place the tuna on a heated serving dish; surround with the vegetables. Discard the bouquet garni and pour the remaining liquid over the fish.

BARBUE À LA CANCALAISE

Brill with oyster and cream sauce

Brittany

Preparation: 1 hour
Cooking: 25 minutes
Complicated

Serves 6:
1 brill or flounder weighing 4–4½ lb
¼ cup butter
2 dozen oysters
⅓ cup heavy cream

For the *fumet* or fish stock:
1 leek, white part only
2 medium-sized onions, peeled
1 carrot, peeled
1 shallot, peeled
Pinch each cayenne pepper, nutmeg, salt, pepper
1 bouquet garni (thyme, bay leaf, parsley)
¾ cup Muscadet or other dry white wine

For the roux:
2 tbsp butter
4 tbsp all-purpose flour

Make the fish *fumet*: wash and slice the leek; slice the onions, carrots, and shallots and put in a large saucepan; if you have any fresh fish trimmings, add them for extra flavor. Season with cayenne, nutmeg, salt, and pepper; add the bouquet garni, and the wine diluted with an equal volume of cold water. Bring to a boil, then boil gently for 45 minutes. Strain and allow to cool.

Shuck the oysters, discarding the shells; save all their juice and strain it into a saucepan. Trim, gut, wash, and dry the brill. Place in a roasting pan or large butter-greased ovenproof dish. Pour in the *fumet* and place the pan on the stove to heat quickly, as soon as the liquid boils, draw aside from the heat, cover tightly with a large sheet of foil, and place in the oven, preheated to 425°F. After 10 minutes, reduce the heat to 300°F for a further 15 minutes.

While the brill is in the oven, add the oysters to their strained juice, heat gently, and draw aside just as the liquid starts to boil; leave to stand for 5 minutes, then drain the oysters and set aside, discarding the liquid.

Fillet the brill, discarding all the bones and dark skin; save and strain all the liquid and juices. Place the fillets on a heated serving dish, garnish with the oysters, cover, and keep warm.

Melt the butter, stir in the flour, and cook for 1–2 minutes; continue stirring while gradually adding the strained liquid; cook and stir for a few minutes until the sauce has thickened. Add the cream, stir briefly, and pour all over the brill fillets.

LOTTE À L'ARMORICAINE

Goosefish with tomatoes and wine

Brittany

Preparation: 10 minutes
Cooking: 30 minutes
Easy

Serves 4:
2½–2¾-lb goosefish tail, skinned
¼ cup all-purpose flour
¾ cup butter
2 medium-sized onions, peeled
¼ cup Calvados or apple brandy
2¼ cups Muscadet or other dry white wine
*1¼ cups sieved fresh tomatoes (*passato*)*
2 cloves garlic, peeled
pinch each salt, pepper, cayenne pepper

Remove the second, transparent skin; fillet the fish if wished. Cut into 1¼-in sections, roll these in the flour, shake off excess and sauté in hot butter (½ cup) with the finely sliced onions in a fireproof casserole dish. Add the Calvados, heat, and flame. Pour in the wine and the tomato (use *passato* sold in cartons), add the whole garlic cloves and the seasonings. Cover and simmer for 30 minutes.

Lightly grease an ovenproof dish with a little of the remaining butter; transfer the pieces of fish into it to keep hot while you make the sauce. Strain the remaining contents of the casserole into a saucepan, add more seasoning if necessary; stir in the remaining butter over low heat, adding a small piece at a time. Pour over the fish and serve with steamed rice.

MORUE BRESTOISE

Salt cod and vegetable pie

Brittany

Start preparation 24 hours in advance
Preparation: 40 minutes
Cooking: 10 minutes
Easy

Serves 6:
2–2½ lb salt cod (1¾ lb if filleted)
½ cup butter
3 onions, peeled
4 leeks, white part only
3 tbsp all-purpose flour
1¾ lb waxy potatoes
½–¾ cup fine, dry breadcrumbs
pepper

Soak the salt cod in frequent changes of cold water for 24 hours if using whole salt cod, for 12 hours if using filleted. Bring to a boil in a large saucepan of fresh cold water, reduce the heat and simmer until tender. Drain well, reserving the liquid. Remove the skin and bones if present. Boil the potatoes in their skins until tender. Cook the finely sliced onions and leeks in half the butter until tender and lightly browned. Sprinkle with the flour and stir. Once the flour has turned pale golden brown, stir in 1½ cups of the cooking liquid and plenty of freshly ground pepper. Continue stirring over low heat until thickened.

Peel the cooked potatoes and slice. Drain the cod and break into large, thick flakes with a fork. Grease a deep ovenproof dish with butter; spread a layer of cod flakes over the bottom, cover with a layer of potato slices, repeat this layering, then spoon the onion and leek sauce all over the top. Sprinkle with a topping of breadcrumbs, dot with butter and bake in a preheated oven at 450°F for 10 minutes.

MORUE GUINGAMPOISE

Salt cod fritters

Brittany

Start preparation 24 hours in advance
Preparation (including marinating): 2¼ hours
Cooking: approx. 5 minutes
Easy

Serves 6:
2–2¼ lb salt cod (1¾ lb if filleted)

Marinade:
6 tbsp white wine vinegar
1 clove garlic, peeled and lightly minced
2 onions, peeled
2 cloves
3 tbsp mixed chopped parsley and chives
pepper

For the coating batter:
1 cup all-purpose flour
3 eggs, separated
1 cup milk
½ cup finely grated Gruyère cheese

See previous recipe for preparation and cooking of salt cod. Drain and set aside to cool. Remove any skin and bones.

Make the marinade, mixing all the ingredients with 1½ pints cold water in a nonmetallic dish or bowl. Soak the cod in this for 2 hours.

Make a thick coating batter: sift the flour into a bowl and make a well in the center; pour in the egg yolks beaten with the milk. Gradually work into the flour; add the Gruyère cheese mixing well (if preferred, this batter can be made in the blender). Beat the egg whites until firm but not dry. Use kitchen towels to dry the pieces of cod thoroughly; try to ensure that these are evenly sized.

Heat the fat or oil in a deep fryer until hot (355°F). Dip the cod pieces in the batter, then in the beaten egg whites, lower into the deep fryer, and cook until the batter is golden brown and crisp. Remove with a slotted ladle or spoon, draining well. Serve immediately, sprinkled with the herbs.

MAIN COURSES

OIE EN DAUBE
Pot roasted goose

Normandy

Preparation: 25 minutes
Cooking: 3 hours
Easy

Serves 6:
1 young goose weighing 6½–7 lb
1½ lb piece smoked bacon
¼ cup butter
4 carrots, peeled and thinly sliced
3 onions, peeled and finely chopped
1 stick celery, chopped
1 leek, white part only, sliced
1 bouquet garni (thyme, bay leaf)
1 quart still, dry cider
2–2½ lb Rennet apples
salt and pepper

A young goose is best for this recipe as it will not have too much fat on it; joint it into 10–12 pieces using a very sharp knife and poultry shears. Remove the skin and tough pieces of cartilage from the bacon; if in one piece, cut into lardons, if sliced, cut across these into small pieces. Heat the butter in a large, heavy-bottomed fireproof casserole dish; brown the goose portions and bacon.

Add the carrots, chopped onions, the celery, leek, and bouquet garni. Season with salt and pepper. Add the cider. Cover and simmer over very low heat for 3 hours.

While the goose is cooking, peel, core, and quarter the apples; cook them with a sprinkling of water in a covered nonstick saucepan until nearly tender; cook uncovered for a few minutes more to eliminate all excess moisture.

Take the goose pieces out of the casserole dish and place on a serving platter. Moisten with some of the strained cooking liquid and serve with the apple compote.

COTES DE VEAU À LA NORMANDE*
Veal chops with cider and cream sauce

Normandy

Preparation: 10 minutes
Cooking: 30 minutes
Easy

Serves 6:
6 milk-fed veal loin chops
4 Rennet apples (or any firm apple)
¼ cup butter
¼ cup Calvados
½ cup still, dry cider
¼ cup heavy cream
salt and pepper
small pinch nutmeg

Peel, quarter, core, and slice the apples evenly.

Heat the butter over moderate heat until it starts to turn golden brown in a large, heavy-bottomed saucepan or skillet, add the chops, and cook for 10 minutes on each side. Season with a little salt, freshly ground pepper, and the nutmeg then transfer to a heated serving dish, leaving all the juices and fat in the pan.

Cover the chops with foil and keep hot in a slow oven or over a pan of hot water.

Add the apple slices to the hot fat and juices in the pan and sauté briefly over high heat, turning them with a spatula. Take out of the pan, draining well, and arrange around the chops; replace the foil and keep warm.

Pour the Calvados into the pan, heat, and flame. Add the cider; keep the heat high and work all the caramelized deposits free with a wooden spoon. Boil for 3 minutes; reduce the heat to very low; stir in the cream, adjust the seasoning, and pour over the chops.

ANDOUILLE DE VIRE À L'OSEILLE*

Sausage with sorrel

Normandy

Preparation: 20 minutes
Cooking: 30 minutes
Easy

Serves 6:
12 slices Vire sausage (or a good quality smoked boiling sausage)
2½ lb sorrel
10 spinach leaves
1 stick butter
2 eggs
¾ cup heavy cream
salt and pepper

If sorrel is not available, use all spinach or Swiss Chard or spinach beet; the dish will lack the sharpness of the sorrel but will still taste very good. Remove the stalks and large ribs from the sorrel and spinach, wash the leaves and dry thoroughly before blanching in 2 quarts boiling water in a nonmetallic saucepan. Boil, uncovered, for 10 minutes, drain, and press down hard on the leaves to eliminate all excess moisture.

Heat half the butter in a saucepan, add the sorrel and spinach; cook over moderate heat for a few minutes, stirring occasionally. Season with salt and pepper. Reduce the heat to very low. Mix the eggs and cream in a small bowl, pour over the sorrel mixture, and stir; cover and cook extremely gently for 30 minutes (use a heat diffuser if necessary to prevent the mixture approaching boiling point).

Slice the sausage. When the sorrel mixture is about halfway through its cooking time, heat the remaining butter and fry the sausage slices for 1 minute on each side. Serve in a heated serving dish, on a bed of the sorrel and spinach mixture.

TRIPES À LA MODE DE CAEN

Tripe with cider and onions

Normandy

Preparation: 30 minutes
Cooking: 15 hours
Easy

Serves 10:
7½–8 lb blanched beef tripe
1 cooked cow's foot, 2 raw calf's feet
1 2-lb piece fresh pig's skin
2–2½ lb carrots, peeled and sliced
2 very large onions, peeled and quartered
1 leek
8 cloves garlic, peeled
3 cloves
20 peppercorns, coarsely crushed
1 bouquet garni (thyme, bay leaf, parsley)
1 bottle dry, still cider or dry white wine
¼ cup Calvados
¾ cup all-purpose flour
salt

The original recipe calls for tripe from the four sections of the ox's stomach but is equally good made with just the rumen (covered with *villi* or tiny protuberances) and/or reticulum (honeycomb) tripe. Rinse the blanched tripe and cut into 2–2½-in squares. Split the cow's foot or calf's feet lengthwise down the middle.

Line a very large earthenware casserole dish with the pig's skin, so that the fat side is against the bottom and sides of the casserole dish. Arrange the ingredients in alternating layers, starting with the tripe, half a cow heel or calf's foot, carrots, onion, and so on, burying a cheesecloth bag containing the sliced leek, garlic, cloves, pepper, and bouquet garni deep among them. Pour in the cider or wine and top up with a little water if necessary so the liquid covers all the ingredients.

Make a thick flour and water paste and seal the lid onto the casserole with it to prevent any steam escaping.

Cook for 15 hours at 220°F: the tripe should barely simmer.

When this time has passed, break the seal, remove the lid, and allow to stand for a few minutes; remove excess fat from the surface. Remove the bones from the cow heel, the cheesecloth bag, and the onion quarters. Pour in the Calvados, stir, and serve very hot.

In pre-Revolutionary times one of the most unpopular taxes in Brittany was the "gabelle" *levied on salt, giving rise to the nick-name of* "gabelous" *for customs officers. When the Duchy of Brittany became part of France, it was exempted from this fiscal burden. Appropriately, the best French salt is Breton sea salt from Guérande.*

POULE AU BLANC

Poached chicken in cream sauce

Normandy

Preparation: 15 minutes
Cooking: 2 1/2 hours
Easy

Serves 6:
1 3–3 1/2-lb chicken
1 sprig tarragon
2 carrots, peeled
2 onions, 1 studded with 3 cloves
2 leeks, white part only
1 stick celery
1 bouquet garni (thyme, bay leaf, parsley)
1/4 cup butter
1/2 cup all-purpose flour
1 egg yolk
3/4 cup crème fraîche *or heavy cream*
salt and pepper
nutmeg

Prepare the vegetables. Drop the tarragon into boiling water, leave for 10 seconds and drain; place in the cavity of the washed, dried chicken, together with the chicken's liver if this is available (trim off any discolored parts), and a little salt and pepper.

Put the chicken in a fireproof casserole dish or heavy-bottomed saucepan with sufficient cold water to cover. Bring slowly to a boil, add a little salt and the carrots, onions, the leeks (tie these in a bundle), celery, and bouquet garni. When the liquid has returned to a boil, cover and simmer gently for 2 hours.

When the chicken is done, melt the butter in a saucepan, stir in the flour and cook over low heat, stirring continuously, until the roux turns a pale golden brown. Gradually stir in 2 1/4 cups of the cooking liquid and continue stirring after the sauce has thickened and boiled for a few minutes. Draw aside from the heat. Combine the egg yolk with the cream in a bowl, add a pinch of salt, pepper, and nutmeg. Lightly beat in 1/2 cup of the sauce, mix well, then stir into the sauce in the pan. Stir over gentle heat for a minute or two; do not allow to boil.

Take the chicken out of the casserole dish, carve into portions and arrange these in a heated serving dish; coat with a few spoonfuls of sauce. Surround with the well drained vegetables (untie the leeks) and discard the cloves and bouquet garni; serve the remaining sauce in a sauceboat.

POULARD À L'ANGEVINE*

Chicken with wine, cream, and mushroom sauce

Anjou

Preparation: 25 minutes
Cooking: 1 hour
Easy

Serves 8:
1 3–3 1/2-lb chicken
1/4 cup butter
3/4 cup dry white Anjou wine
1 large, ripe tomato, skinned
2 shallots, peeled
1 medium-sized onion, peeled
2 cloves garlic, peeled
1 1/2 cups chicken broth
1/2 lb small wild or button mushrooms
2 1/4 cups crème fraîche *or heavy cream*
juice of 1 lemon
1 egg yolk
salt and pepper

Joint the chicken into 8 pieces and add to the hot butter in a large, heavy-bottomed, fireproof casserole dish; once the outer layers of flesh have whitened and "set," season with salt and pepper, cover, and cook over very low heat for 40 minutes, turning now and then to brown lightly and evenly. Transfer to a heated dish, cover, and keep hot.

Add the wine to the juices and butter in the casserole dish, and place over high heat, scraping the bottom to loosen the deposits; reduce the heat and add the coarsely chopped, deseeded tomato, the finely

chopped shallots, onion, and garlic. Add half the broth, cover, and simmer until the liquid has reduced by half.

Sauté the mushrooms for 5 minutes in a little extra butter in a saucepan, add the remaining broth, cover, and simmer for 20 minutes, then add to the casserole dish.

Reduce the heat to very low; stir in the cream and adjust the seasoning. Do not allow to boil. Add the chicken pieces, turn in the sauce, and cover. Keep gently warm until just before serving. Transfer the chicken to a heated serving dish. Beat the lemon juice and egg yolk together in a small bowl; quickly stir this into the creamy mixture and then spoon over the chicken.

POULET VALLÉE D'AUGE

Chicken braised in cider

Normandy

Preparation: 15 minutes
Cooking: 45 minutes
Easy

Serve 6:
1 4½-lb chicken
¼ cup butter
¼ cup Calvados
2 shallots, peeled
2¼ cups still, dry cider
½ lb large field mushrooms
1 cup crème fraîche *or heavy cream*
salt and pepper

Joint the chicken into 12 portions. Rub these all over with a seasoning of salt and freshly ground pepper. Heat 1–1½ tbsp of the butter in a large casserole dish or heavy-bottomed saucepan and place the chicken pieces, starting with the skin side down, to brown lightly, then turn several times to brown all over. Drain off any fat, add the warmed Calvados, heat, and flame.

Add the coarsely chopped shallots. Pour in the cider; once this has come to a boil, reduce the heat to fairly low, cover, and simmer for 30 minutes. Turn the chicken pieces once, after 15 minutes' cooking.

Slice the mushrooms and place in a saucepan with 1 tbsp of the remaining butter. Cover and sweat for 4 minutes, shaking the saucepan several times. Remove the lid and allow the moisture to evaporate, taking care that the mushrooms do not stick. Set aside and add to the chicken after it has cooked for 25 minutes. Add the cream.

Take the chicken pieces out of the casserole (draining off any liquid back into the casserole) and keep hot. Reduce the creamy liquid, stirring over moderate heat, until it is smooth and velvety. Adjust the seasoning. Draw aside from the heat and beat in the remaining butter a small piece at a time with a balloon whisk.

Return the chicken portions to the casserole and turn them in the sauce to coat thoroughly. Transfer to a heated serving dish and cover with the sauce.

GÉLINE À LA LOCHOISE*
Chicken with wine and mushrooms

Touraine

Preparation: 30 minutes
Cooking: 1 hour
Easy

Serves 6:
1 3–3½-lb young chicken
½ cup butter
½ lb wild mushrooms or button mushrooms
1 Bermuda onion, peeled
¾ cup dry white wine (e.g. Vouvray, Montlouis)
2¼ cups heavy cream
salt and pepper

Joint the chicken into 6 or more pieces. Heat the butter in a large, heavy-bottomed fireproof casserole dish and brown the chicken in it over moderately high heat. Quarter the mushrooms or cut in half, depending on their size. Add to the chicken, together with the thinly sliced onion. Season with salt and pepper, stir for a few minutes, then cover and place in the oven, preheated to 300°F for 45 minutes. Take the casserole out of the oven and pour in the wine.

Place the casserole over moderate heat for 10 minutes, uncovered. Test that the chicken pieces are done then transfer to a heated dish with the mushrooms and onion, straining the sauce and returning it to the casserole dish. Stir in the cream and correct the seasoning. Heat through but do not allow to boil. Return the chicken, mushrooms, and onions to the casserole and stir to coat with the sauce over very low heat. Serve immediately.

QUEUES DE COCHON AUX HARICOTS ROUGES
Pigs' tails with red kidney beans

Orléanais

Start preparation 24 hours in advance
Preparation: 10 minutes
Cooking: 3½ hours
Easy

Serves 6:
6 fresh pigs' tails
1½ lb dried red kidney beans
1 large onion, studded with 2 cloves
3 cloves garlic, peeled
3 large carrots, peeled
1 bouquet garni (thyme, bay leaf, parsley)
1 bottle dry red Loire wine
salt and pepper

The day before you plan to cook this dish, rinse the beans and put them to soak in a large bowl of cold water. The following day, drain them and transfer to a large heavy casserole dish with the clove-studded onion, the garlic cloves, the carrots (cut these lengthwise in four), and the bouquet garni. Add the wine and sufficient cold water to cover the beans completely. Season with freshly ground pepper. Bring slowly to a boil then cover and simmer for 1 hour. When the beans are tender, add salt to taste (beans salted when raw will be tough, however long they are cooked). Add the pigs' tails. Cover and simmer for a further 2½ hours.

Other cuts of pork (such as pig's feet or pork belly) can be used instead of pigs' tails.

CUL DE VEAU À L'ANGEVINE*

Pot-roasted veal

Anjou

Preparation: 20 minutes
Cooking: 2½ hours
Easy

Serves 8:
1 4-lb rolled boneless rump roast of milk-fed veal
½ lb fresh pig's skin
8 oz onions, peeled
1¾ lb carrots, peeled
½ bottle dry white Anjou wine
¼ cup Anjou marc *or brandy*
2 cups beef broth
1 bouquet garni (thyme, bay leaf)
1 cup crème fraîche *or heavy cream*
salt and pepper

Line the bottom of an earthenware or enameled cast iron cooking pot with the piece of pig's skin cut to size, fat side downward.

Arrange the carrots and onions in layers on top of this lining, put the veal on this bed of vegetables and place, uncovered, in the oven, preheated to 340°F. Cook for 10 minutes then turn the veal and cook for a further 10 minutes.

Take the casserole dish out of the oven, pour in the wine, *marc* or brandy and the broth. Add the bouquet garni, and season with salt and pepper. Cover with a tight-fitting lid or with foil and cook for 2 hours, turning the meat after 1 hour and reducing the temperature to 300°F for the last hour's cooking.

Take the veal out of the casserole dish and keep hot. Remove and discard the pig skin, leaving behind all the juices and vegetables, stir the cream into this mixture and return the dish to the oven while carving the veal. Use an extremely sharp carving knife or the veal will tend to break up into shreds.

Cover the sliced veal with the creamy sauce and serve.

POULET EN BARBOUILLE

Chicken in blood sauce

Berry

Preparation: 25 minutes
Cooking: 1 hour 20 minutes
Complicated

Serves 6:
1 3-lb chicken
3 tbsp red wine vinegar
1 chicken liver
1 stick butter
1/4 lb semisalted, unsmoked bacon
3 carrots, peeled and finely sliced
2 tsp sugar
3 tbsp all-purpose flour
1 large onion, peeled
1 bouquet garni (thyme, bay leaf, parsley)
3/4 cup dry red wine (eg. Sancerre)
3/4 cup chicken broth (see glossary)
3/4 cup crème fraîche *or heavy cream*
1 egg yolk
salt and pepper

For most American cooks and for all town-dwellers, the original recipe for this dish has to be modified: traditionally, it calls for a live chicken, its legs and wings firmly tied; the head is chopped off and and a bowl quickly placed beneath, to catch the blood that drains from the neck. The blood is then mixed with the vinegar. Remove any discolored parts from the chicken liver and cut into 6 or more pieces. Set aside.

Remove any skin or cartilage from the bacon, chop, and sauté in the butter in a large fireproof casserole dish.

Add the carrots and sugar and continue cooking, stirring, until lightly browned. Add the chicken pieces and brown over high heat, turning several times.

Turn down the heat, sprinkle in the flour, and stir until a pale golden color.

Season with salt and pepper, add the whole, peeled onion and the bouquet garni. Pour in the wine and broth.

Stir, cover, and once the liquid has come to a boil place in the oven, preheated to 350°F, for 1 hour.

When the chicken is done, take the casserole out of the oven; add approx. 3/4 cup of the hot liquid into the vinegar; beat with a balloon whisk as you add it, then add this mixture to the contents of the casserole, stirring all the ingredients. Keep hot but do not allow to boil.

Blend the chicken liver in the food processor with the cream and egg yolk (or chop very finely and mix with the cream and egg); stir into the contents of the casserole dish with a wooden spoon. Heat very gently for a few minutes; serve immediately.

Saint Martin of Tours is supposed to have introduced the Vouvray grape to France in the fourth century: as he set out on his long journey home from eastern Europe he placed the vine shoot in a hollowed bird's bone for safe-keeping. As it grew he transferred it to a lion's bone, then to an ass's bone. When the grapes were first harvested, the wine makers are said to have first sung, then roared, and finally brayed.

RAGOÛT DE PRÉ-SALÉ DE CROZON

Lamb shoulder with spring vegetables

Brittany

Preparation: 45 minutes
Cooking: 2 1/4 hours
Easy

Serves 6:
1 boned lamb shoulder weighing 2–2 1/2 lb
1/2 cup lard
3 onions, peeled
1/2 cup all-purpose flour
1 clove garlic, peeled
1 bouquet garni (thyme, bay leaf, parsley)
l lb baby carrots, peeled
1 lb baby turnips, peeled
1 lb new potatoes
1 lb frozen petit pois *or fresh peas*
coarse sea salt and pepper

Cut the lamb into 2-in cubes and brown all over in the lard in a large fireproof casserole dish. Add the sliced onions and brown lightly. Sprinkle in the flour and stir into the fat with a wooden spoon. Add the chopped garlic, bouquet garni, a generous pinch of sea salt, and freshly ground pepper. Pour in sufficient cold water to barely cover the meat. Stir. Bring to a boil, cover, and simmer gently for 30 minutes. Add the carrots and turnips. Cover again and simmer for 45 minutes. Add the potatoes and the peas and continue simmering for a further 45 minutes.

Serve from the casserole dish.

BEUCHELLE TOURANGELLE*

Kidneys and sweetbreads with creamy mushroom sauce

Touraine

Start preparation 24 hours in advance
Preparation: 40 minutes
Cooking: 40 minutes
Complicated

Serves 6:
2 sets veal sweetbreads
juice of 1 lemon
2 veal kidneys
3 tbsp cognac
1/2 cup butter
1 cup crème fraîche *or heavy cream*
1 lb cèpes (boletus edulis), *fresh, canned or dried*
salt and pepper

Prepare the sweetbreads 12–24 hours in advance if possible: wash thoroughly under running cold water; soak in a bowl of cold water for several hours. Place them in a saucepan of cold water, add the lemon juice and a small pinch of salt. Bring very slowly to a boil; barely simmer for 5 minutes; drain and place the sweetbreads in a large bowl of cold water for 10 minutes. When cold gently pull off any elastic sinews. Spread the sweetbreads between 2 layers of kitchen towel, place a cookie sheet on top and a weight to flatten them slightly and express their pink liquid; leave overnight if possible. Cut the kidneys lengthwise in half, remove most of their central strip of fat and gristle, and cut across into slices about 1/4 in thick.

Heat 1/4 cup of the butter in a skillet; when foaming, add the kidneys and sauté briefly, to seal and color them all over (2 minutes at most). Reduce the heat to very low, season with salt and pepper, and simmer for a further 2 minutes. Add the warmed cognac, heat briefly, and flame. Transfer the kidneys to a heated dish to keep gently warm.

Slice and sauté the sweetbreads in the same way, using the remaining butter; remove from the pan and keep them warm. Add 1/4 cup of the cream to the pan, stirring and scraping the bottom to loosen deposits for 5 minutes. Pour over the sweetbreads.

If using fresh *cèpes* (*boletus edulis*), make sure they are very well rinsed to eliminate any grit; dry well. Drain well and dry if canned or if soaked, dried mushrooms are used. Sauté over high heat in an extra tablespoon of butter for a minute or two. Cover and sweat for 10 minutes, then take out of the pan, draining off all the butter and keep hot. Discard the butter and juices left in the pan; pour in the remaining cream; simmer to reduce and thicken for 10 minutes. Pour all over the mushrooms. Mix all the cooked ingredients together, correct the seasoning, and transfer to a heated serving dish.

ANDOUILLETTES AU VOUVRAY*

Sausages with mushrooms and white wine

Touraine

Preparation: 15 minutes
Cooking: 35 minutes
Easy

Serves 4:
4 andouillettes de Touraine *or other good-quality sausages*
1/4 lb shallots, peeled
1/2 lb field or cultivated mushrooms
cup butter
1/2 1 bottle Vouvray or other dry white wine
1/4 cup Touraine marc *or brandy (optional)*
1 cup fine fresh breadcrumbs
2–3 tbsp chopped parsley
salt and pepper

If you are using *andouillettes* or delicately flavored sausages, they will be improved by a sprinkling of *marc* or brandy; leave to stand, turning now and then, for 24 hours.

Mix the chopped shallots and the sliced mushrooms and sprinkle into an ovenproof dish that has been liberally greased with butter. Pour in some wine to moisten the vegetables thoroughly. Season with salt and pepper.

Place the sausages flat, in a single layer, on this bed. Dot the remaining butter in flakes all over the sausages and vegetables.

Preheat the oven to 300°F, place the dish in the oven and cook uncovered for 20 minutes then turn the sausages and increase the temperature to 350°F; add a little more wine if the vegetables look a little dry and cook for a further 10 minutes. Sprinkle the breadcrumbs over the sausages, moisten with a little of the cooking liquid and brown under a hot broiler for 5 minutes. Sprinkle with chopped parsley.

CANETON FARCI

Stuffed roast duck

Anjou

Preparation: 40 minutes
Cooking: 2 hours
Complicated

Serves 4:
1 3–3 1/2-lb duck with its liver
4 shallots, peeled
1/2 cup butter
1 bottle dry white wine
1/2 lb pork tenderloin
1 1/2-lb piece fresh pork belly or unsmoked bacon
2 1/2–3 oz duck foie gras, *fresh or canned*
3 cooked sweet chestnuts, fresh or canned
1/4 cup Anjou marc *or brandy*
1/4 lb rillettes, *homemade or canned*
1 large leaf (sheet) barding fat
3 carrots, peeled
3 onions, peeled
salt and pepper

With a very sharp knife, slit all along the line of the duck's breastbone and work the flesh and skin neatly away together from the plate-like bone underneath, down to where the bone is joined to the rest of the carcass; detach and discard this bone.

Make the stuffing: soften the thinly sliced shallots over gentle heat in 2 tbsp of the butter. Add 1 cup of the wine and simmer until reduced to about one third of its original volume. Cut the pork tenderloin and the pork belly or bacon into fairly small pieces; place in the food processor with the shallots and remaining liquid and chop them coarsely; add the *foie gras* and the fresh duck liver, cut into fairly small pieces, and the cooked, drained chestnuts (despite their name these should be *au naturel*, i.e. unsweetened). Process until fairly smooth, add the *marc* or brandy and the rillettes and blend briefly. Fill the duck cavity with this mixture, pull the flesh and skin back into position, enclosing the stuffing, and sew up securely with a trussing needle and trussing thread. Wrap in the piece of barding fat (fresh pork back fat, cut in a thin sheet), and tie with kitchen string.

Cut the remaining butter into small pieces and distribute half of these all over the bottom of a large casserole dish. Scatter the carrots and onions on top, place the duck on this vegetable layer, and smear the remaining pieces of butter all over its exposed surfaces. Cover and place in a preheated oven at 350°F.

When the duck has cooked for 1 hour, turn it over so it is breast side down, add 1 cup wine, and season with salt and pepper. Replace the lid (or foil) and cook for a further hour, basting now and then with the wine and juices in the casserole.

Carve off the legs and the wings with a little breast; carve the breast and stuffing into slices, cutting straight down, at right angles to the carving board. Surround these slices with the leg and wing portions on a heated serving platter.

Unsweetened chestnut purée is a traditional accompaniment to this dish.

GIGOT À LA BRETONNE*

Roast lamb leg with white beans

Brittany

Start preparation 24 hours in advance
Preparation: 15 minutes
Cooking: 1¼ hours
Easy

Serves 8:
1 4½-lb lamb leg
1lb dried white navy beans
1 bouquet garni (parsley, bay leaf, summer savory)
2 large, ripe tomatoes
2 cloves garlic, peeled
½ cup butter
3 onions, peeled
2 shallots, peeled
salt and pepper

The dried white kidney beans must be soaked overnight in cold water. The following day, place them in a large saucepan with just enough unsalted cold water to cover, with the bouquet garni (use thyme if savory is unavailable) and the whole tomatoes. Bring to a boil and cook for 45 minutes before adding a generous pinch of salt, then continue cooking until tender.

Make slits between the bone and flesh at the knuckle end of the lamb leg and push in the garlic cloves.

Grease a roasting pan with butter and place the lamb in it, rounded side up. Dot small pieces of butter all over it; season with salt (preferably coarse sea salt) and pepper. Roast at 375°F for 45 to 50 minutes (depending on whether you like your lamb slightly pink inside or not).

When the beans are very nearly done, heat ¼ cup butter in a saucepan, add the finely chopped onions and shallots and the tomatoes extracted from among the beans (skin and chop coarsely); sauté until the onions and shallots are tender. Add the drained beans and ¼ cup of their reserved cooking liquid. Season with pepper and place in a large, fairly deep, heated serving dish. Keep hot while you carve the lamb into fairly thick slices; arrange these on top of the beans.

Pour some of the remaining cooking liquid into the roasting pan and use a wooden spoon to scrape the caramelized juices free over a moderate heat. Pour this gravy over the lamb and serve.

CANETON NANTAIS AUX PETITS POIS

Duck with peas, lettuce, and savory

Brittany

Preparation: 25 minutes
Cooking: 1 hour
Easy

Serve 6:
1 3–3½-lb oven-ready duck
1 5-oz piece semisalted bacon
½ cup butter
10 baby onions, peeled
2 lb peas
1 large round lettuce heart, shredded
1 small bunch summer savory
salt and pepper

Remove the skin and any tough pieces of cartilage from the bacon; cut, at right angles to the lines of fat and lean, into strips (lardons). Blanch in boiling water for 10 minutes; drain well.

Heat the butter in a large, fireproof casserole dish and brown the duck well all over. Take out the duck and keep hot in the oven, preheated to 350°F. Place the bacon pieces and baby onions in the hot butter and brown over high heat. Replace the duck in the casserole dish. Season with salt and pepper, cover, and roast in the oven for 30 minutes. Bring a pan of unsalted water to a boil; add the peas and cook until just tender. Drain and reserve.

Take the casserole dish out of the oven; surround with the peas and shredded lettuce, mixing these well to coat with fat and juices. Bury the savory, tied in a bundle, in the peas. Moisten with a little water and add salt and pepper to taste. Cover the casserole and return to the oven for a further 30 minutes. When the duck is done to your liking, serve without delay.

POTÉE QUIMPEROISE

Beef and pork winter casserole

Brittany

Preparation: 15 minutes
Cooking: about 2$^1/_2$ hours
Easy

Serve 6:
2–2$^1/_4$ lb boiling beef (e.g. chuck, beef short ribs
1 1-lb piece semisalted pork breast or belly or unsmoked bacon
1 large onion, peeled, studded with 1 clove
1 bouquet garni (thyme, bay leaf, parsley)
2 leeks, chopped
2 carrots, peeled, and chopped
1 small turnip, peeled and diced
$^1/_2$ rutabaga, peeled and cubed
1 large cabbage heart, shredded
1 full-flavored smoked boiling sausage

Place the beef, the pork or bacon, the clove-studded onion and the bouquet garni in a very large cooking pot. Add sufficient cold water to cover and bring slowly to a boil. Skim off any scum from the surface. Simmer gently for 1$^1/_2$ hours. Add the vegetables (blanch the quartered cabbage heart briefly in boiling water before adding it). Allow to return to a very gentle boil, then simmer for a further 20 minutes, then add the sausage, pricked in several places to prevent the skin bursting. Once the liquid has reached boiling point again, skim off any scum. Simmer for 30–35 minutes, depending on the size of the sausage.

VEGETABLES

GALETTE DE POMMES DE TERRE

Potato cake

Berry

Preparation: 1$^1/_2$ hours
Cooking: 20 minutes
Very easy

Serves 4:
$^1/_2$ lb floury potatoes
3 oz unmatured Valençay cheese (fresh white goat's cheese)
$^1/_4$ cup butter, softened
1 whole egg + 1 yolk
1 $^3/_4$ cups all-purpose flour
3 tbsp vegetable oil

Bake the potatoes in the oven in their skins until well done. Scoop the soft, floury potato out of the skins and work in the finely crumbled cheese by hand, as soon as the potato is no longer too hot to handle (or use a food processor); work in the butter, then add the egg yolk and blend thoroughly. Finally work in the flour. Knead the mixture until it is very smooth and homogenous. Shape into a ball and leave to stand for 1 hour, wrapped in foil.

Roll out into a sheet $^3/_8$ in thick on a lightly floured pastry board or slab. Use a 4-in diameter pastry cutter to into disks. Beat the remaining whole egg and brush the surface to glaze.

Place on one or more lightly oiled cookie sheets and bake in a preheated oven at 350°F for 20 minutes.

Popular tradition credits Marie Harel with the invention of Normandy's Camembert, but the cheese already existed well before her day (it is mentioned as early as 1700). Madame Harel greatly improved the cheesemaking process, however, and deserves the statue erected in her honor by the employees of the world's largest Camembert factory, located, rather improbably, in the state of Ohio, U.S.A.

NAVETS AU CIDRE*

Stuffed turnips baked in cider

Normandy

Preparation: 15 minutes
Cooking: 30 minutes
Easy

Serves 6:
6 large turnips or 12 small turnips
$^1/_2$ lb good-quality sausage meat
2 shallots, peeled
1 sprig tarragon
few chives
2 egg yolks
$^1/_2$ cup butter
1 cup still, dry cider
$^1/_2$ cup light broth
1 sprig each thyme, tarragon, 1 bay leaf, few chives
salt and pepper

Peel the turnips; use an apple corer to hollow out the center. Mix the sausage meat in a bowl very thoroughly with the finely chopped shallots, tarragon leaves, and chives; work in the egg yolks and season. Pack this stuffing into the hollow centers of the turnips.

Grease a shallow ovenproof or gratin, which that will contain all the turnips in one layer, using all the butter. Place the turnips in it and pour in the cider mixed with the broth. Sprinkle with the thyme leaves and crumbled bay leaf. Have the oven preheated to 425°F and bake the turnips for about 30 minutes, basting frequently with the cooking liquid. Test with a thin skewer after 25 minutes and take out of the oven when very tender.

KIG HA FARS

Meal-in-a-pot with buckwheat pudding

Brittany

Preparation: 20 minutes
Cooking: 3 hours
Complicated

Serves 10:
3–3$^1/_2$ lb salt-cured lower arm or leg of pork
4$^1/_2$ lb semisalted pork breast or piece of unsmoked bacon
1 bouquet garni (thyme, bay leaf, parsley)
1 large cabbage heart, blanched
1 lb carrots, peeled
2 onions, peeled
1 lb leeks, white part only
salt and pepper

For the pudding:
9 cups buckwheat flour
3 tbsp salt
1 $^3/_4$ cups heavy cream

2 eggs
2–2¼ cups milk

Soak both cuts of salted meat in several changes of cold water overnight, drain, rinse, and place in a very large, wide saucepan with the bouquet garni; add 4 quarts cold water. Bring to a boil, reduce the heat, and simmer for 1 hour.

Add the cabbage, carrots, onions, and the leeks tied in a bundle.

While the stew is simmering, make the pudding: heap up the flour in a very large mixing bowl, make a well in the center and in it place the cream, eggs, and salt. Gradually work these into the flour then add the milk a little at a time, stirring well. Use a pudding boiling bag or a large piece of clean, closely woven cotton or linen cloth for the covering; transfer the pudding mixture to this, leaving plenty of air space inside when you tie it up. Add to the cooking pot containing the meat; make sure it is submerged in the liquid and simmer for 2 hours, then take out the bag, drain briefly in a colander, unwrap, and slice.

Serve the broth first; follow with the meat, vegetables, and pudding.

DESSERTS

SABLÉS DEAUVILLAIS
Butter cookies

Normandy

Preparation: 15 minutes + 2 hours resting time for the dough
Cooking: 7–8 minutes
Easy

Serves 4:
1 cup all-purpose flour
1 cup butter
2 egg yolks + 1 whole egg
1/3 cup superfine sugar
pinch salt
1/3 cup ground almonds
3 tbsp Calvados (optional)

Soften the butter at room temperature and cut into small pieces. Sift the flour onto a pastry board or marble slab; make a well in the center, to hold the butter, the egg yolks, sugar, salt, ground almonds, and the Calvados if used. Use a pastry scraper and/or your fingertips to combine these with the flour; "knead" the dough very briefly by pushing a little at a time away from you with the heel of your hand, crushing it as you do so, just enough to make it homogenous.

Shape into a ball, wrap in foil, chill for 2 hours, then roll out to a thickness of 1/8 in. Use a 4-in pastry cutter to cut out into disks (gather up the off-cuts, roll out and cut out more disks). Brush with a glaze of the lightly beaten remaining egg. Place on a cookie sheet and bake for only 7–8 minutes (sablés burn very easily) at 375°F.

BOURDELOTS*
Apple dumplings

Normandy

Preparation: 30 minutes
Cooking: 30 minutes
Fairly easy

Serves 6:
6 small, firm apples (e.g. Rennet, Granny Smith)
2 1/2 cups all-purpose flour
3 sticks butter
1/4 cup superfine sugar
generous pinch ground cinnamon
1 large egg
1/2 cup milk

Sift the flour into a mixing bowl, add 1 1/4 sticks butter, softened at room temperature and cut into small pieces. Rub the butter into the flour (or use the food processor) until the mixture looks like breadcrumbs; gradually sprinkle in sufficient cold water to make a smooth, firm pie dough that leaves the sides of the bowl cleanly. Wrap and chill. Peel the apples, removing the cores with an apple corer. Beat the remaining butter in a bowl with the sugar and cinnamon; place an equal amount inside each apple.

Roll out the pie dough into a square or rectangular sheet; divide this into equal squares, large enough to completely enclose an apple; place an apple in the center of each and bring the corners up and over the apple to meet on top; moisten all the edges and pinch these together securely, decorate the top with a leaf cut out of any leftover dough.

Beat the egg yolk into the milk and brush over the pastry cases. Place in the oven (preheated to 400°F) and cook for 30 minutes, reducing the heat to 350°F if the pastry browns too quickly. Serve with cream.

GÂTEAU NORMAND

Apple Cake

Normandy

Preparation: 1 1/2 hours
Cooking: 40 minutes
Easy

Serves 6:
6 firm apples (e.g. Rennet, Granny Smith)
1/4 cup Calvados
1 cup superfine sugar
1 1/4 sticks butter, softened
5 eggs, separated
2 1/2 cups all-purpose flour
1 cup milk
2 tsp baking soda

Peel, quarter, core, and slice the apples; mix the Calvados and 3 tbsp of the sugar in a bowl, stir in the apples and leave to stand. Beat 1/2 cup of the sugar with generous 1/4 cup of the butter until light and pale. Spread all over the inside of a springform cake pan. Place the apple slices in a neat arrangement on the mixture.

Beat the egg yolks with the remaining sugar until very pale and frothy; continue beating

while gradually adding the sifted flour, followed by the remaining, melted, butter. Beat the egg whites stiffly; fold the flour mixture into these 1 tbsp at a time, using a mixing spatula to avoid crushing the air out of the whites. Sprinkle in the baking powder; fold in gently but thoroughly. Fill the cake pan with this mixture. Make sure the oven is preheated to 350°F; bake the apple cake for 40 minutes or until a thin knife blade inserted deep into the center of the cake comes out clean but slightly damp.

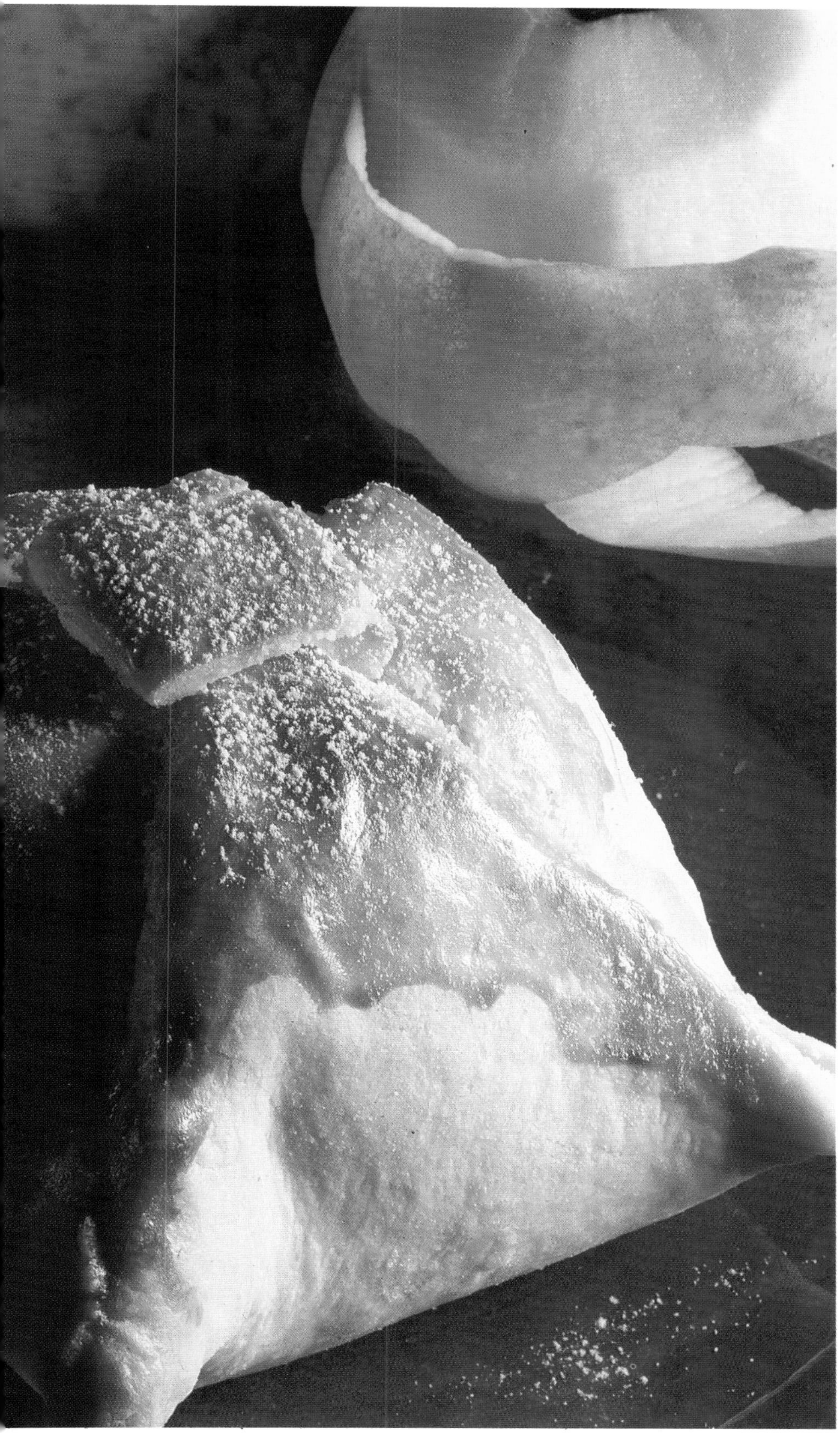

BIGOUDENS

Almond and Calvados cookies

Brittany

Preparation: 45 minutes
Cooking: 20 minutes
Easy

Serves 6:
2 1/2 cups all-purpose flour
1/4 cup butter
3/4 cup superfine sugar
4 egg yolks
2/3 cup ground almonds
3 tbsp heavy cream
3 tbsp Calvados or applejack

Sift the flour into a large mixing bowl; make a well in the center and add the butter (softened at room temperature and cut into small pieces), sugar, egg yolks, almonds, cream, and Calvados.

Mix all these gradually into the flour with a wooden spoon, then knead briefly by hand. Shape into a ball, wrap in foil, and chill for 30 minutes.

Roll out on a lightly-floured board to just over 1/8 in thick and cut out 2-in diameter discks with a plain pastry cutter; place these on a greased cookie sheet and brush lightly with a glaze of cold milk. Bake in a preheated oven at 425°F for 20 minutes or until pale golden brown.

FAR AUX PRUNEAUX*

Prune flan

Brittany

Start preparation 24 hours in advance
Preparation: 15 minutes
Cooking: 45 minutes
Very easy

Serves 6:
20 plump, moist prunes
1/4 cup rum or 1 cup weak, strained tea
1 quart hot milk
3/4 cup butter
3/4 cup superfine sugar
6 eggs
2 1/4 cups all-purpose flour

Soak the prunes overnight in the rum mixed with a little cold water or in cold tea; stir occasionally. Stir the butter and sugar into the hot milk to melt and dissolve. Leave to cool. Drain the prunes thoroughly. Beat the eggs in a mixing bowl; gradually add the sifted flour, stirring well. Continue stirring as you slowly add the milk. Stir in the prunes.

Grease a fairly deep pie dish liberally with extra butter, ladle the batter into it, then make sure the prunes are evenly distributed. Bake at 400°F for 45 minutes or until a knife blade inserted deep into the flan comes out cleanly. Can be eaten hot, warm or cold.

BOURDONS

Apple purses

Maine

Preparation: 25 minutes
Cooking: 30 minutes
Easy

Serves 6:
6 small, firm apples (e.g. Rennet, Granny Smith)
1 1/4 sticks butter
1 cup superfine sugar
1 egg yolk
1/2 cup milk

For the sweet pie dough:
4 cups all-purpose flour
2 sticks butter

1/4 cup superfine sugar
pinch salt

Make the sweet pie dough (see page 20 for method), wrap, and chill for 1 hour.

Peel and core the apples. Stop up the bottom of each core hole with a little chilled butter; fill the hole with sugar (or use jam) and then stop up the top with more butter.

Roll out the pie dough into a sheet just over 1/8 in thick; use a pastry cutter to cut out disks twice the diameter of the apples. Place an apple in the center of each disk, gather up the edges enclosing the apple without stretching the dough; pinch and seal tightly (moistening where necessary with your fingers, dipped in water) on top of the apple. Mix the egg yolk with the milk and brush this over upper half of each pastry purse.

Place on a cookie sheet sheet that has been greased with butter and bake for 30 minutes at 400°F, reducing the heat to 350°F and extending the time if the pastry browns too quickly.

CRÉMETS D'ANJOU

Creamy fresh cheese molds

Anjou

Preparation: 20 minutes
Chilling time: 12 hours
Very easy

Serves 6:
1 cup crème fraîche *or heavy cream*
1 cup soft cream cheese
2 large egg whites
1/2 cup superfine sugar

Beat the cream until firm. Beat the cream cheese with a wooden spoon. Beat the egg whites until stiff but not "dry" with an electric beater; beat in the sugar. Combine the cream and cream cheese; fold in the egg whites with a mixing spatula.

Line *coeur à la crème* molds or similar small, pierced porcelain molds with pieces of cheesecloth; fill with the mixture; fold the cheesecloth over the top and chill for 12 hours.

Fold back the cheesecloth and turn out the molded shapes. Serve with sieved fresh fruit such as raspberries.

TARTE TATIN*

Upside-down apple tart

Orléanais

Preparation: 30 minutes
Cooking: 45 minutes
Complicated

Serves 6:
3 1/4–3 1/2 lb firm apples (e.g. Rennet, Granny Smith)
1 stick butter, softened at room temperature
3/4 cup superfine sugar
1/2 lb sweet pie dough (see glossary)

Spread two thirds of the butter all over the inside of a 9 1/2-in straight-sided fairly deep tart pan; sprinkle two thirds of the sugar evenly all over the butter. Peel, core, and slice the apples vertically in half, pack them upright in the pan, sprinkle with the remaining sugar, and dot with flakes of the remaining butter.

Place the pan over moderate heat and cook until the sugar and butter have turned to a pale golden brown caramel (about 20 minutes, but this will vary). Have the oven preheated to 450°F and place the pan in it for 5 minutes, then take out. By now the apples should have softened and sunk level with the lip of the pan. Reduce the oven temperature to 400°F.

Roll out the pie dough to a thickness of 1/8 in and place over the pan; cut round the edge, leaving an overlap hanging over the edge of 3/8–1/4 in all round. Place in the oven for 20 minutes or until the pastry is a golden brown. Allow to stand for a few minutes then place a serving plate upside down over the pan, hold both together, and turn the right way up, releasing the tart onto the plate, apples uppermost.

Atlantic Coast

Bordelais
Périgord
Quercy
Angoumois
Aunis
Saintonge
Poitou

The coastal region that runs southward, with the River Loire as its northern border and the Garonne river marking out its southernmost boundary, has three natural subdivisions, three different landscapes, each with its own produce and distinctive style of cooking. The first is called the Bordelais or Bordeaux country, the second is the ancient duchy of Guyenne (comprising the provinces of Périgord and Quercy). The third runs all the way down the Atlantic coast south of Brittany: first, and northernmost, Poitou, then Angoumois, Aunis, and Saintonge.

The Bordeaux country is known the world over for its wines. Its other products have been overshadowed by the wine industry, the most important in France, producing more than a quarter of all the fine wines produced worldwide.

Raymond Dunay, a respected writer on matters gastronomic, described these great wines as the product of man's partnership with nature and personified them as "smooth, mysterious and unassuming, like a woman, yet possessing a man's strong frame, vitality and astonishing vigor. All the great growths, despite their great diversity of character, can survive for a hundred years."

Bordeaux can boast at least thirty-six "*appellations controlées*" or designated wines which fall into very distinct categories. The vineyards of Sauternes, Barsac, Médoc (Haut-Médoc, Margaux, Pauillac, Saint-Julien, Saint-Estèphe), Pomerol, Saint-Emilion and Graves produce a large number of *crus nobles* (the very best growths). Among which the most remarkable white is Château d'Yquem and among the red wines, the Châteaux of Lafite-Rothschild, Mouton-Rothschild, Latour, Margaux, Haut-Brion, Ausone, Cheval-Blanc, and Pétrus. Bottles of these wines sometimes fetch astronomical prices but the Bordeaux region produces superb wines in such quantity that the most discerning palate will find plenty of choice at a much less prohibitive cost. All these fine wines need food worthy of them and Bordelais cooks (both in the town itself and in the surrounding countryside) respond magnificently to the challenge. Despite some excellent local products, the administrative and commercial capital of the Gironde *département* is not associated with such a distinctive and distinguished cuisine as say, the city of Lyons and its surroundings. The Bordelais area can boast only one truly great and original creation: sauce Bordelais made with beef bone marrow and shallots (the latter are as popular here as they are in Nantes in Brittany; the shallot is to Bordeaux cookery what the onion is to Lyons and Lille, and garlic to Marseille and Nice). The other great dishes which appear on Bordeaux menus are borrowed from neighboring regions.

In Périgord and Quercy the menus bear witness to the southern French fondness for goose and duck and for that glory of the local cuisine, the truffle.

On the previous pages: *many Périgord farmers derive a large proportion of their income from their flocks of geese.* Below: *looking out over the tiled roofs of a village in southwestern France toward an old dovecote built before the French Revolution.*

Above: *in the cellars of a Sauternes winery hundreds of casks lie in long rows, full of the strong, luscious, yellowy-gold white wines often drunk with another regional product,* foie gras. Right: *the head cellarman takes a sample of cognac out of the barrel to check how well it is ageing.*

These greatly sought after fungi grow underground and have become increasingly expensive during recent years: they impart a sumptuous richness to a wide variety of foods, be they simple and cheap (as in *brouillades*, a five-star version of scrambled eggs) or expensive and elaborate (*foie gras*, or crammed goose liver).

Another local product, walnut oil, gives a pleasantly different accent to dressings for salads.

Among the other specialists of Périgord and Quercy are its soups or *potages tourains* made with goose fat which is also used a great deal for such dishes as Sarlat potatoes (*pommes de terre sarladaises*); stuffed, potted pork (*porc farci et confit*); salsify pie and stuffed savory pancakes. Another great regional creation is *lièvre à la royale* (a version of jugged hare which is indeed fit for a king's table), as elaborate as its name would suggest, for which a partially boned, whole hare is stuffed with *foie gras* and truffles. The wines of Périgord and Quercy are not in the same class as those of Bordeaux but Cahors, Monbazillac, and Bergerac wines are very drinkable.

A different culinary tradition has developed in the Charente (comprising the old provinces of Angoumois, Aunis, and Saintonge) and in Poitou, where the four local products that have determined its character are oysters, mussels, snails, and kidney beans.

Anyone who has visited the Charente region or who is fond of fine brandy will already be well aware of the most famous product of Angoumois: cognac, made in a delimited area around the town of Cognac. Less widely known but extremely popular with the Charentais people are the *petits-gris* snails, once found in large quantities in local vineyards and known as *cagouilles* in Charentais dialect; these are no longer found in sufficient quantities to satisfy demand and an ever growing proportion of the snails consumed locally is imported, such is the enthusiasm for this delicacy in an area where the locals refer to themselves as *cagouillards*, partly because of their fondness for eating snails and partly because they think life is best lived at a slower pace. No decent meal would be complete here without snails, whether they come in the form of soup; cold with a vinaigrette dressing; stewed with a mixture of chopped pork fat and garlic; braised with ham and white wine; in omelets; casseroled; with shallots . . . but if snails reign supreme away from the sea, on the coast oysters and mussels receive star treatment.

Special oyster-rearing beds in coastal reserves at Marennes, Bourcefranc and La Tremblade produce vast numbers of these bivalves which are served with broiled local sausages and the marvelous Charentais and Poitevin butter which has a sweetness and flavor to rival or surpass that of Normandy.

Mussels are gathered from hurdles on which they are cultivated along the coast; these rearing frames are called "bouchots" (after the branches laid between the posts). Local mussel preparation methods include *éclades* (the mussels are placed on a wide, thick plank of olive wood, covered with pine needles which are then set alight and burned to ashes, after which the mussels are ready to eat), or *mouclades* (with a cream sauce).

Along the coast and around the nearby islands of Oléron, Ré, Yeu, and Noirmoutier there is an abundance of good seafood: delicious little soles, baby cuttlefish, and small rays; mackerel, bream, bass; excellent

Above: *Gujan-Mestras has seven main sites where the typical wooden sheds and pontoons betray the presence of oyster beds which were established in the first half of the nineteenth century.* Left: *Périgord's reputation for fine food and a largely unspoilt architectural heritage attracts tourists all the year round.*

shrimp *langoustines* (scampi); several types of clams, crabs, lobsters, and the local sardines, so fresh and full of flavor that they are often eaten raw, with bread and butter, or broiled and sprinkled with sea salt.

The local eels, caught in the salt marshes, are also a treat when broiled, and just as delicious when sautéed in butter and moistened with a little white wine, or stewed in red wine; cut into pieces, browned and covered with a savory white sauce in a *fricassée*, or served *au gratin*.

Above: *the Pilat sand dune is the highest in Europe (373 ft); the long, arduous climb to its crest is rewarded by the magnificent view over the Landes pine forests to the bay of Arcachon.*

In Poitou, further inland, other products take the place of seafood: pork products, beef from the lush Vendée countryside with its shady copses, poultry (chickens, pigeons, geese, turkey, and, notably, the superlative duck reared around Challans). Vegetables are very good and plentiful, especially cabbages which are cooked and finished with butter, with cream or given a dressing of vinaigrette, while the local white kidney beans are also prepared with cream, or with butter and onions, or walnut oil.

SOUPS

SOUPE AUX HUÎTRES*
Oyster soup

Aunis et Saintonge

Preparation: 30 minutes
Cooking: 15 minutes
Easy

Serves 6:
3 dozen oysters
$^1/_4$ cup butter
6 tbsp all-purpose flour
3 pints court-bouillon *(see glossary)*
1 cup milk
1 egg yolk
6 slices French bread
1 small bunch chervil
salt and pepper

Shuck the oysters; save and strain their juice. Melt the butter in a saucepan, stir in the flour and cook, stirring continuously, until the roux is a pale golden brown. Reserve 1 cup of the *court-bouillon*, mix the rest with the milk and gradually stir into the roux over moderate heat as the mixture comes to a gentle boil.

Beat the egg yolk into the reserved *court-bouillon* and then stir into the saucepan. Do not allow the contents to boil from now onward. Heat the strained oyster juice in a large saucepan to boiling point; add the oysters, cover, and simmer very gently for 3 minutes. Remove from the heat and stir in the thickened *court-bouillon* mixture.

Pour onto crisply baked slices of French bread and serve immediately, sprinkled with chopped chervil.

CHAUDRÉE
Atlantic fish soup

Aunis and Saintonge

Preparation: 10 minutes
Cooking: 55 minutes
Easy

Serves 4:
10 oz flounder or sole fillets
10 oz filleted ray
10 oz small eels
10 oz cleaned cuttlefish body cases
10 oz filleted, sliced striped mullet
$^1/_2$ cup butter
2 onions, peeled
2 cloves garlic, peeled
$2^1/_4$ cups dry white wine
1 bouquet garni (thyme, bay leaf, parsley)
few small, peeled potatoes (optional)
6 slices French bread fried in butter
salt and pepper

Prepare all the fish. Slice the cuttlefish into thin strips and sweat gently in $^1/_4$ cup of the butter in a large saucepan with the very finely sliced onions and the whole garlic cloves in a covered pan for 15 minutes, shaking the saucepan now and then.

Add the wine, 1 quart water, and the herbs. Bring to a gentle boil and simmer for 30 minutes, then add the firmest, largest fish pieces first to the pan, together with the potatoes if used. Simmer for 5 minutes. Remove and discard the bouquet garni and the garlic; add the remaining, more delicate fish and simmer for a further 5 minutes. Chop the fried bread into croûtons and serve with the soup.

SOUPE À L'OSEILLE ET AUX HARICOTS
Sorrel and bean soup

Périgord

Preparation: 10 minutes + 4 hours soaking time for the beans
Cooking: $2^1/_4$ hours
Easy

Serves 6:
1 lb dried white navy beans
3 tbsp goose fat or lard
2 onions, peeled
3 tbsp all-purpose flour
$^1/_2$ lb sorrel (or watercress or spinach)
6 slices coarse white bread
salt and pepper

Soak the beans for 4 hours in cold water, drain, and bring to a boil in a large saucepan with 3 quarts fresh cold, unsalted water (adding salt to beans when they are raw makes them tough). Boil gently for 1 hour. Soften and lightly brown the thinly sliced onions in half the goose fat. Stir in the flour and cook until a good, deep golden brown. Pour in 1/2 cup of the cooking water from the beans; leave to cook for 2 minutes, then stir, scraping the bottom of the pan to free any onions and deposits. Add this sauce to the saucepan of undrained, cooked beans.

Remove the sorrel stalks and large ribs; wash the leaves, squeeze out excess moisture, chop coarsely, and cook in the remaining goose fat for 3 minutes. Mix with the beans. Simmer for a further hour, adding salt to taste after 50 minutes. Traditionally the beans are cooked until extremely tender and almost mushy. Add pepper to taste just before serving. Place the bread slices (best if stale and dry) in heated bowls and ladle the soup on top. Add a little more soup after a minute or two if wished, as the bread absorbs much of the liquid.

SOUPE AUX MOULES ROCHELAISE

Mussel soup

Aunis

Preparation: 30 minutes
Cooking: 40 minutes
Easy

Serves 6:
1 1/2–2 lb porgy
1–1 1/2 lb goatfish
1 1 1/2-lb slice conger eel
1 quart mussels
6 scampi
2 carrots, peeled
1 clove garlic, peeled
1 onion, peeled
2 tomatoes, peeled and sliced
1/4 cup peanut oil
2 1/4 cups dry red wine
1 bouquet garni (parsley, thyme)
3 threads real saffron
salt and pepper

Prepare the fish (remove the scales from the porgy and red mullet, gut, trim; rinse and dry these and the conger eel slice). Scrub the mussels, removing all breads and barnacles; discard any that are open. Slice the carrots, garlic, and onion. Remove the seeds from the tomato slices.

Heat the oil in a very large saucepan, add the vegetables, and cook, stirring, over moderate heat for 5 minutes. Add the fish and brown lightly over slightly higher heat for 5 minutes, turning once. Pour in the wine, 1 1/2 quarts water; add the bouquet garni, salt, and pepper. Bring to a boil, cover, and simmer gently for 15 minutes. Rinse and drain the scampi. Place the mussels in a large saucepan with 1/2 cup water and place over high heat; as soon as they have opened, take them off the shell and set aside. Discard any that remain closed. Save all their juices, strain and add to the fish in the saucepan. Add the crustaceans and the saffron.

Cook over moderate heat, uncovered, for 10 minutes to reduce the liquid. Take the pieces of fish and the scampi out of the saucepan with a slotted spoon; take any bones out of the fish and peel the crustaceans; strain the soup into a clean saucepan. Return the fish pieces, crustaceans, and mussels to the soup and serve, with slices of French bread fried in butter, if wished.

TOURAIN PÉRIGOURDIN*

Tomato soup

Périgord

Preparation: 10 minutes
Cooking: 40 minutes
Easy

Serves 6:
2 large onions, peeled
1 1/2 tbsp goose fat or lard
1 clove garlic, peeled
3 tbsp all-purpose flour
1–1 1/4 lb ripe tomatoes, blanched and peeled
6 slices 2-day old French bread
salt and pepper

Bring 1 1/2 quarts water to a boil in a large pot; remove all the tomato seeds, chop the flesh coarsely and add to the boiling water. Cook for 10 minutes. Slice the onions very finely and cook in the goose fat or lard in a fairly small saucepan until soft and lightly browned. Add the minced clove of garlic. Sprinkle with the flour and cook, stirring continuously, until the roux turns a pale golden brown.

Stir in 1/2 cup of the liquid from the cooked tomatoes. Scrape the bottom of the saucepan with a wooden spoon to loosen any deposits and add to the tomatoes. Season with salt and pepper; simmer for 30 minutes.

Pour the soup through a vegetable mill, milling the solid ingredients (alternatively, process briefly in the blender, or sieve). Reheat and ladle into heated soup bowls. Cut the slices of bread into cubes and sprinkle onto the soup.

ENTRÉES

CAGOUILLES À LA CHARENTAISE
Snails with herbs, wine, and garlic

Angoumois

Preparation: 10 minutes (for prepared snails)
Cooking: 1 hour 45 minutes
Easy

Serves 6:
6 dozen snails
2 onions, 1 studded with 2 cloves
4 cloves garlic, peeled
2 leeks, white part only
2 carrots, peeled
1 bouquet garni (thyme, bay leaf, parsley)
3/4 cup dry white wine
3/4 cup light broth (see glossary)
1/4 lb pork breast or unsmoked bacon
8 shallots, peeled
1/4 lb raw, cured ham
1/4 cup butter
1 1/4–1 1/2 cup fine, dry breadcrumbs
3/4 cup finely chopped parsley
salt and pepper

If the snails are alive, make sure they have been purged and prepare as described on page 48 (*Escargots à la bourguignonne*). If using canned snails, often sold with their cleaned shells, drain and rinse briefly.

If live or raw snails are used, place in a saucepan of water with a finely chopped mixture of: 1 onion, 2 cloves garlic, chopped leeks, and the finely sliced carrots. Add the bouquet garni and the peeled whole, clove-studded onion. Sprinkle with a very little water, cover tightly, and place on extremely low heat for 10 minutes. Season with salt and pepper. Add the wine and broth, cover tightly again, and return to a gentle heat for 1 1/2 hours. If using canned snails, join the recipe here. Chop the pork or bacon, the remaining garlic cloves, the shallots and ham very finely; sweat together in a tightly covered large saucepan or deep skillet. Add the snails (in Charente these are left in their shells, to be sucked out or extracted at table, with finger bowls provided). Cover and cook gently for 5 minutes. Add the breadcrumbs and parsley; cook, stirring for a further 5 minutes. Serve immediately.

PÂTÉ DE PÂQUES*
Easter pie

Poitou

Preparation: 1 hour
Cooking: 45 minutes
Easy

Serves 6:
1 3/4 sticks butter
1 3/4 cups all-purpose flour
10 oz boned chicken or rabbit
1 1/4-lb piece from veal leg
1/4 lb pig's liver
1/4 lb pork belly or fresh bacon
3 tbsp finely chopped parsley, chervil, and chives
8 eggs
3 tbsp cognac
salt and pepper

Make the pie dough, working half the butter (softened at room temperature and cut into small pieces) into all the flour, using a processor or rubbing in with your fingertips. Gradually moisten with only just enough water to form a smooth, homogenous dough and knead briefly, until it no longer sticks to your fingers. Shape into a ball, wrap, and chill while you prepare the filling. Wash, dry, and trim the chicken or rabbit and veal. Cut into small cubes. Finely chop the pork belly or bacon and the pig's liver (do not grind) and mix in a bowl with the chopped herbs, salt, and pepper; using your hands, shape into walnut-sized balls. Heat most of the remaining butter in a skillet and brown the meatballs all over, followed by the cubed meat.

Hard boil 7 of the eggs (10 minutes). Cool quickly in cold water, peel, and cut lengthwise in half.

Roll out two thirds of the pie dough to line a 9 1/2-in deep tart pan or fairly shallow springform cake pan greased with butter, allowing an extra 3/8 in overlap all round the edge.

Arrange the meat and meatballs in this pie shell and season with salt and pepper; place the halved eggs on top, dot with flakes of butter, and sprinkle the meat with the cognac.

Roll out the remaining dough to form a lid, bring the overlap up and over the lid edges, and pinch the layers together with fingertips dipped in cold water. Brush the surface with a beaten egg. Place in the oven, preheated to 375°F and cook for 45 minutes or until the pastry is done and pale golden brown (reduce the heat to 350°F if it browns too quickly). Serve hot or cold.

MIQUE SARLADAISE

Bread, ham, and egg dumpling in broth

Périgord

Preparation: 10 minutes
Cooking: 20–30 minutes
Easy

Serves 6:
7 oz stale, dry white or brown bread
2 eggs, lightly beaten
1/4 cup finely chopped bacon fat
1 cup all-purpose flour
salt and pepper
1 quart beef broth

Cut the stale bread into small dice, place in a mixing bowl and pour the eggs over it.

Stir in the finely chopped fat (traditionally this recipe uses up fat trimmed from *prosciutto*-type cured raw ham, giving the dumpling a delicious flavor). Season to taste, mix well, and shape the mixture into a ball; roll in the flour to coat all over.

Bring the beef broth to a boil in a deep saucepan (the original recipe makes use of leftover broth from boiled beef) and add the dumpling. Boil over moderate heat for 20–30 minutes.

COU D'OIE FARCI À LA QUERCYNOISE

Goose neck sausage

Quercy

Start preparation 2 days in advance
Preparation: 30 minutes
Cooking: 1 hour
Easy

Serves 4:
Skin from a goose neck (see method)
1/4 cup Armagnac or brandy
2 cups (1 lb) good pork sausage meat
1/2 lb fresh foie gras *or canned semicooked, pasteurized* foie gras
1 1/2 oz truffles or truffle peelings
1/4 cup dry white wine
salt and pepper
1 lb goose fat for cooking the sausage

Carefully remove the skin from a goose neck, ideally with a flap of the breast skin as well; make sure it is all in one piece, with no punctures or tears (a cylinder with a flap at one end). Marinate in a small bowl in the Armagnac for 2 days, turning occasionally.

To make the filling for this casing, place the sausage meat in the food processor and process with the *foie gras* and truffles (both truffles and peelings are sold in tiny cans), salt, pepper, the Armagnac used to marinate the skin casing, and the wine. (If you do not have a processor, chop the *foie gras* and truffle and stir very thoroughly in a bowl with the sausage meat and other ingredients). Fill the neck casing with this mixture, tying securely with kitchen string at both ends. Heat the goose fat in a deep fryer to 275°F and add the sausage; fry for 1 hour or until the sausage floats up to the surface of the fat, the signal that it is done. Take out of the fat and serve at once, hot, or transfer to a suitable deep, rectangular terrine, pour the goose fat all over it and leave to cool and solidify. Refrigerate until needed. This keeps well for several days.

BROUILLADE AUX TRUFFES

Truffled scrambled eggs

Périgord and Quercy

Start preparation 24 hours in advance
Preparation: 20 minutes
Cooking: a few minutes
Complicated

Serves 6:
7 oz truffles, preferably fresh
9 eggs
3 tbsp crème fraîche *or heavy cream*
1 1/2 tbsp goose or duck fat
salt and pepper

This recipe dates back to the days when fresh truffles were more plentiful and less expensive than they are now; if you can buy air-freighted truffles they are at their best at the beginning of the new year. Clean the truffles, brushing off any impurities and wipe with a clean cloth; place them in a hermetically sealed container (e.g. a large cookie tin) with the eggs. Leave for 24 hours, until shortly before you prepare this dish; their scent and flavor will penetrate the permeable eggshells and impart a marvelous taste to the eggs inside.

Slice the truffles thinly and place in a small saucepan with 3/4 cup very lightly salted water. Simmer uncovered for 10 minutes so that the liquid reduces as it absorbs the truffle flavor.

Beat the eggs and cream together with a balloon whisk; add to the truffles and the remaining liquid off the heat. Grease the inside of the top container of a double boiler with the fat; place over gently simmering water in the lower part of the boiler. Stir very slowly but continuously with a wooden spoon. The eggs and cream will gradually thicken and become creamier. Take the double boiler off the heat when they have nearly reached the required thick, almost set consistency and stir for a few moments more. Serve immediately.

CAGOUILLES À LA SAINTONGEAISE

Snail, herb, and wine casserole

Saintonge

Preparation: 15 minutes (for prepared snails)
Cooking: 3 hours 20 minutes
Fairly easy

Serves 6:
6 dozen prepared snails
2 onions, peeled
2 carrots, peeled
3 cloves garlic
1 bouquet garni (thyme, bay leaf, parsley)
1/2 bottle dry white wine
1/4 cup butter
4 shallots, peeled
1/2 lb smoked slab bacon
6 tbsp all-purpose flour
2 1/4 cups dry red wine
1 small bunch parsley
1 small bunch chives
salt and pepper

If you are using live snails, see page 48 (*Escargots à la bourguignonne*) for preparation instructions. Place the prepared snails in a saucepan with the sliced onions and carrots, one garlic clove, the bouquet garni, white wine, and 3/4 cup cold water. Season with salt and pepper and simmer gently for 2 hours.

When the snails are cooked, chop the remaining 2 garlic cloves and the shallots finely and cook with the bacon (skin removed, trimmed, and cut into lardons, or into strips if you have bought sliced bacon) until lightly browned in the butter. Sprinkle in the flour and stir over low heat to blend and cook the roux mixture. Stir in the red wine and one third of the snails' cooking liquid, strained.

Add the drained snails to this mixture, cover, and simmer for 1 1/4 hours. Serve with a sprinkling of chopped parsley and chives.

Pierre Coste was among the most eloquent of wine experts but one evening, during a wine tasting of some of the greatest Bordeaux wines, he came across a superb claret that defied even his descriptive powers: "Why, it's Marilyn Monroe!" he exclaimed in a fitting tribute to a full-bodied, luscious wine.

FISH

ÉCREVISSES À LA BERGERACOISE

Freshwater crayfish in wine and tomato sauce

Périgord

Serves 6:
4 dozen freshwater crayfish
3 carrots, peeled
1 clove garlic, peeled
3 shallots, peeled
2 onions, peeled
6 tbsp olive oil
1/4 cup brandy (Armagnac or cognac)
1 bottle dry white wine (e.g. Montravel or Bergerac)
3 large, ripe tomatoes, blanched and peeled
1 bouquet garni (thyme, parsley, bay leaf)
8–10 sprigs parsley, tied in a bunch
salt and pepper

Cut the carrots into small dice, and the garlic, shallots, and onions into thin slices. Season with salt and pepper and cook over low heat for 15 minutes in 1 1/2 tbsp of the oil until tender and lightly colored. Set aside. Have the crayfish ready prepared and gently scrubbed under running cold water (see page 85, *Demoiselles de Cherbourg à la nage*, for method of extracting the bitter alimentary tract).

Heat the remaining oil in a large fireproof casserole dish or heavy-bottomed saucepan, add the crayfish, cover, and shake the pan over fairly high heat to ensure that they cook evenly. Turn them if necessary. As soon as all the crayfish have turned scarlet, add the warmed brandy and flame. When the flames have subsided, add the wine, the reserved chopped, cooked vegetable mixture, the coarsely chopped, deseeded tomatoes, the bouquet garni, and the separate, larger bunch of parsley. Season with more salt and pepper to taste. Cover and cook over moderate heat for 15 minutes.

Take the crayfish out of the pan with kitchen tongs and keep hot in a serving dish. Boil the liquid left in the pan to reduce and thicken; remove and discard the bouquet garni and the extra bunch of parsley. Pour the sauce all over the crayfish.

SOLE À LA MARAÎCHINE

Sole with cream, wine, and shallots

Aunis

Preparation: 35 minutes
Cooking: 10 minutes
Easy

Serves 4:
4 English soles or flounders
3/4 cup all-purpose flour
6 shallots, peeled
1/2 lb small button mushrooms
2 1/2 cups dry white wine
1 stick butter
1/2 cup crème fraîche *or heavy cream*
salt and pepper

Ask your fishmonger to trim, gut, and skin the soles. Coat with flour, shaking off excess. Slice the shallots and the mushrooms thinly. Cook both in the white wine in an uncovered saucepan over moderately high heat for 20 minutes.

Cut the butter into small pieces and use to cook the fish for 3–5 minutes on each side, depending on their thickness, in a wide skillet over moderately high heat; do not allow the butter to brown. Turn the fish once, carefully. Cook in 2 batches or one at a time if necessary. Keep them hot while you season the reduced wine mixture with salt and freshly ground white pepper; stir in the cream and then pour over the soles.

HUÎTRES FARCIES

Oysters with savory butter

Aunis and Saintonge

Preparation and cooking: 15 minutes
Very easy

Serves 2:
2 dozen large oysters
3 cloves garlic or 3 shallots
6 tbsp finely chopped parsley
1/2 cup butter, slightly softened
3/4 cup fine breadcrumbs (optional)
pepper

If you have bought flat oysters, spread them out in a roasting pan or broiler pan; if rounded, place a bed of crumpled foil in the bottom of the pan, place the oysters on it and they will not tip over. Turn the oven to very high. As soon as the oysters open, take them out of the oven, remove and discard the top shell. Blend or mix the peeled and very finely chopped garlic or shallots with the parsley and the butter (use breadcrumbs as well if wished) very thoroughly. Spread a little on each oyster in its half shell. Season with freshly ground pepper. Place the oysters under a very hot broiler for a minute or two, then serve.

HUÎTRES À LA BORDELAISE*
Oysters and sausages

Bordelais

Preparation: 15 minutes
Cooking: 5–10 minutes
Fairly easy

Serves 6:
3 dozen oysters
2 dozen crépinettes *(very small flat truffled sausages)*

Open the oysters and place on a bed of crushed ice in a serving dish or on individual plates. Broil the *crépinettes*. Tiny cocktail sausages can replace these, or you can serve a coarse pork paté with the oysters, as they do in the coastal region of Charente; canned, truffled *foie gras* would also be suitable.

Serve the oysters and the sausages (or your chosen alternative) with coarse, brown rye bread.

The idea is to alternate between oysters, sausages, and sips of dry white wine.

BOUILLITURE D'ANGUILLES
Eel, red wine, and herb stew

Aunis and Saintonge

Preparation: 15 minutes
Cooking: 20 minutes
Easy

Serves 6:
2–2½ lb eels
¼ cup butter
4 cloves garlic or 4 shallots
3 tbsp all-purpose flour
1 quart dry red wine
1 bouquet garni (thyme, bay leaf, parsley)
salt and pepper

Wash, trim, and cut off the heads and tails of the eels, gut them and scrub well, up and down the length of their bodies and across, to eliminate the thin, slimy outer membrane (the skin is traditionally left on in Charente). Cut into 2-in lengths. Cook the peeled and finely sliced garlic or shallots in the butter in a large saucepan until lightly browned; sprinkle in the flour and cook, stirring, for a few minutes. Remove from the heat and gradually stir in the red wine. Return to the heat and bring to a boil. Add the eel pieces at once, then the bouquet garni, salt, and pepper. Cook over moderately high heat for 15 minutes.

Serve with steamed or boiled potatoes.

MOUCLADE
Mussels in wine and cream sauce

Aunis and Saintonge

Preparation: 30 minutes
Cooking: 35 minutes
Easy

Serves 6:
3 quarts mussels
1 bouquet garni (thyme, bay leaf, parsley)
1½ cups dry white wine
2 onions, peeled and thinly sliced
2 shallots, peeled and thinly sliced
¼ cup butter
2 threads real saffron
½ cup crème fraîche *or heavy cream*
3 egg yolks
¼ cup cognac
salt and pepper

Scrub the mussels removing the beards. Discard any that do not close when handled. Place in a wide saucepan with the bouquet garni and wine, cover, and place over high heat. Discard any that have not opened after 5 minutes.

Remove the empty half of each mussel and discard; spread the mollusks on their half shells in a single layer in shallow ovenproof dishes. Strain the juices and wine.

Preheat the oven to 425°F. Sweat the onions and shallots in the butter until tender; add the strained liquid and boil gently, uncovered, for 30 minutes to reduce. Season with salt and pepper, add the saffron, and simmer for a few minutes more. Draw aside from the heat and stir in the cream. Mix the egg yolks with the cognac and beat into the cream sauce with a balloon whisk for a minute or two. Spoon a coating of this sauce over each mussel. Place in the hot oven for 5 minutes, then serve.

MOULES À LA BORDELAISE

Mussels with tomato, herb, and wine sauce

Bordelais

Preparation: 30 minutes
Cooking: 25 minutes
Easy

Serves 6:
2 quarts mussels
1½ cups dry white wine
6 tbsp soft, fine breadcrumbs
3 tbsp milk
1½ tbsp butter
3 tbsp all-purpose flour
3 tbsp finely chopped parsley
2 shallots, peeled and finely chopped
3 tbsp tomato paste
salt and pepper

Clean and prepare the mussels, scrubbing them well under running cold water, removing their beards and rinsing them thoroughly to eliminate all traces of sand. Discard any that are open. Place in a large, wide saucepan with the wine over high heat; shake the pan or turn them so that they all heat and open. Discard any that do not open within a few minutes. Remove and discard the empty half shells; spread the mussels on the half shell in a single layer in a very wide, shallow fireproof dish or pan. Strain all the juice and liquid and reserve.

Sprinkle the breadcrumbs with the milk, stir, and squeeze out any excess moisture. Melt the butter in a saucepan, stir in the flour and continue stirring while cooking the roux until it turns a pale golden brown. Stir in ½ cup of the reserved liquid followed by the moistened breadcrumbs, the parsley, shallots, and the tomato paste. Season with salt and pepper and cook over low heat while stirring for about 10 minutes.

Stir in the remaining reserved liquid; pour this sauce evenly all over the mussels, cover, and heat gently for 10 minutes. Serve immediately.

MOULES À LA SAINTONGEAISE*

Mussels with breadcrumbs and garlic

Saintonge

Preparation: 20 minutes
Cooking: 10 minutes
Easy

Serves 4:
4 quarts mussels
¾ cup dry white wine
¼ cup butter
3 cloves garlic, peeled and finely chopped
6 tbsp finely chopped parsley
1¾ cups soft white breadcrumbs
sea salt and pepper

Clean and prepare the mussels (see previous two recipes for method). Place in a very wide saucepan with the wine over high heat and turn with a slotted ladle or spoon. Discard any that have not opened after 5–6 minutes. Take the mussels out of their shells (discard the shells).

Melt the butter in a skillet or large, heavy-bottomed saucepan and cook the garlic and parsley gently until the garlic has colored very lightly. Add the breadcrumbs and stir well. Add the mussels, stirring continuously over high heat for a few minutes. Season with sea salt and freshly ground pepper, cover the pan, and turn off the heat. Serve very hot.

LAMPROIE À LA BORDELAISE

Lamprey stewed in red wine

Bordelais

Preparation: 50 minutes
Cooking: 2 hours
Complicated

Serves 6:
1 live lamprey weighing 4½ lb
12 small leeks
½ cup peanut oil
¾ lb Bayonne, cured raw ham
6 shallots, peeled
12 very small onions, peeled
6 tbsp all-purpose flour
1 bottle dry red Bordeaux wine
¾ cup fish broth (see glossary)
2 cloves
1 bouquet garni (thyme, bay leaf, parsley)
4 cloves garlic, peeled
¼ cup Armagnac or brandy
6 slices coarse white bread
½ cup butter
salt and pepper

For most American cooks this recipe will be an interesting curiosity rather than a practical proposition, either for humanitarian reasons or because lampreys are not marketed commercially nowadays. Eels could be substituted for lamprey and the bleeding stage omitted. Tie the lamprey tightly round its head and hang up over a wide bowl; cut off the end of the lamprey's tail and leave it to bleed into the bowl for 30 minutes. When it has stopped bleeding add the lamprey to a large saucepan of boiling water and blanch for 1 minute. Remove and lay flat on a board or working surface; scrape off its skin with the back of a heavy knife blade; cut off the head just below the gills, take hold of the dorsal nerve (which looks rather like a strip of raffia and is not edible) and pull it out. Wipe the lamprey all over with a clean dry cloth and cut into 1½-in sections placing these in the bowl of blood.

Use the white part and just the first ½ in of the green of the leeks; leave these sections whole and sweat them in the oil in a large, fireproof casserole dish, stirring occasionally. Add the Bayonne ham, cut into small dice, the sliced shallots and the whole onions. When these start to brown lightly, sprinkle in the flour and cook gently, stirring, until golden brown. Gradually stir in the wine and broth, the cloves, and the bouquet garni. Season with plenty of freshly ground pepper and just a little salt. Add the two garlic cloves, minced with the flat of a knife. Bring to a boil, cover, and simmer gently for 45 minutes before adding the lamprey sections; cover once more and simmer for a further 45 minutes. Take out the lamprey pieces with a slotted spoon, place in another saucepan, and add the heated Armagnac; flame.

Stir approx. 1 cup of the hot sauce into the bowl of blood; add as much again, stirring continuously and then return to the casserole dish and stir. Add the flamed lampreys; adjust the seasoning, cover and simmer gently for 10 minutes while you toast the bread slices till crisp and then rub them with the cut surfaces of the remaining garlic cloves.

Cover the bottom of a deep, heated serving dish with the garlic toast, place the lamprey pieces on top and surround with the leeks; cover with the sauce.

Cognac is said to have been invented during the seventeenth century by one Chevalier de la Croix-Marron.

This nobleman thought that the local wines left a lot to be desired and that the brandy distilled from them was equally disappointing. He decided to experiment with a second distillation … and cognac was born.

MEAT

TOURTIÈRE DE POULET AUX SALSIFIS

Chicken and salsify pie

Périgord

Preparation: 40 minutes + 2 hours resting time for the pie dough
Cooking: 1 hour 10 minutes
Complicated

Serves 6:
5 cups all-purpose flour
1¼ cups lard or shortening (see method)
2 eggs
1 3¼–3½-lb chicken
1 lb salsify
¾ cup white wine vinegar
1 medium-sized onion, peeled
1 large, ripe tomato, peeled
¾ cup dry white wine
¾ cup chicken broth
1 egg yolk
salt and pepper

Make the pie dough. Measure out 4 cups of the flour into a mixing bowl, make a well in the center, and in it place 1 cup 2 tbsp of the lard (or your usual pie dough shortening) cut into small pieces, 2 eggs, and ¾ cup cold water. Mix these into the flour, quickly and not too carefully with your fingers. Work the dough briefly, just enough to blend it evenly and make it smooth and homogenous. Shape into a ball, wrap in a floured cloth, and leave to rest for 2 hours in the refrigerator.

While you are chilling and resting the pastry, scrape or peel the skin off the salsify roots, cut them in half and immediately drop into a large bowl containing water mixed with the vinegar to prevent discoloration. Cut off the leg, thigh, wing and 2 breast portions from the chicken and brown them well all over in the remaining, very hot lard. Reduce the heat a little, sprinkle in the remaining ½ cup flour, stirring well, add the quartered onion and the halved, deseeded tomato. Continue stirring as the sauce thickens; as soon as it begins to darken, add the white wine and broth. Season with salt and pepper and simmer for 30 minutes.

Grease a large, deep pie dish or springform pie mold with lard; it must be big enough to hold all your chicken pieces and the salsify.

Roll out the pie dough to a thickness of just under ¼ in and cut out 2 pieces, one to line the base and sides of the springform pie mold and overlap its edges by about ⅜ in (if using a pie dish you will allow for the lip, so there is no need for an overlap). The second piece is for a lid, cut exactly to size, with no overlap needed.

Place a ceramic pie chimney in the dish if you use one. Arrange the chicken pieces in the pie dish (just as they are, do not remove the bones) with the salsify and the sauce. Cover with the pastry lid, dampening the edges and bringing the overlap back over the edge of the lid if using a pie mold, pinching the lid all the way round the edge to seal. Brush the surface of the lid with the egg yolk. If you are not using a ceramic pie chimney, cut a neat circle in the center of the cover ½–¾ in wide, and place a cylinder of foil in it.

Place in the oven, preheated to 425°F and bake for 30 minutes.

JARRET DE VEAU AU PINEAU

Casseroled veal shin

Angoumois

Preparation: 10 minutes
Cooking: 2 hours
Easy

Serves 6:
1 veal shin sawn into 2-in sections
1 cup all-purpose flour
½ cup butter
2 onions, peeled and sliced
2 carrots, peeled and sliced
1 bottle Pineau des Charentes (see method)
2 cloves garlic, peeled
1 lb tomatoes, blanched and skinned
1 bouquet garni (thyme, bay leaf, parsley)
finely grated peel of 1 lemon
salt and pepper

Ask your butcher to saw the veal shin across the bone into pieces for you. Season these with salt and pepper and coat lightly with flour, shaking off excess. Brown them all over in 3 tbsp hot butter in a fireproof casserole dish, then take them out and set aside. Discard all the butter and juices and wipe the casserole dish.

Cook the onions and carrots in the remaining butter for 10 minutes over low heat, until lightly browned.

Place the veal pieces on top of the vegetables, add the Pineau (if you cannot buy this white wine and brandy mixture, use any white wine and ¼ cup brandy) and bring to a boil. Add the minced garlic cloves, the deseeded and coarsely chopped tomatoes, the bouquet garni, and the grated lemon peel. Reduce the heat, adjust the seasoning and leave to simmer for 1½ hours over gentle heat.

DAUBE DE BOEUF À LA SAINTONGEAISE*

Beef and calf's foot casserole

Saintonge

Preparation: 45 minutes
Cooking: 5 hours
Easy

Serves 6:
3½ lb braising beef (e.g. flank or brisket)
1 boned calf's foot
½ lb semisalted pork breast or pork belly or slab unsmoked bacon
¾ cup butter
20 shallots, peeled
4½ lb carrots, peeled
2 quarts dry red wine
¼ cup cognac or brandy
4–5 strips pork skin or fresh bacon
4 cloves garlic, peeled
1 bouquet garni (thyme, bay leaf, parsley)
salt and pepper

This casserole is best made a day in advance and reheated when you wish to serve it.

Trim off the skin or rind from the pork breast or bacon and remove any tough pieces of cartilage; cut across the strips of fat and lean into ¾-in lardons. Fry these gently in ½ cup of the butter with the calf's foot for 20 minutes in a fireproof casserole dish. Remove the lardons and calf's foot with a slotted spoon and set aside.

Cut the beef into 1½-in cubes and add to the hot fat and butter in the casserole dish. Cover and cook, turning now and then, for 15 minutes to brown all over.

Cook the sliced shallots and carrots in the remaining butter in a saucepan over low heat until tender and lightly browned.

Bring the wine and cognac to a boil in another saucepan, set a taper to this mixture and flame as soon as it starts to reach boiling point.

Add the shallots, carrots, calf's foot, lardons, and strips of pig's skin to the beef when browned. Add the boiling hot wine and cognac, the whole garlic cloves, and the bouquet garni. Cover and simmer very gently for 5 hours.

After 4 hours of simmering, taste and season with pepper, and a little salt if needed.

LIÈVRE FARCI À LA POITEVINE

Stuffed braised hare

Poitou

Start preparation 1 or 2 days in advance
Preparation: 40 minutes
Cooking: 1 hour 40 minutes
Complicated

Serves 8:
1 large, young hare
1 bottle dry white wine
2 onions, peeled and sliced
2 carrots, peeled and sliced
1 bouquet garni (thyme, bay leaf, parsley)
5 oz boned blade end of pork
5 oz boned veal shoulder
5 oz fat fresh bacon
1 large, thin piece barding fat (a leaf of pork flair or back fat)
1 egg
¼ cup cognac or brandy
1 large thin slice cured raw ham
½ cup butter
few chives
salt and pepper

Clean and skin the hare, saving all its blood, the liver, lungs, heart, and kidneys. Cut off the head and paws. Marinate for 1 or 2 days in a large, nonmetallic bowl in the white wine, onions, carrots, bouquet garni, salt, and pepper. Turn from time to time. On the day you plan to cook the hare, make the stuffing: chop the hare giblets, pork, veal, and fresh bacon finely in the food processor or by hand (do not grind). Mix in a very large bowl, seasoning with salt and pepper; stir in the lightly beaten egg, the hare's blood, and the cognac.

Take the hare out of the marinade and wipe dry all over with kitchen towels. Brown the slice of ham lightly in 1½ tbsp butter and line the abdominal cavity with it; sprinkle with chopped chives and fill with the stuffing. Truss the hare, folding the hind and forelegs neatly, making it easy to wrap in the leaf of barding fat; tie this securely in two or more places with kitchen string. Use some of the remaining butter to grease a roasting pan or ovenproof casserole dish and place the hare in it; smear the remaining butter in small pieces all over the hare. Place in the oven, preheated to 425°F and roast for 30 minutes, sprinkling with ¼ cup of the marinade at 10-minute intervals to keep the hare moist. Reduce the heat to 375°F and roast for a further 1 hour.

Pour the remaining marinade into a saucepan and boil gently, uncovered, until it has reduced to half its original volume. Strain.

When the hare is done, take off the barding fat, carve into portions, and arrange these on a heated serving plate around the sliced stuffing. Serve the sauce in a sauceboat. This dish is often served with wild mushrooms (*cèpes*); see recipes on pages 128 and 129.

CANARD À LA POITEVINE*

Roast duck with baby turnips

Poitou

Preparation: 30 minutes
Cooking: 1¼ hours
Complicated

Serves 6:
1 3½-lb duckling
½ cup butter
20 baby onions, peeled
3½ lb baby turnips, peeled
1 cup light broth
1½ tbsp superfine sugar
¼ cup crème fraîche *or heavy cream*
¼ cup cognac or brandy
1½ tbsp chopped fresh chervil
salt and pepper

For the stuffing:
¼ lb chicken livers
¼ lb pig's liver
¼ lb trimmed fresh bacon or pork belly
2 shallots, peeled
few fresh herbs (rosemary or sage, bay leaf, parsley)
6 small button mushrooms
2 eggs
¼ cup butter
salt
pinch cayenne pepper

You will need some of the duck's giblets for this recipe: the liver and the cleaned, trimmed gizzard.

Chop the chicken livers, duck liver, and pork liver finely together with the fresh bacon or pork belly, the shallots, and herbs (use a food processor if you have one but do not grind). Chop the mushrooms and mix with the meats; blend in the eggs, ¼ cup slightly softened butter, salt, and cayenne pepper. Stuff the duck with this mixture and sew up both ends with a trussing needle and thread.

Heat generous ¼ cup of the remaining butter in a large fireproof casserole dish and brown the duck well all over. Cover and cook over brisk heat for 30 minutes, starting with the breast uppermost, turning the duck once after 15 minutes.

Cook the onions and turnips in the remaining butter over gentle heat for 10 minutes, then add the broth and sprinkle the sugar all over them. Continue cooking slowly for 20

minutes, then gently stir in 2–3 tbsp of the juices from the duck followed by the cream; transfer the vegetables and all the liquid to the casserole dish containing the duck which should now be turned breast side uppermost again; take out approx. ½ cup of the liquid and mix with the cognac; pour this over the duck; put the lid on the casserole and place in the oven, preheated to 425°F, to cook for 15 minutes.

Carve the duck and arrange the pieces on a heated serving platter surrounded by the vegetables. Skim excess fat from the surface of the liquid and pour the sauce over the duck. Sprinkle with chopped chervil.

SAUCE BORDELAISE

Wine, marrow, and shallot sauce

Bordelais

Preparation: 10 minutes
Cooking: 1 hour 10 minutes
Easy

Serves 4:
2 medium-sized onions, peeled
2 medium-sized carrots, peeled
½ cup butter
2½ tbsp all-purpose flour
2½ cups veal or beef broth (see glossary)
1 bouquet garni (thyme, bay leaf, parsley)
1½ oz shallots, peeled
1¼ cups red wine (Bordeaux)
¼ lb beef marrow
salt and pepper

Slice the onions and carrots finely and cook in 1 tbsp of the butter over moderate heat until lightly colored; stir in the flour and cook until it turns a pale golden brown. Gradually stir in the broth; when the mixture has boiled, cover the saucepan and leave to simmer gently for 15 minutes.

Slice the onions very thinly and place in another small saucepan with the wine, a pinch of salt, and pepper. Boil gently for 30 minutes to reduce by one third, then stir into the simmered sauce and cook gently for a further 15 minutes. Strain into a pan placed in hot water to keep warm.

Extract the marrow from the beef bones neatly and cut into small dice, dipping the knife blade into very hot water; add the diced marrow to a small saucepan of barely simmering water and leave for 5 minutes while you stir all the remaining butter into the sauce a very small piece at a time, to thicken and enrich it. Stir in the drained marrow and serve.

FOIE GRAS AUX CÂPRES

Crammed goose liver with capers

Quercy and Périgord

Preparation: 25 minutes
Cooking: 40 minutes
Easy

Serves 6:
1¼ lb fresh foie gras *or canned, semicooked, pasteurized* foie gras
¼ cup Armagnac or cognac
1½ tbsp goose fat
2 oz capers
¾ cup madeira
salt and pepper

Prepare the fresh, raw *foie gras* by the method described on page 224. Season it with salt and pepper, place in a bowl, and sprinkle all over with the Armagnac or cognac. Lightly brown the *foie gras* all over in the goose fat in a heavy-bottomed fireproof casserole dish. Add the capers. Cover and cook very gently for 35 minutes. Take out the *foie gras* and keep hot in a serving dish. Pour the madeira and the remaining Armagnac into the casserole and scrape the deposits loose with a wooden spoon over high heat; pour the resulting liquid all over the goose liver and serve.

CONFIT D'OIE À L'OSEILLE*

Preserved goose with sorrel

Périgord

Preparation: 20 minutes
Cooking: 45 minutes
Easy

Serves 4:
2 thighs or 1 breast and wing portion of preserved goose
1 lb sorrel (or watercress or spinach)
½ cup chicken broth (see glossary)
1 small bunch parsley
1 small bunch chervil
1 sprig fresh tarragon
salt and pepper

Place the preserved goose in a heavy-bottomed fireproof casserole dish and heat gently; the aim is to gradually melt the fat and heat through without browning or frying at all.

While the goose is warming, remove the sorrel stalks, rinse the leaves in cold water and then add to a large saucepan of boiling salted water. The moment the water returns to the boil, drain the sorrel, refresh by immediately rinsing in a sieve under running cold water; squeeze the leaves by hand to express all the excess moisture. Cut the leaves with a knife (do not chop).

Take the preserved goose out of the casserole dish, set aside, and drain off all but $1\frac{1}{2}$ tbsp of the fat. Return the goose to the casserole, place over slightly higher heat, and add the sorrel and broth. Season with salt and freshly ground pepper. Sprinkle with the coarsely chopped parsley, chervil, and tarragon leaves, cover, and simmer gently for 20 minutes.

Slice the goose meat and serve on a bed of the sorrel.

LIÈVRE À LA ROYALE*

Rich hare casserole

Périgord

Start preparation 24 hours in advance
Preparation: $1\frac{1}{2}$ hours
Cooking: 6 hours 40 minutes
Very complicated

Serves 8:
1 young hare weighing $4\frac{1}{2}$ lb
3 tbsp red wine vinegar
2 carrots, peeled
2 onions, peeled
6 cloves garlic peeled
1 bouquet garni (thyme, bay leaf, parsley)
4 cloves, minced (not ground)
1 bottle good dry red wine (Cahors or Bergerac)
3 tbsp peanut oil
$\frac{1}{2}$ lb pork tenderloin or boned blade end
$\frac{1}{2}$ lb fresh slab bacon
2 shallots, peeled
few chives
3 sprigs each chervil and tarragon tied in a bunch
1 truffle (fresh or canned)
1 egg
$\frac{1}{2}$ lb boned veal leg or shoulder (or fresh foie gras*)*
10 oz barding fat (leaves of flair or pork back fat)
$\frac{1}{4}$ cup goose fat
$\frac{1}{4}$ cup Armagnac or brandy
$\frac{3}{4}$ cup veal or chicken broth
salt and coarsely crushed peppercorns

Prepare the hare the day before you plan to cook this dish. (see hare recipe on page 120, *Lièvre farci à la Poitevine*). Mix the blood with the vinegar in a bowl to prevent it coagulating and add the liver, heart, and kidneys.

Marinate the hare in a very large nonmetallic bowl. Make the marinade by combining the sliced carrots and onions with 4 of the garlic cloves, minced with the flat of a knife blade, the bouquet garni, a little salt, a generous pinch of the coarsely crushed peppercorns, the cloves, red wine, and oil. Leave overnight.

Carefully take out the rib cage, working the meat away from the bones. Make the stuffing:

in a processor or by hand, chop the pork, bacon, shallots, and the hare's kidneys and heart, with the chives, chervil, tarragon, and a seasoning of salt and pepper. (Do not grind.)

Slice the veal or the *foie gras* thinly. Cut the leaves of barding fat so that they will neatly cover the whole of the hare.

Line the ventral cavity of the hare with a neat, single layer of barding fat, place a layer of veal or foie gras slices on top of the fat, then another layer of barding fat, fill the cavity with the stuffing, cover with a layer of barding fat; place another layer of veal (or *foie gras*) on top and then a final layer of barding fat; sew up the ventral cavity with a trussing needle and thread, bringing the thin, boned layers of flesh to meet in the middle. Wrap the whole hare in the remaining leaves of barding fat and tie up tightly at several points with kitchen string to ensure the fat stays in place. Heat the goose fat in a very large fireproof casserole dish and add the hare in its wrappings; cook over high heat, turning several times, until the barding fat is browned all over. Take out the hare "parcel" and keep hot.

Line the casserole dish with the remaining barding fat, spread out the carrots and onions from the marinade over the fat and place the hare on top. Pour in the marinade and the Armagnac. Heat slowly to boiling point, then simmer, uncovered, for 30 minutes to reduce by half. Add the broth, cover, bring back to a boil, and simmer gently for 6 hours.

Take the hare carefully out of the casserole dish, snip, and remove the string and outer wrapping of barding fat; remove the bones. Cover the meat and keep hot.

Take the liver out of the blood and vinegar and pound it to a smooth paste; stir the blood and vinegar into the liquid in the casserole dish, then stir in the liver and the remaining, finely minced 2 cloves of garlic. Boil very gently, uncovered, for 10 minutes, then strain and pour all over the hare.

ENTRECÔTE BORDELAISE

Rib of beef with Bordelais sauce

Bordelais

Preparation: 20 minutes
Cooking: approx. 20 minutes
Easy

Serves 4:
2 thick rib steaks of beef, each weighing 1 lb
1/2 cup butter
4 shallots, peeled
1/2 cup Bordeaux or other good red wine
1 bouquet garni (thyme, bay leaf)
2 oz beef marrow
1–1 1/2 tbsp finely chopped parsley

1/2 lemon
salt and pepper

The steaks should be about 1¼–1½ in thick. Melt 2 tbsp of the butter over a gentle heat, add the finely chopped shallots and cook until tender and lightly browned. Add the wine and bouquet garni and season with salt and pepper. Reduce by boiling over high heat for a few minutes.

Keep on dipping the blade of a sharp kitchen knife in very hot water as you cut the marrow into thick slices. Poach these for exactly 2 minutes in gently boiling, salted water. Remove with a slotted spoon, drain on kitchen towels, and keep warm. Strain the reduced liquid and keep hot.

Heat another 2 tbsp of the butter in a very wide skillet and cook the steaks for anything from 3–6 minutes on each side over high heat, depending on whether you like them very rare or just pink in the center. Just before removing them from the skillet, season with salt and freshly ground black pepper. Keep hot on a serving plate. Pour the wine mixture into the skillet and deglaze over high heat, using a wooden spoon. Stir in 1 tsp lemon juice and the chopped parsley. Reduce the heat to very low and gradually beat in the remaining butter, adding a small piece at a time. Place the marrow slices on the steaks and pour the sauce all over them. Carve each rib of beef to serve 2.

CANARD AUX OIGNONS

Braised duck with onions, garlic, and herbs

Périgord

Preparation: 25 minutes
Cooking: 1 hour 40 minutes
Easy

Serves 6:
1 2¼–2½-lb duckling
20 baby onions, peeled
2 cloves garlic, cut in half
crust from 1 very thick slice stale bread
5 fresh sage leaves, blanched
2 sprigs thyme
¼ cup oil
3 oz fresh bacon rind or pork skin
¾ cup chicken broth
salt and pepper

You will need the duck's gizzard and liver for this recipe (trim off the bile duct and any bile discoloration). Season the cleaned duck with salt and pepper inside and out. Rub the cut surfaces of the garlic cloves all over the bread crust; tear the latter into small pieces and then chop it (or use a food processor) with the gizzard, liver, 4 sage leaves, and the leaves from 1 sprig thyme. Stuff the duck's cavity with this mixture and sew up the vent and loose neck skin. Brown the duck well all over in the hot oil over high heat in a large, fireproof casserole dish.

Cut the pork skin or bacon rind into 2-in squares, lift the duck out briefly, and spread the squares over the bottom of the casserole, skin side uppermost. Replace the duck and surround with the onions. Add salt and pepper, the remaining sprig of thyme, and 2 blanched sage leaves. Pour in the broth.

Cover with a very tight-fitting lid and place in the oven, preheated to 350°F, to cook for 1½ hours. Just before serving, carve the duck with a very sharp knife and poultry shears, arranging the legs and thighs to one side, wings and breast to the other, with the sliced stuffing in the middle of a hot serving platter and surround with the onions. Remove excess fat from the surface of the cooking liquid and sprinkle the latter over the duck.

The novelist Colette likened the truffle to an exceedingly capricious, much sought-after black princess, worth her weight in gold but often sadly misused. Why, she wondered, was its scent and flavor so often masked with the cloying richness of foie gras *or buried in over-fattened chickens; or, worse still, chopped up and drowned in brown sauces; served with ill-assorted vegetables, or smothered in mayonnaise? Truffles are best enjoyed for themselves alone and served with magnificent simplicity. In short, feast royally on them . . . or leave them alone.*

CONFIT D'OIE AUX CÈPES

Preserved goose with wild mushrooms

Périgord

Preparation: 15 minutes
Cooking: 45 minutes
Easy

Serves 4:
2 leg portions or 1 wing and breast portion preserved goose
*2–2¼ lb fresh or canned cèpes (*boletus edulis*) (see glossary)*
1 clove garlic, peeled
1 small bunch parsley
salt and pepper

Place the preserved goose in a heavy-bottomed fireproof saucepan; cover and place over very low heat so that it heats through gently and the fat melts without frying.

While the goose is heating, separate the stalks from the caps of the mushrooms. Brush and wipe the caps carefully with a clean, dampened cloth. Slice any very large mushrooms; cut the smaller ones in half.

Take the goose out of the casserole dish when ready and keep hot. Leave the fat behind in the pan and sauté the mushroom caps in it over high heat for 5 minutes, stirring and turning them. Reduce the heat to low, cover, and cook gently for 20 minutes, then sprinkle with a pinch of salt. Clean the stalks and chop together with the garlic and parsley. Add this mixture to the caps, increase the heat and cook for a further 10 minutes.

During these final 10 minutes, cook the goose over high heat or in a very hot, preheated oven in a very little extra fat to make the surface crisp and crunchy. Serve on a bed of the mushrooms.

ENCHAUD

Pork and pig's feet casserole

Quercy and Périgord

Start preparation 24 hours in advance
Preparation: 15 minutes
Cooking: 4 hours 10 minutes
Very easy

Serves 8:
3½ lb boned pork loin
6 cloves garlic, peeled
3 tbsp lard
1 bouquet garni (thyme, bay leaf, parsley)
1 cup light broth (see glossary)
2 pig's feet, cut lengthwise in half
salt and pepper

Ask your butcher to give you the bones from the pork loin if possible. Lay the pork on the working surface, fat side downward; season with salt and pepper, place the garlic cloves at intervals in incisions along the inner (uppermost) side of the loin and then roll up and tie securely as if for roasting. Wrap in foil and chill in the refrigerator overnight.

Heat the lard in a fireproof casserole dish and brown the pork all over with the bones if you have them. Season with a little more salt and pepper, add the bouquet garni, the broth, and the pig's feet. Heat to boiling point, cover, and simmer gently for 4 hours. Top up the water from time to time.

Remove the pieces of string and the bones and discard; place the pork in a terrine or deep bowl; pour the liquid from the casserole all over it; leave to cool completely and then place in the refrigerator. The pork is carved and served cold, with its firm jelly cut into small dice. The pig's feet are delicious boned and served with a vinaigrette sauce.

VEGETABLES

SAUCE PÉRIGUEUX
Truffle sauce

Périgord

Preparation: 20 minutes
Cooking: $2^1/_4$ hours
Easy

Serves 6:
3 shallots, peeled
1 medium-sized onion, peeled
$1^1/_2$ tbsp goose fat or lard
3 tbsp all-purpose flour
$2^1/_4$ cups Monbazillac sweet white wine (or madeira)
1 cup chicken broth (see glossary)
$2^1/_2$ oz truffles, fresh or canned
3 tbsp Armagnac or brandy
salt and pepper

Slice the shallots and onion very finely; cook them in the fat in a fairly small, heavy-bottomed saucepan until they are very tender indeed but not at all browned. Stir in the flour with a wooden spoon and as soon as this begins to turn a pale golden color, stir in the wine and the broth. Season with salt and pepper and barely simmer over extremely low heat for 2 hours. Stir from time to time.

Twenty minutes before you intend serving the sauce, strain it and add the very finely sliced truffles (if canned, add the juice as well). Stir in the Armagnac and return to a very low heat for another 15 minutes.

This sauce is often served with beef, in which case degrease any available beef juices and stir them into the sauce.

POMMES SARLADAISES*
Sauté potatoes with garlic and parsley

Périgord

Preparation: 25 minutes
Cooking: 30 minutes
Easy

Serves 8:
$3^1/_2$ lb firm, waxy potatoes
$^1/_4$ cup goose fat
4 cloves garlic, peeled, chopped
3 tbsp finely chopped parsley
salt and pepper

Peel, rinse, and thoroughly dry the potatoes with kitchen towels. Cut into slices under $^1/_8$ in thick. Heat 3 tbsp of the goose fat in a very wide skillet, add the potatoes and fry for 15 minutes. Turn carefully once or twice but allow them to brown; use a spatula to avoid breaking them up.

Sprinkle the slices with salt, pepper, the mixed chopped garlic, and parsley and add the remaining goose fat. Fry for a further 15 minutes, turning them over carefully from time to time. Serve immediately.

CÈPES À LA BORDELAISE

Mushrooms and shallots in olive oil

Bordelais

Preparation: 20 minutes
Cooking: 55 minutes
Easy

Serves 6:
*2–2½ lb cèpes (*boletus edulis*) (see glossary), preferably dark, closed-cap specimens*
1½ cups olive oil
3 shallots, peeled
3 tbsp finely chopped parsley
salt and pepper

Separate the stalks from the caps. Brush the caps carefully to eliminate any grit or impurities. Trim off any damaged sections. Wipe with a clean, slightly dampened cloth, and season with salt and pepper. Sauté the caps over moderately high heat in the olive oil, using a large skillet, for 10 minutes, turning them several times. Transfer the mushrooms and about half of the visible oil (the caps will have absorbed a good deal) to a fireproof casserole dish. Simmer over very low heat for 45 minutes, turning from time to time while you trim, peel, and wipe the stalks and chop them finely with the shallots.

Ten minutes before the caps are ready, pour the reserved oil into a small saucepan; sauté the chopped mixture briskly, stirring and turning it; season with salt and pepper, stir and spoon all over the caps. Sprinkle with the parsley and serve very hot.

MOJETTES FRAÎCHES À LA CRÈME*

White navy beans with cream sauce

Poitou, Saintonge, Aunis, Angoumois

Preparation: 20 minutes + 4 hours' soaking time if dried beans are used
Cooking: 3¼ hours
Very easy

Serves 6:
3½ lb fresh white navy beans or 1 lb dried beans
3 tbsp oil
¼ cup butter
2 carrots, peeled and sliced
3 cloves garlic, peeled and sliced
1 bouquet garni (parsley and thyme)
2 peeled onions, each studded with 1 clove
¾–1 cup crème fraîche *or heavy cream*
salt and pepper

The original recipe calls for fresh beans; if using dried beans, soak in plenty of cold water for 4 hours, drain and dry. Heat the oil and 2 tbsp of the butter in a large fireproof cooking pot or casserole dish. Add the beans and cook over low heat for 15 minutes, stirring from time to time.

Add the carrots, garlic cloves, bouquet garni, the clove-studded onions and enough boiling water to cover the beans completely. Do not add salt yet. Bring to boiling point then simmer very gently for 2 hours; add a generous pinch of salt and continue the slow simmering for a further hour. Top up the liquid with more boiling water whenever necessary to ensure the beans are submerged.

When the beans are very tender, remove and discard the bouquet garni and the clove-studded onions. Drain the beans.

Place the remaining butter and the cream in a very hot, deep serving dish; add the beans, mix well, seasoning with freshly ground pepper and serve.

RAGOÛT DE TRUFFES
Truffles braised in white wine

Périgord and Quercy

Preparation: 15 minutes
Cooking: 35 minutes
Easy

Serves 6:
6 even-sized large black fresh truffles
½ cup butter
1½ tbsp all-purpose flour
1 bottle Monbazillac sweet white wine
salt and pepper

A princely dish to serve in celebration of inheriting a large fortune! Melt the butter in a small, heavy-bottomed casserole dish. Stir in the flour with a wooden spoon and cook over gentle heat until it starts to color; add the wine, stirring continuously. If you cannot buy this wine, which is slightly less sweet than Sauternes, use a good madeira. Simmer, uncovered, over moderate heat to reduce while you brush the truffles gently with a dampened, soft brush, wipe them with a clean cloth and then cut each into quarters. Place the truffles in the sauce; season with a little salt and some freshly ground pepper and cook very gently for 20 minutes.

EMBEURRÉE DE CHOUX
Cabbage stewed in butter

Poitou and Angoumois

Preparation: 10 minutes
Cooking: 1 hour
Very easy

Serves 6:
1 large, white cabbage
1 cup very fresh best butter
salt and pepper

This recipe is a great deal more delicious than it sounds but everything depends on the freshness of the cabbage and on the quality of the butter which is, of course, as in all these recipes, unsalted. Remove the wilted outer leaves of the cabbage and cut out the hard stem. Wash briefly in cold water. Bring 3 quarts lightly salted water to a boil in a large saucepan, add the whole cabbage, cover, and simmer gently for 1 hour.

When the cabbage is very tender indeed, drain well, place in a drum hair sieve and crush the cabbage with a fork (or use a vegetable mill) to form a coarse purée.

Transfer to a deep, heatproof serving dish, place the dish in a pan of very hot water and season with salt and plenty of freshly ground pepper. Gradually stir in the butter, cut into small pieces, using a fork; make sure that all the butter is absorbed by the cabbage. Serve very hot.

CÈPES À LA PÉRIGOURDINE
Mushrooms with garlic, shallot, and parsley

Périgord

Preparation: 20 minutes
Cooking: 1½ hours
Easy

Serves 6:
2–2½ lb cèpes (boletus edulis) *(see glossary)*
½ cup peanut oil
3 cloves garlic, peeled
1 shallot
1 small bunch parsley
salt and pepper

Separate the stalks from the caps with a sharp knife; trim off any damaged pieces from the caps, brush to remove any grit, and wipe them with a slightly dampened cloth.

Heat the oil in a fireproof casserole dish, place the caps upside down in the oil and cook over high heat for 10 minutes, turn and continue cooking for another 10 minutes; they should be lightly browned on both sides. Season with salt and pepper, reduce the heat to very low, cover and leave to cook gently.

Trim off any damaged parts from the stalks and clean. Chop finely with the garlic, shallot, and parsley. Season with salt and pepper. When the caps have simmered gently for 30 minutes, spread half the chopped mixture over them, cover again and continue cooking gently for 20 minutes. When this time is up, stir and turn the mushrooms thoroughly and spread the remaining chopped mixture on top; cook for a final 20 minutes.

Drain off excess oil and serve.

In the eleventh century an Irish sailing ship was wrecked off the coast near Esnandes. The sole survivor, one Patrick Walton, settled in that neighborhood and invented a special net, called the allouret, *to trap birds along the tideline. Drawing in his nets, he noticed that the tiny baby mussels, or "fry" clinging to them were flourishing and growing fast. This led him to construct the prototypes of today's "bouchots," a system of posts and wattle fencing on which mussels are reared to this day.*

DESSERTS

GÂTEAU À L'ANGÉLIQUE
Orange, brandy, and angelica cake

Poitou

Preparation: 10 minutes
Cooking: 45 minutes
Very easy

Serves 6:
2¼ cups (4½ sticks) softened butter
3 cups superfine sugar
¼ cup cognac or brandy
1 tsp orange flower water
small pinch salt
5 eggs, separated
4½ cups cake flour or all-purpose flour
2 oz candied angelica, finely diced

Preheat the oven to 350°F. Using a food processor or mixing by hand with a wooden spoon in a mixing bowl, combine the butter with the sugar, beating until pale and light; gradually beat in the cognac, the orange flower water, and the salt. (If orange flower water is unavailable, substitute 1½ tsp finely grated orange peel.) Beat in the egg yolks one at a time. Beat the egg whites until stiff but not "dry." Using a mixing spatula, fold the egg whites into the cake batter; then sift in the flour and fold in gently but thoroughly. Have a fairly deep, rectangular ovenproof dish or a cake pan ready greased with a little extra butter. Turn the cake batter into it, making sure it is level, then sprinkle the angelica over the surface.

Bake for 45 minutes or until a sharp knife inserted deep into the cake comes out clean.

GÂTEAU DE NOIX
Walnut and vanilla cream pie

Périgord and Quercy

Preparation: 20 minutes + 1 hour resting time for the batter
Cooking: 35 minutes
Easy

Serves 6:
2¼ cups cake flour
½ cup butter
¾ cup superfine sugar
¼ lb walnuts

1 cup crème fraîche *or sour cream*
1/2 tsp pure vanilla extract
1 cup confectioners' sugar
1/4 cup rum

Combine the flour, softened butter, and 1/4 cup of the sugar to make a sweet pie dough mixture (see glossary for method). Mix quickly and not over-thoroughly using your fingers, then work the mixture very briefly with your fingertips. Shape into a ball, wrap, and chill for 1 hour in the refrigerator.

Preheat the oven to 375°F. Roll out the sweet pie dough sufficiently to line a 9 1/2-in diameter tart pan or porcelain flan dish.

Reserve 3 or 4 walnuts for decoration; chop the rest coarsely but evenly in the food processor or with a knife. Mix the chopped nuts with the cream, vanilla, and the remaining superfine sugar; fill the pie shell case with it, leveling it with a palette knife. Place in the oven and bake for 35 minutes.

Take out of the oven and leave to cool completely. Mix the confectioner's sugar and rum until smooth and pour evenly over the surface of the filling. Decorate with the reserved walnuts. Leave until the frosting has set and dried somewhat before serving.

TOURTEAU FROMAGÉ

Baked goat's cheese cake

Poitou

Preparation: 30 minutes
Cooking: 45 minutes
Easy

Serves 4:
1 cup fresh goat's cheese
2 1/4 cups all-purpose flour
1/2 cup butter
1/2 cup superfine sugar
5 eggs
1/2 cup potato flour

Drain the cheese well if it has a noticeable amount of whey in it (substitute cottage cheese or fresh ricotta if preferred for a milder, sweeter taste). Make the pie dough: place 1 3/4 cups of the flour in a large mixing bowl and add all but 2 tbsp of the butter, cut into small pieces; cut or rub the butter into the flour and when the mixture looks rather like breadcrumbs, work in just sufficient cold water to make a fairly firm dough. Knead the pastry briefly and slap it against the sides of the bowl so that it becomes smooth and elastic; as soon as it no longer sticks to your hands, shape into a ball and leave to rest in the bowl, covered with a clean cloth or wrapped in a lightly floured cloth while you make the filling.

Preheat the oven to 450°F. Work the cheese with a fork. Gradually blend in the sugar, 2 whole eggs, and 3 yolks (this can all be done in a food processor or blender if preferred). When the cheese mixture is smooth, stir in the remaining flour and potato flour thoroughly. Beat with a balloon whisk.

Beat the egg whites until very firm, fold in the cheese mixture with a mixing spatula, adding 1 tbsp at a time. Grease a fairly deep cake pan with butter.

Roll out the pie dough and use to line the pan. Trim off the edges and fill with the cheese mixture. Place in the oven and bake for 45 minutes. When you remove the cheese cake from the oven it will be burnt black on the surface; this is normal. Peel off this layer carefully just before serving.

CRUCHADES

Rum-flavored cornmeal fritters

Aunis, Saintonge, Angoumois

Preparation: 20 minutes + 1 hour for resting the pie dough
Cooking: a few minutes
Easy

Serves 6:
1 quart rich milk
1/3 cup superfine sugar
pinch salt
1 lb 2 oz fine cornmeal
1/4 cup rum

Pour the milk into the top of a double boiler, add the sugar and salt. Place over moderate heat and when the milk is just below boiling point, sprinkle in the cornmeal or polenta, stirring continuously as you do so. Place the double boiler top over its lower compartment containing gently simmering water, and keep stirring at frequent intervals during the next 10 minutes as the mixture thickens and cooks. It should be very thick. Stir in the rum.

Spread the mixture out on a pastry board. Smooth the surface and leave for 1 hour.

Use a triangular pastry cutter to cut triangles out of the cold mixture. Dust these lightly with flour on both sides and then deep fry in very hot oil. Drain, then place on kitchen towels.

Sprinkle with superfine sugar and serve.

CROQUANTS DU PÉRIGORD

Orange flower and walnut cookies

Périgord

Preparation: 30 minutes
Cooking: 30 minutes
Easy

Serves 6:
4 eggs
1 1/2 cups superfine sugar
1 1/2 cups all-purpose flour
3 tbsp crème fraîche *or heavy cream*
1 cup (1/4 lb) chopped walnuts
1 tsp orange flower water

Beat the eggs and sugar together very thoroughly; add the flour and cream and beat the thick mixture well until smooth and homogenous; work in the chopped walnuts and orange flower water, slapping the dough against the sides of the bowl to make it elastic; when it no longer sticks to your hands or to the bowl, knead for a few minutes, shape into a ball, wrap and chill for 15 minutes.

Preheat the oven to 320°F. Roll out the dough into a thick sheet (3/4 in thick). Cut into rectangular pieces 3/4 in wide and 4 in long; grease cookie sheets with butter and spread the pieces out on them. Bake for 30 minutes.

TARTE AUX PRUNEAUX*

Prune tart

Quercy and Périgord

Preparation: 20 minutes + 4 hours' soaking time for prunes
Cooking: 30 minutes
Easy

Serves 4:
14 oz large, moist prunes
3/4 cup red wine
3/4 cup superfine sugar or brown cane sugar
2 oz seedless white raisins
1/4 cup rum
1/4 cup butter
1 cup all-purpose flour

Soak the prunes in cold water for 4 hours. Drain well, pit as neatly as possible, and cook, uncovered, for 10 minutes in the wine mixed with an equal volume of water and 1/4 cup of the sugar over moderately high heat. Cool. Soak the raisins in the rum.

Make the pie dough: cut or rub the remaining butter into the flour and add sufficient cold water to make a firm dough. Shape into a ball, wrap in a lightly floured cloth and chill for 1 hour.

Preheat the oven to 400°F. Roll out the pie dough into a roughly circular shape a little less than 1/4 in thick. Grease a fairly deep tart pan or shallow cake pan with butter and line the base and sides with the pastry. Prick lightly with a fork. Fill the pie shell with the prunes and raisins; sprinkle with a little of the prunes' cooking liquid; cover with a lattice made from the remaining pie dough and sprinkle with the remaining sugar. Cook for about 30 minutes, reducing the heat to 375°F if the pastry browns too quickly.

Alpine East

Lyonnais
Bresse
Bugey
Savoie
Dauphiné

The Romans made Lugdunum (now Lyons) the capital of ancient Gaul, a better choice than Paris for the French capital city from a strategic and economic standpoint.

History, however, decided otherwise. Only the Roman Catholic Church perpetuates the former supremacy of the city of Lyons in continuing to recognize the Cardinal Archbishop of Lyons as the Primate of France.

Lyons is one of the two gastronomic "capitals" of France, ranking second to Paris, or taking precedence depending on whether a Parisian or Lyonnais is talking!

The city's location was both its *raison d'être* and the chief reason for its prosperity: surrounded by fertile countryside and known to have been at a crossroads of important trade routes since the earliest records of this part of western Europe, Lyons became a natural magnet for travelers and goods from far and wide.

Fairly close at hand, Bresse is a center for rearing deservedly famous poultry with "blue feet" and snowy white plumage.

Plump hens and capons are cosseted to ensure their outstanding quality. A pie made with the local "white" chicken livers is a revelation for those who come to taste them for the first time. Pigeons are also reared for maximum flavor and tenderness.

In the efficiently managed and strictly supervised fish farms in the Dombes lakes, once an unhealthy marshy region but long since free of all its disease-bearing insects, freshwater fish are reared for the delectation

On the previous pages: *in the fall the trees glow with a magical warmth among the foothills of the Alps in Haute-Savoie.* Above: *a medieval castle in the Alpine province of Dauphiné where the traveler feels the warm south drawing ever closer.*

of discerning Lyons gourmets.

In Bugey, home to the world-famous gastronome Anthelme Brillat-Savarin, cooking is elevated to a minor art form, with such intricate creations as chicken cooked in a pig's bladder and the crayfish sauce that has immortalized the town of Nantua. The southern, or lower Dauphiné (home of Fernand Point, France's most famous chef during the first half of this century) sends turkeys from Crémieu and Saint-Marcellin cheeses to Lyons. Fruit, goat's cheeses, sausages, and chestnuts arrive at the city's markets from the northern part of the Vivarais province (Haut Vivarais) as does *charcuterie* from Forez and the beautiful white eggs from the neighboring province, Charolais.

The inhabitants of Lyons combine knowledge and love of food with the necessary touch of greed. Both in the city and in surrounding areas superb chefs have been attracted by such discerning appreciation of culinary excellence as much as by the unrivaled quality of local raw materials. Some of the most famous French chefs work in the region's restaurants but none is too grand to prepare the delicious local, rustic recipes: such tripe dishes as *gras-double*, or the *tablier de sapeur* and many others, the *saladier* assortment of poultry livers, lamb's feet, herrings, Cervelas sausages among them.

Until World War II there was a strong Lyonnais tradition of female chefs and restaurateurs whose vegetable cookery was unrivaled: onion soup, cardoons with beef marrow, gratins of baby marrows, all a feast of freshness and flavor.

Left: *a sheepdog waits patiently while his master digs potatoes from the Alpine slopes, perhaps to be transformed into a delectable* gratin Savoyard *or* Dauphinois. Below: *the tiny vineyard of Château-Grillet, where the vines grow on terraces sloping down toward the River Rhône, produces a superb white wine.*

Good wines are produced in the Lyonnais; to the south of Lyons are the vineyards of Condrieu and Château-Grillet and the heady, sensuous growths of Hermitage, Côte-Rotie, Cornas and Saint-Joseph.

To the north, great white wines come from Mâcon and the Côte Chalonnaise; then there are the red wines of the Côte Roannaise and the pleasant but less distinguished wines of Beaujolais: these last are light reds, drunk the world over and produced in vast quantities, indeed there is an old saying that the city walls are washed by the rivers of the Rhone, the Saône . . . and the Beaujolais.

Two local customs are associated with Beaujolais: the *boules* players' habit of having a small bottle of this wine (containing about 1 pint) standing by to quench their thirst when they enjoy a game of this version of bowls on a hot summer's day. It also accompanies a substantial late breakfast or *machon* eaten mid morning, consisting of sausages, cheese, and often much else.

Below: *looking out over vast rolling stretches of vineyards in Beaujolais country near Beaujeu, a designated wine-producing area where a light red wine is made, drunk as* Beaujolais nouveau *very soon after it is made or allowed to mature.* Opposite above: *the Dombes region with its countless lakes is a paradise for birds.* Opposite below: *the river Rhône flows through many areas that are famous for their widely varying styles of fine cooking, including Savoie, Bugey, Bresse, Lyonnais, Dauphiné, and Provence among others.*

Lyons has been the main, voracious market for food products of the countryside for many miles around and has therefore influenced the cooking of a very wide area, from Belley to Roanne and from Mâcon to Vienne. Savoie and Dauphiné have, however, managed to retain their distinctive styles of cookery.

When Savoie became part of France only 130 years ago, French gourmets were quick to appreciate the province's excellent cheeses: Beaufort, Reblochon, Abondance, and Aravis and its captivating wines: Apremont, Crépy, Mondeuse, Roussette, and Ripaille, which deserve to be much more widely known. Savoie's lake fish are superb: perch, tench, laveret (a type of pollan) and shad, as well as the increasingly rare *omble chevalier* which lives near the bottom of the deepest lakes.

Few traces remain of Savoie's Italian past (a version of polenta among them) but northern Dauphiné (Brianconnais and Queyras) is full of Italian echoes: lasagna, potato gnocchi, and ravioli with fresh white

goat's cheese and herb stuffing.

These Alpine provinces have given their names to two delicious creamy baked potato dishes: *gratin Savoyard*, made with Beaufort cheese (also used in the local version of fondue), and *gratin Dauphinois* which omits the cheese but adds a subtle hint of garlic to the potato slices cooked with cream and onions.

Desserts and confectionery are under-represented in the traditional repertoire of the region. Savoie can boast of its Savoy sponge cake, Dauphiné of its brioches (*pognes*) and Lyonnais its beignets (*bugnes*) and rather heavy, indigestible pancakes (*matefaims*, literally hunger killers!) So, even in this gastronome's paradise, there is still room for improvement.

GRATINÉE LYONNAISE*

Onion soup with cheese topping

Lyonnais

Preparation: 30 minutes
Cooking: 2 hours 40 minutes
Easy

Serves 6:
For the broth:
3½ lb fresh veal and chicken bones and chicken giblets
2 carrots, peeled
2 baby turnips, peeled
2 leeks
4 sticks celery
1 bouquet garni (thyme, bay leaf, parsley)
1 large onion studded with 2 cloves
10 peppercorns
3 cloves garlic, peeled
1 small fresh red chili pepper
1½ tbsp coarse sea salt

For the soup:
1¾–2 lb large onions, peeled

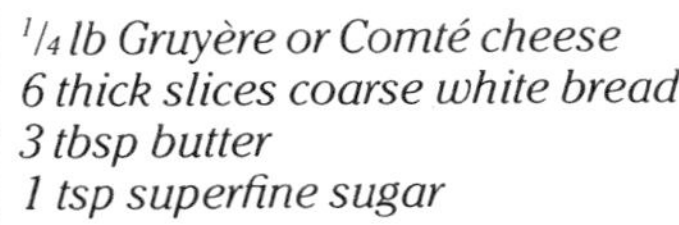
¼ lb Gruyère or Comté cheese
6 thick slices coarse white bread
3 tbsp butter
1 tsp superfine sugar

Put the veal and chicken bones in a very large kettle or saucepan with the giblets, add sufficient water to completely cover, and bring slowly to a boil. Boil gently for 20 minutes, skimming off any scum. Peel and prepare all the vegetables, leaving them whole; tie the leeks together in a bundle. When the 20 minutes are up, add the vegetables to the broth with the bouquet garni, the studded onion, peppercorns, garlic, chili pepper, and salt. Cover and simmer very gently for 2 hours.

Just over an hour before you intend serving the soup, slice the onions into thin rings and sweat in the butter in a saucepan with a tightly fitting lid for 15 minutes. While they are cooking, place the slices of bread in the oven at about 275°F to dry out and crisp without coloring. Grate the cheese. Take the lid off the onions after 15 minutes and continue to cook over gentle heat for a further 30 minutes, stirring frequently. Sprinkle in the sugar and stir until dissolved. Add the broth, bring to a boil, then simmer very gently for a final 15 minutes.

Preheat the broiler; pour the soup into a deep ovenproof bowl or casserole dish, place the bread on the surface, sprinkle the cheese all over it and place under the broiler for 5 minutes to melt and brown the surface. Serve at once.

PÂTÉ DE FROMAGE DE CHÈVRE

Goat's cheese pie

Savoie

Preparation: 25 minutes
Cooking: 45 minutes
Easy

Serves 6:
2¾ cups all-purpose flour
¾ cup sugar
4 egg yolks
¼ cup lard or shortening, diced
½ cup butter, diced
2¼ cups milk
1 thick slice cooked ham
3 small fresh goats' cheeses (weighing 2½–3 oz each)
¼ cup grated Beaufort (semihard) cheese
salt and pepper

Make the pie dough: place 2¼ cups of the flour in a mixing bowl, make a well in the center, and in it place ½ cup of the sugar, 2 egg yolks, a pinch of salt, all the lard, and ¼ cup of the butter (the fats should be slightly softened at room temperature). Mix all these ingredients together just enough to make a smooth, well blended dough. Do not knead at all. Shape into a ball, wrap, and chill while preparing the filling.

Melt 2 tbsp of the remaining butter in a saucepan, stir in the flour and, stirring continuously, cook the roux for a few minutes without allowing it to color. Continue stirring as you gradually add the milk; bring to a boil, cook for a few minutes, then remove from the heat and stir in the two remaining egg yolks.

Dice the ham and cut the goat's cheeses into thin slices; stir into the sauce, followed by the grated Beaufort. Add plenty of freshly ground pepper.

Preheat the oven to 375°F. Roll out the pastry and line a fairly deep tart pan or flan case, greased with butter. Spoon in the cheese filling and sprinkle with the remaining sugar. Bake for 45 minutes. Serve hot or cold.

SALADIER LYONNAIS*

Mixed cold platter

Lyonnais

Start preparation 24 hours in advance
Preparation: 15 minutes
Cooking: 1 hour 40 minutes
Easy

Serves 4:
For the marinade:
6 tbsp white wine vinegar
6 tbs oil (peanut or olive)

For the court-bouillon:
1 quart water
1/2 bottle dry white wine or 1/2 cup white wine vinegar
1 1/2 tbsp coarse sea salt
2 carrots, peeled
1 leek
1 stick celery
1 shallot, peeled
2 medium-sized onions, peeled, each studded with 1 clove
1 bouquet garni (thyme, bay leaf, parsley)
10 peppercorns

Cold platter ingredients:
2 fresh herring fillets
2 lamb's feet
2 trimmed chicken livers
4 hard-boiled eggs

For the dressing:
1 1/2 tbsp white wine vinegar
1 tsp strong mustard
6 tbsp peanut or olive oil
3 tbsp chopped fresh herbs
salt and pepper

The day before you plan to serve this dish, marinate the herring fillets in a bowl in the vinegar and oil.

The next day, place all the *court-bouillon* ingredients in a large saucepan (slice all the vegetables with the exception of the peeled, clove-studded onions). Skim off any scum and simmer, uncovered, for 40 minutes. Add the meticulously cleaned and washed lamb's feet, bring back to a boil and boil gently for 1 hour. When cool enough to handle, take out the lamb's feet, remove all the bones, and cut into small pieces.

Meanwhile, sauté the chicken livers in 1 1/2 tbsp oil for 5 minutes over moderately high heat. Take out and leave to cool. Cut both livers in half or quarters.

Make the vinaigrette dressing in a salad bowl; add the lamb pieces, the well drained herring fillets cut into fairly small pieces; sprinkle with the fresh herbs (such as parsley, chives, and chervil or tarragon) and mix well. Place the quartered eggs on top.

TABLIER DE SAPEUR

Breaded tripe with tartare sauce

Lyonnais

Preparation: 4 hours + 3 hours marinating
Cooking: approx. 10 minutes
Easy

Serves 4:
For the breaded, fried tripe:
1 scalded ox stomach (honeycomb tripe)
2 onions, peeled and quartered
2 carrots, peeled and sliced
2 baby turnips, peeled
2 leeks, sliced
1 small stick celery
1½ cups dry white wine
juice of 1 lemon
1 tsp strong (Dijon) mustard
6 tbsp peanut oil
salt and pepper
2 eggs, lightly beaten
½–¾ cup breadcrumbs

For the tartare sauce:
2 egg yolks
2 tsp strong mustard
1 cup peanut oil
2 gherkins, chopped
1 tsp capers, chopped
fresh herbs (parsley, chives, and chervil or tarragon)
salt and pepper

Rinse the cleaned and blanched tripe well under running cold water. Make a broth with the onions, carrots, turnips, leeks, and celery and 2 quarts water. Simmer the tripe very gently in this for 4 hours; drain, dry thoroughly, and marinate in a mixture of the wine, lemon juice, mustard, 1½ tbsp oil, salt, and pepper for 3 hours. Toward the end of this time, make the sauce: mix the egg yolks in a bowl (or a blender) with the mustard, salt, and pepper. Gradually beat in the oil, adding this in a very thin stream (use an egg beater if you do not have a blender, to give a light, thick mayonnaise-like consistency). Stir in the gherkins, capers, and herbs.

Drain the tripe, pat dry with kitchen towels, and cut into large 6-in equilateral triangles. Mix the beaten eggs with the remaining oil and an equal quantity (4½ tbsp) of cold water; dip the triangles in this and then coat all over with the breadcrumbs; shallow fry until very lightly browned on both sides in a little oil over moderately high heat.

Serve immediately with the tartare sauce.

Gnafron, a character from Lyonnais folklore, reflects the local love of good food. A cobbler, he drank like a fish and was wont to dispense such gems of wisdom as: "It is better for a man to keep warm by eating than to catch cold working," and, "At work we can only do our best but at table we should spare no effort."
According to one source, the quaintly named "tablier de sapeur" (sapper's apron) was originally called Gnafron's apron. This tripe dish acquired its present name in the mid nineteenth century from the military governor of Lyons, Field-Marshal Castellane who originally served in the Engineers' (always known as the sappers') regiment.

CAILLETTES DAUPHINOISES

Pork and chard meatballs

Dauphiné

Preparation: 30 minutes
Cooking: 20 minutes
Easy

Serves 6:
1 lb Swiss chard or spinach beet
1 stick celery
5 oz pig's liver
10 oz pork tenderloin
¼ lb fresh bacon or pork belly
3 cloves garlic, peeled
3 pigs' cauls, or as required
¼ cup lard
salt and pepper

Wash the chard or spinach beet well and boil in lightly salted water for 10 minutes with the celery. Drain, dry, then chop finely (use a food processor if wished) with the liver, pork, bacon or pork belly; and the garlic. Do not grind: chopping gives a much better consistency and taste. Season with salt and pepper.

Divide the mixture into equal portions; roll each of these into a ball (dip your hands in cold water and roll between your palms), wrap in sufficient pig's caul to cover the meat completely. Grease an earthenware or roasting dish with some of the lard; melt the remainder and pour all over the meatballs. Place in the oven, preheated to 375°F, for 20 minutes, basting the meatballs 3 or 4 times with their juices and fat. Serve hot or cold.

CERVELAS EN BRIOCHE

Saveloy in a brioche bread case

Lyonnais

Preparation: 1 hour + 2 hours rising time for the dough
Cooking: 20 minutes
Complicated

Serves 4:
1 1¾-lb imported French Cervelas sausage or a good Saveloy

For the brioche dough:
⅓ of a cake (⅙–⅕ oz) compressed fresh yeast
2½ cups all-purpose flour
3 eggs
¼ cup butter, melted
salt

Add the Cervelas sausage to a pan of gently boiling water and as soon as it nears boiling point again, lower the heat, and barely simmer for 45 minutes. Leave in the water.

Mix the yeast with 3 tbsp lukewarm water; mix in just enough of the flour to make a soft, moist starter dough, or leaven; cover with a clean, damp cloth and leave to rise at warm room temperature for 1 hour; when this time is up, place the remaining flour in a mixing bowl, make a well in the center and into it break 2 eggs; add a generous pinch of salt, the melted butter, and the leaven and combine thoroughly.

Shape this brioche dough into a ball, dust the inside of the bowl lightly with a little extra flour, cover with a clean, damp cloth and leave at warm room temperature again for 1 hour to double in bulk.

When the sausage is just cool enough to handle, take it out of the water and remove its skin carefully. Preheat the oven to 375°F. Roll out the risen brioche dough on a lightly floured board into a rectangle in which you can encase the sausage neatly, pinching the edges firmly for a tight seal without having to stretch or pull the dough.

Place seam side down on a cookie sheet greased with extra butter; beat the remaining egg and brush this all over the exposed surface of the "parcel." Bake for 20 minutes or until done and golden brown.

Serve hot, cut into thick slices with a very sharp serrated knife.

SAUCISSON OU CERVELAS À LA LYONNAISE

Sausage baked with potatoes and onions

Lyonnais

Preparation: 20 minutes
Cooking: 1½ hours
Very easy

Serves 4:
1 imported Lyons sausage (pure pork, smoked or the Lyons Cervelas sausage with truffles and pistachio nuts)
$1^1/_4$ lb new potatoes
3 onions, peeled
$^1/_4$ cup butter
salt and pepper

Peel the potatoes, rinse them, slice about $^3/_8$ in thick, and pat dry with kitchen towels.

Brown the finely sliced onions lightly in 3 tbsp of the butter, mix with the potatoes, and place in an ovenproof dish greased with butter. Season lightly with salt and freshly ground pepper. Preheat the oven to 425°F. Prick the sausage skin in several places with a needle and half bury it in the potatoes and onions. Add sufficient light broth or water to cover. Cook for $1^1/_2$ hours, sprinkling with a little more broth or water if the sausage or potatoes start to become at all dry. After 1 hour 20 minutes dot the surface with flakes of the remaining butter and allow to brown lightly.

SAUCISSON CHAUD, POMMES À L'HUILE*

Hot sausage and warm potato salad

Lyonnais

Preparation: 30 minutes
Cooking: 30 minutes
Very easy

Serves 4:
$1^1/_4$ lb new potatoes
1 $1^3/_4$-lb Lyons sausage or Cervelas (see previous recipe)

For the dressing:
2 shallots, peeled
2 tbsp white wine vinegar
2 tbsp dry white wine
$^1/_4$ cup olive or peanut oil

Place the potatoes in a pan of salted cold water, and boil in their skins for 30 minutes.

Prick the sausage skin in several places with a needle; place in a saucepan and add sufficient cold water to cover and a small pinch of salt. Bring slowly to just below boiling point and barely simmer for 25 minutes. Make the dressing, gradually adding the oil to the mixed wine and vinegar in a blender or beating with a whisk. Chop the shallots when the potatoes are nearly done. Drain the latter and peel while very hot, using a cloth to avoid burning yourself. Cut into thick slices and place in a salad bowl. Sprinkle with the shallots and the dressing.

Mix the potato salad with two salad spoons, taking care not to break up the slices. Cut the hot sausage into thick slices and arrange on a heated serving plate. Serve with the warm potato salad.

FONDUE SAVOYARDE*

Cheese fondue

Savoie

Preparation: 10 minutes
Cooking: 20 minutes
Very easy

Serves 4:
14 oz Comté or Gruyère cheese
14 oz Beaufort cheese
1 large 2–3-day old coarse white loaf or pan loaf
1 tsp potato flour
1/4 cup kirsch
1 clove garlic, peeled
1 bottle dry white wine
freshly ground white pepper

Cut the bread into 1-in cubes. Mix the potato flour well with the kirsch. Cut the garlic clove in half and rub the cut surface all over the inside of a fondue dish or a deep, fireproof casserole dish, pressing hard so that the garlic clove is gradually worn away to nothing.

Slice the cheeses and spread out in loose, uneven layers in the fondue dish. Place on a heat diffuser over low heat and melt, stirring slowly and continuously, gradually adding half the wine, a little at a time. Blend in the well mixed potato flour and kirsch and then stir in the remaining wine a little at a time. When the cheese mixture is hot and completely melted, add plenty of freshly ground white pepper.

Place the fondue dish on a fondue stand over a burner in the middle of the table. Use long-handled forks to spear bread cubes and dip them in the melted cheese mixture.

GÂTEAU DE FOIES BLONDS*

Chicken liver mousse molds

Bresse

Preparation: 20 minutes + 2 hours for marinating the chicken livers
Cooking: 15 minutes
Easy

Serves 6:
12 chicken livers
1/2 bottle dry white wine
1/2 cup butter
4 eggs
1/2 cup crème fraîche *or heavy cream*
1/4 cup cognac or brandy
salt and pepper

Clean and trim the livers thoroughly, removing all the membranes and blood vessels; place in a bowl and cover with the white wine. Leave to marinate for 2 hours then purée in the processor or blender or pound to a paste. Gradually add the butter a little at a time, processing after each addition. Do likewise with the eggs. Season with salt and pepper. Mix the cream and cognac together, add to the liver mixture and process until very smooth. Grease fairly shallow molds, ramekin dishes or timbales with butter; fill these three-quarters full with the mixture and place in a steamer over boiling water; steam for 5 minutes, partially covered, to allow some of the steam to escape, then cover each mold with a disk of waxed paper, close the lid and steam for another 10 minutes. They can also be cooked in a bain-marie at 325°F until set. Unmold if to be served hot. Can also be served cold.

CERVELAS À LA BEAUJOLAISE

Sausage with red wine sauce

Lyonnais

Preparation: 5 minutes
Cooking: 20 minutes
Very easy

Serves 4:
1 1¾-lb fresh Cervelas or Saveloy sausage
¼ cup butter
4 shallots, peeled
4 tbsp finely chopped parsley
¾ cup good, dry red wine (ideally Beaujolais)
salt and pepper

Grease a wide shallow gratin dish generously with all the butter. Chop the shallots very finely, mix with the parsley, and sprinkle over the bottom of the dish. Place the sausage, pricked in several places with a needle, on this bed and season with a little salt and plenty of freshly ground pepper. Sprinkle in the wine. Cover with a sheet of foil and place in a preheated oven at 350°F for 20 minutes.

Serve with a warm potato salad or a brown lentil salad.

RAVIOLES

Ravioli

Dauphiné

Preparation: 25 minutes + 2 hours resting time for the pasta dough
Cooking: a few minutes
Complicated

Serves 6:
2¼ cups all-purpose flour
4 eggs
pinch salt
4 tbsp finely chopped parsley
1 tbsp butter
1 fresh, drained goat's or sheep's cheese
1 cup finely grated Gruyère cheese

Prepare the pasta dough 2 hours before you plan to make the ravioli. Place the flour (a hard [durum], unbleached flour will absorb more moisture and is best for pasta) in a mixing bowl, make a well in the center, break 2 eggs into it, and add a pinch of salt.

Gradually add up to ½ cup lukewarm, lightly salted water as you stir the eggs into the flour. Mix vigorously then knead until the dough is very smooth and homogenous. Shape into a ball, cover with a slightly dampened cloth, and leave to rest for 2 hours.

Cook the chopped parsley for a few minutes in the butter over low heat. Break up the goat's cheese (weighing about 2½–3 oz) with a fork in a mixing bowl, work in the remaining 2 eggs, beating with a wooden spoon, then all but 3 tbsp of the Gruyère, the parsley, and a pinch of salt. Roll out the dough on a lightly floured working surface into a thin, rectangular sheet twice as long as it is wide. Cut in half, into 2 squares. Place teaspoonfuls of the cheese mixture at regular intervals 1¼ in apart on one sheet. Cover with the other sheet and press the two together firmly in a grid pattern between all the little heaps of filling. Cut through both layers of pastry in lines, equidistant between the heaps, again in a grid pattern, with a plain or fluted pastry wheel cutter.

Bring a large pan of chicken broth or salted water to a boil, add the ravioli, and cook for 3-5 minutes.

Drain, place in a lightly buttered or oiled serving dish, and sprinkle with the remaining Gruyère.

FISH

QUENELLES DE BROCHET*

Pike dumplings

Lyonnais

Preparation: 1 hour
Cooking: 25 minutes
Very complicated

Serves 4:
For the panada:
1 cup milk
2 tbsp butter
1/2 cup all-purpose flour
1 egg

For the fish mousse:
9 oz filleted pike
3/4 cup butter
3 whole eggs + 3 extra whites
3 1/2 cups crème fraîche
1 tsp all-purpose flour
pinch each salt, white pepper, and nutmeg

For the white sauce:
1/2 cup butter
1 cup all-purpose flour
2 1/4 cups milk
2 1/4 cups crème fraîche *or heavy cream*

Make the panada: heat the milk and butter in a saucepan and when the milk reaches boiling point, sprinkle in the flour while beating vigorously with a balloon whisk; the mixture should be completely smooth, without lumps. Draw aside from the heat. Beat in the egg. Return to a very low heat and continue beating energetically for a few minutes until the mixture is glossy and comes away cleanly from the sides and base of the pan. Set aside to cool.

Prepare the fish mousse: pound the raw filleted fish or rub through a drum sieve; do not process in a food processor or blender or grind (other types of white fish or salmon can be used but the traditional Lyonnais recipe calls for pike). Place in a mixing bowl and gradually work in the panada with a wooden spatula until perfectly blended. Melt the butter and beat into the fish mousse in a thin stream. Beat in 3 eggs, one at a time, then fold in 3 stiffly beaten egg whites. Finally fold in the cream and season with salt, freshly ground white pepper, and a very small pinch of nutmeg. Cover and chill in the refrigerator.

Make the white sauce: melt the butter gently in a saucepan; sprinkle in the flour, stirring over low heat to form a smooth roux. Gradually stir in the milk, followed by the cream; take care to scrape the spoon across the bottom of the pan to prevent the sauce catching and burning or forming lumps. Continue cooking and stirring for 10 minutes. Remove from the heat. Cover and keep warm in a bain-marie of hot water.

With 35–45 minutes to go before you plan to serve the dumplings, divide the chilled mixture into 8 equal parts; shape and roll with your palms on a lightly floured board into cylindrical, sausage-shaped pieces (see illustration below). Bring 4 quarts salted water to an extremely gentle simmer, just below boiling point. Add the dumplings and poach for 10 minutes. Have the oven preheated to 375°F, and pour the white sauce into a warmed ovenproof dish. Remove the dumplings from the water with a slotted ladle as soon as they are cooked, drain well, and arrange in the sauce. Place in the oven for 15 minutes, then serve.

OMBLE CHEVALIER À L'ANCIENNE

Baked char with mushrooms, wine, and cream

Savoie

Preparation: 20 minutes
Cooking: 20 minutes
Easy

Serves 4:
2 Arctic char or lake char, each weighing approx. 3/4 lb
1 egg
1/4 cup all-purpose flour
10 oz fresh cèpes (boletus edulis) *or 5 oz dried*
1 cup dry white wine
1/2 cup crème fraîche
1/4 cup butter
juice of 1 lemon
salt and pepper

Trim, gut, wash, and dry the fish. Pour the lightly beaten egg into a large, shallow plate and coat the fish all over, then roll in the flour, shaking off excess. Grease a large, ovenproof dish with extra butter, place the fish in it, head to tail, and season with salt and pepper.

Have the mushrooms ready cleaned if fresh, slice the caps (presoak and squeeze to get rid of excess moisture if dried) and fill the spaces around and between the fish with them. Sprinkle with the wine and lemon juice, then the cream. Dot the butter, in flakes, all over the fish and mushrooms and bake for 20 minutes at 400°F, basting frequently with the liquid in the dish.

TRUITE GRENOBLOISE
Butter-fried trout with capers, lemon, and parsley

Dauphiné

Preparation: 10 minutes
Cooking: 15 minutes
Easy

Serves 4:
4 medium-sized trout
1/2 cup butter
2 slices rye bread
2 tbsp capers
3 tbsp all-purpose flour
2 lemons, 1 divided into peeled segments
3 tbsp finely chopped parsley
salt and pepper

Gut, wash, and dry the trout. Season with salt and pepper and coat lightly with flour shaking off excess. Fry gently in the butter for about 10 minutes or until done, turning once halfway through. Transfer to a heated serving plate and keep hot, leaving all the butter behind in the pan. Cut each slice of bread into 2 triangles and brown on both sides in the butter. Place with the fish and garnish with the lemon segments (removed from their inner skin).

Add the capers, parsley, and juice of the other lemon to the remaining hot butter, heat briefly, stir, and pour over the fish.

FÉRA À LA CHABLAISIENNE
Freshwater fish with wine and tomato sauce

Savoie

Preparation: 10 minutes
Cooking: 30 minutes
Easy

Serves 4:
Any fine white-fleshed freshwater fish weighing 1 1/2–1 3/4 lb
1 clove garlic, peeled
1 shallot, peeled
2 tomatoes, peeled and deseeded
1/4 cup butter
1 1/2 cups dry white wine
juice of 1 lemon
breadcrumbs
salt and pepper

The *féra*, a lake fish of the *salmonidae* family with delicate white flesh with very few bones, is now very rare. Use any good, very fresh lake or brook fish; trim, descale if necessary, gut, wash, and dry. Chop the garlic and shallot. Chop the tomatoes coarsely. Grease an ovenproof dish liberally with butter; sprinkle the chopped mixture and the tomatoes over the bottom, place the fish on top. Season with salt and pepper.

Add the wine and lemon juice; sprinkle breadcrumbs over the fish, followed by the remaining, melted, butter. Bake in a preheated oven at 400° for 30 minutes or until the fish is done.

GRATIN DE QUEUES D'ÉCREVISSES
Freshwater crayfish in cream and white wine sauce

Dauphiné

Preparation: 30 minutes
Cooking: 30 minutes
Complicated

Serves 4:
24 freshwater crayfish
2 carrots, peeled and finely sliced
4 shallots, peeled and finely sliced
1/4 cup butter
1/2 cup cognac or brandy
1/2 cup dry white wine
1 large, ripe tomato, peeled and deseeded
1 sprig fresh thyme
1 small bay leaf
1 cup crème fraîche *or heavy cream*
1 1/2 tbsp all-purpose flour
salt and pepper

Rinse the crayfish thoroughly under running cold water; grasp the center tail flipper, give it a half twist while pulling firmly and it should come away, together with the bitter, black intestinal tract (can also be done by pulling away the whole of the last ring of shell on the tail). Sweat the carrots and shallots for 10 minutes in a very large covered saucepan with 1 1/2 tbsp of the butter. Add the crayfish, cover, and cook over high heat for 5 minutes, shaking them inside the pan.

Add the warmed cognac and flame. Stir the crayfish; pour in the wine. Add the tomato, thyme, and bay leaf; season with salt and pepper. Cover and cook for 5 more minutes.

Take the crayfish out of the pan, detach their meaty tails and keep hot while you crush the heads thoroughly in the pan (use a meat bat or wooden rolling pin). Cook for 5 minutes. Stir in the cream and when it has reached a gentle boil, strain through a fine sieve, crushing the contents to extract all the liquid. Transfer this liquid to a saucepan and heat gently; have the remaining, solid butter ready kneaded with the flour, add to the liquid, beating with a balloon whisk as it thickens and cooks for a few minutes.

Peel the crayfish tails. Pour a thin layer of the sauce into a shallow ovenproof (gratin) dish, place the tails in this and cover with the remaining sauce. Place under a preheated broiler for 2 minutes; serve.

BOEUF SAUTÉ LYONNAIS
Quick beef

Lyonnais

Preparation: 10 minutes
Cooking: 20 minutes
Very easy

Serves 4:
1¾–2 lb leftover boiled beef
2 large onions, peeled
¼ cup butter
3 tbsp finely chopped parsley
salt and pepper

This recipe is a delicious way of using up leftovers from a large piece of boiled beef. Slice the onions and cook in half the butter in a large skillet until tender but not browned; remove from the pan and set aside while you carve the beef into thin slices.

Heat the remaining butter in the skillet and sauté the beef briefly, just sufficiently to heat it thoroughly; stir in the onions and cook for a further 5 minutes over high heat. Season with salt and freshly ground black pepper and serve, sprinkled with the parsley.

Once the beef and onions have been transferred to a heated serving plate, the skillet can be quickly deglazed with a very little red wine vinegar; sprinkle the resulting juice over the beef then add the parsley.

POULARDE DEMI-DEUIL
Chicken with truffles and madeira

Lyonnais

Start preparation 48 hours in advance
Preparation: 15 minutes + 3 hours' marinating
Cooking: 4 hours
Easy

Serves 8:
1 4–4½-lb capon or plump, young chicken with giblets
3 medium or 4 small fresh or canned black truffles
¼ cup madeira
6 quarts chicken broth (see method)
8 small carrots, peeled
8 baby turnips
1 large, peeled onion studded with 1 clove
1 small stick celery
salt and pepper

If using fresh truffles clean by brushing them carefully, cut into thin slices, and place in a small bowl with a pinch each of salt, freshly ground pepper, and the madeira. Leave for 3 hours.

Cut off the last 2 joints of the chicken wings; reserve. Pierce the chicken's skin with the point of a sharp knife at various evenly spaced points all over the chicken, matching one side with the other, slitting the skin just enough to slide in the truffle slices immediately underneath the skin, flat against the underlying flesh. Chill for 48 hours in the refrigerator so that the chicken absorbs the scent and flavor of the truffles. On the day you plan to serve the chicken, make your own chicken broth with 1 fresh chicken carcass if available and the trimmed, washed giblets, wingtips, neck and 8 quarts cold water. Bring to a gentle boil and continue cooking, uncovered, for 3 hours. Add the vegetables and the chicken, securely tied in a piece of cheesecloth; simmer gently for 1 hour.

Unwrap the chicken, place (whole or jointed) on a heated serving platter surrounded by the vegetables and sprinkled with a little of the liquid. Have some coarse sea salt on the table, for people to help themselves.

POULET AU VINAIGRE
Chicken with tarragon vinegar

Lyonnais

Preparation: 5 minutes
Cooking: 45 minutes
Easy

Serves 4:
1 3¼–3½-lb capon or plump, young chicken
¼ cup butter
1 cup best tarragon vinegar
1 tsp all-purpose flour
salt and pepper

Cut the chicken into 8 pieces, using a carving knife and poultry shears. Brown these, skin side down, in ¼ cup of the butter in a large skillet over high heat for 5 minutes, then season with salt and pepper. Sprinkle with half the vinegar. Cover with a tight-fitting lid and simmer gently for 30 minutes. Transfer the chicken pieces to a heated serving dish; add the remaining vinegar to the juices in the pan; boil, uncovered, for 4 minutes. Reduce the heat to very low; have the remaining tablespoon of solid butter kneaded with the flour, stir into the liquid in the skillet with a wooden spoon and continue stirring while the sauce thickens and cooks for a few minutes.

Pour over the chicken and serve.

ENTRECÔTE BEAUJOLAISE*
Rib steaks with wine sauce

Lyonnais

Preparation: 5 minutes
Cooking: 15-20 minutes
Easy

Serves 4:
2 rib steaks, each 14 oz trimmed weight
¼ cup butter
¾ cup Beaujolais or other good dry red wine
1 medium-sized onion, finely chopped
3 shallots, finely chopped
salt and pepper

The steaks should be about 1–1½ in thick; trim off most of the fat. Season with salt and freshly ground pepper. Heat the butter in a skillet large enough to take both the steaks and cook them over moderately high heat for 5–8 minutes on each side (depending on whether you like them very rare or medium rare). Transfer them to a heated serving dish, leaving the butter behind in the skillet.

Add the onion and shallots to the skillet and fry until they are golden brown; pour in the

wine and scrape the deposits free with a wooden spoon as it boils. Add a little salt or pepper if needed and pour over the steaks. Carve the steaks at table. Paul Bocuse's version of this recipe calls for an anchovy fillet to be crushed into the browned onions and shallots; no more salt is needed.

ÉPAULE DE VEAU FARCIE À LA BUGISTE

Stuffed rolled veal shoulder

Bugey

Preparation: 30 minutes
Cooking: 2 hours 10 minutes
Complicated

Serves 4:
2¼–2½ lb boned veal shoulder
½ cup butter
1 lb flat field mushrooms or cultivated button mushrooms
¼ lb blade end of pork
¼ cup very fat fresh bacon
2 oz trimmed chicken livers
2 oz shallots, peeled
2 large sprigs parsley
1 wide, thin leaf barding fat
1 cup dry white wine
½ cup chicken broth (see glossary)
1 stick celery
1 onion, peeled and studded with 1 clove
1 cup crème fraîche *or heavy cream*
salt and pepper

Sweat ¼ lb of the mushrooms in half the butter for 5 minutes. Remove a piece weighing approx. ½ lb from the middle of the inside of the shoulder and chop this finely together with the pork, fat bacon, chicken livers, shallots, and parsley (use a processor if wished, but do not grind); add the mushrooms (leave the butter and juices behind in the pan) and chop them too; season with salt and pepper. Spread the inside of the shoulder with this mixture, roll it up, cover with the barding fat and tie securely in 3 or more places with kitchen string.

Brown the rolled shoulder all over in the remaining butter over high heat. Add the wine and broth, reduce the heat, and add the celery and onion. Add a little more salt and pepper. Cover and simmer gently for 2 hours, turning the meat after 1 hour. Ten minutes before it is done, sweat the remaining mushrooms in the butter and juices reserved in the pan. Transfer the veal to a heated serving platter and keep hot. Add the cream and the mushrooms to the veal cooking liquid and juices. Boil gently to reduce and thicken; carve the veal into thick slices and pour over the sauce.

This stuffing can be used for veal parcels (*paupiettes de veau*) which should then be wrapped in pig's caul instead of barding fat, to baste them naturally as they cook (for only 1¼ hours instead of 2, turning halfway through).

Reblochon, a delicious semisoft cheese, is made by cowherds who graze their cows on the high summer pastures in the Grand-Bornand region of the Alpine foothills. The name is said to derive from "reblâche," dialect for a second milking. The landowners in Savoy used to tax the peasants very heavily and would have their land agents measure the milk yields every milking time. The cowherds would avoid milking their cows dry, in order to finish the milking later, in secret, and make their cheeses from this clandestine milking.

DÉFARTE CRESTOISE*

Lamb's feet and tripe

Dauphiné

Preparation: 15 minutes
Cooking: 5 hours
Easy

Serves 6:
6 lambs' feet
12 4-in square pieces blanched sheeps' tripe

For the court-bouillon:
1/2 lb carrots, peeled, sliced
2 onions, peeled and sliced
2 leeks, white part only, sliced
1 stick celery, sliced
3 tbsp white wine vinegar
1 onion, peeled and studded with 1 clove
1 bouquet garni (thyme, bay leaf, parsley)
4 quarts water
salt and pepper

For the sauce:
1 onion, peeled and finely chopped
2 cloves garlic, peeled and finely chopped
1/4 cup butter
1/4 cup all-purpose flour
3/4 cup dry white wine
1 1/2 tbsp tomato paste
3 tbsp finely chopped parsley

Clean the lamb's feet very thoroughly, split lengthwise in half with a cleaver, and then tie together again with kitchen string. Add, with the tripe, to the *court-bouillon*, bring to a boil, cover, and boil gently for 4 hours. When the meat has only about 20 minutes more to cook, sweat the onion gently in the butter until tender; stir in the flour with a wooden spoon; cook this roux for a few minutes, then stir in

half the chopped garlic and parsley, the wine, just under 1/2 cup water, the tomato paste, and salt and pepper to taste. Take the lamb's feet and tripe out of the *court-bouillon*, and drain well. Untie the lamb's feet and take all flesh off the bones. Transfer the meat and tripe to a fireproof dish, pour the sauce over them and simmer gently for 1 hour. Sprinkle with the remaining finely chopped garlic and parsley and serve.

GRAS-DOUBLE LYONNAIS

Tripe with onions, parsley, and white wine

Lyonnais

Preparation: 15 minutes or 6 1/2 hours (see method)
Cooking: 30 minutes
Easy

Serves 4:
3 1/4–3 1/2 lb cleaned, scalded tripe
1/4 cup lard or butter
1 1/2 tbsp peanut oil
4 large onions, peeled
2 cloves garlic, peeled
2 tbsp butter
6 tbsp finely chopped parsley
1/2 cup dry white wine
1 tsp white wine vinegar
salt and pepper

If the tripe has been cleaned, blanched but not cooked, place in a kettle or large, heavy-bottomed saucepan with 2 quarts cold water, 2 onions, 1 clove garlic, salt and pepper. Bring to boiling point and then barely simmer for 6 hours.

Cut the tripe into thin strips and sauté these in very hot lard (or butter and oil) for a few minutes in a large saucepan. Gently fry the very finely sliced onions and the remaining, chopped, clove of garlic in 1 tbsp of butter until soft and pale golden brown. Stir in the parsley. Add these to the tripe and mix well; transfer to an ovenproof dish. Preheat the oven to 350°F.

Pour the wine into the hot pan used to fry the tripe, scraping any deposits free with a wooden spoon over high heat. Pour over the tripe and place in the oven to cook for 30 minutes.

Just before serving, stir in the vinegar.

POULARDE EN VESSIE*

Chicken cooked in a pig's bladder

Lyonnais

Start preparation 24 hours in advance
Preparation: 30 minutes
Cooking: 1 1/2 hours
Complicated

Serves 4:
1 3 1/2–4-lb capon or plump, young chicken
1 pig's bladder
3/4 cup white wine vinegar
1 bottle dry white wine or 3/4 cup madeira and 1/4 cup cognac or brandy
4 carrots, peeled
4 baby turnips, peeled
4 leeks, white part only
coarse sea salt

Wash the pig's bladder very thoroughly, turn inside out, and rinse well; marinate overnight in a small bowl of water mixed with the vinegar and coarse sea salt.

The following day, place the neatly trussed chicken inside the pig's bladder; tie one end of the pig's bladder tightly closed with kitchen string, pour the white wine or mixture of madeira and cognac into the other end and then tie up this end of the bladder tightly. Use a needle to prick the bladder at about 10 well spaced points to prevent it bursting during cooking.

Add to a kettle full of gently simmering water and barely simmer for 1 1/2 hours (the water must cover the chicken). Boil or steam the vegetables separately and arrange around the unopened chicken on a large heated serving platter. Cut open at table, and the delicious aroma will be released.

DAUBE DAUPHINOISE
Pork, veal, and beef casserole

Dauphiné

Preparation: 40 minutes + 3 hours soaking time for the tongue
Cooking: 12 hours
Fairly easy

Serves 10:
4½ lb good lean braising or stewing beef
1 lb fresh bacon rind or pork skin
3 pig's feet
1 calf's foot
1 ox tongue
6½ lb carrots
3 large onions, each studded with 1 clove
2 large, ripe tomatoes, peeled and deseeded
2 cloves garlic, peeled
3 bottles dry red wine
1 bottle dry white wine
2¼ cups chicken broth (see glossary)
2 small, red chili peppers
peel of 1 orange
1 bouquet garni (thyme, bay leaf, parsley)
salt and peppercorns
¾ cup cognac or brandy
½ cup sieved tomatoes
1 lb small button mushrooms

This gargantuan stew is also known as *daube à la boulonnière* and *marmite des Lesdiguières*.

Place the ox tongue in a large bowl to soak for 3 hours in sufficient cold water to cover mixed with white or red wine vinegar; this will eliminate any unpleasant slime or smell. You will need an extremely large, heavy kettle or cooking pot or your largest saucepan. Line the base and sides with the pieces of blanched bacon rind or pork skin, fat side placed against the surface of the cooking receptacle.

In each of two separate large saucepans, heat 2 quarts cold water to boiling; place the feet, split lengthwise in half, in one and boil for 15 minutes. Place the drained ox tongue in the other and boil gently for 20 minutes. Place the drained calf's and pig's feet and ox tongue on the lining in the bottom of the kettle or cooking pot with the beef in one piece on top (lard the beef with lardons or pork fat and a larding needle if possible), or make deep incisions in it and insert pieces of very fat bacon. Season with salt and pepper.

Add the sliced carrots and onions, placing them between and on top of the pieces of meat. Add the coarsely chopped tomatoes and the garlic cloves, crushed with the flat of a knife blade, the peppers, bouquet garni, orange peel (with no white pith on it) and the peppercorns. Pour in the red and white wine and the broth. The liquid should cover the meat; if it does not add more in the same proportions (2 parts red to 1 part white wine and ½ part broth). Cover and simmer extremely slowly for 12 hours. Check the liquid level every 2 hours, adding more in the above proportions to keep the meat covered. When the meat has cooked for 10 hours, add the cognac, sieved tomatoes and the washed, dried, and quartered mushrooms.

Just before serving remove and discard the bouquet garni, orange peel, and the onions and cloves. Carve the meat and serve with the vegetables and some of the reduced cooking liquid.

Any leftover meat can be boned where necessary, cut into smaller pieces and packed into a terrine or pâté mold; pour sufficient strained cooking liquid over them to completely cover, which will set to a jelly, making a most attractive and delicious cold dish.

Rearing the famous capons of Bresse is an art. These neutered birds are fattened on rice, wheat, and milk in the farmhouse kitchens. As the famous cook, Alain Chapel described it:
"These capons fetch a very high price, partly because of the time and skill needed to pluck them; they are not scalded or waxed before plucking and yet the feathers must be removed without tearing the skin at all. Anything but the lightest touch will mar their whiteness with a blue fingerprint-shaped bruise. A countrywoman will sometimes have to spend an entire day plucking just one chicken."

NOIX DE VEAU À L'AIXOISE
Veal with spring vegetables

Savoie

Preparation: 25 minutes
Cooking: 1¼ hours
Easy

Serves 4:
1¾–2¼-lb boneless top round of veal
2 celery hearts, trimmed
12 baby onions, peeled
12 baby carrots, peeled
12 small round new potatoes, peeled or washed
12 baby turnips
¼ cup butter
½ cup beef or chicken broth (see glossary)
3 tbsp dry white wine
salt and pepper

Prepare all the vegetables (baby root vegetables can have a little of their stalks left on), wash and dry them. Heat the butter in a large fireproof casserole dish and brown the veal all over lightly, take out and keep hot. Add all the vegetables and cook in the butter over moderately high heat for a few minutes, turning them several times. Return the meat to the casserole dish, season with salt and pepper and pour in the broth. Cover tightly and simmer for 1 hour.

Serve the veal carved into fairly thick slices (the French cut is known as the *noix*) on a heated serving platter surrounded by the vegetables. Pour the wine into the casserole dish and scrape the deposits free with a wooden spoon over high heat for a minute or two; pour over the meat.

POTÉE SAVOYARDE*
Pork and sausage casserole

Savoie

Preparation: 45 minutes
Cooking: 2½ hours
Easy

Serves eight:
¾ lb fresh or semisalted slab bacon, pork breast or pork belly
1 fresh or semisalted pork hock or tapering end of arm shoulder cut
8 small vegetable and pork or pure pork sausages or 1 large pork boiling sausage
10 oz smoked slab bacon
1 Savoy cabbage
14 oz carrots, peeled
14 oz small, waxy potatoes, peeled
½ lb baby turnips
2 onions, peeled, each studded with 1 clove
1 bouquet garni (thyme, bay leaf, parsley)
2 cloves garlic, peeled
salt and pepper

Remove the outermost leaves of the cabbage; cut out the stem and plunge the cabbage into a large pan of boiling salted water. Cook for 10 minutes, drain in a colander and immediately refresh under running cold water. Blanch any semisalted meats. Prepare all the vegetables, leaving them whole.

Arrange all the meats in a very large kettle or cooking pot, ideally earthenware or cast iron. Add the bouquet garni, the studded onions, garlic, carrots, and turnips. Season with salt and pepper; add sufficient cold water to completely cover; heat slowly to boiling, skimming off any scum; simmer gently for 1½ hours. Add the cabbage and potatoes. Simmer for a further hour. Add a little salt and pepper if necessary.

Arrange the meat, carved into slices, in a very large heated serving dish with the vegetables.

VEGETABLES

CARDONS À LA MOELLE
Cardoons with beef marrow

Lyonnais

Preparation: 15 minutes
Cooking: 1 hour
Easy

Serves 6:
2 1/4–2 1/2 lb cardoons
1 lemon
1/2 cup butter
marrow from a large beef shin bone, sawn into short sections
3 tbsp finely chopped parsley
salt and pepper

Cardoons are related to the artichoke and prized for their creamy white stalks. Trimming off the leaves and the woody sections of the stalks; cut the tender remaining portions into sections 2–4 in long.

Remove all the stringy bits from these and immediately rub with the cut surface of the lemon to prevent them discoloring. Bring a large pan containing 3 quarts salted water to a boil and add the cardoons; boil, uncovered, for 45 minutes. Drain in a colander and immediately rinse well under running cold water.

Add the well drained cardoons to a saucepan containing 1 tbsp butter, cover, and sweat over moderate heat for 5 minutes.

Preheat the oven to 450°F. Run the sharp point of a knife round the inside of the beef marrow bones and then press down on the marrow to extract it neatly. Poach in salted water for 5 minutes; drain on a clean cloth and then cut across into round slices.

Butter a wide ovenproof dish generously, place the cardoons in it, place the slices of marrow on top and dot with small flakes of butter. Place in the oven for 5 minutes; serve, sprinkled with the parsley.

GRATIN SAVOYARD*
Cheesy potatoes

Savoie

Preparation: 20 minutes
Cooking: 1 hour
Very easy

Serves 6:
2 1/4–2 1/2 lb firm waxy potatoes
1/4 cup butter
5 oz grated Beaufort (semihard) cheese
3 1/4 cups pints chicken broth (see glossary)
salt and pepper

Peel the potatoes and cut into very thin, round slices. Dry very thoroughly in a clean cloth. Grease a wide, shallow ovenproof dish with some of the butter. Preheat the oven to 350°F. Arrange the potatoes in layers, seasoning with salt and freshly ground pepper and sprinkling each layer with grated cheese.

Add the boiling hot broth. Sprinkle the surface of the potatoes with the remaining grated cheese and dot with flakes of butter. Bake, uncovered, for 1 hour.

GRATIN FORÉZIEN

Potatoes with cheese, garlic, and cream

Lyonnais

Preparation: 20 minutes
Cooking: 1½ hours
Easy

Serves 4:
2¼–2½ lb waxy potatoes
3¼ cups crème fraîche *or heavy cream*
1 clove garlic, peeled
10 oz grated Gruyère or Comté cheese
salt and pepper

Peel the potatoes, cut into very thin slices, and dry thoroughly in a clean cloth or with kitchen towels. Spread out in a gratin dish greased with butter, season the layers with salt and pepper and sprinkle with finely chopped garlic. Preheat the oven to 400°F. Heat the cream to boiling point; meanwhile sprinkle the grated cheese all over the surface of the potatoes. Pour the cream slowly over the potatoes. Bake, uncovered, for 1½ hours, turning the oven down to 375°F if the top browns too quickly.

FONDS D'ARTICHAUT AU FOIE GRAS

Artichoke hearts with foie gras

Lyonnais

Preparation: 40 minutes
Cooking: 20 minutes
Easy

Serves 4:
4 large Breton artichokes (8 if very small)
juice of 1 lemon
4 thick slices canned foie gras *(see method)*
¼ cup butter
6 tbsp madeira
salt and pepper

Trim off the stems and hard, outer layer of the artichoke bases, remove the lower leaves, and snip off the tips of the remaining leaves, covering all the cut surfaces immediately with lemon juice to prevent discoloration; add to a very large pan of boiling salted water and boil for 30 minutes. Remove and discard all the leaves and the hairy choke.

Heat the butter gently in a saucepan, add the artichoke hearts and season with salt and pepper. Add the madeira. Cover and sweat for 15 minutes over low heat. Transfer the hearts to a heated serving dish with a slotted spoon, placing them the right way up (they will look like shallow dishes) and place a thick, round disc of foie gras (cut to the size of the artichoke hearts) in each. Serve.

GRATIN DAUPHINOIS*

Potatoes with milk, cream, and garlic

Dauphiné

Preparation: 20 minutes
Cooking: 1½ hours
Easy

Serves 6:
2¼–2½ lb waxy potatoes
1 clove garlic, peeled and cut in half
¼ cup butter
1 cup rich milk
1 cup crème fraîche *or heavy cream*
salt and pepper

Peel, wash, and dry the potatoes. Cut into very thin slices; dry these thoroughly in a clean cloth. Rub the garlic hard against the inside of a wide, shallow ovenproof dish, pressing it hard against the surface so that it is gradually worn away to nothing. Grease the dish liberally with slightly softened butter. Heat the oven to 350°F.

Arrange the potato slices in layers, seasoning each of these with salt and freshly ground pepper. Mix the cream with the milk (use 1¾ cups half-and-half if preferred) and pour all over the potatoes to just cover them. Dot the surface with remaining butter, in flakes. Bake for 1½ hours.

DESSERTS

RÉZULES DE POIRES
Pastry fritters with pear filling

Savoie

Preparation: 2¼ hours
Cooking: 6–15 minutes
Easy

Serves 8:
2¼–2½ lb pears
1¾ cups preserving or granulated sugar
½ cinnamon stick
14 oz puff pastry
1 cup confectioner's sugar

Peel, quarter, and core the pears, dropping them into a deep, heavy-bottomed saucepan or fireproof casserole dish containing 1¾ cups cold water, the sugar, and the cinnamon (substitute a generous pinch of ground cinnamon if necessary).

Cover and simmer gently for 2 hours. Remove the lid, take the saucepan off the heat, and leave to cool. There should be no visible liquid left. Remove the cinnamon stick (if used).

Roll out the pastry into a sheet just under ¼ in thick. Use a 4-in diameter fluted or plain circular pastry cutter to cut into disks. Place 1 heaping tbsp of the very thick stewed pear compote in the center of half the disks, cover these with the remaining disks, moistening and pressing the edges with your fingers to seal tightly.

Either deep fry in very hot oil or lard for 6–8 minutes, then drain well, or place in a preheated oven (450°F) and cook for 15 minutes.

It used to be an old Dauphiné tradition, when baking bread, to set aside a small ball of dough to cook for the children.

*Since then it has become the custom to add various simple flavors and sugar to what was once just a fistful (*poignée*) of bread dough (for which the dialect word *pougne* is still used).*

BUGNES LYONNAISES
Lemon, rum, and vanilla fritters

Lyonnais

Preparation: 30 minutes + 3 hours resting time for the pastry
Cooking: a few minutes
Easy

Serves 4:
Peel of ½ lemon
¼ cup butter
½ cup superfine sugar
3 eggs
1½ tbsp rum
2¼ cups all-purpose flour
salt
oil for deep frying
3 tbsp vanilla-flavored confectioner's or superfine sugar

Peel off the skin of the lemon, leaving all the white pith behind; blanch half this peel in boiling water for 5 minutes. Drain, dry, and chop very finely. Beat the butter (slightly softened at room temperature) with the sugar until pale and creamy; beat in a pinch of salt, the lemon peel, the eggs (adding 1 at a time) and the rum. Stir in the sifted flour; mix this stiff dough thoroughly, adding a very little milk if it is too dry. Shape into a ball, using your hands, cover with Saran wrap, and chill in the refrigerator for 3 hours.

Divide the dough into 8 equal portions and roll each one out as thinly as possible on a lightly floured board; cut into rectangles measuring 3 × 6 in and, one at a time, lower these into very hot oil: they should puff up as they turn crisp and pale golden brown. Drain well on kitchen towels and sprinkle with vanilla sugar.

MATEFAIM
Apple and orange flower pancake

Lyonnais

Preparation: 15 minutes + 3 hours resting time for the pastry
Cooking: 30 minutes
Easy

Serves 6:
1¾ cups all-purpose flour
2 eggs
½ cup sugar
1½ tbsp peanut oil
pinch salt
1 cup milk
1½ tbsp orange flower water
4 firm apples (e.g. Rennet, Calville, Granny Smith)

Make the batter; place the flour in a large mixing bowl, make a well in the center, and break the eggs into it; gradually stir these into the flour with a wooden spoon. Mix in two thirds of the sugar, 1 tsp of the oil, and the salt. Mix very thoroughly, then gradually add the cold milk and orange flower water. See that there are no lumps. Leave to stand for 3 hours.

Just before you plan to cook the pancake, peel, core, and grate the apples into a bowl. Stir in the remaining sugar very thoroughly. Combine with the batter. Heat the rest of the oil in a very wide, non stick skillet. Mix the batter briefly and pour into the skillet. Cook for a total of 30 minutes over moderate heat, turning carefully every 8 minutes until the final 6 minutes.

Serve this thick pancake warm, sprinkled with superfine sugar or with *crème fraîche*.

CERVELLE DE CANUT*
Fresh herb cheese

Lyonnais

Preparation: 15 minutes
Very easy

Serves 4:
14 oz fresh white cheese
2 shallots (or 1 Bermuda red onion) peeled
1 clove garlic, peeled
5 sprigs each parsley (flat-leaved if possible), chervil, tarragon
1 small bunch chives
½ cup olive oil
½ cup dry white wine
1 cup crème fraîche *or heavy cream*
salt and pepper

Drain the cheese if there is a lot of whey with it; beat well in a mixing bowl, then beat in the very finely chopped shallots, garlic, and whatever fresh herbs are available as listed above. Continue beating as you gradually add the oil, then the wine, salt, and freshly ground pepper. Beat the cream and fold into the cheese mixture. Transfer to a serving bowl and chill in the refrigerator, taking it out just before serving.

If a little oil should ooze out onto the surface, beat again briefly.

BRIOCHE DE SAINT-GENIX

Sweet yeast bread

Savoie

Start preparation 24 hours in advance
Preparation: 50 minutes
Cooking: 45 minutes
Easy

Serves 6:
$^3/_4$ cake compressed fresh yeast
$4^1/_2$ cups all-purpose flour
2 tbsp sugar
pinch salt
6 eggs
$3^3/_4$ sticks (2 cups) butter
$^1/_2$ lb pink pralines (knobbly sugared almonds)

Make the brioche dough the day before: mix the yeast with $^1/_2$ cup lukewarm water. Place the flour in a mixing bowl, make a well in the center and pour the dissolved yeast into it, add the sugar, salt, and the eggs. Stir with the fingers of your slightly cupped hand held together or with a wooden spoon, gradually incorporating all the flour. Work the dough, slapping it against the sides of the bowl until it is smooth and elastic; work in $3^1/_4$ sticks ($1^3/_4$ cups) of the butter, softened or kneaded and cut into small pieces. Work well to blend thoroughly. Cover the bowl with a cloth and leave to stand in a warm place. When the dough has doubled in bulk, knock down with the flat palm of your hand, return to the bowl, cover with a dampened cloth and chill in the refrigerator overnight.

The following day, work three quarters of the pralines evenly into the dough, shape into a ball and place in a large brioche mold greased with butter. Preheat the oven to 400°F. Leave the dough to rise again for 30 minutes in a warm place then bake for 45 minutes.

The invention of the Savoy sponge cake is said to date back to the end of the fourteenth century when the chief pastrycook at the court of Amédée VI, Count of Savoy, served the delicacy at a banquet in honor of Count Amédée's overlord, the Holy Roman Emperor. So impressed was the illustrious guest by this featherlight cake, that he promptly appointed his host to the important post of Imperial Vicar-General.

GÂTEAU DE SAVOIE*

Savoy sponge cake

Savoie

Preparation: 15 minutes
Cooking: 40 minutes
Easy

Serves 6:
4 eggs, separated
$^1/_2$ cup superfine sugar
2 tbsp vanilla sugar or a few drops pure vanilla extract
$^1/_2$ cup all-purpose flour
$^1/_2$ cup potato flour
2 tbsp butter
2 tbsp confectioner's sugar

Preheat the oven to 350°F. Place the yolks in a mixing bowl with the superfine sugar and the vanilla sugar or vanilla essence. Beat with a balloon whisk until the mixture is very pale and creamy and forms an unbroken flat ribbon when dropped from the whisk or beater into the bowl. Sift in the flour a little at a time, stirring in gently but thoroughly; do likewise with the potato flour. Beat the eggs until stiff but not dry; fold them into the cake batter using a mixing spatula to avoid crushing out the air.

Grease a rectangular, square or round shallow cake or sponge sandwich pan and sprinkle the granulated sugar all over the buttered surface; turn the mixture into it, making sure the level comes only two thirds of the way up the sides of the pan. Bake for 40 minutes. Test by inserting the point of a knife into the center of the cake; if it comes out clean the cake is done.

Turn out of the pan carefully, leave to cool on a cake rack and serve with whipped cream or jam.

POGNE DE ROMANS

Sweet bread ring

Dauphiné

Preparation: 15 minutes + 6 hours resting time for the the dough
Cooking: 30 minutes
Complicated

Serves 6:
1 tbsp salt
$^1/_2$ cup sugar
$1^1/_2$ cakes compressed fresh yeast
$4^1/_2$ cups all-purpose flour
3 tbsp orange flower water
6 eggs
$1^1/_4$ cups butter
$1^1/_2$ tbsp extra flour for shaping the dough
$1^1/_2$ tbsp peanut oil

Pour just under $^1/_2$ cup lukewarm water into a bowl, stir in the salt, 2 tbsp of the sugar, and the yeast until they have dissolved. Sift 1 cup of the flour into a mixing bowl and gradually stir the yeast mixture into it to make the starter dough or leaven.

Cover with a damp cloth and leave in a warm place to double in volume, then mix the remaining flour and sugar in a large mixing bowl. Make a well in the center, pour in the orange flower water and stir into the flour and sugar, followed by the eggs, adding one at time. Blend in the leaven; knead the dough, slapping it against the sides of the bowl until it is smooth and elastic and no longer sticks to your fingers. Work in the butter, still solid but softened at room temperature or kneaded. Shape into a ball and leave to rise for 2 hours in the bowl, covered with a damp cloth in a warm place.

Knock down the risen dough with floured hands. Shape into a ball again, cover, and leave to rise once more, this time for 4 hours.

Flour your hands again and push your thumbs down into the center of the dough, pulling it away from this central hole to form a ring. Leave to rise again for 30 minutes.

Dip the tip of a knife blade in water and make slanting slashes all round the top of the ring. Bake for 30 minutes or until a thin skewer or trussing needle pushed deep into the cake comes out clean and dry. Three smaller rings can be made instead of a single large one and the baking time adjusted.

Massif central

Bourbonnais
Auvergne
Velay
Vivarais
Gévaudan
Rouergue
Limousin
Marche

Despite being situated right in the center of France, this high plateau has until modern times been relatively inaccessible, cut off from the rest of the country, with all the important trade and communication routes skirting round it. The Massif Central is a patchwork of old and historically very isolated provinces: Bourbonnais, Velay, and Vivarais in the east; Gévaudan and Rouergue in the south; to the west Limousin and Marche, and Auvergne at its center.

With the exception of some fortunate areas, the soil here is thin and lacking in fertility, and much of the region has always been poor, reflected in the raw materials used in its cooking. The inventiveness of the inhabitants has, however, more than compensated for the deficiencies of nature.

On the previous pages: *the fertile Limagne plain is bordered by the high Auvergne hill country and lends itself to mixed farming: among the arable crops, cereals predominate, mainly wheat with barley and corn, all grown on a large scale by European standards.* Above: *the fortified Château de Val's fifteenth-century towers are reflected in the lake formed by the Bort-les-Orgues dam.*

The variety of basic foodstuffs and products may not be very wide but those available are of fine quality. Freshwater fish are still plentiful in most of the lakes, streams, and rivers of the region, saved from over-exploitation by depopulation (people continue to leave the land in large numbers, moving away from the countryside to seek more remunerative work in the towns and cities elsewhere in France).

Good grazing is to be had on the grassy plains of the Aubrac and Millevaches plateaux and in the *causses* of Rouergue and Gévaudan; beef cattle are reared in the Limousin and Salers regions, while the sheep farmers of Larzac and Brioude produce lamb and mutton.

Besides fattening these animals for meat,

Above: *haymaking on the western slopes of the Massif central.* Left: *milk warm from the cows is poured through cheesecloth stretched over deep, narrow vats called "gerles." Milk from a single milking of thirty cows is needed to make one Cantal cheese.*

dairy cows and ewes are kept, their milk used to make superb cheeses such as Saint-Nectaire, Murols; the *Fourmes* d'Ambert and Montbrison, the Bleu d'Auvergne and des Causses (blue cheeses), Cantal and Laguiole, all of which are made with cow's milk while ewe's milk is used for the incomparable and inimitable Roquefort. Excellent goat's milk cheeses are also produced in this region.

The local culinary repertoire is rustic, peasant cooking typified by the cabbage soup of Auvergne and hearty stew-like soups for which the ingredients vary in different parts of the Massif Central. The Bourbonnais pork scratchings and pastry (or bread dough) ring reflects the frugal habits of local countrywomen, using up leftovers and baking them into delicious, substantial dishes. The same principle of making do with very little has resulted in the rather heavy dumplings made with crisp pieces of fat bacon and flour or potato, the Limousin *farcidures*.

The poor peasant origin of most of the area's recipes results in such economical, filling and nourishing dishes as Limousin chestnut soup and hog's jowls with lentils from Velay, while the Auvergne's specialties include *pounti* (a mixture of chopped fat bacon, cured raw ham, chard and herbs mixed with flour and eggs), and *falette* (stuffed, boned veal breast); the equally sustaining *Aligot* (a potato purée mixed with fresh, melted Cantal cheese) comes from Rouergue; *pouytrolle* (stuffed pig's stomach or tripe) and *caillettes* (pork variety meat and spinach pie from Vivarais), to say nothing of the Gévaudan's lamb's heads (*cabassols*).

Many of the region's dishes may reflect their simple rural origins in their lack of sophistication, but they more than make up for this in fine and well-balanced flavors.

Looking westward across the wide Artense granite plateau toward the Dordogne, a farming landscape with both arable land and grazing pastures, hedgerows, spinneys and copses, kept well watered and green by numerous rivers such as the Rhue and the Tarentaine. This is good dairying and meat livestock rearing country.

Good examples of this flair for enhancing unexciting basic ingredients are provided by the Auvergne dish *tripous*, little mutton or veal tripe parcels filled with meat and herb stuffing, sometimes cooked with sheeps' or lambs' feet. Leg of lamb *Brayaude* style emerges in triumph from its long, slow simmering.

The most exacting gourmets enjoy *poulet au fromage* (chicken with a velvety cheese sauce) and the Rouergue dish of *estofinado*, a distant cousin of Nice's *stoficada*, made with dried salt cod. The Bourbonnais method of preparing hare and duck "*à la Duchambais*" with a sauce made with vinegar, cream, and shallots results in a dish to rival the finest regional cooking in France.

The Vivarais wines deserve a mention (Cornas, Saint-Joseph, Saint-Péray) while the

desserts of the Massif Central are delicious: Limousin's renowned fruit flans, made with cherries (*clafoutis*), or apples or prunes or pears (*flognarde*). Vivarais is famous for marrons glacés (candied chestnuts) and Auvergne for sweet pastries and cakes: *cornets de Murat*; cookies such as *sablés de Salers* and *croquants* from Mauriac. Some of France's best brioches are said to be baked in Riom and Gannat.

A sumptuous sweet walnut pastry pie with the quaint name of *piquenchagne* is a traditional specialty of the Bourbonnais, filled with pears, redcurrant jelly, and cream.

If the enthusiastic gourmet finds he or she has been a little too self-indulgent in tasting and savoring all these substantial dishes, the elegant spa town of Vichy is close at hand where the medicinal waters will soon restore the greediest visitors' appetites and make them feel fit and ready to set out again on their gastronomic adventures.

Above: *tourists provide a very important source of revenue, attracted by the dramatic scenery of the Gorges du Tarn region; visitors can reach these deep ravines by car, on foot, or navigate the twists and turns of the river by boat or in kayak canoes. As the Tarn winds its way through the gorges it has worn away, sheer rock faces tower above the river over 300ft in places.* Left: *flocks of sheep graze the slopes of Puy de Laschamp to the south of the famous Puy de Dôme national park.*

SOUPE AUX CHOUX*

Boiled bacon, pork, and vegetables

Auvergne

Start preparation 24 hours in advance
Preparation: 25 minutes
Cooking: $2^1/_4$ hours
Easy

Serves 6:
$1^1/_4$ lb salt pork, boned and rolled (Boston butt or shoulder butt, blade end or picnic shoulder, or breast or belly)
1 large onion, peeled, studded with 1 clove
1 salted knuckle raw ham
2 green cabbages
10 oz carrots, peeled
3 leeks, white part only
$1^1/_2$ tbsp lard
1 bouquet garni (thyme, bay leaf, parsley)
1 pork boiling sausage
$1^1/_4$ lb firm waxy potatoes
thick slices coarse rye bread
salt and pepper

The day before you plan to cook this dish, soak the salt pork and ham separately in plenty of cold water to eliminate the excess salt. The following day, drain, rinse, and place in a very large kettle or saucepan with the clove-studded onion. Add enough cold water to completely cover the meat, bring to a boil, turn down the heat, cover, and leave to boil gently for 10 minutes.

Remove and discard the outer leaves of the cabbages, remove their stems, quarter, and blanch in a large pan of boiling water for 5 minutes. Drain and refresh under running cold water in a colander.

When the meat has cooked for 10 minutes, skim off any scum and add the cabbages, carrots, bouquet garni, and lard. Cover and leave to simmer for 1 hour.

Add the sausage, the peeled potatoes, and the leeks. Simmer for a further hour.

Pour off most of the liquid and serve as a soup (do not strain), ladling it onto bread slices placed in heated soup bowls, then serve the meats and vegetables as the main course.

SOUPE AU CANTAL

Cheese, bread, and onion soup

Auvergne and Rouergue

Preparation: 15 minutes
Cooking: 1 hour 10 minutes
Easy

Serves 6:
6 onions, peeled
2 tbsp butter or lard
1½ quarts broth (see glossary)
½ lb coarse rye bread
10 oz fresh, unmatured Cantal cheese
salt and pepper

Slice the onions very finely and brown lightly in the butter or lard in a large saucepan. Add the broth, a pinch of salt, and plenty of freshly ground pepper. Cover and boil gently for 30 minutes. Cut the bread into thin slices and slice the cheese very thinly. Arrange the bread and cheese in alternating layers in a deep, ovenproof tureen or casserole dish. Pour the broth and onions all over them, cover and place in the oven, preheated to 300°F and leave for 30 minutes.

The liquid will soak into the bread, which will have disintegrated by the time you take the "soup" out of the oven.

SOUPE AUX MARRONS

Chestnut soup

Limousin

Preparation: 10 minutes
Cooking: 1 hour 10 minutes
Easy

Serves 6:
2 leeks, white part only
1 onion, peeled
2 tbsp butter
24 prepared fresh or dried sweet chestnuts (see method)
2 sprigs fresh thyme
1 small stick celery
1 quart broth (see glosssary)
1 cup crème fraîche *or heavy cream*
4 toasted slices coarse white bread
salt and pepper

Trim, wash, and slice the leeks. Slice the onion finely. Sweat the leeks and onion in the butter in a large saucepan for 10 minutes until very tender; do not brown at all.

If using fresh chestnuts, have them ready peeled (both the tough outer casing and the bitter thin skin) or use dried chestnuts, soaked in water overnight and drained. Add to the saucepan; pour in the broth, and add the thyme and celery. Season with salt and pepper. Bring to a boil and then boil gently for 45 minutes.

Remove and discard the thyme and celery; pour the contents of the saucepan through a vegetable mill into a clean saucepan, reducing the vegetables and chestnuts to a purée. Reheat the soup over moderate heat; gradually stir in the cream, adding a little at a time. Simmer for 10–15 minutes and then ladle onto the slices of toast in heated soup bowls.

Saffron, the dried pistils of a variety of crocus, is the world's costliest spice. Used in a number of dishes in central and southwestern French cooking, it is thought to have been introduced by the Moors when they invaded southwestern France from Spain. Their dreams of conquest were shattered by Charles Martel in 732 when his army defeated the Moslem invaders at Poitiers. Saffron may well be the spice referred to as karkhom in the Bible.

During the Middle Ages it was one of the ingredients used in concoctions sold as love potions.

ENTRÉES

POMPE AUX GRATTONS

Bacon and pastry ring

Bourbonnais

Preparation: 20 minutes
Cooking: 1 hour
Easy

1 lb sliced smoked bacon
3½ cups all-purpose flour
3 eggs
¼ cup butter
pinch of salt
just under 1 cup boiled, cooled milk

Cut the bacon across the lines of fat and lean into short strips. Fry these until crisp and brown. Drain well and dry with kitchen towels. (The original recipe uses up pieces of pork called *grattons* left over from home-rendered pork fat). Make the pastry dough: place the flour in a mixing bowl, make a well in the center and add the eggs one at a time, mixing each one into the flour before adding the next. Add the butter, softened at room temperature and cut into small pieces. Work into the flour and egg mixture. Add the cold milk a little at a time to make a smooth dough; knead in the crisp bacon pieces.

Shape the dough into a ring on a greased cookie sheet and place in the oven, preheated to 400°F. Bake for 1 hour.

OMELETTE BRAYAUDE

Cheese, ham, and potato omelet

Auvergne

Preparation: 10 minutes
Cooking: 30 minutes
Easy

Serves 6:
½ lb waxy potatoes
7 oz raw cured Auvergne ham
¼ lb Cantal cheese
3 tbsp lard
9 eggs
2 tbsp butter
3 tbsp crème fraîche *or heavy cream*
pepper

Peel, wash, and dice the potatoes then dry them in a clean cloth. Dice the ham (substitute

Parma ham if necessary). Cut the cheese into wafer-thin slices.

Heat the lard in a very wide skillet over high heat, add the potatoes, and fry for 5 minutes, turning as they brown. Cover, reduce the heat to very low, and cook for 15 minutes, shaking the pan from time to time to prevent the potatoes catching and burning. Add the diced ham and stir gently to distribute evenly among the potatoes. Cover and leave to cook while you beat the eggs with freshly ground pepper and then stir in the butter, softened at room temperature and cut into very small pieces. Pour this mixture (with the butter pieces still solid) all over the potatoes and ham. When the omelet is lightly browned underneath, draw aside from the heat, place a large, round plate on top and turn the skillet upside down; slide the omelet back into the skillet to brown the other side lightly.

Sprinkle the piping hot omelet with the cream and cheese slivers and serve immediately, cut into wedges.

OMELETTE AU ROQUEFORT*

Roquefort cheese omelet

Rouergue

Preparation: 10 minutes
Cooking: approx. 5 minutes
Very easy

Serves 6:
2½ oz Roquefort cheese
¼ cup crème fraîche *or heavy cream*
9 eggs
2 tbsp butter

Place the coarsely crumbled cheese and the cream in a heatproof bowl over simmering water or in the top of a double boiler; stir as you heat the mixture until the cheese has completely melted.

Beat the eggs with a balloon whisk and pour into a wide skillet coated with the hot butter. As soon as the eggs start to set, pour the cheese mixture all over the surface, mixing carefully with the tine tips of a fork to blend with the liquid egg on the surface.

When the omelet is done (completely set underneath, still creamy on top) slide onto a heated serving plate and fold over, in half (see below).

The word "brayaude" which appears in the name of many of the regional dishes of the Auvergne is derived from the old word for the short pants worn by the ancient Gauls. The Auvergne was the native province of the barbarian Arverne tribe, of which Vercingetorix was chieftain, beaten by Julius Caesar in the Battle of Alesia; all his troops would have worn these breeches as everyday apparel.

FEUILLETÉ AU ROQUEFORT
Roquefort pastries

Rouergue

Preparation: 10 minutes (+ time for making the pastry)
Cooking: 30 minutes
Easy

Serves 6:
4 1/2 cups all-purpose flour
2 1/4 cups butter
1 lb 2 oz Roquefort cheese
1 egg yolk
1/4 cup milk

Make the puff pastry dough (see glossary for method) or use thawed frozen puff pastry dough. Roll out into a sheet about 1/8 in thick on a lightly floured working surface; cut into 6-in squares; cut the Roquefort into thin, rectangular slices (it does not matter if it crumbles) and place a piece on one side of each square, leaving a wide border round the sides and the other side of the square empty; fold the uncovered half of each square over the cheese and press the 3 cut edges together firmly. Trace a lattice pattern on the surface of each pastry by running the point of a sharp knife lightly over it in a criss-cross design. Brush the surface with the beaten egg and milk mixture.

Place the pastries, well spaced out, on 1 or 2 lightly floured cookie sheets and bake for 30 minutes, or until puffed up and deep golden brown.

FARCIDURE
Cheese, egg, and potato cake

Limousin and Marche

Preparation: 20 minutes
Cooking: 30 minutes
Easy

Serves 6:
12 potatoes
2 eggs
1/4 cup grated Cantal cheese
1 clove garlic, peeled
1 thick slice raw cured Auvergne ham or Parma ham
1/4 cup peanut oil
salt and pepper

Peel the potatoes and grate them onto a clean, dry cloth; blot them dry thoroughly with the cloth and place in a mixing bowl with a little salt and plenty of freshly ground pepper.

Beat the eggs with a balloon whisk and mix with the grated potatoes. Stir in the grated cheese and the minced garlic, followed by the finely chopped ham. Heat the oil in a large skillet over moderate heat. Add the mixture and cook until the underside is lightly browned; turn carefully (see method of *Omelette Brayaude* on page 165) and brown the other side. Serve immediately.

RISSOLES DE SAINT-FLOUR*
Pastry fritters with cheese filling

Auvergne

Preparation: 20 minutes + 3 3/4 hours for the pastry
Cooking: a few minutes
Easy

Serves 6:
4 1/2 cups all-purpose flour
1 1/4 cups butter
pinch salt
3/4 cup grated Cantal cheese
few chives
1 small bunch fresh chervil
3 eggs
1 cup fromage frais *(soft cow's milk cheese)*
salt and pepper

Make the shortcrust pie dough: place the flour in a mixing bowl, make a well in the center and in it place the butter, cut into small dice, and the salt. Rub or cut the fat into the flour and add just enough cold water for a firm dough. Work the dough as little as possible, just enough to make sure it is homogenous and no longer sticks to your fingers (it should not be elastic); shape into a ball and leave in the lightly floured bowl, covered with a cloth, in the refrigerator for 3 hours.

Mix the Cantal with the finely chopped chives and chervil in a mixing bowl; work in the *fromage frais* and the eggs until very smooth.

Roll out the pie dough into a sheet just over 1/8 in thick. Cut out into disks 4 in in diameter. Place a small, slightly flattened ball of the cheese mixture slightly to one side of the center of each disk, fold the free half-circle over to make a pasty or turnover, sealing the edges very carefully.

Chill in the refrigerator for 45 minutes; shortly before you intend serving the fritters, heat plenty of oil in a deep fryer until very hot (350°F) and fry a few at a time until crisp and golden brown. Drain well and keep hot, uncovered, on kitchen towels in the oven while you fry the rest. Serve immediately.

FISH

ESTOFINADO*

Stockfish with potatoes and garlic

Rouergue

Start preparation 4 days in advance
Preparation: 30 minutes
Cooking: 40 minutes
Easy

Serves 6:

2¼–2½ lb stockfish (dried salt cod) or dried cod
1 bouquet garni (thyme, bay leaf, parsley)
2¼–2½ lb potatoes
5 eggs
6 cloves garlic, peeled
1 bunch parsley
½ cup walnut oil
1 cup crème fraîche *or heavy cream*
salt and pepper

Place the stockfish in a large bowl of water and soak for 4 days or change the water frequently. If you cannot buy stockfish, use dried cod and soak for 36 hours, changing the water 2 or 3 times. Place the fish in a large saucepan of cold water with the bouquet garni; bring slowly to a boil, cover, and immediately remove from the heat; leave to stand for 20 minutes.

Wash the potatoes well and boil them in their skins for 20–30 minutes, depending on their size. Hard boil 3 of the eggs (boil for 10 minutes) and cool quickly under running cold water. Chop the garlic and parsley finely. Peel the potatoes while still hot, transfer them to a deep heatproof dish standing in simmering water and crush them coarsely with a fork or potato masher. Remove the skin and bones from the stockfish and break up into small flakes, mixing roughly with the potato with a wooden fork. Heat the oil and cream separately in 2 small saucepans over low heat.

Stir the chopped garlic and parsley and the 2 remaining, lightly beaten eggs into the fish and potato mixture. Season with a little salt and plenty of freshly ground pepper. Keep stirring the mixture as you add the hot oil in a very slow trickle, then the cream. Cut each of the peeled hard-boiled eggs lengthwise into 8 sections and place these on top of the fish mixture. Take the dish out of the bain-marie and serve very hot, straight from the dish.

MEAT

TRIPOUS
Tripe parcels simmered in white wine sauce

Auvergne and Rouergue

Preparation: 30 minutes
Cooking: 8 hours
Complicated

Serves 6:
1 calf's stomach (rumen section of tripe)
8 lambs' feet
2¼ lb calf's sweetbreads
½ lb hog's jowl
½ lb pork breast or belly
8 oz raw cured ham
5 oz onions, peeled
6 cloves garlic, peeled
1 bunch parsley
sufficient fresh pork skin to line a large casserole dish
1 bouquet garni (thyme, bay leaf, parsley)
2 cloves
½ bottle dry white wine
2 quarts light broth (see glosssary)
salt and pepper

Buy the tripe, lamb's feet, and sweetbreads ready cleaned and blanched from the butcher if possible. Cut the tripe into eight matching rectangular pieces, each about 6 × 3 in, fold in half, and sew up 3 sides with a large needle and linen thread to make bags measuring 3 in square. Take the flesh off the lamb's feet and dice.

Use a sharp, heavy kitchen knife to coarsely chop the sweetbreads, hog's jowl, the breast or belly of pork (remove the skin and cartilage), the ham, offcuts from the tripe, ¼ lb of the onions, the garlic, and parsley. Mix with the diced flesh from the lamb's feet and season well with salt and pepper. Fill each tripe bag loosely with one eighth of this mixture and sew up the open side.

Line the inside of a deep, heavy fireproof casserole dish (earthenware or cast iron is traditional) with the pork skin, fat side against the surface of the casserole dish; place the tripe bags in a single layer. Add the bouquet garni, the remaining onions (quartered and studded with the cloves), the wine, and broth. Make a hermetic seal for the lid by using a luting paste of flour and water. Cook at 275°F for 8 hours.

FALETTE*
Stuffed, rolled veal breast

Auvergne

Preparation: 25 minutes + 2 hours for soaking the raisins
Cooking: 2 hours
Easy

Serves 6:
7 oz seedless white raisins
1 lb hog's jowl
¾ lb pork breast or belly
¾ cup chopped parsley
¼ lb stale bread soaked in milk
3 eggs
pinch each of salt, pepper, and nutmeg
4½ lb boned veal breast, in one piece
½ cup lard
½ lb onions, peeled
1 clove garlic, peeled
1½ cups dry white wine
1½ cups broth
1 bouquet garni (thyme, bay leaf, parsley)

Soak the seedless white raisins in lukewarm water then drain. Finely chop the hog's jowl and pork breast or belly with the parsley and well-squeezed breadcrumbs. Place in a large mixing bowl and stir in the eggs and the drained raisins. Season well with salt and pepper and a small pinch of nutmeg. Insert a sharp knife between the layers of flesh and membrane, dividing the thickness of the veal breast as close to the center as possible; stop short of the sides and far end so that the meat forms a large, long bag or pocket. Fill this evenly with the prepared mixture and sew up the open edge.

Heat 1½ tbsp of the lard in a roasting pan, place the stuffed breast of veal in it and turn to coat with fat; place in the oven, preheated to 375°F, for 45 minutes to brown well (do not cover). Sprinkle with a little salt when this time is up.

Brown and cook the sliced onions and crushed garlic clove in the remaining lard in a large ovenproof casserole dish; place the breast of veal on top, add the wine and broth, and the bouquet garni. Cover and return to the oven for a further 1¼ hours. Take out of the oven and leave to stand for 5 minutes before removing the trussing thread from the ends of the roll. This dish is traditionally served with green lentils from Puy but small brown lentils, cooked until tender, are a good substitute.

CHOU FARCI*

Cabbage stuffed with beef and pork

Auvergne

Preparation: 45 minutes
Cooking: 1 hour
Complicated

Serves 6:
1 large, green cabbage
1¾ lb boiled or casseroled beef leftovers
1 lb Boston butt or bone, rolled shoulder of pork
½ lb onions, peeled
3 shallots, peeled
1 clove garlic
1 small bunch parsley
1 sprig thyme
2 eggs
5 oz pig's caul
salt and pepper

For the cooking liquid:
2 carrots, peeled
2 large onions, peeled
1 cup beef stock
3 tbsp butter

Remove and discard the outermost leaves of the cabbage. Blanch the whole cabbage in a large pan of boiling salted water for 15 minutes. Place upside down in a colander and rinse well under running cold water.

Make the stuffing: process the meat with the onions, shallots, garlic, parsley, and thyme in the food processor until finely chopped. Add the eggs and salt and pepper and process until very well blended.

Open out the outer layer of leaves, easing them away very carefully to avoid breaking them off, just enough to enable you to remove the next layer or two of leaves, detaching them from the base and laying them flat, in order of size, on a clean cloth; cut out the heart of the cabbage from the stem with a sharp knife and "replace" it with a ball of meat stuffing of matching size. Surround this ball with the smallest of the leaves you have removed and laid out on the cloth, in their natural order. Place some of the meat carefully on the remaining detached leaves, spreading it out a little and replace the leaves in the correct order, so the cabbage is restored (approximately) to its original appearance. The heart can be used for another dish.

Heat the oven to 425°F. Rinse the caul after soaking it in vinegar and water, drain, and spread out flat on a large, clean, dry cloth.

Hold the cabbage securely and place upside down in the center of the caul; wrap the cabbage in it, then wrap in the cloth, squeezing gently to remove any remaining water. Heat the butter in a large, deep fireproof casserole dish; cook the sliced onions and carrots until browned, add the broth and the cabbage, having first removed the cloth (but not the caul). Cover and place in the oven to cook for 1 hour.

Remove the cabbage, draining well, and carefully take off the caul. Serve on a heated platter, cut into slices like cake.

MOURTAYROL*

Saffron soup and chicken poached with vegetables

Auvergne and Rouergue

Preparation: 10 minutes
Cooking: 2½ hours
Very easy

Serves 6:
1 4-lb chicken
4 leeks
2 carrots, peeled
3 medium-sized onions, peeled, each studded with 2 cloves
1 baby turnip
generous pinch real saffron powder
6 slices 2-day old French bread
salt and pepper

If you wish to stuff the chicken, use a lightly seasoned and flavored stuffing and sew up both ends. Place the chicken in a deep, fireproof casserole dish or cooking pot with the vegetables around it, add sufficient cold water to cover and bring to a boil. Reduce the heat and season with salt and pepper. Simmer gently for 2½ hours, removing any scum that rises to the surface. Take the chicken and vegetables out of the casserole dish and transfer to a heated serving dish; keep hot. Strain the cooking liquid and stir in the saffron; serve this broth as a first course, ladling it onto the bread slices placed in heated soup bowls. Serve the chicken and vegetables as the main course.

GIGOT BRAYAUDE

Lamb leg with vegetables and garlic

Auvergne

Preparation: 15 minutes
Cooking: 4¼ hours
Easy

Serves 8:
1 4½-lb lamb leg
3 cloves garlic
1½ tbsp lard

2 carrots, peeled
2 onions, peeled
3/4 cup lamb or vegetable broth
salt and pepper

Have the leg part boned by your butcher, removing the tail and hipbone in one piece (which you can use to make the stock) leaving the bone that juts out at the thin, tapering end in place. Trim off all the thick fat. Peel 2 garlic cloves, cut lengthwise in quarters and insert these into deep, narrow, well spaced incisions in the lamb flesh. Tie the boned section of the lamb so that it keeps its shape during cooking. Heat the lard in a fireproof casserole dish large enough to take the lamb leg; brown the leg well all over, add the third garlic clove, unpeeled, and the sliced onions and carrots. Cook until browned.

Add the hot broth. Cover tightly and place in the oven, preheated to 325°F and cook for 4 1/4 hours. Carve and serve with the vegetables. Other traditional accompaniments include red kidney beans, cooked until very tender, or braised cabbage or lentils.

JAMBON À L'AUVERGNATE

Glazed ham

Auvergne

Preparation: 15 minutes + 12 hours for soaking raw ham
Cooking and glazing: 2 3/4 hours
Complicated

Serves 12:
1 8 1/2–9-lb raw smoked, salted ham
2 carrots, peeled, sliced
2 onions, peeled, 1 studded with 4 cloves
2 leeks, white part only
1 1/2 quarts dry white wine
1 bouquet garni (thyme, bay leaf, parsley)
5 peppercorns
1 1/4 cups veal broth (see glossary), reduced
1/2 cup confectioner's sugar

Soak the ham in plenty of cold water for 12 hours, making sure it is completely immersed.

Transfer the ham to a very large kettle or saucepan, add sufficient cold water to cover and bring to a boil. While the water is heating, slice the carrots and 1 onion; leave the leeks in large pieces. As soon as the water boils, take the ham out of it and discard the water. Rinse the kettle, return the ham to it with 3 quarts cold water, 1 quart of the wine, the carrots, sliced onion, whole clove-studded onion, leeks, and bouquet garni.

Bring slowly to a boil and reduce the heat so that the liquid barely simmers; cover and cook for 1 1/2 hours, then add the peppercorns and cook for a further 30 minutes. Preheat the oven to 400°F. Take the ham out of the liquid and place on a large chopping board; remove all the skin and much of the fat, leaving a covering layer only about 3/8 in thick. Transfer the ham to a very large roasting pan or shallow ovenproof dish, pour 1 1/4 cups of the remaining wine mixed with the veal stock all over it then sprinkle the exposed surface evenly with half the confectioner's sugar. Put the ham in the oven and cook for 20 minutes, basting frequently (use some more of the wine if necessary). Take the ham out of the oven, turn it over, sprinkle the freshly exposed surface with the remaining sugar, and return to the oven to finish glazing for a further 25 minutes. Serve hot with the reduced basting liquid handed round separately as a sauce. This dish is also good served cold.

Roquefort is known to date back further than any other French cheese. The Roquefort cheesemakers were granted a special license in 1407 by King Charles VI. As early as the sixth century, Gregory of Tours described how the Causse pasturelands, frozen during the bitter winters but covered with wildflowers in springtime, were home to flocks of ewes which were milked to make this cheese. Earlier still, when Pliny describes a cheese made in ancient Gaul that surpassed all others, sought after by sophisticated Romans with their discerning palates, he is almost certainly referring to Roquefort.

POULET AU FROMAGE

Chicken with creamy cheese sauce

Bourbonnais

Preparation: 15 minutes
Cooking: 1 hour
Easy

Serves 6:
1 2 1/4–2 1/2-lb chicken
2 leeks, white part only
2 carrots, peeled
1 medium-sized onion, peeled
2 cloves
1 bouquet garni (thyme, bay leaf, parsley, a little celery)
1 clove garlic, peeled
1 quart chicken broth (see glossary)
1/2 cup butter
1/2 cup all-purpose flour
3 cups milk
salt and pepper
pinch nutmeg
3/4 cup grated Gruyère cheese
1/4 cup crème fraîche

Slice the leeks and carrots; quarter the onions, stud 2 quarters with 1 clove each. Place the vegetables in a large, deep fireproof casserole dish with the cleaned, washed, and dried chicken, bouquet garni, and whole garlic clove. Add sufficient chicken broth to cover and season with salt and pepper. Bring slowly to a boil and then simmer very gently for 45 minutes. Make a white sauce: melt the butter, stir in the flour, and cook for a few minutes then add the milk, continuing to stir and cook as the sauce thickens. Add a pinch each of salt, freshly ground white pepper, and nutmeg. Remove the saucepan from the heat, stir in the grated cheese and the cream, and continue stirring until very smooth and velvety. Use a very sharp carving knife and poultry shears to joint the chicken into 4 pieces. Pour just under half the sauce into a gratin dish large enough to take the chicken pieces in one layer, place the chicken on the sauce and coat with the remaining sauce. Sprinkle with the rest of the cheese and place in the oven, preheated to 400°F, for 15 minutes.

POUNTI*

Ham, bacon, and chard pie

Auvergne

Preparation: 20 minutes
Cooking: 1 hour
Easy

Serves 4.
5 oz semisalted pork belly or bacon
5 oz raw cured Ardennes ham
5 or 6 very large Swiss chard or spinach beet leaves
1 bunch parsley
2 1/4 cups all-purpose flour
4 eggs
3/4 cup milk
1–2 leaves barding fat (pork back fat)
salt and pepper

Blanch the pork belly (or breast) or bacon, drain, and remove the skin and any tough parts (cartilage). Use only the green, leaf part of the chard for this recipe; wash, dry, and chop with the pork or bacon, ham, and the parsley. Place in a large mixing bowl and gradually stir in the flour, followed by the eggs, blending in one at a time; finally stir in the milk a little at a time. Season with salt and pepper. Line the base and sides of a pie mold or cake pan neatly with the barding fat. Fill with the mixture, level the surface, and cook in the oven, uncovered, at 375°F for 1 hour. The surface should be golden brown when cooked; push a thin skewer or trussing needle deep into the center of the pie: if it comes out clean and dry, the pie is done. Take out of the mold or pan and serve hot.

VEGETABLES

ALIGOT*

Cheesy creamed potato

Rouergue

Preparation: 25 minutes
Cooking: 40 minutes
Easy

Serves 6:
1¼ lb floury potatoes
10 oz fresh Tomme de Cantal cheese (or any mild, semihard cheese)
¼ cup butter
¾ cup crème fraîche
1 clove garlic, peeled
salt and pepper

Wash the potatoes well; do not peel. Boil over moderate heat in a large saucepan of salted water for 20–30 minutes or until they are tender.

While they are cooking, cut the cheese into very thin slices. Peel the potatoes while they are still very hot and push them through a vegetable mill or sieve into a heavy-bottomed saucepan. Stir in the butter until completely melted, with a wooden spatula or spoon, then gradually beat in the cream, followed by the minced garlic. Season with a little salt and plenty of freshly ground pepper. Place over low heat and keep stirring until very hot; add all the cheese at once and continue stirring until it has completely melted and strings form when a spoonful of the mixture is lifted above the pan. Serve immediately in heated dishes.

PÂTÉ DE POMMES DE TERRE
Potato pie

Bourbonnais

Preparation: 30 minutes
Cooking: 40 minutes
Easy

Serves 4:
1¾ lb waxy potatoes
½ cup butter
½ cup dry white wine
salt and pepper
nutmeg
1 lb shortcrust pie dough (see glossary)
1 egg
1 cup crème fraîche *or heavy cream*

Peel the potatoes and cook them in a pan of lightly salted boiling water for 15 minutes (they should be only just tender, not completely cooked). Drain and cut across into round slices about ¾ in thick while still very hot. Place these in a large bowl and distribute ½ cup of the butter, cut into small pieces, over them. Once the butter has started to melt, sprinkle with the white wine, and season with salt, plenty of freshly ground pepper, and a pinch of nutmeg. Stir and turn the potato slices carefully, try not to break them up.

Preheat the oven to 400°F. Roll out two thirds of the pie dough into a very thin sheet and use to line the base and sides of a springform pie mold greased with butter, allowing a ¾-in overlap all round the edge; lightly prick the base here and there with the tines of a fork. Fill the raw pie shell with even layers of potato slices. Roll out the remaining pastry to form a lid, cut to match the overlap of the lining and cover the potatoes, pinching and then rolling the overlaps together so that they form a roll all round the edge of the pie, just inside the pan; brush the surface of the lid with the beaten egg. Cut a ¾-in diameter hole in the center of the lid, place a tube of foil in it. Bake the pie in the preheated oven for 20 minutes, then carefully pour the heated cream down the chimney. Return to the oven for 5 minutes or until the pastry is cooked and golden brown.

DESSERTS

CLAFOUTIS*
Cherry flan

Limousin

Preparation: 10 minutes
Cooking: 25 minutes
Easy

Serves 6:
1 lb fresh black cherries
¼ cup butter
8 eggs
1 cup superfine sugar
1 tsp pure vanilla extract
¼ cup very thick crème fraîche *or heavy cream*
3 tbsp kirsch (optional)

Grease a very wide, shallow ovenproof dish liberally with the butter. Remove the stalks from the cherries (traditionally the pits are not removed: warn your guests!) and place in the dish in a single layer with a little space between them. Preheat the oven to 450°F. Reserve ¼ cup of the sugar and beat the rest energetically with the eggs; beat in the vanilla extract, then the cream and the kirsch, if used. Pour over the cherries.

Bake for 20 minutes, then sprinkle the surface with the reserved sugar and place under a very hot broiler to caramelize.

FLOGNARDE
Apple flan

Limousin

Preparation: 15 minutes
Cooking: 30 minutes
Easy

Serves 4:
1/4 cup butter
1 1/4 cups all-purpose flour
pinch salt
1/4 cup superfine sugar
4 eggs
1 1/2 tbsp rum
1 cup boiled, lukewarm milk
10 oz firm apples or soaked, pitted prunes
1 1/2 tbsp vanilla-flavored confectioner's or superfine sugar

Grease a fairly deep flan or gratin dish with a little of the butter; chill the dish and the remaining butter in the refrigerator. Preheat the oven to 375°F.

Place all the flour except for 1 1/2 tbsp in a mixing bowl with the salt and sugar. Make a well in the center and break the eggs into it. Stir the eggs, gradually incorporating all the flour, stir in the rum a very little at a time and then the lukewarm milk; the batter should be very thick but just pourable.

Dust the greased flan dish all over with the reserved flour, shake out excess. Cover the bottom with the peeled, cored, and thinly sliced apples (Rennet, Calville or Granny Smith are suitable varieties) or with the well-drained, plumped up prunes.

Pour the batter all over the fruit, scraping out the bowl, and dot the leveled surface with small flakes of the remaining, very cold butter. Place in the oven and bake for 30 minutes. Sprinkle with vanilla sugar and serve warm.

CORNETS DE MURAT
Cream-filled wafers

Auvergne

Preparation: 25 minutes
Cooking: about 5 minutes
Easy

Serves 6:
1 cup superfine sugar
1 3/4 cups all-purpose flour
pinch salt
6 eggs, lightly beaten
2 large sugar lumps
1 cup crème Chantilly (see glossary)

Place the sugar, flour, and salt in a mixing bowl and mix well; make a well in the center, pour in the beaten eggs a little at a time, stirring to incorporate the flour and sugar gradually. When smoothly blended, leave to stand while you melt the sugar lumps: place these in a small saucepan, having dipped them very briefly in cold water. Heat gently to make a thick sugar syrup. Dip a wooden spatula into cold water and use it to work the thick syrup into a ball. Continue to dip the spatula into cold water at frequent intervals so that the sugar does not stick to it. Work this sugar into the batter.

Preheat the oven to 425°F. Grease two or more nonstick cookie sheets with butter and drop tablespoons of the mixture onto it, very well spaced out, drawing the spoon upward as the mixture drops to make a pyramid shape. (This quantity should yield about 24 wafers). Carefully flatten these heaps into disks 4 in in diameter. Bake in the oven for about 5 minutes, or until the edges of the disks are light golden brown (they will look like round cats' tongues cookies). Take out of the oven and, working quickly but carefully, loosen the disks with a metal spatula and roll them into cylinders. Leave to cool. If the disks start to harden before you have rolled them, return to the oven for a few seconds to soften.

Pipe a little crème Chantilly into both ends of each cylinder with a fluted piping tip and pastry bag.

GÂTEAU AUX NOIX*
Walnut cake

Auvergne

Preparation: 30 minutes
Cooking: 30 minutes
Easy

Serves 4:
1 cup walnuts
1 cup hazelnuts
6 eggs, separated + 4 extra yolks
1 cup superfine sugar
1/4 cup rum
1/2 cup cake flour or all-purpose flour
approx. 3/4 cup redcurrant jelly

Spread the nuts on shallow baking trays and place in the oven set at 375°F. Roast for 10 minutes or until very pale golden brown; check frequently to ensure they do not overcook or burn. Pound well or process briefly so they are finely ground.

Preheat the oven to 325°F. Place all the egg yolks in a mixing bowl with the sugar, rum, and ground nuts. Mix well; fold in the 6 egg whites beaten until stiff but not at all grainy or dry. Sift in the flour and fold in thoroughly.

Turn this batter into a cake pan greased with butter and lightly dusted with extra flour; bake for 30 minutes or until done.

Turn out carefully onto a cooling rack and when cold, cut horizontally in half and fill with your favorite jelly or jam.

South: the Midi (Mediterranean Coast)

Provence
County of Nice
Corsica
Mediterranean Languedoc
Roussillon

France's Mediterranean seaboard stretches from the Italian frontier in the east, westward to the Spanish border, with the island of Corsica southeast of Nice. Nowadays, with the new freeway, a distance of just under 375 miles, it does not take long to drive from Ventimiglia to Perthus. The landscape does not change much along the coast, nor does the architecture. The ancient Romans held sway here for several centuries and traces of the civilization they brought with them have survived to this day. It would be logical to expect the cooking of this coastal area to vary little from west to east but this is only true up to a point.

To anyone who lives above an imaginary line drawn from Montélimar to Barcelonnette (dismissed as "northerners" by the inhabitants of the Midi), the cooking of the Mediterranean coast and its immediate hinterland is synonymous with garlic, olive oil, wild herbs from the typically sparse vegetation of the Garrigue, and tomatoes.

Like most generalizations, this only sketches the broad lines of the picture. There are plenty of variations on this theme: in the Venaissin district, once the fief of the Avignon papacy, a wide variety of fruits and vegetables grow in profusion and black truffles are plentiful. In contrast, in the high valley of the Durance river, one of the poorer districts, excellent lamb is produced from flocks which graze pastures full of wild herbs around Sisteron, and lavender is cultivated on a very large scale. Marseille and Toulouse draw their wealth mainly from industry, the Côte d'Azur from tourism, the Languedoc from wine, Roussillon from market gardening (especially very early, forced vegetables, and anchovies). Corsica, with its wild, beautiful, and largely unspoiled landscape has many suitably small-scale industries which include agriculture, viticulture and tourism; its cooking, together with that of the former Comté of Nice, is the most distinctive of this warm and sunny region. The historical ties of Corsica and Nice with Italy are reflected in the popularity of such dishes as ravioli, cannelloni, and gnocchi; *soupe au pistou* and Corsican *minestra*, both made with basil, are direct borrowings from traditional Genoese dishes. Nice is famous for its recipes for tripe and red mullet, for its *mesclun* salad lettuce, ratatouille, and salade niçoise but there are plenty of other, equally outstanding but less well known regional specialties such as the delicious velvety smooth bean soup, anchovy fritters, and a salad of *nonats* (these are little fish fry, which only Niçois fishermen have the right to fish, a

On the previous pages: *the famous vines of Châteauneuf-du-Pape flourish in stony soil, stretching out in neat rows below the ruins of the old castle.* Below: *from the* Vieux-Port, *the old harbor of Marseilles, these gleaming fresh fish will soon find their way into a delicious bouillabaisse*

Above: *there are several haunting old and modern popular songs about Provençal markets. The spice seller's stall is crammed with baskets; their aromatic and colorful contents are used with discretion and to great effect in traditional regional recipes.* Right: *perhaps the crisp* baguette *loaf should be France's national emblem, an indispensable accompaniment to meals all over the country.*

privilege granted in 1860, the year Nice became part of France), and *socca* made with fine cornmeal, water, and olive oil.

Other discoveries worth making include the Corsican *figatellu* (pig's liver sausage), omelets made with fresh ewe's milk cheese (*brocciu*), casseroled vegetable mixtures such as ragout of eggplant, tomatoes, and wild marjoram (*nébita*), and potatoes with macaroni.

The French Catalan population of Roussillon have a good deal in common with the Spanish Catalans and, like them, greatly enjoy anchovies, for which Collioure has long been famous; besides indulging their love of snails (and there is even a snail festival), local cooks excel at fish stews made with squid, different types of fish, mussels, saltwater crayfish, onions, tomatoes, and garlic. Distinctively Catalan dishes appear on both sides of the western border: eel stew (*bouillinade d'anguilles*), *fraginat* (beef sautéed with garlic); *boutifare*, blood sausage or black pudding, and the little meatballs called *boles de picoulat*, flavored with herbs, fried and coated with a tomato, olive, and ham or bacon sauce, as well as the less tempting *ouillade*, a stew made with pigs' tails and rancid pork fat or *sagi*.

In common with other coastal regions, the Mediterranean Midi has two styles of cooking, that of the coast proper and that of the hinterland.

The most famous dish belonging to the former is the fish soup-stew known as *bouillabaisse* in Provence, *bouillinade* in Languedoc, *pinyata* in Roussillon, *aziminu* in Corsica, *soupa de péi* in Nice. Another dish that makes the most of the excellent local seafood is *bourride*, which consists of white fish accompanied by a garlic mayonnaise (*aïoli*), and belongs equally to Languedoc and Provence.

Members of the cod family, dried and salted cod or haddock (the latter is called

stockfish), are a great favorite all along the Mediterranean coast: in Nice a dish called *stocaficada* is made with haddock that has been salted and dry-cured whole (entrails included). This has to be soaked for a long time in cold water and is then cooked with olive oil, tomatoes, potatoes, sweet peppers, garlic, black olives, and herbs, a dish with a robust flavor and an overpowering smell.

Dried haddock or cod becomes *pestu* in Corsica. In Nîmes the same fish is turned into the delicious creamed mixture made with olive oil and cream or milk which goes under the name of *brandade de morue*. In Roussillon it is cooked with spinach and called *merenda*, and in French and Spanish Catalonia, it is prepared with olive oil, sweet peppers, and tomatoes. In the hinterland, in Languedoc and Roussillon, the inhabitants have shown equal inventiveness when cooking their beloved snails.

Roussillon and Corsica are renowned for their robustly flavored pork products.

In Provence and Nice, soups are given star billing in the menu, while the superb local vegetables are served when young and tender yet full of flavor, stuffed, fried or baked.

In the hills of Haute-Provence, the lambs graze on meadows full of wild herbs and the meat acquires a delicious flavor, among the best in France. Their intestines and feet are used for traditional specialties of Marseilles.

The best wines produced in this region include those made with the rare Bellet vine around Nice, Roussillon's Banyuls, wines from Provence and Luberon and the slopes of Aix, excellent Cassis, Palette and Bandol, the southern Côtes-du-Rhône wines, especially Gigondas and the great growths of Châteauneuf-du-Pape, as well as the wines from Languedoc: Minervois and Corbières. The region lacks any superb cheeses, producing only the workaday Banon and Picodon from Provence and Niolo and Venaco from Corsica.

Desserts and confectionery are excellent: candied fruit from Apt, caramel candy (*berlingots*) from Carpentras, almond cakes (*calissons*) from Aix, croquants (nut cookies) from Montpellier, *biscotins* from Castelnaudary and, most famous of all, a happy marriage between two of Provence's main products, honey and almonds: nougat from Montélimar.

Secluded beaches and sheltered inlets form much of Corsica's coastline. The island is famous for its breathtaking wild scenery and also for some good wine, especially Ajaccio and Patrimonio, fine accompaniments to the very distinctive local cooking.

Left: *a selection of the thirteen traditional specialties served as desserts at the end of meals during the Christmas festivities.*
Above: *so numerous are the orchards around Apt, with cherry trees predominating, that the town is known as the candied fruit capital of France.*

SOUPS

AÏGO BOULIDO
Garlic soup

Provence

Preparation: 5 minutes
Cooking: 15 minutes
Very easy

Serves 6:
3 tbsp olive oil
6 cloves garlic, peeled
3 sage leaves
1 bay leaf
6 thin slices stale or lightly crisped French bread
6 very fresh eggs (optional)
1/4 cup grated cheese (optional)
salt and pepper

Bring 2 quarts water to a boil with the olive oil and a generous pinch each of salt and pepper. Mince the garlic cloves and add to the water with the sage and bay leaf. Boil for 15 minutes, then remove and discard the sage and bay leaf.

Place the bread in heated bowls, pour the soup onto it.

To make this "poor man's soup" more interesting, beat an egg in each bowl and sprinkle the bread slices with grated cheese before pouring in the hot liquid.

SOUPE DE PINÏAOU
Sharp fish soup

Mediterranean Languedoc

Preparation: 30 minutes
Cooking: 35 minutes
Easy

Serves 6:
6 large sea-robins
2 3/4 lb waxy potatoes
1 bouquet garni (thyme, bay leaf)
5 whole, peeled garlic cloves
1/2 cup olive oil
1/4 cup white wine vinegar
salt and pepper

Peel and quarter the potatoes. Gut the fish and trim off their fins; wash and dry them.

Bring 2 1/2 quarts water to a boil in a kettle or large saucepan, add the bouquet garni, the whole garlic cloves, and a generous pinch each of salt and pepper. Boil for 5 minutes before adding the potato; cover and boil fast for 15 minutes or until tender.

Remove the kettle or saucepan from the heat; add the fish and simmer gently for 15 minutes or until done. Transfer the potatoes to a wide, heated serving dish and carefully place the whole fish on top. Keep hot while you make the vinaigrette, gradually beating the oil into the vinegar with a little salt and pepper; beat in 1/4 cup of the hot cooking liquid and pour all over the fish. Serve at once.

MINESTRA
Bean and mixed vegetable soup

Corsica

If dried beans are used, start 24 hours in advance
Preparation: 15 minutes
Cooking: 1 1/2 hours
Very easy

Serves 6:
1/2 lb fresh white kidney beans or 1/4 lb dried
1/2 lb fresh red kidney beans or 1/4 lb dried
2 potatoes
1 onion, peeled
2 cloves garlic, peeled
1 small Savoy cabbage, stalks removed
1/2 cup finely chopped smoked ham fat or smoked bacon fat
5 oz rice or small soup pasta
3 tbsp olive oil
salt and pepper

Corsican cooking includes an impressive array of wild herbs and edible plants that grow in the maquis *(the scrubland that is the natural vegetation of the island): fool's dandelion, pennyroyal, wild chicory, borage, sorrel, dandelion, pimpernel buds, savory, wild asparagus, capers, sage, bay, corn salad or lamb's tongue (also known as mâche), wild carrot, wild beet or chard, fennel, calamint, salsify, wild radish, juniper, rosemary, myrtle, thyme.*

These wild plants (called erbislies *in Corsican dialect) are used to make a traditional soup with potatoes, beans, garlic, and onions.*

If you are using dried beans, soak them overnight in a large bowl of cold, unsalted water. Trim, peel, and wash all the vegetables where necessary; remove and discard the outer cabbage leaves; cut out the stalk.

Fill a kettle or very large saucepan two-thirds full with water, add the beans, the sliced onion, 1 clove garlic, and half the ham fat. Bring to a boil and then cook over moderate heat for 1 hour 10 minutes, then add a generous pinch of salt, the cabbage cut into small pieces (not shredded), and the rice or pasta and leave to boil for a further 20 minutes while you fry the rest of the ham fat gently in the olive

oil with the remaining, very finely chopped garlic clove. Add this mixture to the soup 5 minutes before serving.

SOUPE AU PISTOU*

Vegetable soup with basil relish

Provence and County of Nice

Preparation: 40 minutes
Cooking: 2 hours
Easy

Serves 6:
5 baby zucchini
5 baby carrots
5 baby turnips or 1 small celeriac
2 medium-sized leeks
2 large onions
2 large, firm tomatoes
7 oz French beans
¼ lb fresh white kidney beans
¼ lb fresh red kidney beans
1 bouquet garni (thyme, bay leaf, parsley)
¼ lb cooked short pasta, e.g. macaroni (optional)
salt and pepper

For the *pistou*:
1 large bunch fresh basil
3 cloves garlic, peeled
½ cup olive oil
½ cup finely grated Gruyère or Parmesan cheese (optional)

Peel, trim, and wash the vegetables and cut into small pieces. (If you have to use dried beans, use half the fresh weight, and soak overnight in plenty of cold water.) Place all the vegetables in a kettle or very large saucepan with the bouquet garni and sufficient cold water to completely cover them. Bring to a boil and simmer for 2 hours. Add a generous pinch of salt 10 minutes before this time is up, together with the pasta and tomatoes (some cooks add the tomatoes to the relish or *pistou* instead).

Make the *pistou*: mince the garlic to a paste with a pestle and mortar; gradually add the washed and dried basil leaves, working them into a smooth paste; blend in the olive oil a very little at a time and the cheese, if used.

Transfer the *pistou* into a small dish (it is never cooked); each person takes a little and stirs it into his or her bowl of steaming hot soup.

ENTRÉES

RAVIOLI*

County of Nice and Corsica

Preparation: 30 minutes + 1 hour for resting the pasta dough
Cooking: about 12 minutes
Complicated

Serves 6:

For the pasta dough:
6 cups all-purpose flour
5 eggs
3 tbsp olive oil
1 tbsp salt

For the filling:
1 lb leftover casseroled beef
2¼ lb Swiss chard leaves
2 eggs
1 sprig thyme
pinch nutmeg
1 clove garlic, peeled
1 medium-sized onion, peeled
approx. 1 cup grated Parmesan cheese
salt and pepper

Make the pasta dough: sift the flour onto a pastry board, make a well in the center, and break the eggs into it then add the oil and salt. Stir the eggs with the fingers of your slightly cupped hand, gradually incorporating all the flour. Work the dough thoroughly for 10 minutes, kneading until it becomes glossy and elastic. Shape into a ball, place in a bowl, covered with a cloth, and leave for 1 hour, then roll out into 2 large, very thin sheets of equal size.

While the dough is resting, make the filling: chop the beef leftovers very finely or process in a food processor with the blanched, well drained Swiss chard leaves; work in the eggs, thyme leaves, nutmeg, and the very finely chopped garlic and onion and process until smooth. Add 2 or 3 tbsp liquid from the beef casserole (or a little cold water) if the mixture is very dry.

Break off small pieces of the meat mixture and roll into balls about ¾ in in diameter; place these in neat rows ¾ in away from each other and with a ¾-in gap between the rows. Carefully cover with the second sheet of pasta dough, pressing the two sheets together between all the balls of filling to seal well; use a fluted pastry wheel to cut out into little square cushions; dust these ravioli with flour to stop them sticking together and spread out on a clean, dry cloth. Cook in a large saucepan of boiling salted water for about 12 minutes, drain and add 1–2 tbsp butter. Serve immediately, with a sprinkling of grated Parmesan. In Corsica grated *brocciu* (the local ewe's milk cheese) and finely chopped raw cured ham are added to the filling, giving it a stronger taste.

GNOCCHI
Potato dumplings

County of Nice and Corsica

Preparation: 50 minutes + 30 minutes resting time for the dough
Cooking: a few minutes
Easy

Serves 6:
2¼–2½ lb floury potatoes, peeled
2¼ cups all-purpose flour
¼ cup butter
1 egg
salt
extra butter and grated Parmesan cheese, or homemade tomato sauce

Boil the potatoes until very tender in a large pan of salted water. Drain well, and while they are still piping hot put them through the vegetable mill with the smallest gauge disk or push through a sieve or potato ricer. Mix in the flour energetically and quickly, then beat in the butter and the egg until well blended. Shape this very stiff dough into a ball and leave to rest for 30 minutes. Break off pieces the size of a large egg; roll into cylinders about ¾ in in

diameter with the palms of your hands on a lightly floured board; cut into 1¼-in lengths.

Crook your index finger and press the center section into each of the dough pieces, slightly flattening them and leaving a shallow lengthwise depression (this will make the dumplings cook more quickly and evenly). Add to a very large pan of boiling salted water; the gnocchi are done when they bob up to the surface. Drain and serve with butter and Parmesan cheese or a homemade tomato sauce.

SALADE NIÇOISE*

County of Nice

Preparation: 35 minutes
Very easy

Many similar substantial salads are served under this name; this is the original recipe:

Serves 6:
10 medium-sized tomatoes
3 hard-boiled eggs
12 anchovy fillets
1 large cucumber
2 sweet green peppers
6 small new, white onions or scallions
½ lb fresh fava beans
12 baby violet artichokes
1 clove garlic, peeled
¼ lb small Provençal black olives
½ cup olive oil
1 bunch fresh basil
salt and pepper

Quarter the tomatoes, remove the seeds if wished and sprinkle the flesh lightly with salt to draw out the moisture; place them on kitchen towels to drain. Quarter the eggs lengthwise. Rinse the salted anchovies (drain if canned in oil), remove any visible bones, and cut each fillet into 3 or 4 pieces. Cut the cucumber into very thin slices; cut the green peppers into rings, removing the pith and seeds; cut the onions into very thin rings. Hull the fava beans and remove the inner casings as well, exposing the bright green beans. Slice the artichokes lengthwise (use baby Italian artichokes canned in oil as a substitute if necessary).

Cut the garlic clove in half and rub the cut surfaces against the inside of a large salad bowl until the clove is completely worn away. Arrange all the ingredients in the bowl. Blot the tomatoes dry; sprinkle with a little more salt and add to the salad. Beat the very finely chopped basil with the oil, freshly ground pepper, and salt for the dressing, saving a few whole basil leaves for decoration. Chill briefly and then serve.

ESCARGOTS À LA LANGUEDOCIENNE

Snails simmered in white wine sauce

Mediterranean Languedoc

Preparation: 25 minutes
Cooking: 30 minutes
Easy

Serves 4:
48 (4 dozen) canned snails
1 large onion
2 cloves garlic
½ lb raw cured ham
3 tbsp olive oil
2 large, ripe tomatoes
1 fresh hot red or green (chili) pepper
1 cup light broth (see glossary)
½ cup dry white wine
1 small bunch flat-leaved parsley
salt and pepper

One hour before you plan to serve this dish, drain the canned snails thoroughly.

Chop the onion and the garlic very finely. Cut the ham into 1-in cubes. Heat the oil in a skillet and cook the ham gently without browning; remove it with a slotted spoon and drain on kitchen towels. Cook the onion and garlic in the oil over low heat until tender and pale golden brown, stirring with a wooden spoon. Return the ham to the skillet, add the peeled, seeded, and very coarsely chopped tomatoes and the chili pepper. Cook briefly, then add the snails, broth, and wine. Cover and simmer very gently for 30 minutes. Season with salt and pepper to taste. Serve with a sprinkling of coarsely chopped parsley.

PISSALADIÈRE*

Onion bread pizza

County of Nice

Preparation: 45 minutes
Cooking: 15 minutes
Easy

Serves 10:
1 lb bread dough
6½ lb large, mild onions
2 cloves garlic, peeled
1 bouquet garni (thyme, bay leaf, parsley)
½ cup olive oil
10 small black French olives
10 anchovy fillets
salt and pepper

Slice the peeled onions into wafer-thin rings; warm 1½ tbsp of the oil in a skillet and spread the onions out in it. Sprinkle with a pinch of salt. Add the garlic cloves, minced, and the bouquet garni. Cover and sweat very gently until very soft and not at all browned.

Roll out the bread dough into a 10-in diameter disk just over ½ in thick, place in a flan dish or shallow cake pan, leave to rise in a warm place until doubled in volume, and then place in a preheated oven at 350°F to bake until just dry and "set" or three-quarters cooked.

Turn the oven up to 450°F. Remove the bouquet garni from the onions; spread these out

on the part-baked base. Decorate with the olives and the anchovies arranged like the spokes of a wheel; sprinkle with the remaining oil.

Bake for 15 minutes or until done. Sprinkle with freshly ground pepper and serve.

PETITS PÂTÉS DE PÉZENAS
Sweet mutton pies

Languedoc – Mediterranean coast

Start preparation 24 hours in advance
Preparation: 30 minutes
Cooking: 30 minutes
Complicated

Serves 6:
5 cups all-purpose flour
$1^1/_4$ cups lard
pinch salt
10 oz mutton or lamb fillet or leg
5 oz veal suet (preferably fresh from veal kidneys)
5 oz lamb suet (from lamb's kidneys)
2 lemons
2 cups raw brown cane sugar
1 egg
salt

Make the pie dough the day before: rub or cut the lard into the flour and a pinch of salt; gradually add enough cold water, a very little at a time, to make a firm, smooth dough mixture; knead until it no longer sticks to your fingers. Shape into a ball, wrap in foil and chill in the refrigerator.

Make the filling: cut the lamb into small pieces; chop both types of suet finely and mix with the lamb (if kidneys come ready trimmed, with all their surrounding fat removed, use ready prepared suet in a packet). Grate the peel of the well washed and dried lemons and mix with the meat; add the sugar. Stir very thoroughly.

Preheat the oven to 400°F. Roll out the pie dough into a sheet $^1/_4$ in thick. Use a 2-in round pastry cutter to cut out 24 disks. Gather up and knead the offcuts very briefly, roll out again, and cut out into long strips $1^1/_4$ in wide, cut these into 5-in long sections: you will need 12 of them. Take each section and overlap one end over the other, dampening and pinching to seal, making a squat cylinder; dampen both edges of this cylinder with cold water or extra lightly beaten egg; place a cylinder on each of 12 disks (there will be an uncovered margin around the cylinder) and fill with the meat mixture. Place the remaining disks on top: they, too, will overlap the edges of the cylinders, making the finished pies look like old-fashioned cotton reels. Brush with egg yolk to glaze and bake on cookie sheets in the oven for 30 minutes. Serve at once.

TAPENADE*
Black olive and anchovy spread

Provence

Soaking the olives: 2 hours
Preparation: 10 minutes
Very easy

Serves 4:
$^1/_2$ lb Provençal black olives
1 can anchovies
5 oz capers
1 cup olive oil
juice of 1 lemon
pepper

Use the small, firm French black olives for this recipe (Nyons is famous for them); pit them and put them to soak in the olive oil. Drain the anchovies and dry with kitchen towels. Gradually pound the capers, anchovies, and well drained olives together with a pestle and mortar to form a smooth, very thick paste; work in the reserved olive oil and the lemon juice a little at a time. Add freshly ground black pepper to taste.

Serve on croûtons of bread that have been crisped in a slow oven.

BEURRE DE MONTPELLIER
Herb butter sauce

Mediterranean Languedoc

Preparation: 25 minutes
Easy

Serves 6:
$^1/_4$ lb watercress leaves
$^1/_4$ lb burnet
2 oz spinach leaves
2 oz parsley (preferably flat-leaved)
2 oz chervil
1 sprig tarragon
2 baby gherkins pickled in wine vinegar
1 tbsp capers
5 anchovy fillets
2 cloves garlic, peeled
1 shallot, peeled
1 sprig thyme
$1^1/_4$ cup butter
3 tbsp olive oil

This is a delicious herb butter to serve with simply cooked, hot or cold fish or cold meats.

Bring 2 quarts water to a boil, remove from the heat and immediately add the watercress, burnet, spinach, parsley, chervil, and tarragon. Cover and leave to stand for 2 minutes. Strain the blanched leaves and pat dry in kitchen towels.

Chop the shallot and garlic very finely; take the thyme leaves off their stem. Place these 3 ingredients on a chopping board and add the blanched leaves, gherkins, capers, and anchovies (rinsed and dried if salted, drained and dried if canned); chop all these ingredients until they form a very fine mixture, transfer to a bowl and work in the butter, softened at room temperature but not at all melted. Beat until smooth, then gradually beat in the olive oil.

BERLINGUETO

Anchovy- and herb-stuffed eggs

Provence

Preparation: 15 minutes
Cooking: 10 minutes
Easy

Serves 2:
4 hard-boiled eggs
½ cup fine, fresh white breadcrumbs
6 tbsp half-and-half or thin cream
6 canned anchovy fillets
2 sprigs parsley
10 basil leaves
1 clove garlic, peeled
1 egg yolk
1½ tbsp olive oil
6 tbsp fine, toasted breadcrumbs
salt and pepper

Cut the peeled, hard-boiled eggs lengthwise in half, take out the yolks and place in a mixing bowl. Slice off a thin piece from the rounded side of the eggs to keep them stable. Sprinkle the thin cream all over the soft breadcrumbs (stale bread is fine for this recipe) and leave to soak in. Drain the anchovies, remove any visible bones, chop the fillets finely and add to the yolks with the coarsley chopped parsley and basil, and the minced garlic. Squeeze the breadcrumbs to expel a good deal of the cream and reserve this. Add the breadcrumbs to the contents of the bowl and work together with a fork, crushing the egg yolks. Season with salt and pepper and work in the raw egg yolk. Lightly oil a shallow ovenproof dish; fill the hollows in the egg whites with the mixture, heaping it up in a rounded mound; place these in the oiled dish and sprinkle with the toasted breadcrumbs and sprinkle with the reserved cream. Place in the oven, preheated to 375°F, for 10 minutes.

FISH

BOUILLABAISSE*

Provence

Preparation: about 30 minutes
Cooking: 1½ hours
Complicated

Serves 6:

For the basic fish broth:
4½ lb assorted small fish and fresh fish trimmings (choose cheap but very fresh, mainly white fish)
1 cup olive oil
½ bunch celery
2 large, ripe tomatoes
1 whole head garlic
1 leek
2 onions, peeled
1 bouquet garni (thyme, bay leaf, parsley, fennel)
1 fresh hot red or green chili pepper
generous pinch real saffron powder or threads
2½ quarts water
salt and pepper

For the fish stew:
8½–9 lb wide assortment of fresh fish, depending on availability (e.g. John Dory, weever fish, sea-robin, scorpionfish, goosefish, red mullet, whiting, red snapper, bass, perch, porgy, flounder, haddock, etc.)

For the relish (*rouille*):
4 egg yolks
6 cloves garlic, peeled
1 small fresh hot red chili pepper
small pinch real saffron powder or threads
1 cup olive oil
salt and pepper

Serve with:
2¼–2½ lb waxy potatoes
1 crusty white long French stick

Make the fish broth: gut, trim, and wash the small fish; rinse any trimmings. Prepare all the vegetables, chop them all coarsely, including the onions and garlic and cook gently in the oil in a very large, heavy-bottomed saucepan or kettle. When they are lightly browned, add the fish etc. and season with salt and pepper.

Increase the heat to fairly high and cook, stirring continuously with a wooden spoon,

until the fish disintegrate and turn mushy. Add the bouquet garni, the chili pepper, and $2^1/_2$ quarts boiling water. Keep stirring until the liquid returns to the boil, then boil very gently for 40 minutes. Strain the soup through a fine, conical sieve into a large saucepan, pressing down hard on the solid matter left in the sieve to extract all the juices. Simmer very slowly, stirring in the saffron.

Peel the potatoes, cut them into thick, round slices and boil gently in a covered pan for 30 minutes in just enough of the fish broth to cover them. Make the *rouille* or relish: mince the garlic to a fine paste with a pestle and mortar together with the trimmed chili pepper (remove the seeds if you wish) and the saffron. Season with salt and pepper. Work in the egg yolks and then, using a wooden spoon or small balloon whisk, gradually incorporate the olive oil, adding a very little at a time. The resulting thick sauce should look like a bright orangey-red mayonnaise.

Prepare all the selected fish for the stew and cook them in the briskly boiling broth for up to 10 minutes, adding the softest, most quickly cooked fish last. Slice the bread into thick rounds, rub both sides all over with the cut surfaces of garlic cloves and toast until golden brown.

As soon as the fish are cooked, transfer them to a heated serving dish (filleted, if wished) together with the potatoes; pour the broth into a heated soup tureen and serve at the same time as the fish and potatoes; hand round the *rouille* and the croûtons separately.

TIAN DE MERLUSSA

Cod, vegetable, and herb pie

County of Nice

Start preparation 36 hours in advance
Preparation: 20 minutes
Cooking: 30 minutes
Easy

Serves 4:
$1^1/_4$ lb dried salt cod
4 onions, peeled
2 cloves garlic, peeled
$^1/_4$ cup olive oil
4 large tomatoes
3 sticks celery
16 Swiss chard leaves
1 small bunch each fresh parsley and mint
salt and pepper

If using dried salt cod, leave to soak for 36 hours in a large bowl of water with running cold water trickling into it (or change the water several times). If dried unsalted cod is used, soak overnight in cold water. Drain. Slice the onions thinly and flatten the garlic cloves with the flat of a knife blade (but keep them whole); add both these to the oil in a large saucepan.

> *Creamed salt cod or* brandade de morue *has earned its place in history. Adolphe Thiers, a nineteenth-century Prime Minister and later President of France described it as "mankind's greatest achievement" and was so addicted to it that he had pots of it sent to Paris from Nîmes which he devoured in secret in his library. Gaston Doumergue, French President in 1924–31, waxed even more lyrical, and said that whenever he ate* brandade *he could hear the crickets singing in the pine trees around the Magne tower (a famous historic landmark in Nîmes).*

Cook gently for 10 minutes until very lightly browned.

Blanch and peel the tomatoes and remove their seeds; slice and drain on kitchen paper. Remove the strings from the celery and cut into 1-in lengths. Blanch these then drain.

Remove the garlic from the oil and place in another saucepan with the cod, add sufficient water to cover the fish, and bring to just below boiling point; immediately turn off the heat, cover, and leave to stand for 5 minutes. Take out the garlic and the cod with a slotted spoon and reserve, replacing them with the Swiss chard leaves; leave these in the water for 1 minute, then drain and set aside. Preheat the oven to 375°F.

Take the onions out of the oil with a slotted spoon and spread half of them out in the bottom of a wide, ovenproof dish (a *tian* or type of gratin dish is traditional); chop the reserved cooked garlic and sprinkle over the onions.

Break up the cod into large flakes, removing any bones as you go. Arrange the tomatoes, onions, celery, Swiss chard leaves, and cod in separate rows in the dish (you will have 2 or more rows of cod separated by the vegetables). Sprinkle with coarsely chopped parsley and mint and sprinkle with the oil left over from cooking the onions. Season with a very little salt and plenty of freshly ground pepper; cover with aluminum foil. Place in the oven for 10 minutes or until very hot; the surface can then be sprinkled with grated Gruyère or Parmesan and browned for 5 minutes, uncovered.

AÏOLI*

Cold platter with garlic mayonnaise

Provence and County of Nice

Start preparation 2 days in advance
Preparation: 1 hour
Cooking: 1 hour + 1 extra hour for dried beans
Complicated or Easy, depending on chosen seafood

The name "aïoli" denotes the mayonnaise but has come to stand for the whole cold platter, by extension. This version is called "le grand aïoli" ("large or special aïoli").

Serves 10:
3–$3^1/_2$ lb dried salt cod
1 lb dried white kidney beans or garbanzos
1 lb French beans
24 whelks or purged, cleaned snails
10 baby violet artichokes
12 small, young carrots
20 small new potatoes
1 bouquet garni (thyme, bay leaf, parsley, fennel)
3 tbsp olive oil
$^3/_4$ cup dry white wine
1 small bunch parsley
6 eggs
salt and pepper

For the aïoli (garlic mayonnaise):
20 cloves garlic, peeled
3 large egg yolks
1 lemon
3 cups olive oil
pinch of salt and pepper

If using dried salt cod, soak for 2 days in a large bowl of cold water with frequent changes of water to eliminate excess salt and soften it. Soak the dried white beans or garbanzos overnight in cold water. If using live whelks or snails, mix well with several handfuls of coarse salt and leave overnight to kill them and extract their slime.

Rinse the whelks very thoroughly under running cold water to eliminate all the slime they have released. Cook in a *court-bouillon* (see glossary) with another bouquet garni. Drain the beans or chickpeas, rinse and cook in plenty of water with pepper but do not add salt until they have boiled gently for 1 hour 50 minutes, then continue cooking for a further 10 minutes.

Trim, wash, and prepare all the vegetables and cook each type separately, boiling them for the required amount of time in salted water until tender; drain well and keep hot, still separated from one another and covered. Do not peel the potatoes until after they have been cooked. Drain the cod, remove any pieces of skin or bones and cut into 2–$2^1/_4$-in squares. Bring 2 quarts water to a boil with the bouquet garni; add the cod and once the water has almost returned to a boil, reduce the heat to very low; simmer gently for 15 minutes.

Take the whelks out of their shells with a large pin or lobster picker; remove the black section. Heat the oil and add the whelks, pour in the wine and sprinkle with a little chopped parsley. Leave to cook gently for 20 minutes,

while you hard-boil the eggs, cool them quickly under running cold water; and peel them.

Make the aïoli sauce: slice all the garlic cloves lengthwise in half and remove the central shoot, if present (this gives a persistent and excessively strong garlic odor and flavor); pound the garlic to a smooth paste in a mortar with a pestle. Add the egg yolks, salt and freshly ground white pepper, followed by 1 tsp cold water. Continue pounding and working together until well blended. Using a wooden spoon (or a small balloon whisk if preferred) beat in the olive oil a very little at a time, as for a mayonnaise. When you have blended in one third of the oil, add the lemon juice, then continue beating in the oil very gradually. The sauce should be creamy and thick but still pourable. Add a few drops more cold water if it is becoming too thick. Arrange all the prepared ingredients on a heated platter and hand round the aïoli in a sauceboat.

CIVET DE LANGOUSTE À LA CATALANE

Casseroled lobster

Roussillon

Preparation: 30 minutes
Cooking: 30 minutes
Complicated

Serves 4:
2 lobsters, each weighing 1½ lb
½ cup olive oil
¼ lb onions, peeled and chopped
¼ lb shallots, peeled and chopped
4 cloves garlic, peeled
4 large tomatoes, peeled and deseeded
¼ cup brandy
½ bottle dry white wine (Banyuls rancio)
1 bouquet garni (thyme, bay leaf, parsley)
½ cup butter
pinch cayenne pepper
salt and pepper

Carefully insert the point of a heavy kitchen knife deep into the center of a cross-shaped depression in the back of the lobster's "head." Save all the juice that runs out when you cut up the raw lobster and reserve it. Twist off the claws from the body; cut the heavily armored heads off where they are joined by the jointed tail; cut the tail into sections at each convenient joint of shell plating. Remove and discard the feelers. Sauté all the lobster pieces (except for the heavily armored head section) in the oil in a fireproof casserole dish over moderately high heat; shake and turn the pieces. As soon as they have all turned red, take out of the casserole with a slotted spoon and set aside. Cut the "head" section lengthwise in half with a heavy knife and spoon out the creamy liver (tomalley) and reserve. Remove and discard the small, leathery stomach sac from this head section. Place the two halves of the head in the oil and cook until they have turned scarlet. Set aside with the other lobster pieces.

Fry the onions and shallots in the oil remaining in the casserole dish until pale golden brown. Add the chopped garlic, cook until tender; add the coarsely chopped tomatoes. Leave to cook gently for 10 minutes.

Return the lobster pieces to the casserole dish, sprinkle with the brandy, flame; add the wine and bouquet garni. Season with salt and pepper; simmer for 10 minutes. Transfer the lobster to a heated serving dish and keep hot; stir the creamy liver into the liquid left in the casserole dish. Cook while stirring for 5 minutes, then strain through a conical sieve into a small saucepan. Beat the butter into this hot liquid with a balloon whisk, adding a small piece at a time; add the cayenne pepper.

Pour over the lobster and serve.

FEUILLETÉ AUX ANCHOIS

Anchovy, egg, and tomato pie

Roussillon

Preparation: 25 minutes + time for making the pastry
Cooking: 20 minutes
Easy

Serves 4:
10 oz homemade (see glossary) or thawed frozen puff pastry
¼ cup olive oil
5 eggs
24 anchovy fillets, canned in oil
2¼–2½ lb firm, ripe tomatoes
1 tsp superfine sugar
2 oz small French Provençal olives, pitted
pinch each cayenne pepper, salt, pepper

Roll out the pastry into a very large, very thin round sheet (just over 1/16 in thick) and use to line a 10-in diameter, 1½-in deep shallow cake pan that has been greased with a little of the olive oil. Beat an egg and brush all over the exposed surface of the raw pastry.

Drain the anchovy fillets well. Boil the remaining 4 eggs for 10 minutes, cool quickly in cold water, and shell.

Preheat the oven to 375°F. Set aside 2 firm tomatoes; blanch and peel the rest, remove the seeds, and cut the flesh into small pieces; place in a wide saucepan with the remaining oil, a pinch each of cayenne pepper, salt, and pepper, and the sugar. Simmer, uncovered, while stirring until a good deal of the moisture has evaporated and the mixture has thickened. Allow to cool a little, then spread out over the bottom of the pie shell. Cut the eggs across into rounds and spread out over the tomato mixture. Blanch, peel, and slice the remaining 2 tomatoes; remove their seeds and spread out over the eggs. Cover with a layer of anchovy fillets, then place the olives (black or green) on top.

Place in the oven and bake for 20 minutes. Serve hot, warm or cold.

BOURRIDE À LA SÉTOISE*

Goosefish and shellfish casserole

Mediterranean Languedoc

Preparation: 15 minutes
Cooking: 30 minutes
Easy

Serves 4:
4 steaks or thick slices goosefish, each weighing approx. ½ lb
12–16 small clams in their shells
1 carrot, peeled
10 celery leaves
1 large Swiss chard leaf
2 leeks, white part only
6 tbsp olive oil
salt and pepper

For the aïoli (garlic mayonnaise):
2 cloves garlic, peeled
2 egg yolks
1 tsp strong mustard
½ cup olive oil

Chop the all the prepared vegetables finely and sweat in the oil for 10 minutes in a fireproof casserole dish without allowing them to brown at all. Add the fish steaks and season with salt and pepper. Cover and leave to cook over low heat for 10 minutes, then turn the fish and cook for 10 minutes more.

Meanwhile, make the aïoli: using a pestle and mortar, pound the garlic to a paste, work in the mustard and egg yolks. Leave to stand for 1 minute, then gradually beat in the oil, adding a very little at a time.

Take the casserole dish off the heat; transfer the fish to a heated serving dish and keep hot while you stir the aïoli into the cooking liquid and juices; pour the resulting sauce over the fish and serve with steamed potatoes.

THON À LA CATALANE

Tuna fish with tomatoes and gherkins

Roussillon

Preparation: 10 minutes
Cooking: 20 minutes
Easy

Serves 4:
1 thick slice or steak fresh tuna weighing 1¾ lb
1¾ lb tomatoes, peeled and deseeded
¾ cup olive oil
1½ tbsp tomato paste or ½ cup sieved tomatoes
¼ lb gherkins pickled in wine vinegar
¼ lb baby onions pickled in wine vinegar
few sprigs parsley and fresh coriander leaves
salt and cayenne pepper

Soak the tuna in a bowl of cold water mixed with 1 tbsp wine vinegar for 45 minutes. Drain. Pour half the oil into a fireproof casserole dish or saucepan, add the tuna and surround it with the tomatoes. Season with a pinch of salt and a small pinch of cayenne pepper.

Mix the tomato paste with the remaining oil in a small bowl and pour over the tuna. Cover and cook over low heat for 20 minutes in all, turning the fish halfway through this time. When the fish is nearly done, add the gherkins sliced into rounds, the onions, and the herbs. Replace the lid and cook for 5 minutes more. Leave to cool slowly. Serve cold.

STOCAFICADA

Salt cod stew

County of Nice

Start preparation 4 days in advance
Preparation: 15 minutes
Cooking: 2 hours
Easy

Serves 10:
3¼–3½ lb stockfish (dried salt cod)
5 oz dried salted cod entrails
1¼ cups olive oil
1 large onion, peeled
1 large leek, white part only
1 bouquet garni (thyme, bay leaf, parsley, fennel)
4 cloves garlic, peeled
5½ lb peeled, deseeded tomatoes
½ lb small, black Provençal olives
2¼–2½ lb new potatoes

Beat the dried salt cod with a meat bat to tenderize before placing it in a large bowl of cold water with the entrails; soak for 4 days, changing the water very frequently. If dried unsalted cod is used, without any entrails, simply soak to soften for 36 hours in several changes of

water. Drain. Remove the skin and bones and break the cod into large flakes.

Heat the oil in a large fireproof casserole dish; fry the sliced onion and leek, stirring with a wooden spoon. Reduce the heat, add the bouquet garni, the finely chopped garlic and the tomatoes, cut into fairly small pieces. Spread the fish, and the entrails if used, on this bed of vegetables. Cover and cook over very low heat for 1½ hours, then add a little pepper if wished (and a little salt if you have used dried unsalted cod). Sprinkle the olives over the surface (there is no need to pit them) and cover with a layer of the sliced, raw, new potatoes. Cover and cook for a further 30 minutes, or until the potatoes are tender.

ROUGETS À LA NIÇOISE

Red mullet with tomato, olive, and caper sauce

County of Nice

Preparation: 20 minutes
Cooking: 25 minutes
Easy

Serves 6:
12 very fresh red mullet
¾ cup all-purpose flour
salt and pepper
¾–1 cup olive oil
2¼–2½ lb tomatoes, peeled and deseeded
5 lemons, peeled with pith removed
juice of 1 lemon
12 anchovy fillets
20 small French (Provençal) black olives
1½ tbsp capers
3 tbsp chopped parsley
¼ cup butter

Use kitchen towels to gently rub off the red mullets' scales (their flesh tears very easily). Traditionally they are not gutted, as only fresh caught fish are used but gut them neatly if preferred. Season with salt and freshly ground pepper, then roll in flour to coat all over.

Heat the oil until very hot, add the fish and fry; turn once carefully, when they are well browned on the underside, then fry until done, sprinkling a little hot oil over the exposed side. They are best fried over very high heat. Coarsely chop the tomatoes and place in a sieve to drain. Preheat the oven to 325°F. Transfer the fish to a heated, fairly shallow ovenproof gratin dish with a slotted spatula. Cover and surround with the tomatoes, place an anchovy on top of each fish; scatter lemon slices, olives and capers over the tomatoes and sprinkle the lemon juice and the chopped parsley all over the fish and tomatoes. Bake for 20 minutes.

When this time is nearly up, melt the butter; sprinkle it over the fish just before serving.

ROUGETS À LA BONIFACIENNE

Red mullet with tomatoes, anchovies, and garlic

Corsica

Preparation: 20 minutes
Cooking: 30 minutes
Easy

Serves 6:
2¼–2½ lb medium-sized red mullet
6 anchovies
1½ tbsp tomato paste
4 cloves garlic, peeled
1 bunch parsley
3 tbsp olive oil
½ cup fine, dry breadcrumbs
salt and pepper

Wipe off the red mullets' scales with kitchen towels, taking care not to tear their delicate flesh. Gut, reserving the livers, rinse, and dry.

Preheat the oven to 400°F. If salted anchovies are used, rinse off excess salt and remove any visible bones. Drain if canned. Pound them to a smooth paste with the tomato paste; work in the finely chopped garlic and parsley and 1½ tbsp of the olive oil. Season with pepper, add a very little salt if wished. Stir in the minced fish livers.

Use the remaining oil to grease the inside of a shallow ovenproof dish, spread the prepared paste all over the bottom and place the fish on it, heads to tails; sprinkle them with the breadcrumbs and bake uncovered in the oven for 30 minutes.

GIGOT DE MER À LA PALAVASIENNE

Roast goosefish with green peppers

Mediterranean Languedoc

Preparation: 25 minutes
Cooking: 55 minutes
Easy

Serves 6:
3–3½ lb goosefish
3 cloves garlic, peeled
3 onions, peeled
4 sweet green peppers
¾ cup olive oil
salt and pepper

Buy one or two whole goosefish tails for this dish and leave them whole. The thin skin should have been removed by the fishmonger. Slice the garlic cloves into slivers and insert these in deep, well spaced incisions in the fish.

Slice the onions into rings. Wash, dry, and slice the green peppers in half; remove the white pith and seeds and cut the flesh into

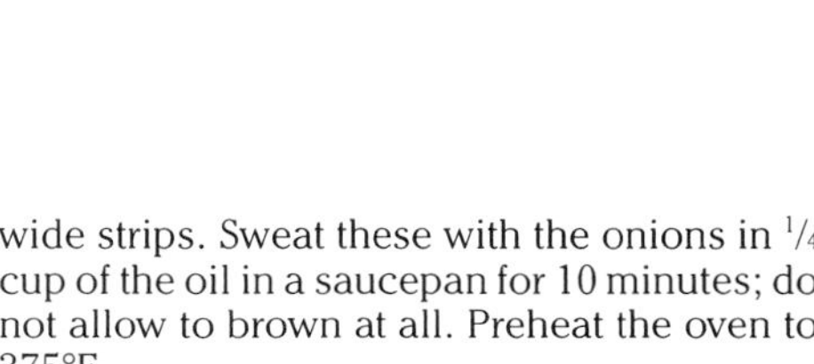

wide strips. Sweat these with the onions in ¼ cup of the oil in a saucepan for 10 minutes; do not allow to brown at all. Preheat the oven to 375°F.

Season the fish with salt and pepper and place in a lightly oiled casserole dish; sprinkle the remaining oil all over it and surround with the green peppers and onions. Place in the oven, uncovered, and roast for 45 minutes, turning halfway through this time and basting frequently with the oil and juices from the casserole dish.

BOURRIDE*

Mixed white fish casserole

Provence

Preparation: 30 minutes
Cooking: 20 minutes
Complicated

Serves 8:
5½ lb assorted white fish (goosefish, sea bass, whiting, John Dory, hake, porgy, etc.)
1 onion, peeled
1 leek

1 carrot, peeled
6 cloves garlic, peeled
1 medium-sized tomato, peeled
1 bouquet garni (thyme, bay leaf, fennel)
peel of 1 untreated orange
2¼ cups dry white wine (ideally Provençal)
3 cups olive oil
8 egg yolks
16 slices toasted French bread
salt and pepper

Trim, gut, wash, and dry the fish. Cut them into thick slices or steaks. Slice the onion, leek, and carrot, peel but do not slice the garlic cloves, and place all these vegetables, with the fish in a very large, fireproof casserole dish or kettle with the quartered and deseeded tomatoes, bouquet garni, and orange peel (oranges treated with fungicide, and most are, will give a bitter taste; use 2 drops essential oil of orange instead if available). Season with salt and pepper. Pour in the wine, 3 tbsp of the olive oil and sufficient boiling water to cover the fish. Bring quickly to a boil and boil briskly for 10 minutes.

Make the aïoli sauce (see page 192; increase the quantity if necessary).

Transfer the pieces of fish to a heated serving dish using a slotted spoon or ladle; pour all the liquid through a conical sieve into a heatproof jug or a lipped saucepan.

Set aside 1 heaping tbsp of the aïoli for each person; place the remaining sauce in the washed and dried casserole dish or a large, heavy-bottomed saucepan and gradually beat in the 8 egg yolks with a wooden spoon away from any heat, blending them in one at a time.

Place the casserole dish on a heat diffuser over very low heat and immediately start beating in the strained liquid, adding this in a very thin stream as you beat. Continue stirring vigorously with the wooden spoon until the mixture is smooth and thickened. Remove from the heat (do not allow to boil at any point or it will separate and curdle).

Place 2 slices of toast in each of 8 large heated soup bowls, ladle the soup over it, and serve. Serve the fish separately, handing round the aïoli sauce.

The inhabitants of Roussillon are true devotees of snails (known as cargols *in the local Catalan dialect from whence comes the name of a method of preparing snails* cargolade, *more of a ritual than a dish). Little brown snails gathered in the vineyards are grilled over fires of vine clippings after pruning has taken place and a little melted salt pork fat is poured into the opening of each snail. They are then served with thick slices of bread spread with aïoli (garlic mayonnaise) and local wine, drunk from rough, gourd-shaped glasses. Next on the menu come little lamb chops, sausages, black (blood) pudding and, finally, a cake called "gipsy's arm."*

BRANDADE NÎMOISE

Creamed salt cod

Mediterranean Languedoc

Start preparation 24 hours in advance
Preparation: 20 minutes
Cooking: 20 minutes
Complicated

Serves 4:
2¼–2½ lb salt cod
1¾ cups olive oil
1¾ cups boiled, lukewarm milk
garlic and nutmeg (optional)
salt and pepper

Soak the cod in a large bowl of cold water for 24 hours to eliminate excess salt. Drain, place in a saucepan of fresh cold water, and bring slowly to boiling point; simmer very gently for 10 minutes. Drain. Remove any pieces of skin or bones, place the cod in an enameled cast iron or stainless steel saucepan (not aluminum or uncoated cast iron which will cause discoloration) over very low heat and break it up into flakes. Gradually work in one third of the oil, stirring constantly until the cod turns into a purée; keep stirring as you add the same quantity of milk a very little at a time.

Repeat this operation twice more, alternating the addition of each third of the remaining two thirds of the oil with the two thirds of the milk. By the time you have finished, the purée should be smooth and light. Add pepper to taste and a little salt if wished.

Serve with toasted or butter-fried slices of French bread.

Some recipes call for the addition of a very little minced garlic, and/or nutmeg.

LOUP FARCI

Stuffed baked sea bass

Provence and County of Nice

Preparation: 20 minutes
Cooking: 45 minutes
Easy

Serves 8:
1 3½-lb sea bass
2 or 3 fresh or dried fennel stalks
*½ lb cured raw ham (*prosciutto *type) or fairly lean salt pork or unsmoked bacon*
¼ lb capers
10 oz small button mushrooms
¼ lb small black or green Provençal olives, pitted
1 large onion, peeled
6 tbsp finely chopped parsley
2 cloves garlic, peeled
½ cup olive oil
1 lb tomatoes, peeled and deseeded
1 quart dry white wine
salt and pepper

Preheat the oven to 375°F. Trim, gut, wash, and dry the fish (leave the head on). Season with salt and pepper inside and out. Make a few well spaced diagonal slashes in both sides of the fish and insert short lengths of fennel stalk; place 2–3 fennel twigs inside the cavity. Lightly oil a roasting pan or ovenproof dish large enough to take the fish lying flat, place the fish in it and cook in the oven for 30 minutes.

While the fish is cooking, chop the ham, capers, mushrooms, pitted olives, onion, parsley, and garlic very finely together.

Pour ½ cup of the olive oil into a saucepan and heat until very hot; add the chopped mixture and stir until lightly browned. Chop the tomatoes very coarsely and add to the mixture, followed by the wine. Cook gently, uncovered, until the wine has reduced to about one third of its original volume. Set aside.

When the fish is just done, take it out of the oven, remove the fennel stalks carefully and fillet it neatly. Spread the prepared mixture all over the lower half and place the two top fillets back in place on top. Return to the oven if necessary for a few minutes to serve very hot.

MEAT

PIGEONS À LA CATALANE

Pigeons with Seville orange sauce

Roussillon

Preparation: 30 minutes
Cooking: 40 minutes
Easy

Serves 4:
2 plump, oven ready pigeons
12 cloves garlic, peeled
2 barding leaves (thinly sliced pork back fat)
*3 oz cured raw bacon (*prosciutto *type)*
2 bitter (Seville) oranges (or ½ sweet orange and ½ lemon)
3 tbsp olive oil
¼ cup butter
1 cup dry white wine
1 cup chicken broth (see glossary)
1½ tbsp all-purpose flour
3 tbsp white wine vinegar
salt and pepper

A traditional dish for January and early February when both pigeons and bitter Seville oranges are in plentiful supply. Add the garlic cloves to a saucepan of boiling water and boil for 10 minutes. Sprinkle the pigeons inside and out with a little salt, wrap them in the barding fat, and tie securely. Cut the ham into dice. Peel the oranges (or orange and lemon), cutting away all the white pith. Cut the flesh into round slices; remove the seeds.

Heat the oil and butter in a fireproof casserole dish; add the pigeons and brown over moderately high heat. Reduce the heat to low, add the diced ham, the drained minced garlic cloves, and the orange (or orange and lemon) slices. Add the wine and broth. Season with freshly ground pepper and a very little salt if necessary. Cover and simmer for 15 minutes; turn the pigeons and cook for a further 15 minutes or until they are just done. Take the pigeons and citrus slices out of the casserole and keep hot. Mix the flour with the vinegar, stir into the liquid in the casserole dish over low heat, and continue stirring as it cooks and thickens for about 5–8 minutes.

Remove and discard the barding fat from the pigeons and cut them in half with poultry shears; lay them cut side downward on a heated serving platter and coat with the strained sauce. Arrange the orange (or orange and lemon) slices around them.

CHOU FARCI*
Stuffed cabbage

Corsica

Preparation: 40 minutes
Cooking: 3 hours
Easy

Serves 4:
1 Savoy cabbage with a large, firm heart
1/4 lb pancetta (cured pork belly) or bacon
1/2 lb figatellu *(a smoked boiling liver sausage)*
4 cloves garlic, peeled
1 1/2 tbsp finely chopped parsley
3 onions, peeled
1/4 lb bread, soaked in milk
2 eggs
3 tbsp olive oil
1 pig's caul, soaked in vinegar and water
2 carrots, peeled
2 leeks, white part only
2 quarts broth (see glossary)
salt and pepper

Remove and discard the outermost leaves and the stalk of the cabbage. Blanch whole in a large saucepan of boiling salted water for 10 minutes. Drain and refresh under running cold water; drain well. Gently pull aside the outer leaves to reach the heart; cut this out and set aside.

Prepare the pork stuffing: remove and discard the sausage skin then chop the pancetta and the liver sausage meat finely together, place in a mixing bowl and add the very finely chopped cabbage heart, the finely chopped garlic, parsley, onions, and the bread, squeezed free of excess moisture. Mix very thoroughly, using your hands, and gradually work in the eggs and the oil. Season with a little salt and plenty of pepper. Shape into a firm ball to match the shape of the removed heart and insert carefully into the center of the cabbage. Press the innermost remaining leaves against the stuffing. Take the pig's caul out of the vinegar and water, drain, and rinse. Wrap the stuffed cabbage in it and tie securely.

Place the cabbage in a deep, fireproof casserole dish, add the carrots, leeks, and sufficient broth to cover; bring to a boil and then simmer gently for 3 hours, spooning the liquid over the top of the cabbage frequently as it cooks. Untie, remove the caul, and cut into slices at table, like cake.

DAUBE DE BOEUF

Slow-cooked beef casserole

Provence, Nice, Corsica

Preparation: 35 minutes
Cooking: 7 hours
Easy

Serves 8:
$4^1/_2$ lb lean braising beef
$^1/_2$ lb fresh pork belly or breast
2 cloves garlic, peeled
3 tbsp very finely chopped parsley
$^1/_4$ lb fat smoked bacon
4 peeled onions, 2 studded with 1 clove each
4 carrots, peeled, cut lengthwise in quarters
$1^1/_2$ tbsp lard
$1^1/_2$ tbsp olive oil
1 calf's foot, split lengthwise in half
1 bouquet garni (thyme, bay leaf, parsley, savory)
3 tomatoes
4 shallots, peeled
peel (no white pith) of $^1/_4$ orange
1 small stick celery
1 quart dry red wine (ideally Provençal or Côtes-du-Rhone)
salt and pepper

Cut the beef into 2-in cubes; cut half the fat bacon into a matching number of little oblong pieces, roll these small lardons in a mixture of 1 garlic clove very finely chopped with the parsley, make a deep slit in the center of each beef cube, and insert a lardon into it.

Remove the skin and any pieces of cartilage from the belly of pork and dice it and the remaining fat bacon. Quarter the 2 unstudded onions. Place the diced bacon in a very large, fireproof casserole dish with the lard and oil. Cook over low heat for 5 minutes, then add the diced pork belly and brown lightly over fairly low heat. Add the beef cubes, the clove-studded onions, the quartered onions, and the carrots. When the beef cubes are well browned all over, add the calf's foot and the bouquet garni. Cook, stirring, for a further 5 minutes.

Add the quartered tomatoes, the shallots, the remaining garlic clove, the orange peel, and the celery cut into small pieces. Stir as you add the wine. Season with salt and pepper and bring to a boil, then place in the oven at 275°F and simmer for $6^1/_2$ hours. Stir occasionally; if the liquid is evaporating too quickly, add a little boiling water.

TRIPES À LA NIÇOISE*

Tripe with vegetables and lemons

County of Nice

Preparation: 25 minutes
Cooking: 10 hours
Complicated

Serves 6:
$5^1/_2$ lb cleaned, blanched honeycomb tripe
6 unsprayed, untreated juicy lemons
1 lb shin of veal or 1 calf's foot, split lengthwise in half
4 large onions, peeled
12 small carrots, peeled
5 sticks celery, trimmed
6 cloves garlic, peeled
10 ripe tomatoes, peeled, and deseeded
1 bouquet garni (thyme, bay leaf, parsley)
pinch chopped fresh or dried oregano
$^1/_4$ cup brandy
$^1/_2$–1 cup grated Parmesan cheese
salt and pepper

Rub the tripe all over with the cut surfaces of the lemons and cut into ¾ × 2-in strips. Season with salt and pepper.

The traditional earthenware tripe pot (*tripière*) is very wide and shallow with a small opening on top and a tightly fitting lid; any heavy-bottomed fireproof casserole dish will do, however. Place a plate upside down to cover the bottom and prevent the tripe sticking. Place the tripe on top, mixed with the shin of veal or calf's foot and the onions and carrots sliced into rounds, the celery cut into small pieces, the garlic cloves, and the quartered tomatoes. Add the bouquet garni, the oregano, the brandy, and sufficient water to completely cover all these ingredients. Make a thick flour and water luting paste and seal the lid onto the *tripière* or casserole dish. Place in the oven, at 250°F and cook very gently for 10 hours, then break the seal on the lid, transfer all the contents to a wide, shallow very hot gratin dish, taking all the flesh off the shin of veal or calf's foot and dicing it before mixing with the tripe.

Sprinkle the surface with plenty of Parmesan cheese and place under a very hot broiler to melt and brown. Serve.

POULE FARCIE PROVENÇALE

Poached stuffed chicken

Provence

Preparation: 30 minutes
Cooking: 4 hours 20 minutes
Complicated

Serves 6:
1 5½-lb chicken (reserve the liver and gizzard)
1¾ cups soft, stale breadcrumbs
¾ cup milk
3 onions, peeled
½ cup peanut oil
5 oz Swiss chard leaves
2 cloves garlic, peeled
½ lb ham
1 large bunch parsley
3 eggs
1 shin of veal or veal shank
6 carrots, peeled
6 leeks, white part only
6 baby turnips, peeled
6 medium-sized white (strong) onions
salt and pepper

For the poaching broth:
2¼ lb beef (bottom round, blade)
1 carrot, peeled
1 onion, peeled and studded with 1 clove
1 bouquet garni (thyme, bay leaf, parsley)

For centuries whole, boned, stuffed Provençal lamb used to be the traditional Easter dish. The custom of serving the French king with this roast for Easter luncheon died out after the reign of Louis XV in the eighteenth century.

For the relish:
3 tbsp red wine vinegar
1 tsp strong mustard
½ cup olive oil
3 tbsp coarsely chopped flat-leaved parsley
1 finely chopped hard-boiled egg
salt and pepper

Make the poaching broth: cut the beef into small pieces or grind it and place with the prepared vegetables and flavorings listed above in a large saucepan or kettle, add 2½ quarts cold water, bring to a boil, and skim off any scum. Boil gently for 2 hours. Strain.

While the broth is cooking, mix the breadcrumbs with the milk and leave to stand. Chop the onions finely and cook in a little of the oil until tender and pale golden brown; add the trimmed and finely chopped chicken liver and gizzard and sauté for 2 minutes. Blanch the Swiss chard leaves in boiling water for 1 minute, drain, refresh under running cold water and drain again. Place the garlic, ham, parsley, Swiss chard leaves, the cooked onion mixture, the breadcrumbs (squeezed to eliminate excess moisture), and the 3 eggs in the food processor and process until smooth, seasoning with salt and pepper (or chop and then stir in the eggs and seasoning).

Preheat the oven to 450°F. Stuff the chicken with this mixture and then sew up very securely at both ends with a trussing needle and thread (otherwise the stuffing will become waterlogged when the bird is poached). Brush the entire surface of the chicken with the remaining oil and place uncovered in a roasting pan in the oven for 20 minutes. Heat the broth to just below boiling point in a kettle or saucepan, add the chicken to it straight from the oven and simmer gently for 1 hour, then add the veal shank and the prepared vegetables. Simmer for a further hour.

Make the relish by gradually beating the olive oil into the vinegar, mustard, parsley, and chopped egg; season and serve this vinaigrette in a sauceboat. Carve the chicken into portions; slice the stuffing and serve on a heated serving platter.

CARBONADE D'AGNEAU

Lamb casserole

Provence

Preparation: 40 minutes
Cooking: 2 hours 20 minutes
Easy

Serves 6:
1 3¼–3½-lb boned lamb shoulder
¼ lb pork belly or breast
5 baby carrots, peeled
5 baby turnips
1 celery heart
12 baby onions, with green leaves if possible
15–20 small, round new potatoes
3 ripe tomatoes or ½ cup sieved tomatoes
3 tbsp olive oil
1 bouquet garni (thyme, bay leaf, parsley)
¾ bottle dry white wine (ideally Côtes-du-Rhône or Provençal)
1 small bunch basil
salt and pepper

Remove and discard the skin and any tough pieces of cartilage from the pork belly, cut across the graining of fat and lean of the flesh into little lardons. Cut the lamb into 2-in cubes.

Cut the prepared carrots, turnips, and celery heart into small pieces; scrub the potatoes but leave them whole; leave half the length of the green leaves attached to the onions, if present.

Skin the tomatoes, quarter, and deseed; simmer in a pan with half the oil and a little salt and pepper until they have liquefied and thickened. Brown the lardons lightly on all sides over moderate heat in the remaining oil in a large, heavy-bottomed fireproof casserole dish for 5 minutes; remove with a slotted spoon and set aside. Brown the cubed lamb all over in the oil and fat left in the casserole, then remove these and set aside. Reheat the oil and fat for 2 minutes, then add the onions and cook fast for 2 minutes, stirring. Lower the heat a little and add all the other vegetables except for the potatoes; cook, stirring, for 5 minutes. Return the lardons and lamb to the casserole and add the bouquet garni and the wine.

Cover and simmer over low heat for 1½ hours (or cook at 350°F in the oven). When this time is up, remove and discard the bouquet garni, add the potatoes and season generously with freshly ground pepper. If a lot of the liquid has evaporated, add a little hot water so that the potatoes can cook evenly. Stir in the creamed tomatoes, cover, and cook for 30 minutes more or until the potatoes are tender. Sprinkle with coarsely chopped basil leaves and serve.

STUFATU*

Beef, ham, and lamb casserole

Corsica

Preparation: 30 minutes
Cooking: 3 1/2 hours
Easy

Serves 6:
1 1/2 lb lean braising beef
*10 oz smoked raw ham (*prosciutto *type)*
1 1/4 lb boned lamb shoulder
1/2 lb fat salt pork or fresh bacon
6 cloves garlic, peeled
1/4 cup lard
3 onions, 1 studded with 2 cloves
1 1/2 tbsp sieved tomato
1 1/2 cups dry white wine
1 mixed fresh bouquet garni (including all or some of the following: thyme, bay leaf, sage, rosemary, peppermint, savory)
2 juniper berries
salt and pepper

Cut the beef and lamb into 2-in cubes. Cut the raw, smoked ham into short, fat strips (see illustration left), make 1 or 2 slits in each meat cube and insert a piece of ham in each. The more robustly flavored raw hams of France (ideally Corsican) give a more authentic flavor than delicate Italian *prosciutto*. Cut 2 garlic cloves into small, very thin pieces and spike the meat cubes with these also. Roll the cubes in a mixture of salt and freshly ground pepper, shaking off excess.

Lightly brown 2 sliced onions in the lard over moderate heat, add the meat cubes, and brown all over, stirring.

Mix the tomato and wine and stir into the contents of the casserole. Add the bouquet garni, the clove-studded onion, and juniper berries. Cover and cook for 20 minutes, then pour in sufficient water to cover the meat; dice the rest of the ham (if there is any left over), chop the salt pork or bacon and the remaining garlic cloves; stir all these into the casserole. Cover and simmer very gently for 3 hours. In Corsica, short pasta is often added to the casserole, to cook slowly in the liquid and juices and the finished dish sprinkled with mixed grated Parmesan and Gouda or Edam cheese.

BOLES DE PICOULAT*

Beef and pork meatballs in rich sauce

Roussillon

Preparation: 25 minutes
Cooking: 1 hour
Easy

Serves 4:
1 cup finely chopped lean beef (e.g bottom round)
2 cups finely chopped blade of pork
6 cloves garlic, peeled
1/2 cup finely chopped parsley
2 eggs
salt and pepper
6 tbsp all-purpose flour
1/4 cup olive oil for shallow frying

For the sauce:
1/2 cup fresh bacon or breast or pork belly
1/4 cup cured raw ham
1 onion, peeled
1 large tomato, peeled
1 fresh hot red (chili) pepper
1/2 lb pitted small green French olives
pinch each nutmeg, salt, and pepper

Mince the garlic cloves lightly with the flat of a knife blade then chop them finely with the parsley and place in a large mixing bowl with the beef and pork. Beat the eggs lightly and add to the bowl; mix well, using your hands, and shape into oval meatballs the size of a small egg. Roll these in the flour, shaking off excess. Heat the oil in a fireproof casserole dish wide enough to take the meatballs in a single layer; brown them on all sides over moderately high heat, turning frequently.

While they are cooking, cut the pork belly or bacon and the raw ham into small dice. Chop the onion finely. When the meatballs are browned (do not overdo this, they have yet to be cooked through), remove them from the oil and keep hot on kitchen towels, covered with foil.

Add the diced pork belly or bacon to the oil left behind and brown lightly all over. Sprinkle in a little more flour to absorb some of the fat, add the onion, and cook until lightly browned; stir in $1\frac{1}{2}$ cups warm water, and continue stirring as the sauce comes to a boil. Season with pepper and a little salt, stir in the tomato, the sliced chili pepper, nutmeg, olives, and diced ham. Finally, add the meatballs; the liquid should half cover them, but add more water if necessary.

Simmer gently for 45 minutes, turning the meatballs after the first 20 minutes' cooking.

ESTOUFFADE DE BOEUF PROVENÇALE

Casseroled steak with anchovies and red wine

Provence

Preparation: 15 minutes
Cooking: 2 hours 20 minutes
Easy

Serves 6:
$3\frac{1}{4}$–$3\frac{1}{2}$ lb boned rib of beef, cut into 5-oz steaks
3 tbsp olive oil
$\frac{1}{2}$ cup best red wine vinegar
$1\frac{1}{2}$ tbsp tomato paste
1 onion, peeled, sliced
1 bouquet garni (thyme, bay leaf, parsley)
$1\frac{1}{2}$ tbsp capers
2 cloves garlic, peeled
1 small wine vinegar-pickled gherkin
2 bottles full-bodied dry red wine (e.g. Châteauneuf-du-Pape or Gigondas)
8 anchovy fillets
salt and pepper

Heat the oil in a wide skillet; add the steaks and brown over high heat for just over 2 minutes on each side, to seal; take them out of the skillet, drain briefly on kitchen towels, and place in a fireproof casserole dish.

Add the vinegar to the oil and juices in the skillet and stir; reduce the heat, add the tomato paste, the thinly sliced onion, the bouquet garni, and the chopped mixed capers, garlic, and gherkin. Pour in the red wine and cook, uncovered, for 15 minutes over moderately high heat, then pour over the steaks. If salted anchovies are used, rinse them under running cold water and remove any visible bones; if canned, drain; add these to the casserole dish, cover and simmer gently for 2 hours.

Serve with blanched Swiss chard leaves, stewed in a very little butter with a whole, peeled clove of garlic.

VEGETABLES

RATATOUILLE*

County of Nice

Preparation: $1\frac{1}{4}$ hours
Cooking: 35 minutes
Easy

Serves 8:
$2\frac{3}{4}$ lb eggplants
1 large onion, peeled
2 celery hearts
1 lb firm, ripe tomatoes
$\frac{1}{2}$ cup olive oil
$\frac{1}{2}$ cup wine vinegar
$1\frac{1}{2}$ tbsp superfine sugar
3 tbsp capers, drained
5 oz pitted small black French olives
3 tbsp coarsely chopped fresh basil
3 tbsp coarse sea salt
pepper

Many inhabitants of the Nice region prefer to leave out the celery hearts and substitute strips of sweet green pepper and sliced zucchini (if you choose to do the same, fry the peppers after the onions, followed by the zucchini). Wash and dry the eggplants, but do not peel. Cut lengthwise into slices and place in a colander, sprinkling each layer with coarse salt; place a plate and a weight on top and leave to stand for 1 hour to draw out all their bitter juices. Rinse and dry the slices. Slice the onion and celery hearts thinly into rounds.

Cut the tomatoes into quarters, remove the seeds; chop coarsely. Heat the oil in a saucepan or large skillet and when very hot brown the eggplant slices lightly on both sides. Remove them, draining well, and set aside; replace with the onion and celery; cook over moderate heat for 3 minutes to brown lightly. Add the tomatoes, stir and turn; sprinkle with the vinegar, sugar and a pinch of salt.

Simmer for 15 minutes, stirring. Return the eggplants to the pan, allow to come to a boil, then add the capers and olives. Simmer for 10 minutes, then remove from the heat. Serve hot or cold. A sprinkling of freshly chopped basil is particularly good with cold ratatouille.

BARBOUILLADE DE LÉGUMES

Mixed vegetables and lardons

Provence

Preparation: 40 minutes
Cooking: 25 minutes
Easy

Serves 4:
5 oz fresh pork belly or breast or unsmoked bacon
2¼ lb fava beans in the pod
12 small new white onions
8 fat, fresh green asparagus spears
12 baby violet artichokes
1 large onion, peeled and chopped
3 tbsp olive oil
juice of 1 lemon
salt and pepper

Remove the skin and any pieces of cartilage from the bacon or pork belly and cut across the graining of fat and lean into lardons. Hull the fava beans from their pods and remove and discard their casing as well, exposing the bright green cotyledons inside. Peel or just wash and dry the little onions and leave 2 in of the green leaves attached. Wash and peel the asparagus; cut off and reserve the tips and cut about 4 in of the stem into ⅜-in sections; discard the woody, tough end. Strip off the lower, outer leaves of the artichokes, trim off the stalk and a thin layer from the base if necessary and snip off the top 1 in (the pointed, upper half) of the leaves. Rub the cut surfaces with lemon juice.

Heat the oil in a large skillet, add the lardons, and brown all over for 5 minutes. Add the chopped onion and fry, stirring for 2 minutes. Add the artichokes and the little onions, stir while cooking for 2 minutes, then add the fava beans and the sliced asparagus spears. Cook gently for 10 minutes while stirring. Add the reserved asparagus tips and sprinkle with the lemon juice, salt and pepper. Stir carefully once or twice and continue cooking slowly for 5 final minutes, or a little longer if the vegetables are hard rather than pleasantly crisp.

AUBERGINES À LA BITERROISE*

Stuffed eggplants

Mediterranean Languedoc

Preparation: 35 minutes
Cooking: 1 hour 10 minutes
Complicated

Serves 6:
6 large, firm eggplants
5 oz raw ham (prosciutto *type)*
5 oz dry cured pork belly or pancetta or bacon
1 onion, peeled
2 cloves garlic
2 shallots
7 oz soft white breadrumbs
6 tbsp lukewarm milk
1 lb pork sausage meat
2 eggs
pinch ground cloves
1 sprig thyme, pinch powdered bay leaf
3/4 cup all-purpose flour
1/2 cup olive oil
2 1/4 cups sieved or creamed tomatoes, simmered with 1 whole, peeled clove garlic and 1 1/2 tbsp coarsely chopped fresh basil
salt and pepper

Try to buy the more rounded, squat eggplants for this recipe. Take off the stalk and cut a large "plug" out of the other, fatter end; use a serrated grapefruit knife or spoon or sharp pointed knife to scoop out the pulp from inside, leaving a layer about 1/4 in thick inside the skin. Alternatively, cut the eggplants in half and scoop out the flesh as shown below.

Chop the ham, pork belly, onion, garlic, and shallots finely together in the food processor or with a sharp knife. Soak the breadcrumbs in the milk; squeeze out excess moisture. Process the bread and meat, or mix by hand, with the sausage meat, eggs, a pinch each of salt, pepper, and cloves, the thyme leaves, and powdered or finely crumbled bay leaf. When well blended, pack into the hollowed eggplants, replace the "plug" or first piece cut from the fatter end and place in a fireproof casserole dish greased with half the oil. Cook over high heat for 10 minutes. Meanwhile, shape the remaining stuffing mixture into small meatballs, roll in the flour and brown all over in half the oil. Drain and set aside. Pour the hot garlic-flavored sieved tomato all over the stuffed eggplants, cover, and simmer gently for 30 minutes. Turn the eggplants, place the meatballs in the spaces between them and simmer for another 30 minutes. Garnish with fresh basil if wished and serve.

ARTICHAUTS À LA BARIGOULE*

Baby artichokes braised with mixed vegetables

Provence

Preparation: 20 minutes
Cooking: 2 1/2 hours
Easy

Serves 6:
18 baby violet artichokes
3/4 cup olive oil
2 onions, peeled, finely diced
2 carrots, peeled, finely diced
3/4 cup dry white wine
2 cloves garlic, minced
salt and pepper

Only the youngest, freshest artichokes are suitable for this recipe, picked long before they start to develop a "choke." Rinse under running cold water, pulling the leaves apart a little; drain upside down. Remove the outer, tougher leaves and trim off the tops of the remaining leaves. Cut off the remains of the stalk so that the artichokes will stand upright. Rub the cut surfaces with lemon juice.

Pour just over 1/2 cup of the oil into a wide, fireproof casserole dish. Spread out the mixed, diced onions and carrots in it. Place the artichokes upright on top. Season with salt and pepper, pulling their leaves apart in order to do so. Sprinkle with the remaining oil.

Cover the casserole dish tightly and place over low heat. Cook without removing the lid for 15 minutes, shaking the casserole from side to side at intervals to prevent the vegetables sticking.

Remove the lid, pour in the wine and increase the heat to boil the liquid and reduce by one third. Add the minced garlic and 3/4 cup water. Cover and simmer gently for 2 hours. From time to time, remove the lid and check that the vegetables are not sticking or burning, shaking the pan now and then.

Frédéric Mistral, the Provençal poet, described how each of seven towns in Provence had its own way of cooking eggplants:

*"In Sérignan they are served as a fricassée; in Carpentras they prefer them baked in an earthenware dish (*a tian*); in Thor, casseroled; the inhabitants of Isle like them stuffed and sautéed; in Maillanne, dipped in batter and deep-fried; in Apt they turn them into jam, and in Pertuis they are broiled over glowing embers ..."*

BAGNA CAUDA or ANCHOÏADE

Vegetables with anchovy dip

Provence and County of Nice

Preparation and cooking: about 30 minutes
Very easy

Serves 4:
Assorted fresh, tender seasonal raw vegetables (e.g. baby violet artichokes, deseeded sweet peppers cut lengthwise into strips, small sticks celery, baby carrots, very young fava beans in the pod, very small fennel bulbs, radishes, cauliflower, small tomatoes, mushrooms etc.)

For the sauce:
1/4 lb salted anchovies
2 cloves garlic, peeled
pepper
1 tsp wine vinegar
1 cup olive oil

Wash and wipe the vegetables dry, having trimmed them where necessary and arrange them attractively in a basket (or bowl).

Make the sauce: rinse salted anchovies under running cold water, dry, and remove any visible bones; drain if canned.

Chop the garlic and pound with the anchovies in a pestle with a mortar or use the food processor. Transfer to a fondue dish or small, heavy-bottomed casserole with a little freshly ground pepper. Keep beating with a balloon whisk over very gentle heat as you add first the vinegar and then the oil, adding the latter a very little at a time. The mixture should be very smooth and light. Place the fondue dish or casserole over a burner in the middle of the table. Each person takes a selection of raw vegetables and dips them in the sauce.

GRATIN D'AUBERGINES

Eggplant and tomato pie

Provence and County of Nice

Preparation: 20 minutes
Cooking: 30 minutes
Easy

Serves 4:
4 eggplants
5 tomatoes, peeled
3 onions, peeled
1 clove garlic, peeled
1 bouquet garni (thyme, bay leaf, parsley)
1 cup olive oil
salt and pepper

Peel the eggplants and cut them lengthwise into thin slices; arrange these in a bowl or colander with a little fine salt sprinkled between each layer. Remove the seeds from the tomatoes and cut into small pieces. Chop the onions; crush the garlic clove.

Preheat the oven to 500°F. Pour 3 tbsp of the oil into a fireproof casserole dish or saucepan, add the tomatoes, onion, garlic, bouquet garni, and salt and pepper. Simmer, uncovered, for 20 minutes over low heat. Use this time to squeeze the eggplant slices to draw out as much of their bitter juice as possible; heat the remaining oil in a wide skillet and fry the eggplants until they are golden brown on both sides. Drain briefly on kitchen towels.

Arrange the eggplant slices in layers in a wide, fairly shallow ovenproof casserole or gratin dish. Pour the tomato mixture all over the top and place in the oven for 10 minutes.

DESSERTS

FIADONE

Fresh cheese and lemon mold

Corsica

Preparation: 30 minutes
Cooking: 30 minutes
Easy

Serves 8:
1 lb fresh ewe's milk cheese
peel (no white pith) of 1 lemon
6 eggs, separated
2/3 cup superfine sugar
1 tsp oil

Place the cheese in a sieve to allow the whey to drain off. In Corsica *brocciu* (fresh sheep's milk cheese) is used; very fresh ricotta may be substituted. Add the lemon peel to a saucepan of boiling water; leave for 3 minutes, then drain. Chop very finely. Beat the egg yolks with the sugar until very pale and the mixture forms an unbroken ribbon when dropped from the balloon whisk back into the bowl. Stir in the chopped lemon peel, using a wooden spoon. Work in the cheese with a fork until smoothly blended. Beat the eggs until stiff but not grainy or dry in appearance. Fold carefully into the cheese mixture with a mixing spatula.

Grease a deep mold with the oil (sweet almond oil is ideal but any oil with a delicate flavor will do) and fill it with the cheese mixture, tapping the bottom on the work surface to make any large air bubbles rise to the top. Place in the oven, preheated to 350°F (stand in a tray of hot water if wished) and cook for 30 minutes. Allow to cool before unmolding. Serve cold.

BISCOTINS D'AIX

Orange flower water cookies

Provence

Preparation: 20 minutes
Cooking: 15 minutes
Easy

Serves 6:
1 1/4 cups sugar
3 1/4 cups all-purpose flour
2 tsp orange flower water
2 tbsp butter

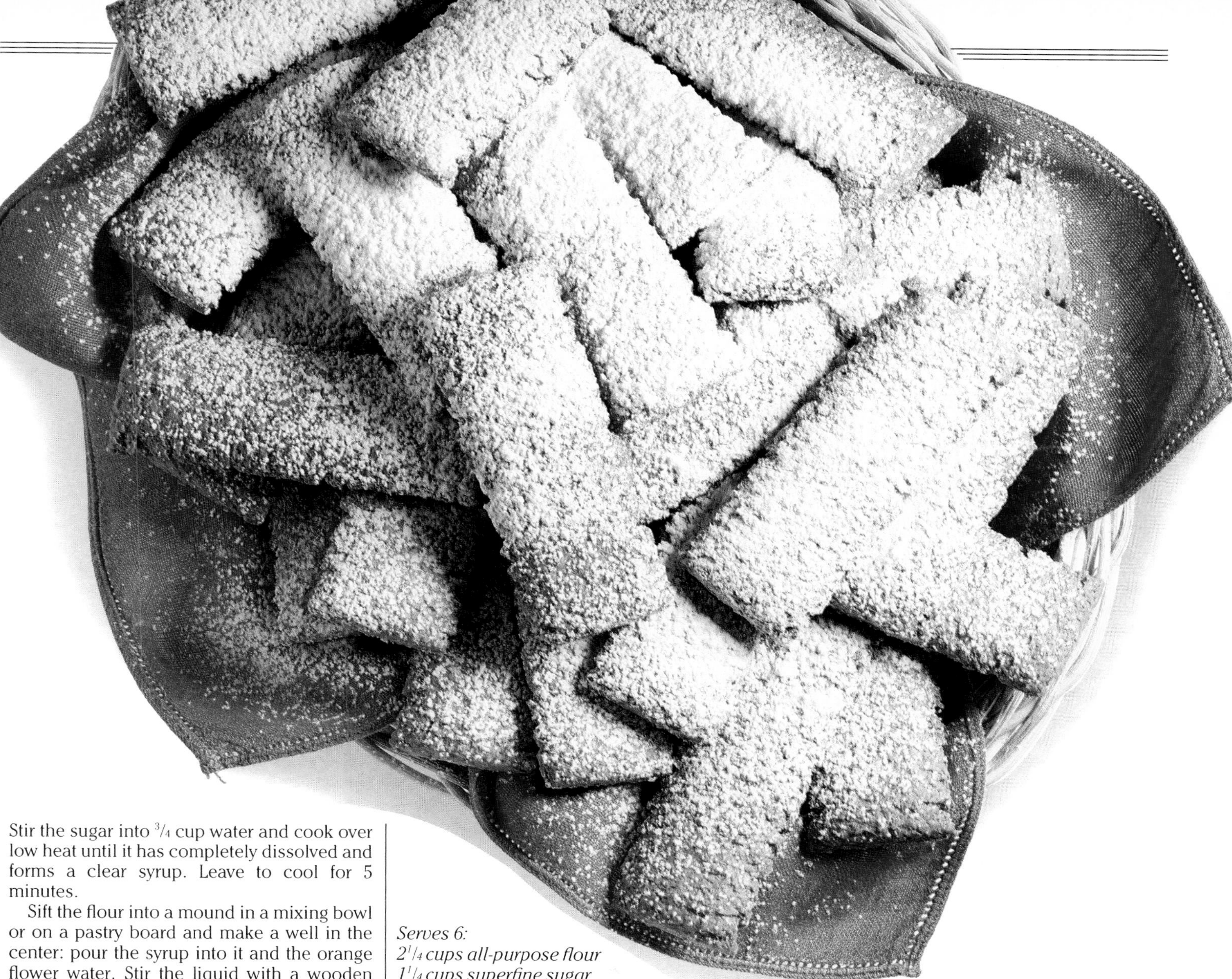

Stir the sugar into $^{3}/_{4}$ cup water and cook over low heat until it has completely dissolved and forms a clear syrup. Leave to cool for 5 minutes.

Sift the flour into a mound in a mixing bowl or on a pastry board and make a well in the center: pour the syrup into it and the orange flower water. Stir the liquid with a wooden spoon, gradually incorporating all the flour. Knead by hand until the dough is firm and smooth.

Preheat the oven to 400°F. Break off walnut-sized pieces of dough and roll into balls between your palms, flatten slightly and place $1–1^{1}/_{4}$ in away from each other on one or more cookie sheets greased with the butter. Sprinkle with a very little water and bake for 15 minutes. Use a palette knife to ease the cookies off the sheets as soon as they are done, while still very hot.

BISCOTINS DU FENOUILLÈDE*

Almond and lemon cookies

Roussillon

Preparation: 10 minutes + 1 hour resting time for the pastry dough
Cooking: 15 minutes
Easy

Serves 6:
$2^{1}/_{4}$ cups all-purpose flour
$1^{1}/_{4}$ cups superfine sugar
3 eggs
1 cup ground almonds
1 untreated lemon (not sprayed with fungicide)
pinch salt
$^{1}/_{4}$ cup butter
$^{1}/_{2}$ cup confectioner's sugar

Heap the flour and sugar in a mound, make a well in the center,and break the eggs into it; stir the eggs with your closed cupped fingers or with a wooden spoon, slowly blending in all the flour and sugar. Work in the ground almonds and finely grated rind of the lemon. Knead until well blended. Wrap in foil and chill in the refrigerator for 1 hour.

Preheat the oven to 350°F. Dust 1 or 2 cookie sheets with flour, shaking off excess, then grease them liberally with the butter, softened at room temperature. Roll out the dough into a sheet $^{3}/_{4}$ in thick and cut into $1^{1}/_{4} \times 4$-in rectangles.

Space these at least 1 in from each other on the cookie sheets and bake for 15 minutes. Dust with sifted confectioner's sugar.

GÂTEAU APTÉSIEN DE NOËL

Rich Christmas cake

Provence

Preparation: 25 minutes
Cooking: $1^{1}/_{2}$ hours
Easy

Serves 8:
3 cups blanched, peeled almonds
$2^{1}/_{4}$ lb assorted candied fruit
$2^{1}/_{4}$ cups all-purpose flour
1 cup butter
$^{3}/_{4}$ cup olive oil
1 cup brown cane sugar
6 eggs, separated
pinch ground cinnamon
1 tsp pure vanilla extract
2 tsps baking soda
peel (no pith) of 1 lemon

¼ cup brandy
pinch salt
butter for greasing

Grease a cake pan generously with butter. Preheat the oven to 400°F. Finely chop the almonds and the candied fruits separately. Place the fruit in a polythene bag with 3 tbsp of the flour and shake vigorously to coat lightly. Use a wooden spoon to beat the butter with the olive oil and the sugar in a mixing bowl until light and creamy; beat in the egg yolks one at a time. Beat the egg whites with a pinch of salt and a couple of drops of lemon juice until stiff but not at all grainy or dry looking. Stir the flour into the egg yolk, butter and sugar mixture, sifting it in with the baking powder, salt and cinnamon. Fold in the egg whites quickly but gently with a mixing spatula, together with the very finely chopped lemon, followed by the vanilla, brandy, and chopped fruit.

Turn the cake batter into the prepared cake pan and bake in the preheated oven for 20 minutes, then reduce the temperature to 350°F and bake for a further hour.

Test for doneness by inserting a thin skewer or sharp knife deep into the center; it should come out clean and dry.

TARTE À LA FLEUR D'ORANGER*

Orange flower water yeast cake with crunchy topping

Provence

Preparation: 10 minutes + 1 hour's rising time for dough
Cooking: 30 minutes
Easy

Serves 6:
½ cake fresh compressed yeast or ½ pkt dried yeast
6 tbsp tepid milk
6 tbsp white sugar
2¼ cup all-purpose flour
½ cup butter
2 eggs
pinch salt
6 drops orange flower water
6 tbsp brown cane sugar or Demerara sugar
6 tbsp crème fraîche *or thick cream*

Dissolve the yeast in the warm milk in a mixing bowl, stir gently; when it starts to foam, add 3 tbsp of the white sugar, followed by the flour, three quarters of the butter, the eggs, salt, and orange flower water. Stir all these ingredients with a wooden spoon or spatula, then knead by hand until smooth and homogenous. Shape into a ball, dust all over with a little flour, and place in a large charlotte mold that has been greased with the remaining butter. Cover with a cloth and leave in a very warm place; after 1 hour the dough should have doubled in bulk. Take the dough out of the oven; turn up the oven to 400°F. Sprinkle the surface of the risen dough in the mold with the brown sugar and place in the oven to bake for 15 minutes.

Take out of the oven, pour ¼ cup of the cream over the surface and return to the oven for 5 minutes. Take it out of the oven again, pour the remaining cream over the surface, then sprinkle with the rest of the white sugar and replace for a final 10 minutes' baking or until the sugar has dissolved and the yeast cake is done.

BRAS DE VÉNUS

Chestnut cake

Mediterranean Languedoc and Roussillon

Preparation: 25 minutes
Cooking: 10 minutes
Complicated

Serves 6:
½ cup superfine sugar
3 eggs, separated
pinch salt
½ cup all-purpose or fine cake flour
½ cup butter
1 tsp baking powder
*1 cup canned vanilla-flavored, sweetened chestnut purée (*crème de marrons à la vanille*)*

Mix and then beat the sugar with the egg yolks in a mixing bowl with a balloon whisk or mixing spatula until they are very pale and form an unbroken ribbon when dropped from the whisk back into the bowl.

Preheat the oven to 425°F. Beat the egg whites with a pinch of salt until stiff but not dry or grainy looking. Transfer half the beaten egg whites to another bowl; alternate beating in half the sugar and egg mixture with sifting in half the flour into one bowl of egg whites. Do the same with the remaining ingredients, then mix both halves together in the same bowl.

Have the butter melted over hot water and cooled (but still liquid); combine with the cake batter and add the baking powder at the same time. Fold in gently but quickly and very thoroughly. Line a jelly roll with lightly oiled waxed paper. Spread the sponge batter out evenly in this, leveling the surface with a spatula. Bake for 10 minutes or until very pale golden brown and done.

Take out of the oven and turn out onto a clean, damp cloth; carefully peel off the waxed paper; working quickly but carefully, spread the exposed surface with the marron purée and then roll up the sponge cake, starting by lifting the nearest end of the cloth and working toward the other end. Leave to cool.

The Southwest and the Pyrenees

Gascony
Western Languedoc (Toulouse)
Béarn
Basque country
County of Foix
Albigeois

Animal fats derived from pigs, geese, and ducks are as much part of the cooking of this region as olive oil is along the Mediterranean coast and in its hinterland. From Périgord to the Basque country, from the Atlantic coast to the Cévennes, the rearing of geese (and increasingly, ducks) plays a very important part in the region's economy.

Traditionally, it was the womenfolk who were responsible for looking after the flocks of geese and that is still true today albeit with some concession to modern living. The geese are driven to the fields, force-fed to fatten them and enlarge their livers, then driven to market when the time comes nowadays, instead of walking beside them in time-honoured tradition, the ladies are more likely to drive a truck, transporting the birds live, or freshly killed, drawn and plucked, their precious enlarged livers sold separately as the supreme delicacy *foie gras*, usually in the weeks leading up to Christmas.

A great many of the region's recipes are for goose and duck, rich food for a historically

On pages 212–213: *the little Pyrenean village of Arragnouet with its slate-roofed houses is built into the hillside by the Spanish border.* Opposite above: *Ainhnoa is the archetypal Basque village with its dark shutters and half-timbering contrasting with the whitewash walls, freshly painted every year;* opposite below: *Toulouse, seen here from the bank of the Garonne river, is called "the pink city" because of the soft, mellow color of the brick buildings. With Castelnaudary and Carcassonne, Toulouse has the best claim to the invention of* cassoulet. Below: *the River Tarn flows through the ancient city of Albi, the birthplace of Toulouse-Lautrec, is surrounded by the river's fertile flood plain where cereals, tobacco, vines (notably Gaillac wine) and fruit trees flourish.*

poor area. Almost every part of these birds can be put to good use, first and foremost their liver, prepared in a hundred different ways both simple and elaborate, part-cooked, pasteurized and canned; cooked with or without port or Armagnac, with garlic or capers or grapes and so on.

Preserved meats (*confits*) feature in all sorts of dishes, including *garbure*, the robust soup from Béarn, which is a meal in itself.

Goose is eaten casseroled, with chestnuts; its legs are broiled, the giblets braised or casseroled and transformed into tasty *ragouts* which go under the name of *alycot* or *alicuit*, the carcass, denuded of most of its flesh, is roasted and turned into tasty morsels not unlike pork spare ribs; even the intestines are cooked and eaten in the local *civet*, a rich, gamey stew.

Cassoulet is most typical dish of the region, in which preserved goose is cooked very slowly with pork or mutton and beans. This famous specialty has been the cause of disputes between three towns for centuries: Toulouse, Castelnaudary, and Carcassonne, each claiming to be the birthplace of *cassoulet*. Prosper Montagné, the great chef, neatly avoided controversy when he diplomatically likened the three feuding municipalities to the Holy Trinity where cassoulet's creation was concerned: "Castelnaudary is God the Father; Carcassonne, the Son, and Toulouse, the Holy Ghost."

There is also the *mounjetado* version of *cassoulet* from the County of Foix.

But *cassoulet*, goose, and duck do not have it all their own way in the cooking of the Pyrenean south of France. They dominate the cooking much less in the Basque country and Béarn than in Gascony and in the Toulouse district of Languedoc. Béarn is famous for its pork butchery, excelling at such charcuterie as Bayonne ham, *andouilles* from Oloron and blood pudding from Orthez. Henry IV, who was king first of Navarre and then of France, declared that he aimed to make the people of his new kingdom prosperous enough to eat

Above: *beneath the historic and legendary Pass of Ronceveaux lies Saint-Jean-Pied-de-Port, almost unchanged by the passing centuries with its old bridge over the River Nive and well preserved buildings;* Left: *good grazing on the slopes of the Pyrenean foothills helped to establish the local tradition of horse breeding.* Above: *the port of Saint-Jean-de-Luz. Local fishermen used to set out on long voyages to faraway cod fishing grounds. Nowadays these hardy Basques fish for tuna nearer to home and there are plenty of regional recipes for their catch.*

chicken every Sunday, and his native region has vaunted its chicken recipes ever since, especially stuffed chicken or capon. The Albi district, and Lacaune in particular, produces superb hams and sausages.

In the extreme southwestern corner of this region, the Basques have clung to their separatism in culinary matters as in so much else. Historically great fishermen, their cooking reflects this: *ttoro*, once a simple fish stew made with cods' heads, has developed into a rival of *bouillabaisse*; salt cod is a great favorite, and there are countless local recipes for it. Cuttlefish are stuffed and served in a sauce made with their ink in the Spanish fashion; fresh tuna is cooked with potatoes and sweet peppers and chili peppers and called *marmitako*.

The Basques are also a peasant people, cultivators of the soil, and this is reflected in their cooking. Recipes such as chicken Basque style, *tripotcha* (calf's tripe), *gachucha* (rice with tomatoes and chorizo hot savory sausages) and *pautxeta* (sausages made with lamb's tripe) all reflect their peasant origins in their homely style.

Both the Basque and Béarnais areas of Gascony produce delicious ewe's milk cheeses. These areas also do not lack for good wine; while the only wine worth mentioning from the real French Basque country is Irouléguy, pleasant and very drinkable but not distinguished, there are nevertheless some very interesting wines, both white and red, Tursan, Pacherenc, and Madiran among them. In some years Jurançon wine achieves true greatness and the Béarnais are justifiably proud of it: Henry IV is said to have been baptized with a drop of this nectar and with a clove of garlic.

Nor must it be forgotten that in two dictricts of Gascony, Landes and Gers, Armagnac is distilled, rivaling its cousin cognac (and there are many people who prefer it) as the world's best spirit distilled from wine.

SOUPS

GARBURE BÉARNAISE

Vegetable, ham, and confit soup

Béarn

Preparation: 30 minutes
Cooking: 2 1/2 hours
Easy

Serves 6:
1/4 lb fresh kidney beans
1 green cabbage
2 geese or ducks' necks (optional)
1 bouquet garni (thyme, bay leaf, parsley)
1/2 lb ham hock or knuckle or piece Bayonne ham
14 oz salt belly or pork breast (optional)
2 preserved goose legs or 3 preserved ducks' legs, with all the fat from the jar
14 oz waxy potatoes, peeled
14 oz carrots, peeled
10 oz onions, peeled
2 cloves garlic, peeled
salt and pepper

If you cannot buy fresh beans, soak 2 oz dried kidney beans overnight in cold, unsalted water. Remove the outer leaves and stem from the cabbage and rinse the heart thoroughly; drain and shred finely, blanch in boiling salted water for 5 minutes then drain, rinse under running cold water, and drain again.

Brown the goose or duck necks lightly in the fat from the preserved goose or duck jar. Add the quartered onions and garlic cloves (minced with the flat of a knife blade) and fry gently until tender and very lightly browned. Pour in 2 quarts water. Season with pepper. Add the bouquet garni, the drained presoaked beans (if dried beans are used) and your chosen cut or cuts of pork. Bring to a boil and skim off any scum. Cover and simmer gently for 2 hours, then add the cabbage, fresh beans (if used), potatoes, and carrots. Simmer for a further 30 minutes, adding a little salt after 20 minutes if necessary (unlikely if you have used salt pork and/or Bayonne ham).

Add the potted goose or duck legs no more than 10 minutes before serving; they need only enough time to heat through.

Serve this substantial soup-stew with toasted slices of coarse white or French bread.

OULIAT

Simple vegetable soup

Gascony

Preparation: 15 minutes
Cooking: 40 minutes
Very easy

Serves 4:
2 large onions, peeled
3 tbsp goose fat or olive oil
2 cloves garlic, peeled
2 large, ripe tomatoes, peeled
1 bouquet garni (thyme and parsley)
1 1/2 quarts vegetable broth
4 slices coarse white bread
2 egg yolks
1 1/2 tbsp wine vinegar
salt and pepper

Traditionally this soup is made from start to finish in a fireproof earthenware cooking pot but any large, enameled cast iron casserole dish or heavy-bottomed saucepan will do. Cook the thinly sliced onions in the goose fat or olive oil until tender and lightly browned. Add the minced garlic, the deseeded and very coarsely chopped tomatoes, and the bouquet garni. Cover and simmer very gently for 30 minutes. Pour in the vegetable broth (ideally left over from cooking legumes such as beans or peas) and season with salt and pepper. Bring to a boil and boil, uncovered, for about 5 minutes.

Place the bread slices in heated soup bowls. Strain the soup through a conical or other fine mesh sieve, pressing hard on the solid ingredients. Beat the raw egg yolks with the vinegar and stir into the very hot (not boiling) soup. Ladle onto the bread and serve immediately, with a sprinkling of grated Gruyère cheese if wished.

TTORO*

Fish head and seafood soup

Basque country

Preparation: 30 minutes
Cooking: 1 hour 10 minutes
Easy

Serves 8:
1 1-lb section conger eel (with its head)
1 sea-robin
1 hake's head
1 lb goosefish
1/4 cup olive oil
2 onions, peeled
2 cloves garlic, peeled
2 1/4 cups dry white wine
1 bouquet garni (thyme, bay leaf, parsley)
1 stick celery
1 sweet red pepper, shredded
1 hot red chili pepper, cut into rings
2 large, ripe tomatoes, peeled
3/4 cup all-purpose flour
1 quart (approx. 2 lb) mussels
8 lobsterettes or scampi
1 bunch parsley
salt

Cut the heads of the conger eel, sea-robin, and hake lengthwise in half and brown lightly all over in half the oil in a large saucepan; add the chopped onions and garlic and cook until tender. Pour in the wine and 1 quart cold water. Add the bouquet garni, the celery stick, the sweet and chili peppers, and the deseeded, chopped tomatoes. Sprinkle with a pinch of salt, cover, and simmer for 1 hour.

Cut the conger eel and goosefish into thick slices and dust all over lightly with flour; brown in a skillet for 1 minute on each side in the remaining oil over high heat. Salt lightly and draw aside from the heat. Transfer the fish pieces to a large fireproof earthenware or enameled cast iron casserole or similar and place the thoroughly washed and scrubbed live mussels on top. Pour in the fish head broth through a sieve, pressing down hard on the solid matter to squeeze out all the juices. Bring to a boil and cook for 6 minutes, add the crustaceans, allow to return to a boil, and cook for 2 minutes more.

Serve with crisp croûtons of bread fried in olive oil.

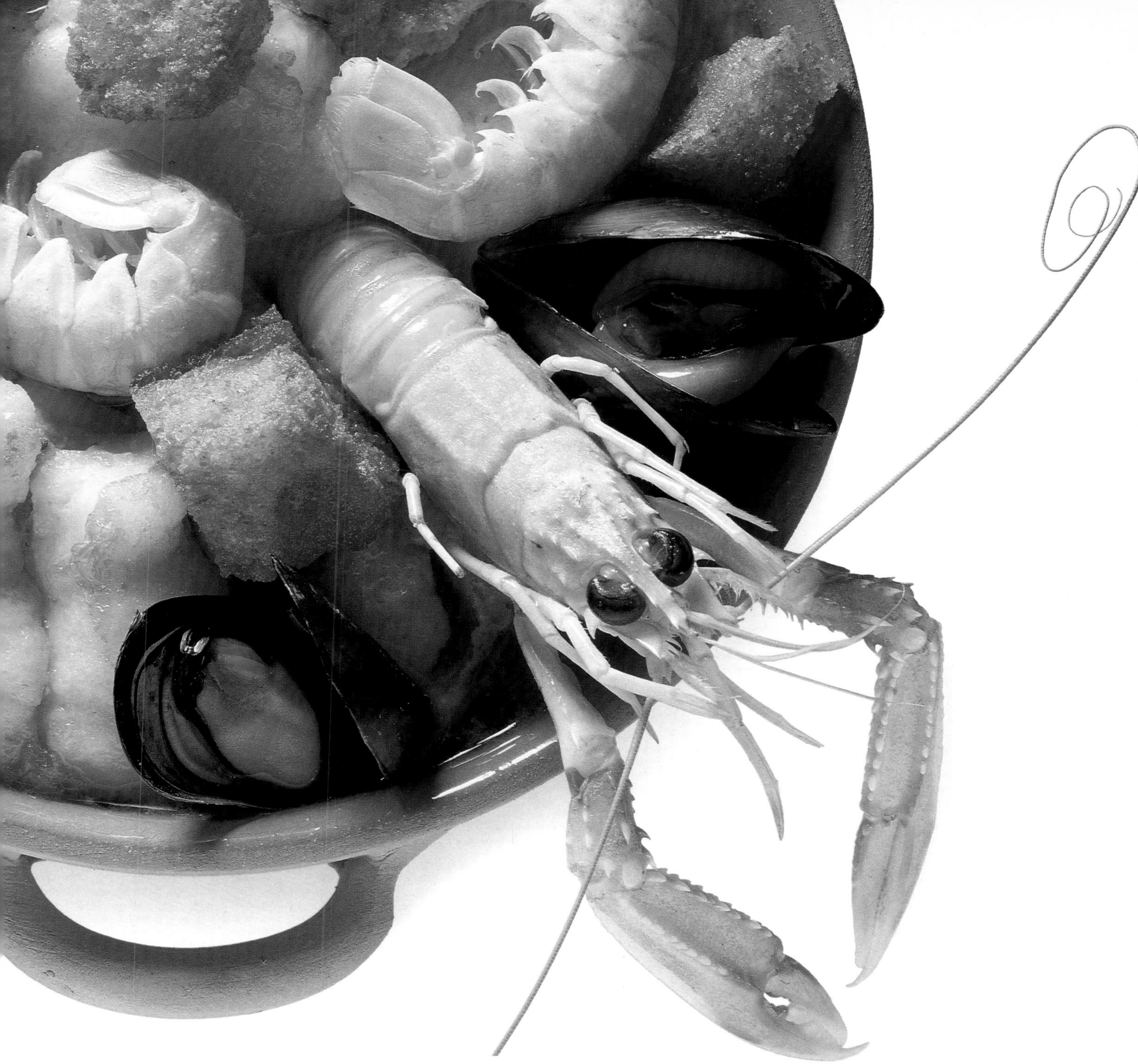

TOURAIN TOULOUSAIN

Garlic, cheese, and egg soup

Languedoc (Toulouse)

Preparation: 20 minutes
Cooking: 30 minutes
Easy

Serves 6:
10 cloves garlic, peeled
1/2 cup goose fat
1 bouquet garni (thyme, bay leaf, parsley, sage)
3 eggs, separated
6 slices toasted coarse white bread
1/2 cup grated Gruyère cheese
salt and pepper

Chop the garlic finely and cook gently in the goose fat in a deep saucepan until very lightly browned. Bring 2 quarts water to a boil and pour into the saucepan containing the garlic and fat. Add the bouquet garni and season with pepper and salt. Allow to return to a boil, cover, and boil for 20 minutes.

Take the broth off the heat, remove and discard the bouquet garni. Pour the egg whites into the broth and place over low heat so that the whites will set.

Beat the yolks in a bowl and continue beating as you gradually add just under 1/2 cup of the hot broth; pour this mixture back into the saucepan, stirring all the while. Do not allow to boil. Add a little salt if necessary and more freshly ground pepper (the soup should be very peppery). Cut or snip the set egg whites into pieces. Place the toasted bread slices in a heated soup tureen, sprinkle with the grated cheese, and pour in the soup. Cover and leave to stand for 3 minutes before serving.

PIPÉRADE*

Scrambled eggs with peppers, tomatoes, and ham

Basque country

Preparation: 40 minutes
Cooking: 20 minutes
Easy

Serves 6:
4 large sweet green peppers
$^1/_2$ cup olive oil
4 large onions, peeled
1 small hot red chili pepper
2 cloves garlic, peeled
$2^1/_4$–$2^1/_2$ lb tomatoes, peeled
1 bouquet garni (thyme, bay leaf, parsley)
6 eggs, lightly beaten
6 slices Bayonne ham (optional)
salt

Broil the sweet peppers to char and loosen their thin, bitter skin which will then peel off easily (rub off with kitchen towels). Cut the peppers in half, remove the seeds, stalk, and white pith and cut the flesh into $^1/_4$-in wide strips.

Heat all but $1^1/_2$ tbsp of the oil in a heavy-bottomed saucepan, add the peppers and cook, stirring, for a few minutes; add the very finely sliced onions, chili pepper, and chopped garlic; cook until nearly tender then add the deseeded, chopped tomatoes and the bouquet garni.

If you are not using Bayonne or similar *prosciutto*-type ham, add a little salt; cook uncovered over low heat for 10 minutes, stirring occasionally (the peppers should be just tender, not mushy, and should keep their shape).

Heat the reserved oil over moderate heat in another large skillet and pour in the lightly beaten eggs. Cook for 2 minutes then, when the underside has just set but the surface is still liquid, add the vegetables and stir, turning the eggs into a creamy scrambled mixture evenly distributed among the vegetables. Serve immediately.

If using Bayonne ham, use fairly thick slices and have them ready, lightly cooked in oil on both sides, to add to the finished dish.

SAUCE BÉARNAISE

Béarn

Preparation and cooking: 25 minutes
Complicated

Serves 8:
$1^1/_4$ cups butter
2 oz shallots, peeled
$^1/_2$ cup wine vinegar
3 tbsp chopped fresh tarragon
1 tsp chopped chervil
1 tsp minced or coarsely ground white peppercorns
5 egg yolks
salt

Take the butter out of the refrigerator in plenty of time and leave to soften at room temperature. Slice the shallots finely and place in a heavy-bottomed, nonmetallic saucepan with the vinegar, tarragon, chervil, and the pepper. Reduce over moderate heat until three quarters of the vinegar has evaporated. Set aside to cool and when cold, beat in the egg yolks with a balloon whisk or hand-held electric beater. Place the saucepan over very low heat or over gently boiling water and keep beating energetically. Increase the heat, still beating continuously, and as soon as the mixture has thickened to the point where the bottom of the pan stays clear for a second or two after the whisk has been drawn across it, start beating in the butter a small piece at a time. Add a pinch of salt and serve immediately.

ROUSOLO

Savory pork, bacon, and egg cake

County of Foix

Preparation: 5 minutes
Cooking: 20 minutes
Very easy

Serves 4:
5 oz finely chopped fat fresh bacon or pork belly
5 oz raw, cured Pyrenean or prosciutto-*type ham, finely chopped*
2 cups 2–3 days-old crumbled stale bread, crust removed
3 eggs
3 tbsp goose fat or lard
2 cloves garlic, peeled and minced
salt and pepper

Mix all the ingredients very thoroughly in a bowl, seasoning with freshly ground pepper and a small pinch of salt. Shape into a fairly thick, flattened cake. Heat the fat in a skillet and cook the savory cake on both sides without browning (to turn, slide out onto a large plate, cover with another plate, turn over and slide the cake back into the skillet).

FISH

THON BASQUAISE
Tuna with peppers

Basque country

Preparation: 5 minutes
Cooking: approx. 15 minutes
Easy

Serves 4:
Ingredients and quantities as listed under Pipérade (opposite page) omitting the ham and eggs
2 tuna steaks, each weighing 14 oz
2 extra cloves garlic, peeled
6 tbsp all-purpose flour
1/4 cup olive oil
salt

Soak the tuna in a bowl of cold water mixed with 1 tbsp wine vinegar for 45 minutes, if wished, to eliminate the strong scent. Drain, rinse, and dry. Cut the extra garlic cloves in half, remove and discard the central shoot if present, and cut the cloves lengthwise in quarters; use these pieces to spike the tuna steaks. Sprinkle with a little salt and coat lightly with flour.

Heat the oil in a large skillet and fry the tuna for 5 minutes over high heat, turn, and fry for a further 5 minutes. Reduce the heat; add the prepared, cooked pipérade. Cover and cook for 2 minutes if the pipérade was added hot, or 8 minutes to heat through from room temperature. Serve.

PIBALES (or CIVELLES) BASQUAISES
Elvers with garlic and chili pepper

Basque country

Preparation: 20 minutes
Cooking: 8 minutes
Very easy

Serves 4:
1 lb elvers (very small eel fry)
1/2 cup white wine vinegar
1 quart court-bouillon *(see glossary)*
1 cup olive oil
4 cloves garlic, peeled
1/2 small dried hot red chili pepper

Rinse the elvers very thoroughly in a deep metal sieve under running cold water. Place them in a bowl with 1/4 cup fresh cold water mixed with the vinegar; stir and turn to coat with vinegar which will kill them if alive; leave to stand for 10 minutes. Return to the sieve and rinse well under running cold water again.

Bring the *court-bouillon* to a boil, dip the sieve into the boiling water so that all the elvers are submerged, and cook for 1 minute only. Drain the elvers and spread out on kitchen towels to dry.

Heat the oil over fairly high heat with the sliced garlic and sliced or crumbled chili pepper for 4 minutes. Add the elvers all at once to the very hot oil and cook for 4 minutes. Serve.

CHIPIRONS À L'AMÉRICAINE*
Cuttlefish with pepper and chili sauce

Basque country

Preparation: 20 minutes
Cooking: 50 minutes
Easy

Serves 6:
12 cuttlefish
1/2 cup olive oil
2 onions, peeled
4 cloves garlic, peeled
3 tbsp all-purpose flour
1 1/2 cups dry white wine
1 1/2 tbsp Armagnac
1 bouquet garni (thyme, bay leaf, parsley)
3 tbsp sieved tomatoes (homemade or imported Italian, sold in cartons)
4 sweet green or red peppers, shredded
2 fresh small hot red or green chili peppers, cut into rings
salt

Prepare the cuttlefish, pulling the tentacles away from the body sac; cut off the tentacles and reserve. Discard the remaining contents of the sac, including the ink bag and the flat, white cuttlebone. Wash the body sac and tentacles well inside and out, rubbing off the thin skin from the sac under running cold water. Dry. Cut into rings. Heat the oil gently in a skillet (preferably nonstick) and add the cuttlefish rings and tentacles. Cook for 15 minutes, stirring occasionally.

Take the cuttlefish out of the oil and set aside. Fry the sliced onions and minced garlic cloves gently in the oil until tender and very lightly browned; sprinkle with the flour and continue cooking, stirring carefully, until the flour is golden brown.

Add the wine, Armagnac, 1/2 cup cold water, and the bouquet garni.

Keep stirring as the liquid thickens and comes to a gentle boil; stir in the sieved tomatoes, the sweet peppers, and chili peppers.

Cover and simmer for 15 minutes, then add the cuttlefish and cook gently for a further 15 minutes. Serve very hot.

MAIN COURSES

OIE EN DAUBE
Casseroled goose

Languedoc (Toulouse)

Start preparation 12 hours in advance
Preparation: 25 minutes
Cooking: 3¼ hours
Complicated

Serves 8:
1 6½-lb goose (not too fatty), jointed
2 sprigs thyme
1 bay leaf
2 cloves, crushed
¼ lb semisalted pork belly or pork breast
¼ lb onions, peeled
3 cloves garlic, peeled
1 bunch parsley
1 bottle dry red wine (ideally Madiran)
approx. 1¾ cups all-purpose flour
salt and pepper

Pull the pieces of hard white fat away from the inside of the goose's cavity before jointing it, put these pieces of fat in a heavy-bottomed saucepan with ¾ cup water and place over moderate heat. The fat will melt; continue cooking until all the moisture content has evaporated (i.e. when no more steam rises from the pan). Pour all but about 3 tbsp of this excellent cooking fat into a pot for later use.

Take the thyme leaves off one stalk and mix them in a large plate with some freshly ground pepper, the finely crumbled bayleaf, and the crushed cloves. Remove the skin and tough bits of cartilage from the salt pork, cut into strips (lardons) across the graining of fat and lean and use to lard the goose flesh with a larding needle (or make incisions with a knife and push the lardons in). Make a marinade in a nonmetallic dish just large enough to accommodate the pieces of goose comfortably, mixing the thyme, half the onions (sliced), 1 clove garlic, chopped parsley, and the wine. The goose must be completely covered by this marinade; add more wine if necessary. Cover and leave in a cold larder or refrigerator for 12 hours.

Take the goose portions out of the marinade, drain, dry, and coat all over with flour, shaking off excess. Brown well all over in the reserved 3 tbsp goose fat, take out of the casserole dish or saucepan, and discard all but 3 tbsp of the fat which has accumulated. Chop the remaining onions and garlic and fry gently in the fat for 5 minutes. Add the goose portions, the remaining sprig of thyme, the strained marinade, and a pinch of salt. Heat almost to boiling point, then place the lid on the casserole dish, sealing with a luting paste made of flour and water.

Place in the oven, preheated to 325°C, and cook for 3 hours.

Take out of the oven, break the luting seal, transfer the goose pieces to a heated serving dish and keep hot while you leave the cooking liquid to settle for 5 minutes and the fat to collect on the surface; skim off as much of the fat as possible, taste the remaining liquid for seasoning, and pour all over the goose.

SALMIS DE PALOMBES
Wild pigeon with red wine and chocolate sauce

Gascony, Béarn, Basque country

Preparation: 15 minutes
Cooking: 1 hour 10 minutes
Easy

Serves 4:
4 wild pigeons
1 tbsp butter
1½ tbsp peanut oil
1 large, thick slice Bayonne ham
2 onions, peeled
10 oz wild girolles or cultivated button mushrooms
1 bottle dry red wine (ideally Madiran, Côtes-de-Buzet or Bordeaux)
1 sprig thyme
pinch each nutmeg, salt, and pepper
1 square bitter (i.e. dark, unsweetened) chocolate
croûtons of white bread fried in butter

Singe off any remaining bits of down from the oven-ready pigeons and use poultry shears to cut them neatly in half lengthwise down the breastbone and backbone. Heat the butter and oil in a fireproof casserole dish, preferably large enough to take the halved birds in one layer and sauté the ham, cut into small dice, with the finely sliced onions and the cleaned and quartered mushrooms for 3–4 minutes, until lightly browned. Take all these ingredients out of the pan with a slotted spoon and set aside. Replace with the pigeons and brown these, allowing 5 minutes for each side. Add the red wine and return the onions, ham, and mushrooms to the casserole. Sprinkle with the thyme, pepper, salt, and nutmeg. Simmer uncovered over low heat for 1 hour. Add the chocolate 5 minutes before this time is up and stir once it has melted. Coat the birds with the sauce and garnish with croûtons.

Most French restaurants close once a week, usually on the same day, except when the major events of life, such as marriages or funerals, disrupt the routine. One very famous French chef, Prosper Montagné, recalled seeing one in Castelnaudary that said: "Closed for preparation of cassoulet*."*

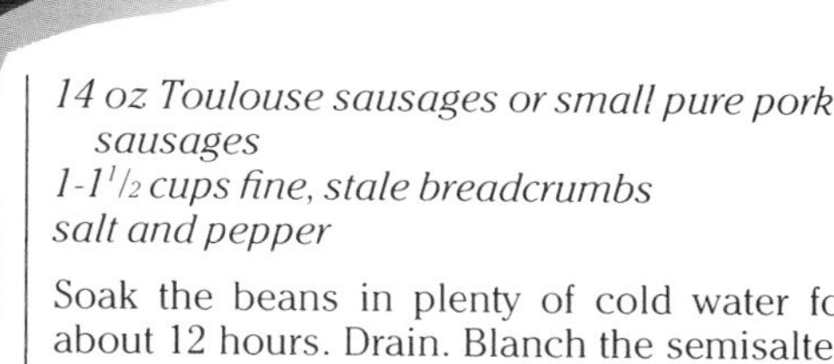

CASSOULET TOULOUSAIN*

Bean, pork, sausage and duck or goose casserole

Languedoc (Toulouse)

Start preparation 12 hours in advance
Preparation: 25 minutes
Cooking: 4 hours
Complicated

Serves 8:
1½-1¾ lb dried white kidney beans
1 semisalted ham hock
¾ lb semisalted or fresh pork spareribs or boned pork shoulder
1 1 lb boiling pork sausage (preferably made with pork rind and garlic)
1 onion, studded with 1 clove
1 sprig thyme
1 medium-sized carrot
1 clove garlic, peeled, cut in half
½ lb fresh pork skin
1 large, firm tomato
3 preserved duck's legs or 2 preserved goose legs
14 oz Toulouse sausages or small pure pork sausages
1-1½ cups fine, stale breadcrumbs
salt and pepper

Soak the beans in plenty of cold water for about 12 hours. Drain. Blanch the semisalted cut(s) of pork. Drain them and place in a kettle or very large saucepan with the beans, large sausage, clove-studded onion, thyme leaves, and the carrot, this last cut lengthwise in quarters. Add sufficient cold water to completely cover. Do not add any salt. Bring slowly to a boil and boil very gently for 1 hour. Rub the inside of a very large earthenware or stoneware casserole dish with the garlic until the half cloves have completely worn away. Line the bottom (and part of the sides if you have sufficient skin) with the pork skin, fat side against the surface of the casserole.

Discard the onion, the clove, and the carrot and transfer half the beans to the casserole dish, using a slotted spoon. Take the ham off the bone and slice; place in a layer on top of the beans. Remove the skin from the large sausage, cut into thick slices, and arrange on top of the ham. Season sparingly with salt if necessary and generously with freshly ground pepper. Spread the remaining beans on top; moisten with 1 cup of the cooking liquid.

Have the oven preheated to 325°F and place the casserole in it, uncovered. Cook for 3 hours. Add a very little more hot liquid at intervals if necessary; the *cassoulet* mixture should be very moist but not soupy, it is enough for the meat to be almost covered with liquid, the beans will cook in the steam. During the last 30–45 minutes, heat the duck or goose with its surrounding fat over very low heat; toast the breadcrumbs and broil the Toulouse sausages until just done.

A skin may form on the surface of the casserole contents as it cooks; press this down gently into the beans with the back of a spoon every 20 minutes, as it will reform; when you have done this for the fifth and last time, add the potted duck or goose pieces and the hot, lightly broiled Toulouse sausages and bury them among the beans. Increase the oven temperature to 400°F. Sprinkle the breadcrumbs all over the surface, pour the melted fat from the potted duck or goose all over them, and return the casserole to the oven, still uncovered, for a final 20 minutes' cooking, when a crunchy, golden brown crust should form.

Serve straight from the casserole dish.

POULE AU POT FARCIE

Stuffed casseroled chicken

Béarn

Preparation: 25 minutes
Cooking: 3 hours
Complicated

Serves 6:
1 3¼–3½ lb kg plump boiling chicken

For the stuffing:
1 egg + 1 extra yolk
2¼ cups stale white breadcrumbs
¼ cup coarsely chopped flat parsley
¼ cup chopped Bayonne ham
½ cup chopped cooked lean ham
1 clove garlic, peeled and minced
the chicken's liver, trimmed and chopped
salt and pepper
cayenne pepper

For the poaching liquid:
2½ quarts water
1 bouquet garni (thyme, bay leaf, parsley)
1 small stick celery, with its leaves
green section of 1 leek, well washed
2 tbsp coarse sea salt
1½ tbsp peppercorns
1 large onion, peeled and studded with 1 clove
pinch cayenne pepper

For the accompanying vegetables:
6 large carrots, peeled
6 large leeks
3 celery hearts, cut lengthwise in half
6 baby turnips, peeled

For the egg vinaigrette sauce:
2 eggs
2 tsp strong mustard
½ cup peanut oil
1 lemon
3 tbsp mixed chopped tarragon, chervil, and chives

Make the stuffing: beat the egg and extra yolk in a mixing bowl. Stir in the breadcrumbs, seasonings, parsley, both types of ham, and a pinch each of salt, freshly ground pepper, and cayenne pepper. When well blended, stir in the chopped chicken liver (trim off any discolored parts of this first). Fill the chicken's cavity with this stuffing and sew up both ends.

Place the chicken breast uppermost in a deep, fireproof casserole dish or heavy-bottomed saucepan; pour in enough cold water to cover the fowl, add the bouquet garni, all the other ingredients listed under poaching liquid above and the rinsed giblets if available. Bring slowly to a boil. Reduce the heat to very low; skim any scum off the surface and simmer very gently indeed for 2 hours. Turn off the heat, remove the bouquet and other flavorings, giblets etc. Skim off as much fat as possible from the surface and add the prepared vegetables, cut into fairly large pieces.

Bring back to a gentle boil and cook for a further 1 hour. Start preparing the egg vinaigrette 30 minutes into this cooking time: add the eggs at room temperature to boiling water and cook for 3½ minutes after the water has returned to the boil. Cool quickly under running cold water. Take off their tops and scoop out the yolks into a bowl with a teaspoon; mix well with the mustard for 5 minutes. Gradually add the oil, trickling it in slowly as you beat energetically with a balloon whisk or hand-held electric beater. Beat in the lemon juice and stir in the herbs and the chopped egg whites. Serve in a sauceboat with the chicken and vegetables. The poaching liquid can be served first as a soup, or kept for another meal.

POULE VERTE

Poached chicken with spinach stuffing

Languedoc (Toulouse)

Preparation: 50 minutes
Cooking: 1½ hours
Easy

Serves 4:
1 2¼–2½ lb chicken with its giblets
1 tsp goose fat or lard
½ lb fresh spinach
2 onions, peeled
2 cups soft, stale breadcrumbs
½ cup milk
1¾ cups ground veal shoulder or breast
1 turkey breast
1 small bunch parsley
1 small bunch chervil
4 carrots, peeled
4 baby turnips, peeled
4 leeks
1 stick celery
1 bouquet garni (thyme, bay leaf, parsley)
1 onion, peeled and studded with 1 clove
salt and pepper
nutmeg

The French still insist that their chickens taste of chicken and a great many are corn-fed, farm-reared and free-range, producing poultry that has plenty of flavor, unlike the bland, watery chickens on sale in so many of our supermarkets.

If you have the chicken's liver (unless the bird has been ready cleaned) trim off the gall bladder and any yellowish discoloration; lightly cook the liver, frying it gently for 5 minutes in the goose fat in a large nonstick or nonmetallic saucepan; take out of the fat and chop finely. Chop the raw, cleaned gizzard if you have it.

Make the stuffing: wash the spinach leaves, removing all the stalks; drain the leaves well and chop; chop the 2 onions. Add to the pan used for frying the liver. Sweat, adding a little more fat, until very lightly browned. Add the spinach, sweat gently, stirring continuously, to cook and eliminate excess moisture.

Moisten the breadcrumbs with the milk and leave to stand for a while; squeeze out excess moisture and mix with the liver, gizzard, veal, and finely diced turkey breast, salt, pepper, and nutmeg, the onions, and the washed, dried, and finely chopped parsley and chervil. Stuff the chicken's cavity with this mixture; sew up securely.

Place the prepared vegetables, the bouquet garni, clove-studded onion and the chicken neck, feet, and wingtips if available, in a very large, deep fireproof casserole dish or cooking pot; place the chicken on this bed and add enough water to come 2 in above the top of the chicken. Bring slowly to boiling point and simmer gently, uncovered, for 1½ hours. Serve the chicken with the vegetables; use the cooking liquid as a soup, or as a rich chicken broth.

FOIE GRAS

Force-fed duck liver

Gascony, Languedoc (Toulouse), Béarn

Start preparation 3–4 days in advance
Preparation: 20 minutes
Cooking: 40 minutes
Complicated

Serves 6:
2 fresh force-fed duck livers, each weighing approx. 1 lb
1 tsp salt
½ tsp superfine sugar
pinch of freshly ground white pepper

Allow the liver to come up to room temperature. Separate the lobes and place each on a separate, clean cloth; use a very sharp, pointed knife to make a very shallow incision (about ⅛ in) down the length of each lobe. Locate the main vein at the larger end of each lobe and pull it away slowly but firmly as you cut carefully with the knife, opening out the lobes: the attached network of smaller blood vessels will come away too, attached to the main vein. The large lobe is supplied with two of these networks. Carefully remove the parts

which were nearest the gall bladder and any areas discolored by bile, and any fatty deposits.

Mix the salt, sugar, and pepper and rub the livers gently inside and out with this seasoning mixture.

Preheat the oven to 300°F. Place one large lobe in the bottom of a bowl, terrine or paté mold, put the two smaller lobes on top of it and cover with the second large lobe, smooth, uncut side uppermost.

Press down gently but firmly with your hand (the bowl should just be big enough to contain the livers) cover with aluminum foil. Place the bowl in a roasting pan, pour in enough hot water to come about halfway up its side and cook for 40 minutes.

Take the bowl or terrine out of the oven; place a small plate on top of the liver (or a piece of board cut so that it will slot easily inside the top of the receptacle) and place a 5–7-oz weight on top to compress the livers and gently squeeze out excess fat. Leave until the livers are completely cold, then chill in the refrigerator, with the weight in place, for 3–4 days. Turn out shortly before serving and slice.

CAPILOTADE DE LAPIN*

Jellied rabbit and white wine casserole

Languedoc (Toulouse)

Start preparation 12 hours in advance
Preparation: 20 minutes
Cooking: 2 hours
Easy

Serves 6:
1 4½ lb rabbit, jointed
1 calf's foot, split lengthwise in half
approx. 1 lb fresh veal bones
2 cloves garlic, peeled
2 shallots, peeled
3 carrots, peeled
5 oz fresh pork belly or breast
3 tbsp butter
2 cloves
1 bouquet garni (thyme, bay leaf, parsley)
2¼ cups dry white wine
¼ cup cognac
salt and pepper

Place the well washed calf's foot and bones (the latter sawn into fairly small pieces) in a large stockpot or saucepan, add sufficient cold water to cover, bring to a boil, then turn off the heat and leave to stand for 5 minutes. Drain. Remove the skin and any tough cartilagenous pieces from the pork belly and cut it into lardons. Slice the carrots into rounds; chop the shallots.

Heat the butter and brown the rabbit portions all over in it; add the lardons and brown them also, then add the shallots, carrots, garlic, cloves, bouquet garni, and the calf's foot and veal bones. Cook for a few minutes, then pour in the wine, cognac, and just enough cold water to come just over three quarters of the way up the rabbit pieces. Season with salt and pepper. Heat to boiling point, cover, and simmer for 2 hours.

Arrange the rabbit portions snugly in a fairly deep earthenware or china serving dish. Strain the cooking liquid through a conical sieve all over the rabbit pieces. Leave to cool; refrigerate for at least 12 hours. The liquid will set into a very savory jelly. Serve lightly chilled with salad.

CONFIT DE CANARD
Preserved duck

Gascony, Languedoc (Toulouse), Béarn

Start preparation 24 hours in advance
Preparation: 1 hour
Complicated

Serves 8:
2 fattened ducks
$4^1/_2$ lb rendered duck or goose fat
7 oz coarse sea salt

To prepare this recipe, buy ducks that have been plucked but not cleaned or ask the butcher to save all the giblets for you, as well as all the solid fat from the inside of the bird's cavity. If you clean the duck yourself, take care to remove the gall bladder without rupturing it and releasing the bitter gall. In France specially fattened, force-fed ducks are used and the liver set aside to make duck *foie gras* (see page 224).

Slit the gizzard and clean it. Cut off the wingtips and reserve; remove the skin from the backbone section where there is little flesh underneath and reserve. Part bone the duck, leaving the bones of the wings and legs, (drumsticks and thighs) in place but taking the skin and flesh off the carcass; reserve the carcass for broth if wished. Cut off the legs and wings.

Rub the salt into the boned legs and wings inside and out by hand, do likewise with the wingtips, gizzard, heart, and neck and place in a bowl in the refrigerator for 24 hours for the salt to penetrate. Chill the solid fat removed from the cavity and the skin removed from the backbone section.

The next day, place the fat and skin in an enameled cast iron saucepan and leave over gentle heat to melt the solid fat and extract the fat from the skin. Pour through a fine sieve and return to the saucepan; add the $4^1/_2$ lb duck or goose fat listed in the ingredients and leave over moderate heat. Wipe the salt carefully from the portions of duck with a clean cloth; there should be no solid crystals of it left adhering to the portions. Add these to the hot fat and cook over gentle heat for $1^1/_4$ hours or until done (when the bone emerges from the receding skin at the ends of the thighs and drumsticks). Leave to cool, then transfer into scrupulously clean, wide-necked stoneware jars or pots. Cover with the liquid fat, up to the lip of the jar; tap gently on the work surface to release any trapped air bubbles. Seal hermetically and keep in a cold larder or refrigerator for up to 2–3 months.

If you choose to sterilize the filled jars (the safest, and recommended method for home canning) cook the duck portions in the fat for 30 minutes only. Then sterilize the sealed jars for $1^1/_4$ hours. Goose can be potted in exactly the same way, allowing a larger quantity of goose fat for larger birds, longer cooking times (approx. 2 hours) and bigger jars. The heart, gizzard, and wingtips can be used in other dishes.

Genuine Bayonne ham is cured and smoked in Orthez, 40 miles from its nameplace and is delicious eaten thinly sliced, with curls of unsalted butter, fresh figs or melon. Other raw, smoked hams or jambons de campagne *cost less and can be substituted when a recipe calls for the addition of coarser flavored ham in casseroles and other dishes.*

AILLADE DE VEAU À LA GASCONNE
Braised veal shoulder

Gascony

Preparation: 10 minutes
Cooking: $3^1/_4$ hours
Very easy
Serves 6:

$2^1/_4$–$2^1/_2$ lb boned veal shoulder
3 large, ripe tomatoes, peeled
$^1/_4$ cup lard
5 cloves garlic, peeled
1 onion, peeled
1 bouquet garni (thyme, bay leaf, parsley)
$1^1/_2$ cups light broth (see glossary)
pinch each sugar, salt, and pepper
$^3/_4$ cup fine, dry breadcrumbs

Cut the veal into $1^1/_2$-in cubes. Slice the tomatoes, deseed, and spread out on kitchen towels to drain.

Brown the meat lightly all over in the lard in a fireproof casserole dish. Add the chopped garlic. Cook for 5 minutes. Add the very thinly sliced onion and the bouquet garni. Season with salt and pepper. Cook, stirring, for a further 5 minutes.

Add the sliced tomatoes, stir, and pour in the broth.

Heat slowly to boiling point, taste for seasoning, add a pinch of sugar, stir, cover, and leave to simmer for 3 hours over moderate heat.

Preheat the oven to 500°F. Transfer the casserole's contents to a preheated, fairly shallow ovenproof serving dish (the liquid should have reduced considerably); sprinkle the breadcrumbs all over the surface and place in the oven for 5 minutes or a little longer to brown.

POULET BASQUAISE*
Chicken with peppers, tomatoes, and Bayonne ham

Basque country

Preparation: 30 minutes
Cooking: 55 minutes
Easy

Serves 6:
1 $2^3/_4$–3 lb oven-ready chicken
$^1/_4$ cup goose fat
1 onion, peeled
2 cloves garlic, peeled
6 sweet green peppers, shredded
4 tomatoes, peeled
$^1/_4$ lb closed cap cultivated mushrooms (optional)
$^1/_2$ cup dry white wine
$^1/_2$ lb Bayonne ham, thickly sliced
6 small garlic, flavored boiling sausages (see method)
salt and pepper
1 small bunch flat-leaved parsley

Cut the chicken into 6 portions. Trim, wash, and dry the giblets if you have them, removing any discoloration from the liver. Heat the goose fat in a fireproof casserole dish or heavy bottomed saucepan and brown the chicken portions and giblets in it over high heat, reducing this as soon as the flesh has firmed and "set." When the chicken pieces have browned, remove from the pan and reserve; leave the giblets in for a further few minutes more. Keep all these hot.

Slice the onion and mince the garlic and add to the fat in the casserole dish, together with the green peppers. Deseed the tomatoes, cutting the flesh into small pieces, add to the casserole, followed by the finely diced mushrooms, if used. Season with salt and pepper and cook briskly over high heat, uncovered, for 10 minutes. Pour in the white wine, allow to return to the boil, cover, and turn down the heat to a simmer and leave to cook for 30 minutes.

Return the chicken pieces to this sauce and continue simmering for 10 minutes, while you dice the ham and slice the sausages (if used, they are an optional extra) into thick rounds: raw Basque *louquenkas* flavored with garlic and the particularly flavorsome local sweet peppers or pimento are traditional, but any small pure pork sausages may be substituted). Brown the ham and sausage slices in a very little extra fat in a skillet and arrange them around or among the chicken pieces coated with the sauce.

Serve with rice, boiled in salted water until tender.

FOIE GRAS AUX RAISINS*

Duck or goose livers with grapes

Gascony

Start preparation 24 hours in advance
Preparation: 1 hour + overnight marinating and seasoning
Cooking: $1^1/_2$ hours
Complicated

Serves 8:
*2 force-fed duck livers (*foie gras*), each weighing approx. 1 lb or 2 goose* foie gras, *each weighing $1^1/_4$ lb*
$2^3/_4$ lb ripe, firm white grapes
1 cup dry white wine (ideally Tursan or Jurançon)
$^1/_4$ cup Armagnac
generous pinch each superfine sugar, salt, and pepper
3 carrots, peeled
2 onions, peeled
$1^1/_2$ tbsp goose fat
1 cup chicken broth
salt and pepper

Wash the grapes, take them off the bunches, peel, and extract the seeds as neatly as possible with a pin or quill toothpick. Place them in a bowl with the wine and Armagnac, stir gently, cover, and leave in the refrigerator overnight.

Prepare the livers as directed in the recipe for *foie gras* on page 224. Rub gently all over with the mixed sugar, salt, and pepper. Place in a bowl, cover with a cloth and chill overnight.

Preheat the oven to 350°F. Cut the carrots and the onions into very thin slices and arrange in an even layer in the bottom of a heavy-bottomed fireproof casserole dish containing the fat.

Place the livers on top of of this vegetable bed and place a sheet of butter-greased waxed paper, buttered side down, on top of the livers. Cover and place in the oven for 25 minutes for duck livers, 30 minutes for goose livers.

Take out the livers and keep hot. Drain off the fat from the casserole dish and pour the broth and the marinade drained from the grapes into it. Boil gently, uncovered, until reduced to half its original volume, then strain and pour back into the casserole dish. Add the grapes and heat gently for 4 minutes. Add salt and pepper to taste if needed.

Serve at once, cutting the livers horizontally into three slices of equal thickness before transferring them to heated plates or a serving dish, with the sauce and grapes spooned over them.

PISTACHE DE SAINT-GAUDENS*

Lamb, bean, and white wine casserole

Languedoc (Toulouse)

Allow 8 hours advance soaking time for dried beans
Preparation: 30 minutes
Cooking: $3^1/_2$ hours
Complicated

Serves 6:
$2^3/_4$–3 lb boned mutton or lamb shoulder
1 lb dried white kidney beans ($2^3/_4$ lb fresh beans in the pod)
3 carrots, peeled
10 oz ripe tomatoes, peeled
5 oz salt pork skin or bacon rind
1 bouquet garni (thyme, bay leaf, parsley)
$^3/_4$ cup goose fat
3 onions, peeled, 1 studded with 1 clove
6 cloves garlic, peeled
1 cup dry white wine
$^3/_4$–1 cup dried breadcrumbs
salt and pepper

If using dried beans, soak them in cold water for 8 hours, drain them shortly before cooking, rinse and place in a kettle or saucepan, pour in enough cold water to cover; do not add salt. Cut the carrots into round slices. Remove the seeds from the tomatoes.

Blanch the pieces of salt pork skin or bacon rind, drain, and refresh; roll them up and tie with string, add them to the beans (they will provide all the salt needed), together with the clove-studded onion, the bouquet garni, and the carrots. Cover and bring slowly to a boil; simmer very gently for 1 hour. Cut the mutton or lamb into $1^1/_2$-in cubes and brown all over in the goose fat, then add the quartered onions and cook these over moderate heat, stirring until lightly browned. Mince 5 of the garlic cloves and add, together with the chopped tomatoes; as these cook and soften, crush them with the back of the spoon, to

reduce them to a coarse purée.

Pour in the wine. Drain the beans when tender (still unsalted) and pour the liquid into the casserole dish or saucepan containing the meat; cover this and cook over very low heat for 1 hour. Add a little salt and plenty of freshly ground pepper halfway through this time.

Use the remaining garlic clove, cut in half, to rub hard all over the inside of an deep ovenproof dish; grease with lard or oil. Preheat the oven to 300°F. Transfer half the beans to this dish, with 1 cup of the cooking liquid from the saucepan containing the meat; place the pieces of mutton or lamb on top and, cover with the remaining beans. Reduce the liquid from the meat saucepan over high heat, and sprinkle 3/4–1 cup of it over the beans. The level of the liquid should be well below the surface of the beans; sprinkle with the breadcrumbs and a little extra melted goose fat. Cook in the oven for 1 1/2 hours. Serve straight from the this casserole dish. Sometimes the pork skin is cut into small squares and mixed with the beans for the final 1 1/2 hours' cooking.

Despite its name, the invention of Béarnaise sauce in 1860 did not take place in that province but in Saint-Germain, a district of Paris; it was created by a cook born in Béarn working in a restaurant called Pavillon Henri IV.

GRAS-DOUBLE ALBIGEOIS

Tripe, ham and mixed vegetable casserole

Languedoc (Toulouse)

Preparation: 15 minutes
Cooking: 10 hours 40 minutes
Complicated

Serves 8:
3¼–3½ lb cleaned, blanched tripe
1½–2 lb fresh bones (e.g. ham, lamb leg or veal)
10 oz carrots, peeled
5 oz onions, peeled
3 cloves
1 whole head garlic
1 bouquet garni (thyme, bay leaf)
1 tsp white peppercorns
10 oz cured raw ham (e.g. Bayonne)
2 tbsp lard
3 tbsp all-purpose flour
pinch real saffron threads or powder
2 tbsp capers
salt and pepper

Traditionally, this recipe is cooked in a very large earthenware cooking pot or *tripière*. A deep earthenware or enameled cast iron casserole dish are both suitable; place the tripe in the casserole dish with the well rinsed bones (whichever your butcher has available), the sliced carrots, quartered onions stuck with the cloves, and the garlic head, left whole with only the outermost dry, papery skin removed; the thyme, bay leaf, and peppercorns enclosed in a cheesecloth bag. Pour in sufficient cold water to come well over the top of the contents. Make a thick luting paste with flour and water and seal the lid to the casserole so that no moisture can escape during cooking. Cook at 250°F and leave to cook for just under 10 hours; 20 minutes before the end of this time, break the luting seal and take off the lid. Gently fry the finely diced ham in the lard for 5 minutes. Sprinkle in the flour, stir for 3 minutes, then stir in 3 cups of the liquid from the tripe dish. Cook, stirring continuously, for 3 minutes; take the garlic out of the tripe dish and squeeze over the ham and sauce to release most of the pulp inside which will have turned to a soft purée. Stir well, adding the saffron. Drain and discard or set aside any remaining liquid from the tripe and cut it into 1½–2-in squares, add to the saffron, garlic, and ham mixture and simmer very gently for a further 30 minutes over low heat, then transfer to a heated serving dish. Drain the capers, sprinkle all over the tripe, and serve at once.

ALYCUIT OR ALYCOT À LA BÉARNAISE*

Giblets braised with ham, vegetables, and white wine

Béarn

Preparation: 25 minutes
Cooking: 1¼–1¾ hours
Easy

Serves 4:
giblets from 1 goose (neck, gizzard, wingtips) or 4 chickens (with their livers)
5 oz raw cured ham, e.g. Bayonne
4 carrots, peeled
2 onions, peeled
2 tomatoes, peeled
¼ cup goose fat
2 cloves
1 bouquet garni (thyme, bay leaf, parsley)
4 cloves garlic, peeled
3 tbsp all-purpose flour
1½ cups dry white wine (ideally Jurançon or Tursan)
salt, pepper, nutmeg

Prepare the giblets: singe off any remaining down from the wingtips, extract any quill ends left behind when the bird was plucked; open and clean the gizzards; trim any gall-discolored parts from the chicken livers, if used, and rinse all these. Cut the ham into small dice. Slice the carrots; cut the onions into fairly thick rings. Cut open the tomatoes and deseed.

Heat the goose fat in a large, fireproof casserole dish and brown the giblets all over in it, stirring. Add the carrots, ham, onions (the largest slices of these studded with the cloves), tomatoes, bouquet garni, minced garlic, salt, pepper, and a pinch of nutmeg.

Cook all these in the fat, stirring, for a few minutes to brown lightly. Sprinkle in the flour and stir until it has turned pale golden brown. Continue stirring as you gradually add the wine and ¾ cup water. Bring slowly to a boil.

Chop the livers very finely indeed, if used, and stir into the contents of the casserole. Once the liquid has come to the boil, turn off the heat, cover and place in the oven, preheated to 350°F, to cook for 1 hour (1½ hours if using goose giblets) or a little longer if the gizzards are not tender enough when tested.

VEGETABLES

RIZ À LA GACHUCHA

Rice with bacon, olives, and sweet peppers

Basque country

Preparation: 15 minutes
Cooking: 35 minutes
Easy

Serves 6:
2½ cups short-grain rice
5 oz onions, peeled
½ cup olive oil
½ cup sieved tomatoes
5 oz green olives, pitted
1 chorizo *sausage*
½ lb smoked bacon
1 lb red or green sweet peppers, shredded
1½ tbsp butter
salt and pepper

Place the rice in a sieve and rinse very thoroughly under running cold water (use Arborio risotto rice if available), drain, and spread out to dry on a clean cloth. Chop the onions very finely and cook them gently in a very large, fairly deep skillet or saucepan in all but 3 tbsp of the olive oil (reserved for later use).

When the onions are very tender, add the sieved tomatoes (homemade or commercially prepared, sold in cartons). Cook, uncovered, stirring for 5 minutes to reduce. Add the rice and cook, stirring, for a few minutes.

Pour in 1½ quarts boiling hot water; add a small pinch each of salt and pepper. Sprinkle in the olives, slice the *chorizo* into rounds and place on the surface. Smear one side of a large piece of waxed paper with a little olive oil and place on top of the rice, oiled side down, cover with a lid as well to prevent most of the steam escaping. Leave to cook over low heat for 25 minutes; the rice should have absorbed all the liquid after this time but should be moist; cook for a little longer if it is still at all sloppy.

While the rice is cooking, cut the bacon into lardons and sauté in the remaining oil until lightly browned. Remove with a slotted spoon and set aside; sauté the peppers until very tender.

Grease a large ring-tube mold with the butter. Take most of the *chorizo* slices out of the rice and press these and the lardons against the inside surfaces of the mold; carefully pack the mold with the risotto. Place a heated plate upside down on top of the mold, turn the plate the right way up, releasing the rice mold onto it and fill the central well with the peppers.

DESSERTS

GIMBLETTES D'ALBI

Citron and orange flower water cookies

Languedoc (Toulouse)

Preparation: 20 minutes + 30 minutes resting time for the dough
Cooking: 30 minutes
Easy

Serves 6:
3½ cups unbleached strong flour or fine cake flour
½ oz (1 packet) dried active yeast
¼ cup butter
¼ cup superfine sugar
1¾–2 tsp salt
6 eggs
grated peel of 1 lemon
2½ oz candied citron peel
1 tsp orange flower water

Mix the flour and yeast in a large bowl. Make a well in the center, pour ½ cup lukewarm water into it, the butter melted over hot water, the sugar, salt, and 2 of the eggs (which should be at room temperature). Stir the contents of the well with your slightly cupped fingers or with a wooden spoon, gradually incorporating all the flour. The dough should be soft and light. Cover with a clean cloth and leave to stand in a warm room for 30 minutes.

While the dough is rising, grate the lemon peel and cut the citron peel into tiny dice. When the 30 minutes are up, work both peels, the remaining eggs, and the orange flower water well into the dough. Knead thoroughly and shape into a ball.

Roll out into a ½-in thick sheet, 5 in wide, on a lightly floured pastry slab or working surface and cut into strips, ½ in wide and 5 in long. Join up the ends of each strip securely to form a ring. Prick lightly in 3 or 4 places with the tip of a sharp pointed knife.

Have a very large kettle or very wide saucepan three quarters full of boiling water; turn down the heat so that the water is simmering gently. Add the rings. Stir gently with a wooden spoon to prevent them sticking. They will soon bob up to the surface; poach them for 5 minutes without stirring after they have done this and they will puff up and expand. Drain on kitchen towels.

Leave to cool. Preheat the oven to 425°F. When the rings are cold, place on cookie sheets greased with butter. Bake in the oven for 20 minutes or until they are golden brown.

GATEAU BASQUE

Vanilla and rum cream tart

Basque country

Preparation: 25 minutes
Cooking: 45 minutes
Complicated

Serves 8:
1 cup rich milk
1 vanilla bean
5 eggs
1 cup superfine sugar
2½ cups all-purpose flour
2 tsp baking powder
¾ cup butter, at room temperature
3 tbsp rum

Make the confectioner's cream first: place the vanilla pod in the milk in a saucepan and bring very slowly to a boil. Set aside to cool slowly. Beat two of the eggs very vigorously with ¼ cup of the sugar until pale and creamy. Keep beating as you sift in ¼ cup of the flour. Remove the vanilla pod from the milk; beat the milk into the mixture and then return to the saucepan in which the milk was heated. Heat over very gentle heat while stirring continuously; at the first sign of the mixture coming to a boil, draw aside from the heat and stir in 1 tbsp of the butter, blending in a very small piece at a time.

Grease a *moule à manqué* (2-in deep cake pan with sides sloping outward from 7–9 in in diameter (or use a straight-sided cake pan of similar size). Preheat the oven to 400°F. Make the dough: beat generous ½ cup or ½ cup + 2 tbsp of the remaining butter until very smooth and creamy; keep beating as you add the sugar. Beat until almost white and very soft and light. (Use a balloon whisk or a hand-held electric beater). Beat in the eggs one at a time, then stir in the flour, sifting this in with the baking powder to make a smooth dough.

Working quickly, dust the greased cake pan with flour, tipping out excess. Beat the rum into the confectioner's cream. Pat out two thirds of the dough on a lightly floured pastry cloth or board into a disk large enough to line the cake pan completely. Press the dough lightly into place against the base and sides. Fill with the confectioner's cream and smooth level. Pat out the remaining dough into another, smaller disk for the lid, place this on top of the filling and pinch the edges very firmly together: there must be no gaps through which the cream could ooze out during cooking. Beat the remaining egg and brush over the surface. Place in the oven and bake for 45 minutes. Leave to cool at room temperature, then turn out carefully. Fresh pitted black cherries and black cherry jam can be used for the filling.

Do not refrigerate this cake, as this ruins its texture. Make on the day you plan to serve it and keep at room temperature for a maximum of 4 hours.

MILLAS LANDAIS*

Orange flower and lemon flan

Gascony

Preparation: 20 minutes
Cooking: 30 minutes
Easy

Serves 6:
1 quart rich milk
$^2/_3$ cup superfine sugar
$1^1/_2$ tbsp orange flower water
5 eggs
1 cup sifted cornstarch or fine cornmeal
finely grated peel of 1 lemon

Preheat the oven to 500°F. Reserve $^1/_2$ cup of the milk and bring the rest to a boil in a saucepan; stir in the sugar with a wooden spoon until it has completely dissolved. Turn off the heat. Stir in the orange flower water. Set aside. Beat the egg whites until stiff but not dry or grainy in appearance.

Sift the cornstarch in a mixing bowl; mix in the egg yolks one at a time. Stir in the grated lemon peel. Beat with a balloon whisk or stir with a wooden spoon as you gradually add the milk (which will still be hot). Make sure there are no lumps. Fold in the beaten egg whites evenly with with a slotted spoon.

Grease a 9-in fairly shallow, wide ceramic soufflé dish or cake pan ($1^1/_2$–2 in deep) with butter; transfer the mixture to it, place in a roasting pan and pour in sufficient boiling water to come about halfway up the sides of the cake pan. Bake for 30 minutes. Allow to cool completely before turning out.

Vine-yards and wines of France

INTRODUCTION

All wines are unique, depending on their provenance, age, the grapes of which they are comprised, the method by which they are produced, and a number of other vital and sometimes indefinable factors. While wine may certainly be drunk on its own, it is really best when judged in relation to food, brought out on special occasions and served in conjunction with specific dishes.

It is not enough to select a wine at random and simply to hope for the best. Some measure of knowledge is always an advantage. It may not be necessary to go to the lengths of connoisseurs' tasting sessions organized according to set rituals and established rules. Recognition of a wine's intrinsic nature, its individual language and expression, comes from years of experience which can be accumulated gradually by sampling different varieties and vintages. Expert terms such as depth, power, firmness, warmth, elegance, seriousness, reticence and so on then acquire meaning. In addition to defining the nuances of appearance, it becomes possible to distinguish the elements of the bouquet or nose, the effect on the palate, the type of finish. One can readily tell a young from a mature wine and decide whether it is ready to drink immediately or worth laying down for the future.

France, of course, is renowned for the quality and variety of its vines, and the French, over the centuries, have transformed the making and consumption of wines into a fine art. Yet these *appellations* range from the most exquisite and expensive vintages, through a seemingly boundless assortment of good to excellent, realistically priced, regional wines, to the simplest of table wines.

The pleasure to be derived from drinking a good French wine is greatly enhanced by some familiarity with the producing regions. The warmth of a Châteauneuf-du-Pape, for example, evokes memories of a vineyard covered with small white stones which store the sun's heat during the day and pass it on to the grapes at night. The fresh, keen, supple expression of Muscadet is perfectly in keeping with the light, flinty soil. The roundness of Burgundy wines stems from the chalky terrain, the delicacy and strength of Médoc from its gravelly hills, and the atmospheric moisture of Sauternes, Vouvray, and Coteaux du Layon favors the development of the *pourriture noble* (noble rot) which makes these great wines so sweet and heady.

Everything, in fact, is encapsulated in a glass of wine: the region, the climate, the grape and, not least, the patient and loving work of man. So it is important to understand the meaning of the name which the proprietor claims for his wine. This name, the *appellation* (A.O.C.: *appellation d'origine contrôlée*; V.D.Q.S.: *vin délimité de qualité supérieure*) is information offered to the consumer: among all food products, wine is only one to stake its claim so openly. The label provides the essential facts and the contents have to speak for themselves.

Despite the overall, generally predictable climate of a wine-producing zone, it is important to remember that each year the weather will vary, so it is wise to be familiar with different vintages. When the vines flower early and the summer is sunny, with a dry period for the harvest, production conditions are right for a wine with a good life expectancy. On the other hand, if there is little sun and the summer is wet, the wine will be more supple and fresh, with a shorter life expectancy; this will go well with a lighter, livelier style of cooking. So one must learn to serve appropriate wines both according to their origin and their age. As a rule it is better to drink a fully mature *grand cru* of a lesser year than a young, still closed wine of a good year.

The serving temperatures recommended for individual wines in the following categories are more or less standard, but the suggested accompanying dishes obviously depend on place and availability, and are capable of almost indefinite extension, according to individual preference. Many are included in the recipe section of this book. It is always worth experimenting, the main purpose being to derive pleasure and satisfaction from a meal, whether a light snack, a business lunch or a formal dinner.

Jacques Puisais

The vineyards of the Southwest

The vineyards which make up the vast and prestigious region of the Bordelais display very similar characteristics and produce wines of similar quality. The soil is subjected to an Atlantic or Aquitaine climate which gives the wines a particular style. A red Bordeaux is notable mainly for its distinctive astringency.

It is a region where the local people know and love the wine which they take so much pride in producing. The connoisseur can revel in a wide range of wines which exhibit all stages of natural evolution from youth to maturity and old age. In the Gironde département *are grouped all the Bordeaux wines, or clarets, white, red, dry, mellow, light, full-bodied, tannic. To the north are the vineyards of Bergerac; up the valley of the Garonne, as far as Toulouse, are the wines of Cahors and Gaillac and then the light, sparkling Limoux; and finally, after crossing the Landes forest, towards the Pyrenees, there are the vineyards of Béarn, made famous by King Henry IV.*

This vast zone of the basin of Aquitaine corresponds roughly to the ancient province of Guyenne and Gascogne (Gascony). The basin of the Garonne is the element common to all the vineyards, except for Béarn, which belongs to the Adour basin.

The Aquitaine region constitutes one of the richest larders in France, with a cuisine which takes particular pride in its foie gras *(goose liver), with its subtle aroma and flavor, and which concocts a delicious variety of dishes based on the local abundance of seafood, sea and river fish, beef, lamb and a marvelous selection of poultry.*

The fine crus *of Bordelais and the Southwest form an ideal accompaniment to this generous cuisine. They are wines to be savored and relished, worthy of the people who have made them and of the soil in which they have been nurtured.*

BARSAC
A.C. White

Grape varieties
Sémillon, Sauvignon, Muscadelle.
Production zone
Commune of Barsac.
Characteristics
Clean color, straw-yellow to golden-yellow as it ages. Well developed bouquet of vegetables, fruit, and flowers; balanced taste, predominantly sugar. The characteristic aromas are strong and persistent. The wines are full-bodied and well blended, slightly astringent, and have very good ageing properties.
Serving temperature and suggested accompaniments
Serve at 50°F (10°C). Goes well with fresh duck *foie gras* or Roquefort omelet.

CÉRONS
A.C. White

Grape varieties
Sémillon, Sauvignon, Muscadelle.
Production zone
Communes or part of communes of Cérons, Illats, Podensac.
Characteristics
Clean color, straw-yellow to golden-yellow as it ages. Well developed bouquet of vegetables, fruit, and flowers; balanced taste, predominantly sugar. The characteristic aromas are very strong and persistent. The wine is full-bodied, delicate, slightly astringent, and has very good ageing propeties.
Serving temperature and suggested accompaniments
Serve at 50°F (10°C). Goes well with lampreys *à la bordelaise*, knuckle of veal, and desserts.

SAINTE-CROIX-DU-MONT
A.C. White

Grape varieties
Sémillon, Sauvignon, Muscadelle.
Production zone
Commune of Sainte-Croix-du-Mont.
Characteristics
Clean color, straw-yellow to golden-yellow as it ages. Well developed bouquet of vegetables, fruit, and flowers; balanced taste, predominantly sugar. The characteristic aromas are very strong and persistent. The wine is full-bodied, well balanced, delicate, slightly astringent, and has good ageing properties.
Serving temperature and suggested accompaniments
Serve at 50°F (10°C) with, say, a warm game salad or *croquants du Périgord*.

SAUTERNES
A.C. White

Grape varieties
Sémillon, Sauvignon, Muscadelle.
Production zone
Communes or parts of communes of Sauternes, Bommes, Fargues, Preignac, Barsac.
Characteristics
Clean, fairly distinct color, straw-yellow to amber-yellow, according to year, as it ages. Well developed bouquet of vegetables, fruit, and flowers; balanced taste, predominantly sugar. The characteristic aromas are very strong and persistent. The wine is full, rich, slightly astringent, and has excellent ageing properties.
Serving temperature and suggested accompaniments
Serve at 50°F (10°C). Goes well with *foie gras*, fish dishes, and Roquefort cheese.

LOUPIAC
A.C. White

Grape varieties
Sémillon, Sauvignon, Muscadelle.
Production zone
Commune of Loupiac.
Characteristics
Clean color, straw-yellow to golden-yellow as it ages. Well developed bouquet of vegetables and fruit; balanced taste, predominantly sugar. The characteristic aromas are strong and persistent. The wine is full-bodied, well balanced, delicate, slightly astringent, and has very good ageing properties.
Serving temperature and suggested accompaniments
Serve at 50°F (10°C) with salmon or with desserts.

ENTRE-DEUX-MERS
A.C. White

Grape varieties
In proportion of 70%: Sémillon, Sauvignon, Muscadelle, Merlot Blanc (max. 30%), Colombard, Mauzac, Saint-Emilion (max. 10%).
Production zone
A.C. zones Premières Côtes de Bordeaux, Loupiac, Saint-Macaire, Sainte-Foy, Bordeaux, Vayres, Arveyres.
Characteristics
The wine, light straw-yellow in color, has a well developed bouquet of vegetables and fruit, the taste balanced without a predominance of sugar (less than 4 g per liter) and strong characteristic aromas. The wine is supple, fresh, and delicate, slightly astringent. It does not age well.
Serving temperature and suggested accompaniments
Serve 50°F (10°C) with seafood.

ENTRE-DEUX-MERS-HAUT BENAUGE
A.C. White

Production zone
Communes or part of communes of Arbis, Cantois, Escoussans, Gornac, Ladaux, Mourens, Saint-Pierre-de-Bat, Soulignac, Targon.

Grape varieties and uses are similar to those of Entre-Deux-Mers.

GRAVES-DE-VAYRES
A.C. White

Grape varieties
Sémillon, Sauvignon, Muscadelle, Merlot Blanc (max. 30%).
Production zone
Communes or part of communes of Vayres, Arveyres.
Characteristics
Light straw-yellow color. Well developed bouquet of vegetables and fruit; balanced taste without a preponderance of sugar. Strong characteristic aromas. The wine is supple, fresh, and delicate, slightly astringent. It does not age well.
Serving temperature and suggested accompaniments
Serve at 50°F (10°C). Goes well with shellfish, particularly cold crab dishes.

GRAVES-DE-VAYRES
A.C. Red

Grape varieties
Cabernet Franc, Cabernet Sauvignon, Carmenère, Merlot, Malbec, Petit Verdot.
Production zone
Communes or part of communes of Vayres, Arveyres.
Characteristics
Medium carmine-garnet color. Well developed fruity bouquet and strong characteristic aromas. The wine is supple and fresh, fairly astringent, and with good ageing properties.
Serving temperature and suggested accompaniments
Serve at 57°F (14°C) with broiled steak.

GRAVES
A.C. White

Grape varieties
Sauvignon, Sémillon, Muscadelle.
Production zone
42 communes of the Gironde.
Characteristics
Color light straw-yellow. Well developed vegetable, mineral, flowery bouquet; balanced, dry taste. Characteristic aromas strong and persistent. The wine is well balanced, fresh, and delicate, with no astringency and has very good ageing properties.
Serving temperature and suggested accompaniments
Serve at 52°F (11°C). Goes very well with baked lobster, served with melted butter and a little lemon juice, with oyster soup, or *caudière de Berck*.

GRAVES
A.C. Red

Grape varieties
Merlot, Cabernet Franc, Cabernet Sauvignon, Malbec, Petit Verdot.
Production zones
Communes or parts of communes of the area for white Graves.
Characteristics
Deep carmine-garnet color. Well developed vegetable, animal, fruity bouquet; balanced taste, without dominance of acid. Characteristic aromas strong and persistent. The wine is full-bodied, well balanced and delicate, fairly astringent. It has excellent ageing properties.
Serving temperature and suggested accompaniments
Serve at 57°F (15°C) with braised veal or tuna *à la concarnoise*.

BLAYE (BLAYAIS)
A.C. White

Grape varieties
Merlot Blanc, Folle, Colombard, Pineau de la Loire, Sémillon, Sauvignon, Muscadelle.
Production zone
Cantons or parts of cantons of Blaye, Saint-Savin-de-Blaye, Saint-Ciers-sur Gironde.
Characteristics
Light color, pale yellow-green; balanced taste without any preponderant element. Typically well developed aromas. The wine is supple and delicate, with little aptitude for ageing.
Serving temperature and suggested accompaniments
Serve at 50°F (10°C) with baked stuffed bream.

BLAYE (BLAYAIS)
A.C. Red

Grape varieties
Cabernet, Merlot, Malbec, Prolongeau, Cahors, Béguignol, Verdot.
Production zone
Identical to area for white Blaye.
Characteristics
Medium garnet-red color, vegetable and fruity bouquet, well balanced taste without any dominant element. Strong characteristic aromas. The wine is supple, fresh, and delicate, fairly astringent, and ages well.
Serving temperature and suggested accompaniments
Serve at 57°F (14°C) with snails in a wine sauce.

BORDEAUX
A.C. White

Grape varieties
Sémillon, Sauvignon, Muscadelle; secondary varieties Merlot Blanc, Colombard, Mauzac, Ondenc, Saint-Emilion.
Production zone
Communes or part of communes not liable to flooding, as laid down by the order of 1911, situated in the Gironde *département*.
Characteristics
Clear pale yellow color, averagely developed vegetable, fruity bouquet, balanced taste, with or without preponderance of sugar. If the wine contains less than 4 g of sugar it is labeled "dry." Strong characteristic aromas. The wine is well blended, fresh, and more or less delicate. It does not age well.
Serving temperature and suggested accompaniments
Serve at 50°F (10°C) with fish, fried or served in a sauce.

BORDEAUX-HAUT-BENAUGE
A.C. White

Grape varieties
Sémillon, Sauvignon, Muscadelle
Production zones
Communes or part of communes of Arbis, Cantois, Escoussans, Gornac , Ladaux, Mourens, Saint-Pierre-de-Bat, Soulignac, Targon.
Characteristics
Light pale yellow color, the wine has a well developed vegetable, fruity, flowery bouquet and a balanced taste with a preponderance of sugar. Strong characteristic aromas. The wine is well blended, delicate, and slightly astringent. It has good ageing properties.
Serving temperature and suggested accompaniments
Serve at 50°F (10°C). Goes well with leeks *au gratin*.

BORDEAUX-CÔTES-DE-FRANCS
A.C. White

Grape varieties
Sémillon, Sauvignon, Muscadelle.
Production zone
Communes or parts of communes of Francs, Saint-Cibard, Salles-de-Castillon, Tayac.
Characteristics
Medium color, straw-yellow to golden-yellow as it ages. Well developed vegetable, fruity, flowery bouquet; balanced taste with preponderance of sugar (min. 27 g sugar per liter). Characteristic aromas strong and persistent. The wine is full-bodied, well balanced, delicate, and slightly astringent. It has good ageing properties.
Serving temperature and suggested accompaniments
Serve at 52°F (11°C). Goes well with plum tart.

BORDEAUX
A.C. Red

Grape varieties
Cabernet Franc, Cabernet Sauvignon, Carmenère, Merlot, Malbec, Petit Verdot.
Production zone
Communes or part of communes of the area for white Bordeaux.
Characteristics
Light to deep garnet-red color, fairly well developed bouquet of vegetables, animal, and fruit, and a balanced taste, without any dominant element. Strong characteristic aromas. The wine is supple and fairly astringent. It ages well.
Serving temperature and suggested accompaniments
Seve at 57°F (14°C) with broiled meats.

BORDEAUX-CÔTES-DE-FRANCS
A.C. Red

Grape varieties
Cabernet, Malbec, Merlot.
Production zone
Identical to area for white Bordeaux-Côtes-de-Francs.
Characteristics
Medium carmine color, well developed bouquet of vegetables and fruit, balanced taste. Strong characteristic aromas. The wine is full, well blended and lively, fairly astringent, and with good ageing properties.
Serving temperature and suggested accompaniments
Serve at 57°F (14°C) with braised meat.

CÔTES-DE-CASTILLON
A.C. Red

Grape varieties
Cabernet Franc, Cabernet Sauvignon, Carmenère, Merlot, Malbec, Petit Verdot.
Production zone
Communes or part of communes of Castillon, Saint-Magne, Saint-Genès, Gardegan, Saint-Philippe d'Aiguille, Manbadon, Belvès, Les Salles, Sainte-Colombe.
Characteristics
Medium carmine-garnet color, vegetable, fruity bouquet, balanced taste with no dominant element, and strong characteristic aromas. The wine is quite full and fairly astringent, with good ageing properties.
Serving temperature and suggested accompaniments
Serve at 57°F (14°C). Goes well with veal.

BORDEAUX
A.C. Rosé and Clairet

Grape varieties
Cabernet Franc, Cabernet Sauvignon, Carmenère, Merlot, Malbec, Petit Verdot.
Production zone
Identical to area for Bordeaux.
Characteristics
Light clear pink color, sometimes verging toward tile-red. The bouquet, of vegetables and fruit, is well developed, the taste balanced without a preponderance of sugar. Strong characteristic aromas. The wine is supple, full, and fresh, slightly astringent. It does not age well.
Serving temperature and suggested accompaniments
Serve at 50°F (10°C) with a *mique sarladaise*, ham omelet or shellfish (particularly mussels *à la bordelaise*).

CÔTES-DE-BORDEAUX-SAINT-MACAIRE
A.C. White

Grape varieties
Sémillon, Sauvignon, Muscadelle.
Production zone
Communes or part of communes of Saint-Macaire, Sainte-Foy-la-Longue, Saint-Pierre-d'Aurillac, Plan-sur-Garonne, Saint-Laurent-du-Bois, Caudrot, Saint-André-du-Bois, Saint-Martin-de Sescas, Saint-Laurent-du-Plan, Saint-Martial.
Characteristics
Light straw-yellow color, well developed mineral, fruity bouquet, balanced taste without predominance of sugar, strong characteristic aromas. The wine is supple, light, delicate, and slightly astringent. It does not age well.
Serving temperature and suggested accompaniments
Serve at 50°F (10°C). It goes well with seafood.

PREMIÈRES CÔTES-DE-BLAYE
A.C. White

Grape varieties
Sémillon, Sauvignon, Muscadelle.
Production zone
Cantons or parts of cantons of Blaye, Saint-Savin-de-Blaye, Saint-Ciers-de-Gironde (see Blaye).
Characteristics
Light straw-yellow color, well developed bouquet of vegetables, fruits, and flowers, balanced taste with preponderance of sugar, strong characteristic aromas. The wine is supple, delicate, slightly astringent, and has good ageing properties.
Serving temperature and suggested accompaniments
Serve at 50°F (10°C) with goose *rillettes*.

PREMIÈRES CÔTES-DE-BLAYE
A.C. Red

Grape varieties
Cabernet Franc, Cabernet Sauvignon, Merlot, Malbec.
Production zone
Cantons or parts of cantons of Blaye, Saint-Savin-de-Blaye, Saint-Ciers-de-Gironde (see Blaye).
Characteristics
Medium clear red color, well developed bouquet of vegetables and fruit, strong characteristic aromas. The wine is well blended, fairly astringent, and ages quite well.
Serving temperature and suggested accompaniments
Serve at 57°F (14°C) with broiled lamb shoulder.

BORDEAUX SUPÉRIEUR
A.C. White

Conditions of production and characteristics are the same as for Bordeaux. Serve at 50°F (10°C) with fish dishes.

BORDEAUX SUPÉRIEUR
A.C. Red

Conditions of production and characteristics are the same as for Bordeaux. Serve at 57°F (14°C) with game or red meat.

PREMIÈRES CÔTES-DE-BORDEAUX
A.C. White

Grape varieties
Sémillon, Sauvignon, Muscadelle.
Production zone
36 communes of the Gironde.
Characteristics
Light straw-yellow color, tending to gold. Well developed fruity, flowery bouquet, balanced taste with preponderance of sugar. Characteristic aromas strong and persistent. The wine is full-bodied, delicate, and fairly astringent. It has good ageing properties.
Serving temperature and suggested accompaniments
Serve at 50°F (10°C). Goes well with warm game salads.

CÔTES-DE-BLAYE
A.C. White

Grape varieties
Sémillon, Sauvignon, Muscadelle, Merlot Blanc, Folle, Colombard, Chenin.
Production zone
Cantons or part of cantons of Blaye, Saint-Sevin-de-Blaye and Saint-Ciers-de-Gironde (see Blaye).
Characteristics
The wine, pale yellow to green in color, has a vegetable, fruity bouquet, a balanced taste with a preponderance of sugar, and strong characteristic aromas. It is supple, delicate, and lively, slightly astringent, with little aptitude for ageing.
Serving temperature and suggested accompaniments
Serve at 50°F (10°C) with cooked meats.

CADILLAC
A.C. White

Grape varieties
Sémillon, Sauvignon, Muscadelle.
Production zone
Communes of Cadillac and 21 other communes of the Gironde.
Characteristics
Color clear straw-yellow to amber-yellow. Well developed bouquet of vegetables, fruit, and flowers; balanced taste with preponderance of sugar (min. 18 g sugar per liter). Characteristic aromas strong and persistent. The wine is well balanced and full-bodied, fairly astringent. It ages very well.
Serving temperature and suggested accompaniments
Serve at 52°F (11°C). It goes well with duck pâté.

PREMIÈRES CÔTES-DE-BORDEAUX
Appellation followed by name of commune
A.C. Red

Grape varieties
Cabernet Franc, Cabernet Sauvignon, Carmenère, Malbec, Petit Verdot, Merlot.
Production zone
Identical to area of white Premières Côtes-de-Bordeaux.
Characteristics
Medium carmine-garnet color. Well developed vegetable, fruity bouquet; balanced taste without preponderance of any element. Characteristic aromas strong and persistent. The wine is light, well balanced, and fairly astringent. It has good ageing properties.

Serving temperature and suggested accompaniments
Serve at 57°F (14°C) with mussels or *entrecôte à la bordelaise*.

BOURG (CÔTE-DE-BOURG or BOURGEAIS)
A.C. Red

Grape varieties
Cabernet Franc, Cabernet Sauvignon, Merlot, Malbec and, in proportion of max. 10%, Verdot, Cahors, Prolongeau.
Production zone
Part of canton of Bourg.
Characteristics
The wine, medium garnet-red in color, has a well developed bouquet of vegetables and fruit, and a balanced taste with no preponderance of any element. Strong characteristic aromas. The wine is supple, light, and well blended, fairly astringent. It ages well.
Serving temperature and suggested accompaniments
Serve at 57°F (14°C) with *entrecôte à la bordelaise* or broiled white meat.

BOURG (COTTES-DE-BOURG or BOURGEAIS)
A.C. White

Grape varieties
Sémillon, Sauvignon, Muscadelle, Merlot Blanc, Colombard and, in proportion of max. 10%, Chenin.
Production zone
Part of canton of Bourg.
Characteristics
Color light straw-yellow, normally developed bouquet of vegetables and fruit, balanced taste with variable preponderance of sugar. Strong characteristic aromas. The wine is supple, delicate, and fresh, with little aptitude for ageing.
Serving temperature and suggested accompaniments
Serve at 50°F (10°C) with fried fish.

CANON-FRONSAC
A.C. Red

Grape varieties
Cabernet, Malbec, Merlot, Bouchet.
Production zone
Part of communes of Saint-Michel-de-Fronsac and Fronsac.
Characteristics
Deep carmine-garnet color. Well developed vegetable, animal, fruity bouquet; balanced taste with no preponderant element. Characteristic aromas strong and persistent. The wine is full, velvety and lively, fairly astringent, and ages well.
Serving temperature and suggested accompaniments
Serve at 57°F (14°C) with roast turkey and chestnut stuffing.

FRONSAC
A.C. Red

Grape varieties
Cabernet, Merlot, Malbec.
Production zone
Communes or part of communes of Fronsac, La Rivière, Saint-Germain-la-Rivière, Saint-Michel-de-Fronsac, Saint-Aignan, Saillans, Glgon.
Characteristics
Medium carmine-garnet color. Well developed vegetable, fruity bouquet; balanced taste with no preponderant element. Strong characteristic aromas. The wine is full, well balanced, and fairly astringent, with good ageing capacity.
Serving temperature and suggested accompaniments
Serve at 57°F (14°C) with *boeuf en daube* or a hotpot.

HAUT-MÉDOC
A.C. Red

Grape varieties
Cabernet Franc, Cabernet Sauvignon, Carmenère, Merlot, Malbec, Petit Verdot.
Production zone
Communes or part of communes of Blanquefort, Le Taillan, Saint-Aubin, Sainte-Helène, Saint-Médard-en-Jalles, Parempuyre, Le Pian, Ludon, Macau, Arsac, Labarde, Cantenac, Margaux, Aversan, Castelnau, Soussans, Arcins, Moulis, Listrac, Lamarque, Cussac, Saint-Laurent-de-Médoc, Saint-Julien, Pauillac, Saint-Sauveur, Cissac, Saint-Estèphe, Vertheuil, Saint-Seurin-de-Cadourne.
Characteristics
Deep garnet color. The bouquet, vegetable, animal, mineral, and fruity, is very strong according to the age of the wine, as are the characteristic aromas, which are also persistent. The wine is well balanced and full-bodied, with typical "noble tannin" astringency. It has an excellent ageing capacity.
Serving temperature and suggested accompaniments
Serve at 57°F (14°C) with duck or lamb.

MÉDOC
A.C. Red

Grape varieties
Cabernet Franc, Cabernet Sauvignon, Carmenère, Merlot, Petit Verdot, Malbec.
Production zone
Zone formed by the peninsula bounded to the east by the Gironde and the Garonne, to the south by the Jalle de Blanquefort, and to the west by the sea, except for the communes of Hourtin, Carcans, Brach, Saumes, Lacanau, Le Temple, Le Porge.
Characteristics
Deep garnet color. The bouquet, vegetable, animal, mineral, fruity or flowery, is very well developed according to the age of the wine. Characteristic aromas are likewise strong and persistent. The wine is full, velvety, well blended, with typical "noble tannin" astringency. It has excellent ageing capacity.
Serving temperature and suggested accompaniments
Serve at 57°F (14°C) with lamb leg or dishes *à la bordelaise*.

MOULIS (MOULIS-EN-MÉDOC)
A.C. Red

Grape varieties
Cabernet Franc, Cabernet Sauvignon, Carmenère, Merlot, Malbec, Petit Verdot.
Production zone
Communes or part of communes of Moulis, Listrac, Lamarque, Arcins, Aversan, Castelnau, Cussac.

Characteristics
Medium carmine-garnet color, well developed vegetable, animal, fruity bouquet. Characteristic aromas likewise strong and persistent. The wine is full, well blended, and typically astringent. It ages very well.
Serving temperature and suggested accompaniments
Serve at 57°F (14°C) with roast or broiled red meat, or pheasant and cabbage.

PAUILLAC
A.C. Red

Grape varieties
Cabernet Franc, Cabernet Sauvignon, Carmenère, Merlot, Malbec, Petit Verdot.
Production zone
Communes or part of communes of Pauillac, Cissac, Saint-Julien, Saint-Estèphe, Saint-Sauveur.
Characteristics
Deep carmine-garnet color. The bouquet, vegetable, animal, mineral, fruity or flowery, according to the year, is well developed, as are the characteristic, persistent aromas. The wine is full-bodied with typical "noble tannin" astringency. It has excellent ageing properties.
Serving temperature and suggested accompaniments
Serve at 57°F (14°C) with saddle of lamb or game.

SAINT-ESTÉPHE
A.C. Red

Grape varieties
Cabernet Franc, Cabernet Sauvignon, Carmenère, Merlot, Malbec, Petit Verdot.
Production zone
Commune of Saint-Estèphe.
Characteristics
Deep carmine color and very well developed animal, vegetable, fruity bouquet. Characteristic aromas very strong and persistent. The wine is full-bodied, with strong and typical "noble tannin" astringency. It has very good ageing properties.
Serving temperature and suggested accompaniments
Serve at 57°F (14°C) with pork or lamb.

SAINT-JULIEN
A.C. Red

Grape varieties
Cabernet Franc, Cabernet Sauvignon, Carmenère, Merlot, Malbec, Petit Verdot.
Production zone
Part of communes of Saint-Julien-Beychevelle, Cussac, Saint-Laurent.
Characteristics
Deep carmine-garnet color, well developed animal, mineral, fruity bouquet. Characteristic aromas likewise strong and persistent. The wine is full, well blended, and fairly astringent. It has excellent ageing properties.
Serving temperature and suggested accompaniments
Serve at 57°F (14°C) with fish or mushroom dishes.

MARGAUX
A.C. Red

Grape varieties
Cabernet Franc, Cabernet Sauvignon, Carmenère, Merlot, Malbec, Petit Verdot.
Production zone
Communes or part of communes of Margaux, Cantenac, Soussac, Arsac, Labarde.
Characteristics
Deep garnet color, well developed vegetable, animal, flowery bouquet. Characteristic aromas strong and persistent. The wine is full, well blended, fairly astringent, with good ageing capacity.
Serving temperature and suggested accompaniments
Serve at 57°F (14°C). It goes perfectly with white meat or steak.

LISTRAC MÉDOC
A.C. Red

Grape varieties
Cabernet Franc, Cabernet Sauvignon, Carmenère, Merlot, Malbec, Petit Verdot.
Production zone
Part of commune of Listrac.
Characteristics
Medium carmine-garnet color. Well developed bouquet of vegetables and fruit. Characteristic aromas strong and persistent. The wine is full, well blended, fairly astringent, with good ageing properties.
Serving temperature and suggested accompaniments
Serve at 57°F (14°C). Goes well with steak and roast chicken.

SAINT-ÉMILION
A.C. Red

Grape varieties
Cabernet Franc, Cabernet Sauvignon, Bouchet, Malbec, Merlot.
Production zone
Communes or part of communes of Saint-Emilion, Saint-Christophe-des-Bardes, Saint-Laurent-des-Combes, Saint-Hippolyte, Saint-Étienne-de-Lisse, Saint-Pey-d'Armens, Vignonet Saint-Sulpice-de-Faleyrens, Libourne.

Within the Saint-Émilion *appellation* there is a Saint-Émilion Grand Cru, corresponding to a qualitative selection of the wines, based on tasting. Certain Saint-Émilion Grand Cru wines are subject to classification, the last of which was in 1986: there are nowadays 11 classified Premiers Grand Crus Classés and 74 Crus Classés.
Characteristics
The color is light to deep carmine-garnet. The vegetable, animal, floral bouquet is very well developed according to the age of the wine. The characteristic aromas are very strong and persistent, particularly for the classified Grand Crus. The wine is velvety, light, well blended, and strongly astringent. It has excellent ageing properties.
Serving temperature and suggested accompaniments
Serve at 57°F (14°C) with pheasant or pigeon.

SAINT-GEORGES-SAINT ÉMILION
A.C. Red

Grape varieties
Cabernet, Malbec, Bouchet, Merlot.
Production zone
Commune of Saint-Georges-Saint-Emilion.
Characteristics
Deep garnet color with well developed vegetable, animal, fruity bouquet. Strong charactertistic aromas. The wine is full-bodied and powerful, with a very typical astringency. It ages extremely well.
Serving temperature and suggested accompaniments
Serve at 57°F (14°C) with roast beef.

LUSSAC-SAINT-ÉMILION
A.C. Red

Grape varieties
Cabernet, Merlot, Malbec, Bouchet.
Production zone
Part of commune of Lussac.
Characteristics
Fairly deep carmine-garnet color. Well developed vegetable, animal, floral bouquet and strong, persistent characteristic aromas. The wine is full, velvety, and strongly astringent. It has good ageing capacity.
Serving temperature and suggested accompaniments
Serve at 57°F (14°C) with roast chicken.

PARSAC-SAINT-ÉMILION
A.C. Red

Grape varieties
Cabernet, Merlot, Malbec, Bouchet.
Production zone
Part of commune of Parsac.
Characteristics
This wine, medium carmine in color, has a well developed vegetable, animal, fruity bouquet and very strong characteristic aromas. The wine is full, velvety, typically astringent, and ages well.
Serving temperature and suggested accompaniments
Serve at 57°F (14°C). It goes well with roast meat, particularly veal or hare.

PUISSEGUIN-SAINT-ÉMILION
A.C. Red

Grape varieties
Cabernet, Merlot, Malbec, Bouchet.
Production zone
Commune of Puisseguin.
Characteristics
Fairly deep color, mainly garnet with a touch of redcurrant. The bouquet of vegetable, animal, and fruit is well developed, as are the characteristic aromas, which are also persistent. The wine is full-bodied and delicate, with typically strong astringency, and it ages well.
Serving temperature and suggested accompaniments
Serve at 57°F (14°C) with roast poultry or quail.

MONTAGNE-SAINT-ÉMILION
A.C. Red

Grape varieties
Cabernet, Bouchet, Malbec, Merlot.
Production zone
Communes or part of communes of Montagne, Parsac, Saint-Georges.
Characteristics
Deep garnet color, well developed vegetable, animal, mineral bouquet. Strong characteristic aromas. The wine is full, velvety, well blended, with very typical astringency. It has good ageing capacity.
Serving temperature and suggested accompaniments
Serve at 57°F (14°C). Goes well with pheasant, eel or beef stew.

POMEROL
A.C. Red

Grape varieties
Cabernet Franc, Cabernet Sauvignon, Bouchet, Malbec, Merlot.
Production zone
Commune of Pomerol and part of commune of Libourne.
Characteristics
Light garnet-redcurrant color. Well developed vegetable, animal, fruity, flowery bouquet. Strong and persistent characteristic aromas. The wine is full, velvety, delicate, typically astringent, with good ageing properties.
Serving temperature and suggested accompaniments
Serve at 59°F (15°C) with mushroom pâté or sweetbreads with truffles.

LALANDE-DE-POMEROL
A.C. Red

Grape varieties
Cabernet Franc, Cabernet Sauvignon, Merlot, Malbec, Bouchet.
Production zone
Communes or part of communes of Lalande-de-Pomerol, Néac.
Characteristics
Fairly deep carmine-garnet color and well developed vegetable, animal, fruity bouquet. The wine is full, well blended, and typically astringent. Characteristic aromas likewise strong and persistent. The wine is full, well blended, with typical astringency. It has good ageing properties.
Serving temperature and suggested accompaniments
Serve at 57°F (14°C) with duck.

NÉAC
A.C. Red

Grape varieties
Cabernet Franc, Cabernet Sauvignon, Merlot, Malbec, Bouchet.
Production zone
Part of commune of Néac.
Characteristics
Fairly deep garnet color and well developed vegetable, animal, fruity bouquet. Characteristic aromas strong and persistent. The wine is full-bodied and typically astringent. It has good ageing properties.
Serving temperature and suggested accompaniments
Serve at 57°F (14°C). Goes well with lamb leg.

BERGERAC
A.C. Red

Grape varieties
Cabernet Franc, Cabernet Sauvignon, Merlot, Cot, Fer Servandou, Mérillé.
Production zone
Communes or part of communes of the Bergerac *arrondissement*.
Characteristics
Medium carmine-garnet color. Fairly well developed bouquet of vegetables and fruit; taste balanced, without preponderance of any element. Strong characteristic aromas. The wine is supple and typically astringent. It does not age particularly well.
Serving temperature and suggested accompaniments
Serve at 57°F (14°C) with roast chicken.

CÔTES-DE-BERGERAC
A.C. Red

Grape varieties
Identical to those of AC Bergerac.
Production zone
Identical to that of the Bergerac area.
Characteristics
Medium carmine-garnet color. Well developed bouquet of vegetables and fruit. Strong characteristic aromas. The wine is full and fresh, with typical astringency. It has reasonable ageing capacity.
Serving temperature and suggested accompaniments
Serve at 57°F (14°C) with preserved duck or potato dishes.

BERGERAC SEC
A.C. White

Grape varieties
Sémillon, Sauvignon, Muscadelle, Ondenc, Chenin.
Characteristics
Communes or part of communes of the Bergerac *arrondissement*.
Characteristics
Light straw-yellow color, well balanced bouquet of vegetables, fruit, and flowers; balanced taste without preponderance of sugar (the wines should contain less than 4 g sugar per liter). Strong characteristic aromas. The wine is supple, well blended, and lively, slightly astringent. It ages reasonably well.
Serving temperature and suggested accompaniments
Serve at 50°F (10°C). Goes well with fried freshwater fish, *mouclade*, cod (*morue brestoise*) or preserved goose with sorrel (*confit d'oie à l'oseille*).

CÔTES-DE-BERGERAC MOELLEUX
A.C. White

Grape varieties
Sémillon, Sauvignon, Muscadelle, Ondenc, Chenin.
Production zone
Communes or part of communes of Bergerac *arrondissement*.
Characteristics
Deep straw-yellow color, well-developed vegetable and floral bouquet, balanced taste with preponderance of sugar (the wines should contain 18–54 g sugar per liter). Characteristic aromas strong and persistent. The wine is full-bodied and delicate, fairly astringent. It has good ageing properites.
Serving temperature and suggested accompaniments
Serve at 52°F (11°C). Goes well with chicken liver omelet or truffled scrambled eggs (*brouillade aux truffes*).

CÔTES-DE-BERGERAC-CÔTES-DE-SAUSSIGNAC
A.C. White

Grape varieties
Sémillon, Sauvignon, Muscadelle, Ondenc, Chenin Blanc.
Production zone
Saussignac, Gageac, Rouillac, Monestier, Razac-de-Saussignac.
Characteristics
Deep color, straw-yellow to golden-yellow with age, well developed vegetable and floral bouquet; balanced taste with preponderance of sugar. Characteristic aromas strong and persistent. The wine is full, rich, and lively, slightly astringent. It ages well.
Serving temperature and suggested accompaniments
Serve at 54°F (12°C). Goes nicely with cheese.

SAINTE-FOY-BORDEAUX
A.C. Red

Grape varieties
Cabernet, Merlot Rouge, Malbec, Petit Verdot.
Production zone
Canton of Sainte-Foy and communes or part of communes of Landerrouat, Gensac, Pessac-sur-Dordogne, Pellegrue, Massugas.
Characteristics
Medium carmine-garnet color, well developed bouquet of vegetables and fruit. Strong charactertistic aromas. The wine, quite full and delicate, is fairly astringent and ages reasonably well.
Serving temperature and suggested accompaniments
Serve at 59°F (15°C) with veal shoulder and cabbage.

SAINTE-FOY-BORDEAUX
A.C. White

Grape varieties
Sémillon, Sauvignon, Muscadelle and, in secondary proportions (max. 10%), Merlot Blanc, Colombard, Mauzac, and Saint-Emilion.
Production zone
Identical to area for red Sainte-Foy-Bordeaux.
Characteristics
Light straw-yellow color, well developed vegetable, fruity bouquet; balanced taste, often with preponderance of sugar. Strong characteristic aromas. The wine is full, delicate, sometimes lively, slightly astringent. It has good ageing properties.
Serving temperature and suggested accompaniments
Serve at 52°F (11°C). Goes well with *pâté en croûte*.

ROSETTE
A.C. White

Grape varieties
Sémillon, Sauvignon, Muscadelle.
Production zone
Communes or part of communes of Bergerac, Lembras, Creysse, Maurens, Prigourieux, Gineste.
Characteristics
Fairly deep amber-yellow color, well developed vegetable, mineral, fruity, flowery bouquet; balanced taste with preponderance of sugar (the wine containing 8–54 g sugar per liter). Characteristic aromas strong and persistent. The wine is full-bodied, delicate, and slightly astringent. It has very good ageing properties.
Serving temperature and suggested accompaniments
Serve at 50°F (10°C). Goes well with chicken liver terrine or duck with onions.

MONBAZILLAC
A.C. White

Grape varieties
Sémillon, Sauvignon, Muscadelle.
Production zone
Communes or part of communes of Monbazillac, Rouffignac-de-Sigoulès, Colombier, Pomport, Saint-Laurent-des-Vignes.
Characteristics
Deep straw-yellow to amber-yellow color, well developed vegetable, fruity bouquet, balanced taste with preponderance of sugar. Strong and persistent characteristic aromas. The wine is rich, well blended, and full-bodied. It has excellent ageing capacity.
Serving temperature and suggested accompaniments
Serve at 52°F (11°C). It goes well with duck liver, truffles, sauce Périgueux, Roquefort pastries or desserts.

MONTRAVEL
A.C. White

Grape varieties
Sémillon, Sauvignon, Muscadelle, Ondenc, Chenin Blanc, Ugni Blanc (max. 25%).
Production zone
Communes or part of communes of Bonneville, Fougeyrolles, La Mothe-Montravel, Montcaret, Montpeyroux, Montazeau, Nastringues, Ponchapt, Port-Sainte-Foy, Saint-Antoine-de-Breuilh, Saint-Michel-Montaigne, Saint-Seurin-de-Prats, Saint-Vivien, Vélines, Saint-Méard-de-Gurçon.
Characteristics
Light straw-yellow color, well developed vegetable, mineral, fruity bouquet; balanced taste with no preponderance of sugar (less than 4 g sugar per liter). Strong characteristic aromas. The wine is quite full, delicate, and slightly astringent. It has good ageing properties.
Serving temperature and suggested accompaniments
Serve at 50°F (10°C). Goes well with poached eggs, shrimp (*à la bergeracoise*) or walnut cake.

PÉCHARMANT
A.C. Red

Grape varieties
Cabernet Sauvignon, Cabernet Franc, Merlot, Malbec.
Production zone
Communes or part of communes of Bergerac, Lembras, Creysse.
Characteristics
Fairly deep garnet-redcurrant color, well developed vegetable, fruity bouquet. Strong characteristic aromas. The wine is supple, velvety, and typically astringent. It has good ageing properties.
Serving temperature and suggested accompaniments
Serve at 59°F (15°C). Goes well with kidneys (*rognons aux croûtons*), duck or mushrooms (*cèpes à la périgourdine*).

BORDEAUX MOUSSEUX
A.C. White and Rosé

Grape varieties
White: Sémillon, Muscadelle, Cabernet Franc, Cabernet Sauvignon, Carmenère, Merlot, Malbec, Petit Verdot, Ugni Blanc, Colombard, Mauzac, Ondenc.
Rosé: Cabernet Franc, Cabernet Sauvignon, Carmenère, Merlot, Malbec, Petit Verdot. Wines made by *méthode champenoise*.
Serving temperature and suggested accompaniments
Serve at 48°F (9°C) as an aperitif.

BLANQUETTE DE LIMOUX
A.C. White

Grape varieties
Mauzac; secondary varieties (max. 20%) Chardonnay, Chenin.
Production zone
Some 40 communes or part of communes around Limoux.
Characteristics
Light pale-yellow or straw-yellow color, well developed vegetable, fruity, floral bouquet, balanced taste with no preponderant element. Strong characteristic aromas, typical of sparkling wines. The wine is supple, delicate, and lively, slightly astringent. It has reasonably good ageing properties.
Serving temperature and suggested accompaniments
Serve at 48°F (9°C) as an aperitif or with desserts.

CÔTES-DE-FRONTONNAIS (FRONTON)
A.C. Red

Grape varieties
Négrette (70%); secondary varieties: Malbec, Mérillé, Fer, Cabernet Franc, Cabernet Sauvignon, Syrah, Gamay, Cinsaut, Mauzac.
Production zone
Communes or part of communes of Fronton, Castelnau-d'Estrétefons, Saint-Rustice, Vacquiers (Haute-Garonne), Bessens, Campsas, Canals, Dieupentale, Fabas, Grisolles, Labastide-Saint-Pierre, Montbartier, Nohic, Orgueil, Pompignan (Tarn-et-Garonne).
Characteristics
Medium carmine-garnet color, well developed vegetable, fruity bouquet. Strong characteristic aromas. The wine is supple, well blended, quite lively, and fairly astringent. It has good ageing properties.
Serving temperature and suggested accompaniments
Serve at 59°F (15°C). Goes with beef (*boeuf en daube*) or poultry dishes.

Under this *appellation* there is also a well made dry rosé type.

CÔTES-DU-FRONTONNAIS-VILLAUDRIC
A.C. Red

Grape varieties
Identical to those of Côtes-du-Frontonnais-Fronton.
Production zone
Following communes or part of communes of Haute-Garonne: Bouloc, Fronton, Villaudric, Villematier, Villemur-sur-Tarn, Villeneuve-lès-Bouloc.
The characteristics of this wine are similar to those of the preceding *appellation*. Serve at 59°F (15°C) with stews.

GAILLAC
A.C. Red

Grape varieties
Principal varieties (min. 60%): Brancol, Duras, Gamay, Négrette, Syrah; secondary varieties: Cabernets, Jurançon, Merlot, Portugais Bleu, Mauzac Blanc and Rosé (max. 5%).
Production zone
73 communes of Tarn.
Characteristics
Fairly deep garnet-redcurrant color, well developed vegetable, fruity bouquet. Strong characteristic aromas. The wine is supple and fairly astringent. It has good ageing properties.
Serving temperature and suggested accompaniments
Serve at 57°F (14°C). Goes well with braised ham or *cassoulet*.
There is also a dry Gaillac Rosé.

GAILLAC
A.C. White

Grape varieties
Len de l'el, Mauzac, Muscadelle, Ondenc, Sauvignon, Sémillon.
Production zone
Identical to area for red Gaillac.
Characteristics
Light to fairly deep color, straw-yellow to golden-yellow for sweet wines. The vegetable, fruity, floral bouquet is well developed, especially in the sweet wines, the taste balanced and with a lesser or greater preponderance of sugar according to type. Characteristic aromas strong and persistent. The wine is supple, the sweet varieties full-bodied, and overall delicate and lively.
There is little astringency and the wines, particularly the sweet varieties, age well.
Serving temperature and suggested accompaniments
Serve at 52°F (11°C). The sweet wines go nicely with cheese soufflé, the drier wines with cooked meats.
The denomination Premières Côtes corresponds to a more restricted production zone of 11 communes.

GAILLAC MOUSSEUX
A.C. White

Grape varieties
The production zone and characteristics are identical to those of the still white wines. The wines are made according to the classic *méthode champenoise*.
Serving temperature and suggested accompaniments
Serve at 48°F (9°C) as an aperitif or with a light picnic meal.

CAHORS
A.C. Red

Grape varieties
Cot (min. 70%); secondary varieties: Jurançon, Merlot, Tannat, Syrah.
Production zone
Cahors and some 40 communes of Lot.
Characteristics
Fairly deep garnet-redcurrant color and well developed mineral, fruity, flowery bouquet. Strong characteristic aromas. The wine is supple, velvety, and lively, with typical astringency. It has good ageing properties.
Serving temperature and suggested accompaniments
Serve at 57°F (14°C). It goes nicely with stuffed poultry or goose pâté with mushrooms (*confit d'oie aux cèpes*).

CÔTES-DE-BUZET
A.C. Red and Rosé

Grape varieties
Merlot, Cabernet Franc, Cabernet Sauvignon, Cot.
Production zone
27 communes of Lot-et-Garonne.
Characteristics
Light to deep color, mainly carmine, garnet for the reds, pale pink for the rosés. Well developed vegetable, fruity bouquet. Strong characteristic aromas. The wines are supple and the reds are full and fairly astringent. They age reasonably well.
Serving temperature and suggested accompaniments
Serve reds at 57°F (14°C), with broiled meats, rabbit or sorrel soup, and rosés at 50°F (10°C) with pâté.

CÔTES-DE-BUZET
A.C. White

Grape varieties
Sémillon, Sauvignon, Muscadelle.
Production zone
Identical to area for red and rosé Côtes-de-Buzet.
Characteristics
Light straw-yellow color, well developed vegetable and floral bouquet; balanced taste with no preponderance of sugar (less than 4 g sugar per liter). Strong characteristic aromas. The wine is supple, light, lively, and slightly astringent. It has good ageing properties.
Serving temperature and suggested accompaniments
Serve at 50°F (10°C) with ham omelet.

CÔTES-DE-DURAS
A.C. Red

Grape varieties
Cabernet Franc, Cabernet Sauvignon, Merlot, Malbec.
Production zone
Communes or part of communes of Duras, Auriac, Esclottes, Sainte-Colombe-de-Duras, Saint-Astier, Loubès-Bernac, Soumensac, Saint-Jean-de-Duras, La Sauvetat-du-Dropt, Moustier, Pardaillan, Saint-Sernin-de-Duras, Savignac-de-Duras, Villeneuve-de-Duras, Baleyssagues.
Characteristics
Fairly deep garnet color, well developed animal, mineral, and floral bouquet. Strong characteristic aromas. The wine is quite full, velvety, well blended and lively, with typical astringency. It has good ageing properties.
Serving temperature and suggested accompaniments
Serve at 59°F (15°C). Goes well with braised tongue.

CÔTES-DE-DURAS
A.C. White

Grape varieties
Main varieties: Sémillon, Sauvignon, Muscadelle, Mauzac, Rouchelein, Ondenc; secondary variety: Ugni Blanc (max. 25%).
Production zone
Identical to area for red Côtes-de-Duras.
Characteristics
Light to deep straw-yellow color, well developed vegetable, mineral, and floral bouquet, balanced taste with preponderance of sugar, except for wines labeled "dry." Characteristic aromas strong and persistent. The wine is full, delicate, and fresh, slightly astringent. It has good ageing properties.
Serving temperature and suggested accompaniments
Serve at 50°F (10°C). The soft wines go well with pork escalopes *à la toulousaine*.

BÉARN
A.C. Rosé

Grape varieties
Tannat, Cabernet Franc, Cabernet Sauvignon, Fer, Manseng Noir, Courbu Noir.
Production zone
In the Pyrenées-Atlantiques: 74 communes; in the Hautes-Pyrenées: Castelnau-Rivière-Basse, Hagedet, Lascazères, Madiran, Saint-Lanne, Soublecasse; in the Gers: Cannet, Manmusson-Laguian, Viella.
Characteristics
Lighty to deep redcurrant pink color, well developed vegetable, mineral, and fruity bouquet, balanced taste with no preponderance of sugar. Strong characteristic aromas. The wine is supple, full-bodied, lively, slightly astringent, and has good ageing properties.
Serving temperature and suggested accompaniments
Serve at 57°F (14°C) with *pipérade* or poultry dishes, e.g. *poulet basquaise*.

BÉARN
A.C. Red

Grape varieties
Tannat (max. 60%), Cabernet Franc, Cabernet Sauvignon, Fer, Manseng Noir, Courbu Noir.
Production zone
Identical to area for Béarn Rosé.
Characteristics
Deep garnet-redcurrant color, well developed vegetable, fruity bouquet. Strong characteristic aromas. The wine is supple, delicate, slightly astringent, and has good ageing properties.
Serving temperature and suggested accompaniments
Serve at 57°F (14°C) with tuna (*thon basquaise*) and poultry (*poule au pot farcie*).

BÉARN
A.C. White

Grape varieties
Petit Manseng, Gros Manseng, Courbu, Lauzet, Camaralet, Raffiat, Sauvignon.
Production zone
Identical to area for red and rosé Béarn.
Characteristics
Light straw-yellow color, well developed vegetable, mineral, fruity bouquet, balanced taste, dry in type. Strong charactertistic aromas. The wine is supple, full-bodied, light, and slightly astringent. It has good ageing properties.
Serving temperature and suggested accompaniments
Serve at 50°F (10°C). Goes well with fish dishes and rabbit.

IROULÉGUY
A.C. Rosé

Grape varieties
Cabernet Franc, Cabernet Sauvignon (max. 50%), Tannat.
Production zone
Following communes or part of communes in the Pyrenées-Atlantiques: Anhaux, Ascarat, Bidarray, Irouléguy, Ispoure, Jaxu, Osses, Saint-Etienne-de-Baïgorry, Saint-Martin-d'Arrossa.
Characteristics
Medium color with pink-carmine nuance. Well-developed bouquet of fruit and flowers; balanced taste, dry in type. Strong characteristic aromas. The wine is supple, full-bodied, fresh, slightly astringent, and has good ageing properties.
Serving temperature and suggested accompaniments
Serve at 52°F (11°C). Goes well with fish soup, rice, *pibales basquaise*, and *pipérade*.
Under the same *appellation* there is a fairly full-bodied red wine and a very fruity dry white wine.

JURANÇON
A.C. White

Grape varieties
Petit Manseng, Gros Manseng, Courbu, Camaralet, Lauzet.
Production zone
Following communes or part of communes in the Pyrenées-Atlantiques: Jurançon, Abos, Arbus, Artiguelouve, Aubertin, Bosdarros, Cardesse, Cuqueron, Estialesq, Gan, Gelos, Haut-de-Bosdarros, Lacommande, Lahourcade, Laroin, Lasseube, Lasseubetat, Lucq-de-

Béarn, Mazères, Monein, Narcastet, Parbayse, Rontignon, Saint-Faust, Uzos.
Characteristics
Light to deep straw-yellow to golden-yellow color. Well developed vegetable, animal, fruity, flowery bouquet; balanced taste, more or less sugary according to year. Characteristic aromas very strong and persistent. The wine is full-bodied, lively, and fairly astringent. It has very good ageing properties.
Serving temperature and suggested accompaniments
Serve at 46°–48°F (8°–9°C) as an aperitif or with *foie gras*, *sauce béarnaise*, goose or goat's cheese.

JURANÇON SEC
A.C. White

Production zone
Identical to area for Jurançon, but this wine is dry in type.
Serving temperature and suggested accompaniments
Serve at 50°F (10°C) with smoked salmon.

MADIRAN
A.C. Red

Grape varieties
Tannat (40–60%), Cabernet Franc, Cabernet Sauvignon, Fer.
Production zone
Following communes or part of communes in the Pyrenées-Atlantiques: Arricau-Bordes, Arrosés, Aubous, Aurions-Idernes, Aydie, Bétracq, Burosse-Mendousse, Cadillon, Castetpugon, Castillon, Conchez-de-Béarn, Corbère-Abères, Crouseilles, Diusse, Escurès, Gayon, Lasserre, Lembeye, Mascaradàs, Moncla, Monpezat, Moncaup, Mont-Disse, Portet, Saint-Jean-Poudge, Séméacq-Blachon, Tadousse-Ussau, Vialer; in the Hautes-Pyrenées: Castelnau-Rivière-Basse, Hagedet, Lascazères, Madiran, Saint-Lanne, Soublecause; in the Gers: Cannet, Maumusson-Laguian, Viella.
Characteristics
Deep color with carmine-garnet nuances. Well developed vegetable, animal, fruity, floral bouquet. Characteristic aromas strong and persistent. The wine is full, velvety, and delicate, with typical astringency. It ages very well.
Serving temperature and suggested accompaniments
Serve at 57°F (14°C). Goes with duck, pigeon or goose.

PACHERENC-DU-VIC-BILH
A.C. White

Grape varieties
Arrufiac, Courbu, Gros Manseng, Petit Manseng, Sauvignon, Sémillon.
Production zone
Communes or part of communes identical to those of Madiran area.
Characteristics
Deep straw-yellow to golden-yellow color. Well developed vegetable, mineral, floral bouquet, balanced taste with preponderance of sugar (sugar content c.10–18 g max. per liter). Characteristic aromas strong and persistent. The wine is full, velvety, and lively, fairly astringent. It has good ageing properties.
Serving temperature and suggested accompaniments
Serve at 50°F (10°C). Serve as aperitif, with *tourain toulousain* or goat's cheese.

CÔTES-DU-MARMANDAIS
A.C. Red

Grape varieties
Abouriou, Fer Servadou, Cot, Gamay Noir à jus blanc, Syrah, and in proportion of max. 50%: Cabernet Franc, Cabernet Sauvignon, Merlot.
Production zone
27 communes of Lot-et-Garonne.
Characteristics
Medium carmine color, well developed fruity bouquet. Strong characteristic aromas. The wine is supple and fairly astringent. It ages reasonably well.
Serving temperature and suggested accompaniments
Serve at 57°F (14°C) with broiled dishes. This appellation includes a dry rosé type.

CÔTES-DU-MARMANDAIS
A.C. White

Grape varieties
Sauvignon (min. 70%), Ugni Blanc (max. 30%).
Production zone
Identical to area for red Côtes-du-Marmandais.
Characteristics
Pale yellow color, well developed fruity bouquet, balanced taste without preponderance of sugar (containing less than 3 g sugar per liter). Strong characteristic aromas. The wine is supple, delicate, and fresh, with little astringency. It ages reasonably well.
Serving temperature and suggested accompaniments
Serve at 50°F (10°C) with fish dishes.

TURSAN
VDQS White

Grape varieties
Ibarroque (90%); secondary varieties (max. 10%): Sauvignon, Petit Manseng, Gros Manseng, Claverie, Cruchinet, Raffiat, Claret du Gers, Clairette.
Production zone
In the Landes: 39 communes; in the Gers: Lannux, Ségos.
Characteristics
Pale yellow color, well developed vegetable, fruity bouquet. Strong characteristic aromas. The wine is supple, lively, and slightly astringent. It has reasonably good ageing properties.
Serving temperature and suggested accompaniments
Serve at 50°F (10°C) with broiled eels.

TURSAN
VDQS Red and Rosé

Grape varieties
Tannat, Bouchy and, in proportion of 25%, Cabernet Franc, Cabernet Sauvignon and Fer.
Production zone
Identical to area for white Tursan.
Characteristics
Medium color, mainly carmine for reds, bright pink for rosés. Well developed bouquet of vegetables, fruit, and flowers. Strong characteristic aromas. The wines are supple, the reds fairly full-bodied, and fairly astringent. They age quite well.
Serving temperature and suggested accompaniments
Serve rosés at 52°F (11°C) with pâté and cooked meats. Serve reds at 57°F (14°C) with variety meats.

VINS D'ENTRAYGUES ET DU FEL
VDQS White, Red, and Rosé

Grape varieties
White: Chenin, Mauzac.
Red and rosé: Cabernet Franc, Cabernet Sauvignon, Fer, Gamay, Jurançon, Merlot, Mouyssaguès, Négrette, Pinot Noir.
Production zone
Aveyron: Entraygues-sur-Truyère, Campouriez, Enguiales, Florentin-la-Capelle, Golinhac, Saint-Hippolyte; Cantal: Cassaniouze, Vieillevie.
Characteristics
Medium color, bright red and pale yellow for reds and whites respectively. The vegetable, fruity bouquet is not very strong, and in the whites the taste is balanced without any preponderance of sugar. Characteristic aromas normally developed. The wines are quite supple, fresh and delicate, the reds fairly astringent. They age reasonably well.
Serving temperature and suggested accompaniments
Serve white and rosés at 50°F (10°C), reds at 57°F (14°C). The former two go well with cooked meats, the latter with roast chicken.

VINS D'ESTAING
VDQS Red, Rosé, and White

Grape varieties
Reds and rosés: Fer, Gamay, Abouriou, Jurançon, Merlot, Cabernet Franc, Cabernet Sauvignon, Mouyssaguès, Négrette, Pinot Noir, Duras, Castet.
Whites: Chenin, Mauzac, Roussellou.
Production zone
Aveyron: Estaing, Coubisou, Sebrazac.
Characteristics
Medium color, mainly redcurrant and straw-yellow for reds and whites respectively. Well developed fruity bouquet, balanced taste without any predominant element. Normal characteristic aromas. The wines are supple, well blended, and lively, the reds fairly astringent. They age reasonably well.
Serving temperature and suggested accompaniments
Serves whites and rosés at 50°F (10°C), reds at 57°F (14°C). All go well with cooked meats.

VINS DE LAVILLEDIEU
VDQS White and Red

Grape varieties
White: Mauzac, Sauvignon, Sémillon, Muscadelle, Blanquette, Ondenc, Chalosse Blanche.
Red: Négrette (max. 35%), Mauzac, Bordelais, Morterille, Chalosse; secondary varieties (max. 20%): Syrah, Gamay, Jurançon Noir, Picpoul, Milgranet, Fer.
Production zone
Communes or part of communes of Lavilledieu, Meauzac, Barry d'Isle-made, Albefeuille, Lagarde, Montbeton, Lacourt-Saint-Pierre, Bressols-Montech, Escatalens, Saint-Porquier, Castelsarrasin, Les Barthes, Labastide-du-Temple.
Characteristics
Reds deep carmine, whites straw-yellow in color. Well developed bouquet of fruit and flowers, the whites balanced in taste without preponderance of sugar. The wines are supple, full and quite lively, fairly astringent and with quite good ageing properties.
Serving temperature and suggested accompaniments
Serve whites at 50°F (10°C), reds at 55°F (13°C). The whites go well with pâtés and the reds with broiled meats.

VINS DE MARCILLAC
A.C. Red and Rosé

Grape varieties
Reds: Fer-Servadou (max. 80%); Cabernet Franc, Cabernet Sauvignon, Merlot, Cot, Gamay, Jurançon, Mouyssaguès, Valdiguié.
Rosès: Fer-Servadou (min. 30%) and other varieties used for red wines.
Production zone
Marcillac-Vallon, Balsac, Clairvaux-d'Aveyron, Goutrens, Mouret, Nauviale, Pruines, Salles-la-Source, Saint-Cyprien-sur-Dourdou, Saint-Christophe-Vallon, Valady.
Characteristics
Deep color, mainly carmine-garnet for reds, bright pink for rosés. Well developed mineral, fruity bouquet. Strong characteristic aromas. The wines are full and delicate, the rosés lively, with fair astringency and reasonable ageing properties.
Serving temperature and suggested accompaniments
Serve rosés at 52°F (11°C) with scrambled eggs and mushrooms and reds at 57°F (14°C) with guinea-fowl.

The regions of the Loire

A sky that is soft, hazy blue, a flat horizon, a variety of soils flanking the valleys, this is the landscape which surrounds the many vineyards of this extensive region.

The first vineyard area is situated at the mouth of the Loire and produces a type of dry white wine: Muscadet A.C. Beside it, forming part of the Brittany region and lying on either side of the Loire, are vineyards which produce a V.D.Q.S., the Gros Plant.

Further up the Loire comes Anjou, and vineyards of white wine on both banks of the river but also on the Coteaux du Layon and de l'Aubance, famed for their mellow whites. Its rosés, too, are internationally renowned. In the Saumurois, a region known mainly for its sparkling and semisparkling wines, the red wines of Champigny are outstanding.

Leaving Anjou, we reach Touraine which, like the Saumurois, is noted for its vines planted in an area of chalky tufa, with caves where the wines can age over many years. They include wines of rare vintage, from the reds of Bourgueil and Chinon to the whites of Vouvray and Montlouis. Beyond these are the V.D.Q.S. vineyards of Haut-Poitou, Valençay, and the Orléannais, and those of the Nivernais, where the Sauvignon grape reigns supreme.

The river is the principal link between all the vine growers of this vast region, the four zones of which are characterized by four different types of climate. Familiarity with these is to understand just how important is the influence of the air which, from generation to generation, has led men to make a wine which is integral to the soil, compelling them to seek, among the innumerable varieties of Vitis vinifera, *the ideal grape to reflect the place and the vintage. Thus, in Muscadet, with its Atlantic climate, the variety of that name gives a dry, supple white wine. In Sancerre and Pouilly, where the climate is continental, a drier but fuller bodied wine is made with the Sauvignon grape. In Anjou, under the Atlantic influence, soft to sparkling wines are produced with the Chenin grape, as also in Touraine, an Atlantic-continental transition zone, where the white wines reflect the climate of that particular year. Mention should also be made of the tannic reds of Bourgeuil and Chinon and, downstream of Tours, of the non-tannic reds prepared from the Gamay variety.*

Drinking these wines in conjunction with local dishes is an enriching gastronomic experience. The local cuisine offers freshwater and sea fish, an abundance of vegetables, meat, and game, and, especially in Touraine, a variety of ingredients which reaps full advantage of the rhythm and generosity of the seasons.

MUSCADET
A.C. White

Grape varieties
One variety, Muscadet.
Production zone
In Loire-Atlantique: Aigrefeuille-sur-Maine, Bouaye, Bourgneuf-en-Retz, Carquefou, Clisson, La Chapelle-sur-Erdre, Legé, Le Loroux-Bottereau, Le Pellerin, Machecoul, Nantes, Nort-sur-Erdre, Paimboeuf, Saint-Père-en-Retz, Saint-Philbert-de-Grand-Lieu, Vertou; in Maine-et-Loire: Montfaucon; in Vendée: Montaigu, Rocheservière.
Characteristics
Muscadet is a dry, lively type of wine with a well developed vegetable bouquet and which fills the mouth well.
Serving temperature and suggested accompaniments
Serve at 50°F (10°C). The wines go well with seafood, particularly scallops. In sunny years the wines age well and can be served with dishes featuring the region's famous sauce, *beurre blanc* or with duckling.

MUSCADET DES COTEAUX DE LA LOIRE
A.C. White

Grape varieties
Same as for Muscadet.
Production zone
Communes or part of communes of Ancenis, Saint-Herblon, Couffé, Mésanger, Thouaré, Le Cellier, Oudon, Saint-Géréon, Anetz, Varades, Ligné, Mouzeil, Teillé, Saint-Florent-le-Vieil, La Chapelle-Saint-Florent, Bouzillé, Liré, Drain, Champtoceaux, Mauves, La Varenne, Landemont, Saint-Sébastien-sur-Loire, Barbechat.
Characteristics
These wines are more full-bodied and vigorous, and age quite well.
Serving temperature and suggested accompaniments
Serve at 50°F (10°C) with seafood.

MUSCADET DE SÈVRE-ET-MAINE
A.C. White

Grape varieties
Same as for Muscadet.
Production zone
Communes or part of communes of Aigrefeuille, Basse-Goulaine, La Chapelle-Heulin, Châteauthébaud, Clisson, Gorges, La Haie-Fouassière, Haute-Goulaine, Maisdon, Monnières, Mouzillon, Le Pallet, La Regrippière, Saint-Crespin-sur-Moine, Saint-Fiacre, Tillières, Valet, Vertou, Le Landreau, Le Louroux-Botteereau, La Chapelle-Basse-Mere, Sainte-Lumine-de-Clisson, Saint-Julien-de-Concelles.
Characteristics
These are fine, supple wines, representing the largest production of wines in the region. Wines bearing on the label the indication "*sur lie*" have been bottled without any filtration, i.e. directly from the vat. This gives the wine a slight sparkling quality.
Serving temperature and suggested accompaniments
Serve at 50°F (10°C) with seafood.

GROS PLANT DU PAYS NANTAIS
V.D.Q.S. White

Grape varieties
Folle Blanche
Production zone
In Loire-Atlantique: 72 communes; in Maine-et-Loire: 16 communes; in Vendée: 5 communes.
Characteristics
This is a young wine, pale greenish-yellow in color with a fair preponderance of acid but well compensated by the fruitiness. The wines are supple and are not

particularly suitable for ageing.
Serving temperature and suggested accompaniments
These wines are best drunk young. They go well with the typical seafood dishes of the Atlantic coast.

COTEAUX-D'ANCENIS

Appellation followed by varietal name: Pineau de la Loire (or Chenin); Malvoisie; Gamay; Pinot Beurrot; Cabernet.
V.D.Q.S. White, Red, and Rosé

Grape varieties
White: Chenin and Pinot Gris (or Malvoisie)
Red and rosé: Cabernet Franc, Cabernet Sauvignon, Gamay Noir à jus blanc, and, in proportion of max. 5%, Gamay Bouze and Chaudenay.
Production zone
In Loire-Atlantique: Ancenis, Anetz, Caquefou, Le Cellier, La Chapelle-Saint-Sauveur, Couffé, Le Fresne-sur-Loire, Ligné, Mauves, Mésanger, Montrelais, Oudon, Saint-Géréon, Saint-Herblon, Thouaré et Varades; in Maine-et-Loire: Bouzillé, Champtoceaux, Drain. Landemont, Liré, La Chapelle-Saint-Florent, La Varenne, Le Mesnil-en-Vallée, Le Marillais, Saint-Florent-le-Vieil, Saint-Laurent-du-Mottay.
Characteristics
The color is light, mainly carmine-redcurrant for the reds, pale straw-yellow for the whites. The rosés are clear pink. The fruity, floral bouquet is normally developed; the taste is balanced and fresh. Characteristic aromas are strong. The wines, supple and lively, with little astringency in the reds, do not age particularly well.
Serving temperature and suggested accompaniments
Serve reds at 55°F (13°C) and whites and rosés at 48°F (9°C). The reds can accompany oysters, soups and *crémets d'Anjou* (cream cheese molds); the whites and rosés go well with shellfish.

ANJOU

A.C. White, Red, and Rosé

Grape varieties
White: Chenin (80%) and, as secondary varieties, Chardonnay and Sauvignon.
Red: Cabernet Franc, Cabernet Sauvignon, Pineau d'Aunis.
Rosé: Cabernet Franc, Cabernet Sauvignon, Pineau d'Aunis, Gamay, Cot, Grolleau.
Production zone
In Maine-et-Loire: more than 170 communes; in Deux-Sèvres: 17 communes; in Vienne: 8 communes.
Characteristics
The white wines are fairly deep in color, from straw-yellow to golden-yellow in the course of ageing. The bouquets, vegetal, are well developed. These wines are delicate, semidry to mellow, with an overall acidity and fair measure of astringency. They fill the mouth well and have a good aptitude for ageing. The rosé wines have a color known as partridge-eye pink. The rosés of Anjou range from slightly sweet to semidry; they persist in the mouth and age extremely well. The reds take their tone from the Cabernets or the Gamay, according to the zones where they are produced. They are slightly tannic where the fruit is dominant. They are best drunk young.
Serving temperature and suggested accompaniments
The white wines can be served as an aperitif at a temperature close to 50°F (10°C). They go perfectly with pike and *beurre blanc* when young. The mellow whites, especially when sufficiently old, are an excellent accompaniment to desserts such as plum tart.
The rosés are many-faceted wines which go nicely with cream caramel and other desserts. The young reds are good with poultry or roast hare.
Since 1987 there has also been an Anjou-Villages *appellation*, exclusively red, made with the Cabernet Franc and Cabernet Sauvignon. The production zone extends to 43 communes. There is in addition another red, Anjou-Gamay.

ANJOU-COTEAUX-DE-LA-LOIRE

A.C. White

Grape varieties
Chenin exclusively.
Production zone
Communes or part of communes of Bouchemaine, Brain-sur-l'Authion, Champtocé, Ingrandes-sur-Loire, Montjean, La Pommeraye, La Poissonnière, Saint-Barthélémy, Saint-Georges-sur-Loire, Savennières, and Chalonnes.
Characteristics
These wines are quite deep in color, yellow with a faint green reflection. As they age, they tend toward golden. The bouquet is very marked by reason of the schistose terrain. In the mouth they are powerful, well balanced, and always with a touch of suppleness. The taste is very persistent and they have an excellent capacity for ageing.
Serving temperature and suggested accompaniments
Serve chilled. It goes particularly well with salmon.

SAVENNIÈRES

"Coulée de Serrant"
"Roche aux Moines"
A.C. White

Grape varieties
Chenin Blanc exclusively.
Production zone
Communes of Savennières, part of communes of La Poissonnière and Bouchemaine.
Characteristics
The wines may bear the complementary denominations of Coulée de Serrant and Roche aux Moines when they come from these places.
Serving temperature and suggested accompaniments
The wines go well with fish, particularly salmon and pike in *beurre blanc*, veal, and chicken. Serve at 52°–54°F (11°–12°C).

COTEAUX-DU-LAYON

A.C. White

Grape varieties
Chenin Blanc exclusively.
Production zone
Communes or part of communes of Aubigné-Briand, Beaulieu-sur-Layon, Brigné, Chalonnes, Le Champ-sur-Layon, Chanzeaux, Chaudefonds, Chavagnes, Cléré, Concourson, Faveraye-Mâchelles, Faye-d'Anjou, La Fosse-de-Tigné, Martigné-Briand, Nueil, Passavent, Rablay, Rochefort, Saint-Aubin-de-Luigné, Saint-Lambert-du-Lattay, Saint-Georges-sur-Layon, Thouarcé, Tigné, Les Verchers.
Characteristics
As a general rule, the wines of this region are semidry to mellow, according to vintage. Before use, the grapes must contain 204 g sugar per liter when harvested. In certain localities, 221 g is stipulated, and thereafter the name of the commune may be associated with that of Coteaux-du-Layon. These are Beaulieu-sur-Layon, Faye-d'Anjou, Rablay-sur-Layon, Rochefort-sur-Loire, Saint-Aubin-de-Luigné, and Saint-Lambert-du-Lattay. The color of these wines ranges from clear to golden yellow according to their development in the bottle. The sugar is in perfect balance with the malic acidity of the Coteaux-du-Layon and a degree of astringency peculiar to the Chenin variety. The aromas linger in the mouth. In the old wines there are particular scents of quince and dried fruits.
Serving temperature and suggested accompaniments
These wines should be served at 52°–54°F (11°–12°C). Older wines can be drunk as an aperitif or with dessert, provided these are appropriate, like nut tart or rhubarb. They also go well with poultry dishes and with freshwater fish such as pike or salmon, or with turbot served with hollandaise sauce.

COTEAUX-DE-L'AUBANCE

A.C. White

Grape varieties
Chenin Blanc exclusively.
Production zone
Communes or part of communes of Brissac, Denée, Juigné-sur-Loire, Mozé, Murs, Saint-Jean-des Mauvrets, Saint-Melaine, Saint-Saturnin, Soulaines-et-Vauchrétien.
Characteristics
The wines are dry to semidry, slightly delicate. The color is yellow with faint nuances of green. They are very fruity, with a characteristic structure and particular aromas in which verbena often appears. They age very well.
Serving temperature and suggested accompaniments
The dry wines make an excellent accompaniment to fried fish, pork *rillettes*, and veal. Serve at 50°F (10°C).

BONNEZEAUX

A.C. White

Grape varieties
Chenin Blanc exclusively.
Production zone
Part of the commune of Thouarcé.
Characteristics
The color of these wines varies from yellow to deep gold. They are mellow, but the sugar is perfectly balanced by the structural elements. They exude vegetable aromas allied with the scent of flowers and ripe fruit. The wines possess excellent ageing properties, and rare vintages are notable for their marvelous bouquet.
Serving temperature and suggested accompaniments
Serve at 45°F (12°C). The wines can be drunk as an aperitif and also make an excellent accompaniment to desserts such as raspberry bavarois.

QUARTS-DE-CHAUME

A.C. White

Grape varieties
Chenin Blanc exclusively.
Production zone
Commune of Rochefort-sur-Loire and especially Les Quarts, Les Rouères, and Le Veau.
Characteristics
These are mellow wines, of a deep yellow to golden color, exhibiting a perfect balance of sweetness and malic acidity. They linger on the palate and have excellent ageing properties.
Serving temperature and suggested accompaniments
Serve at 54°F (12°C). They go well with the dishes complemented by other Anjou wines, notably freshwater fish and white meat.

CABERNET D'ANJOU

A.C. Rosé

Grape varieties
Cabernet Franc and Cabernet Sauvignon exclusively.
Production zone
All the communes listed for the Anjou *appellation* (see above).
Characteristics
The main feature of the wines of this denomination is that the majority are sweet. They are well balanced, with an alcohol content of 11°–12°, their color amber-yellow and the bouquet very fruity, typical of the grapes used. They linger pleasantly in the mouth and age well.
Serving temperature and suggested accompaniments
Serve at 52°F (11°C). They can be drunk as an aperitif and accompany a wide range of foods, going particularly well with strawberries.

CRÉMANT-DE-LOIRE

A.C. White and Rosé

Grape varieties
Chenin Blanc, Cabernet Franc, Cabernet Sauvignon, Pineau d'Aunis, Pinot Noir, Chardonnay, Menu Pineau. Secondary varieties are Grolleau Noir and Grolleau Gris.
Production zone
Identical areas as for the Anjou, Saumur, and Touraine appellations.

Characteristics
Produced by the *méthode champenoise*, this is a pleasant and elegant wine, lightly sparkling, with a fruity bouquet and balanced taste.
Serving temperature and suggested accompaniments
Serve at 50°F (10°C) as an aperitif or at the end of a meal.

SAUMUR
A.C. White and Red

Grape varieties
White: Chenin Blanc.
Red: Cabernet Franc, Cabernet Sauvignon, Pineau d'Aunis.
Production zone
Maine-et-Loire: communes or part of communes of Antoigné, Artannes, Bagneux, Brézé, Brossay, Chacé, Cizay-la-Madeleine,
Le Coudray-Macouard, Courchamps, Dampierre, Distré, Epieds, Fontevrault, Méron, Montreuil-Bellay, Montsoreau, Parnay, Le Puy-Notre-Dame, Saint-Cyr-en-Bourg, Saint-Hilaire-Saint-Florent, Saint-Just-sur-Dive, Saumur, Souzay, Turquant, Les Ulmes, Varrains, Le Vaudelnay, Les Verchers; Deux Sèvres: Tourtenay; Vienne: Berrie, Curçay, Glénouze, Pouançay, Ranton, Saint-Léger-de-Montbrillais, Saix, Ternay, Les Trois-Moutiers.
Characteristics
These wines are harmoniously structured and well balanced by the characteristic aromas of the region, associated as they are with chalky soils, which gives them a preponderantly vegetable tang. They linger pleasantly in the mouth and have excellent ageing properties. The whites are highly reputed for their elegance.
Serving temperature and suggested accompaniments
The whites are served at 50°F (10°C) and go well with broiled salmon in a light lemon sauce, shad or herrings. The reds, served at 55°F (13°C) complement broiled red meat and cheese.

SAUMUR-CHAMPIGNY
A.C. Red

Grape varieties
Cabernet Franc, Cabernet Sauvignon.
Production zone
Chacé, Dampierre, Montsoreau, Parnay, Saint-Cyr-en-Bourg, Saumur, Souzay-Champigny, Turquant, Varrains.
Characteristics
Medium color, predominantly carmine-garnet. Well developed vegetable, fruity bouquet; balanced fresh taste. Strong characteristic aromas. The wine is supple, light, and lively, fairly astringent and with good ageing properties.
Serving temperature and suggested accompaniments
Serve at 55°F (13°C) with veal, eel, kidneys with juniper berries, duck, and goat's cheese.

ANJOU MOUSSEUX
A.C. White and Rosé

Grape varieties
White: Chenin; secondary varieties (max. 60%), Cabernets, Cot, Gamay.
Rosé: Cabernet, Cot, Gamay, Grolleau, Pineau d'Aunis.
Production zone
All the communes listed for the Anjou *appellation* (see above).
Characteristics
The wines are light in color, greenish-yellow to golden-yellow. Well developed vegetable, fruity, floral bouquet; balanced, quite fresh taste and strong characteristic aromas. The wine is full, lively, and sparkling, slightly astringent and with good ageing capacity.
Serving temperature and suggested accompaniments
Serve at 50°F (10°C) as an aperitif or with freshwater fish such as perch. There is also a semisparkling (*pétillant*) Anjou.

SAUMUR MOUSSEUX
A.C. White and Rosé

Grape varieties
White: Chenin Blanc, Chardonnay and Sauvignon, in proportions of max. 20%.
Rosé: Cabernet Franc, Cabernet Sauvignon, cot, Gamay, Grolleau, Pinot Noir, Pineau d'Aunis.
Production zone
Some 60 communes of Maine-et-Loire, 9 communes of Vienne and 17 communes of Deux-Sèvres.
Characteristics
The wines are light in color, straw-yellow to greenish-yellow, with a well developed vegetable, fruity bouquet, a balanced, quite fresh taste, and strong characteristic aromas. They are full, slightly astringent, delicate, lively and sparkling (pressure c. 4.5 kg at 50°F/10°F, with good ageing properties.
Serving temperature and suggested accompaniments
Serve at 46°–50°F (8°–10°C) as an aperitif or with desserts (fresh strawberries, *clafouti*).

SAUMUR PÉTILLANT
A.C. White and Rosé

Grape varieties
Identical to those of Saumur.
Production zone
All the communes of the Saumur *appellation*.
Characteristics
Medium color, pale yellow, these wines possess a well developed vegetable, fruity, flowery bouquet and have a fresh, balanced taste. Very strong characteristic aromas. The wine is supple, slightly astringent, delicate, lively, and semisparkling (pressure c. 2.5 kg at 50°F/10°C), with good ageing properties.
Serving temperature and suggested accompaniments
Serve at 50°F (10°C) as an aperitif; it also goes well with poached fish or white meat.

ROSÉ DE LOIRE
A.C.

Grape varieties
Cabernet Franc, Cabernet Sauvignon with min. 30% of Pineau d'Aunis, Pinot Noir, Gamay, Grolleau.
Production zone
Communes or part of communes qualifying for the *appellations* Anjou, Saumur, and Touraine.
Characteristics
Medium color with dominating redcur-

rant nuance. Well developed fruity bouquet. The taste is balanced with no preponderance of sugar (less than 3 g sugar per liter). Strong characteristic aromas. The wine is supple, lively, slightly astringent, and does not age well.
Serving temperature and suggested accompaniments
Serve at 52°F (11°C) with ham omelet.

THOUARSAIS
V.D.Q.S. White, Red, and Rosé

Grape varieties
White: Chenin.
Red and rosé: Cabernet Franc, Cabernet Sauvignon.
Production zone
Départment of Deux-Sèvres: Bilazais, Coulonges-Thouarsais, Luché-Thouarsais, Luzay, Massais, Maulais, Missé, Oiron, Pas-de-Jeu, Pierrefitte, Rigné, Saint-Jacques-de-Thouars, Sainte-Gemme, Saint-Varent, Taizé.
Characteristics
Light to deep color, the whites straw-yellow, the reds with a dominant carmine-redcurrant nuance; the rosés are quite pale. The bouquet, slightly mineral and fruity, is well developed, the taste balanced, the whites fairly acidic. Strong characteristic aromas. The wines are supple, the whites and rosés delicate and lively, slightly astringent and with little aptitude for ageing, except in sunny years.
Serving temperature and suggested accompaniments
The reds, served at 57°F (14°C) go well with chicken fricassée or with cakes; the whites and rosés, served at 50°F (10°C) with carp or white navy beans with cream sauce.

COTEAUX-DU-LOIR
A.C. White, Red, and Rosé

Grape varieties
White: Pineau de la Loire.
Red: Pineau d'Aunis, Cabernet, Gamay, Cot.
Rosé: Pineau d'Aunis, Cabernet, Gamay, Cot and max. 25% Grolleau.
Production zone
Sarthe: Beaumont-sur-Dême, Chahaignes, Château-du-Loir, Chenu, Dissay, Flée, La Chartre-sur-le-Loir, Lhomme, Marçon, Montabon, Nogent, Poncé, Ruillé, Saint-Germain d'Arcé, Saint-Germain-du-Val, Saint-Pierre-de-Chevillé, Vouvray-sur-Loir; Indre-et-Loire: Bueil, Epeigné-sur-Dême, Saint-Aubin-le-Dépeint, Saint-Christophe, Saint-Paterne-Racan, Villebourg.
Characteristics
Light to deep color, the whites straw-yellow, the reds predominantly carmine, the rosés fairly deep pink. Well developed fruity, floral bouquet, balanced taste, the whites quite sugary in sunny years. Characteristic aromas strong and persistent. The wines are supple, quite full, lively, the reds fairly astringent, and all age well.
Serving temperature and suggested accompaniments
Serve whites and rosés at 52°F (11°C), reds at 57°F (14°C). The former are good with broiled eel, the latter with broiled pork.

JASNIÈRES
A.C. White

Grape varieties
Pineau Blanc de la Loire.
Production zone
Communes or part of communes of Lhomme, Ruillé-sur-Loir.
Characteristics
Deep color, straw-yellow to golden-yellow. Very well developed vegetable and floral bouquet, balanced taste with preponderance of sugar. Characteristic aromas strong and persistent. The wine is full, delicate, and lively, with a typical touch of astringency. It ages very well.
Serving temperature and suggested accompaniments
Serve at 52°F (11°C). It goes particularly well with broiled shad and mackerel *à la quimperoise*.

TOURAINE
A.C. White, Red, and Rosé

Grape varieties
White: Pineau de la Loire, Arbois, Menu Pineau, Sauvignon and Chardonnay (max. 20%).
Rosé: Cabernet Franc, Cabernet Sauvignon, Cot, Pinot Noir, Pinot Meunier, Pinot Gris, Gamay, Pineau d'Aunis, Grolleau.
Red: Cabernet Franc, Cabernet Sauvignon, Cot, Pinot Meunier, Pinot Gris, Gamay, Pineau d'Aunis.
Production zone
Indre-et-Loire: more than 120 communes.
Loir-et-Cher: 42 communes.
Indre: Azay-le-Ferron.
Characteristics
Medium color, the reds with a dominant nuance of carmine-redcurrant, the whites straw-yellow, the rosés pale pink. Well developed bouquet of vegetables, fruit, and flowers, sometimes with a touch of mineral. Strong characteristic aromas. The wines are supple, well blended, rich, delicate, and quite lively, slightly astringent and with good ageing properties.
Serving temperature and suggested accompaniments
Serve reds at 55°F (13°C), whites and rosés at 48°F (9°C). The reds go well with soups, fish, etc., the whites with pork and herring, the rosés with eggs.

TOURAINE-AZAY-LE-RIDEAU
A.C. White and Rosé

Grape varieties
White: Pineau Blanc.
Rosé: Grolleau (min. 60%), Gamay, Cot, Cabernet Franc and, with max. 10%, Cabernet Sauvignon.
Production zone
Communes or part of communes of Azay-le-Rideau, Artannes, Cheillé, Lignières, Rivarennes, Saché, Thilouze, Vallères.
Characteristics
Light to deep color, the whites straw-yellow to golden-yellow with age, the rosés pale pink with a slight touch of brick-red. Very well developed bouquet of vegetables, fruit, and flowers, sometimes with a touch of mineral. Balanced taste, the whites lively and sugary. Characteristic aromas very strong and persistent. The wines are well blended, fresh and delicate, slightly astringent. The whites age very well.

Serving temperature and suggested accompaniments
Serve whites at 52°F (11°C), rosés at 48°F (9°C). The whites are a good accompaniment to salmon, trout or pike, the rosés to pork, quiche, and fish soups.

TOURAINE-AMBOISE
A.C. White, Red, and Rosé

Grape varieties
White: Pineau Blanc de la Loire.
Red and rosé: Cabernet Franc, Cabernet Sauvignon, Cot, Gamay.
Production zone
Communes or part of communes of Amboise, Chargé, Cangey, Limeray, Mosnes, Nazelles, Pocé-sur-Cisse, Saint-Ouen-les-Vignes.
Characteristics
Medium color, the reds mainly carmine-garnet, the whites straw-yellow to amber yellow, the rosés fairly deep pink. Well developed vegetable, fruity, floral bouquet. Balanced taste, the whites fresh and sugary. In older wines, the characteristic aromas are strong and persistent. The wines are full, well blended, and lively, the reds typically astringent. They age well, particularly the whites in sunny years.
Serving temperature and suggested accompaniments
Serve reds at 57°F (14°C), whites at 52°F (12°C) and rosés at 50°F (10°C). The reds go well with partridge and fish, the whites with pork and sole, the softer, older rosés with egg dishes.

TOURAINE-MESLAND
A.C. White, Red, and Rosé

Grape varieties
White: Pineau Blanc, Sauvignon.
Red and rosé: Gamay, Cot, Cabernet Franc, Cabernet Sauvignon.
Production zone
Communes or part of communes of Mesland, Chambon, Chouzy, Molineuf, Monteaux, Onzain.
Characteristics
Medium color, the reds mainly carmine, the whites straw-yellow, the rosés clear, quite deep pink. The fruity bouquet is well developed, as are the characteristic aromas. The wines are supple, delicate, and lively, particularly the rosés, with a pleasantly astringent touch, and they have a good aptitude for ageing.
Serving temperature and suggested accompaniments
The rosés, served at 52°F (11°C) go with pastry, the reds, served at 57°F (14°C) with broiled white meat.

TOURAINE MOUSSEUX
A.C. White, Red, and Rosé

Grape varieties
White: Pineau Blanc, Arbois, max. 20% Chardonnay and max. 30% Cabernet Franc, Cabernet Sauvignon, Pinot Noir, Pinot Gris, Pinot Meunier, Pineau d'Aunis, Cot, and Grolleau.
Red: Cabernet Franc.
Rosé: Cabernet Franc, Cot, Pinot Noir, Gamay, and Grolleau.
Production zone
Communes or part of communes of the Touraine A.C. *appellation*.
Characteristics
Light color, violet-red, and pale yellow. Well developed bouquet of vegetables, fruit, and flowers. Fresh, balanced taste. Characteristic aromas strong and persistent. The wines are supple, light, quite lively, sparkling, with a typical touch of astringency, and a good aptitude for ageing.
Serving temperature and suggested accompaniments
Serve at 48°F (9°C) as an aperitif; they can also be used to make good sorbets.
There is also a semisparkling Touraine, which can be served at 50°F (10°C) as an aperitif or to accompany roast white meat or poached fish.

VOUVRAY
A.C. White

Grape varieties
Pineau Blanc de la Loire exclusively.
Production zone
Communes or part of communes of Vouvray, Rochecorbon, Vernou, Sainte-Radegonde, Chançay, Noizay, Reugny, Parçay-Meslay.
Characteristics
Deep color, straw-yellow to golden-yellow as it ages. The bouquet, of vegetables, fruit, and flowers, with a touch of mineral on certain soils, is well developed, as are the characteristic aromas. The wines are full, well blended, delicate, and lively, with a typical touch of astringency and excellent ageing properties.
Serving temperature and suggested accompaniments
Serve at 54°F (12°C). It goes well with pike, pork, sole, cheeses, and desserts.

VOUVRAY MOUSSEUX
A.C. White

Grape varieties
Pineau Blanc de la Loire.
Production zone
Communes or part of communes of the Vouvray *appellation*.
Characteristics
Deep color, straw-yellow to amber-yellow in older wines. Well developed vegetable, fruity, floral bouquet. Characteristic aromas very strong and persistent. The wines are full, delicate, lively, and sparkling (pressure 4.5 kg at 50°F/10°C), with a typical touch of astringency and an excellent ageing capacity.
Serving temperature and suggested accompaniments
Serve at 50°F (10°C) as an aperitif and for preparing sorbets.

VOUVRAY PÉTILLANT
A.C. White

Grape varieties
Pineau Blanc de la Loire.
Production zone
Communes or parts of communes of the Vouvray *appellation*.
Characteristics
Deep color, straw-yellow to golden-yellow with age, and a very well developed vegetable, fruity, floral bouquet. Characteristic aromas very strong and persistent. The wine is full, delicate, lively, and semisparkling (pressure 2.5 kg

at 50°F/10°C), with a typically astringent touch and an excellent aptitude for ageing.
Serving temperature and suggested accompaniments
Serve at 52°F (11°C) as an aperitif. Softer, older wines can accompany desserts such as plum tart, etc.

MONTLOUIS
A.C. Rosé

Grape varieties
Pineau Blanc de la Loire.
Production zone
Communes or part of communes of Montlouis, Saint-Martin-le-Beau and Lussault.
Characteristics
Light color, straw-yellow to golden-yellow with age. Very well developed vegetable, fruity, floral bouquet. Characteristic aromas very strong and persistent. The wine is full, delicate, and lively, with a typically astringent touch and an excellent aptitude for ageing.
Serving temperature and suggested accompaniments
Serve at 54°F (12°C) to accompany pork, omelets, quiches, roast chicken, pheasant, cheese, etc.

MONTLOUIS MOUSSEUX
A.C. White

Grape varieties
Pineau de la Loire.
Production zone
Communes or part of communes of the Montlouis *appellation*.
Characteristics
Light color, pale yellow, with a well developed bouquet of vegetables and fruit, and a fresh, balanced taste. Strong characteristic aromas. The wine is light, delicate, lively, and sparkling (pressure 4.5 kg at 50°F/10°C), typically astringent, with a good aptitude for ageing.
Serving temperature and suggested accompaniments
Serve at 50°F (10°C) as an aperitif; it can also accompany roasted white meats and pike.
There is also a Mountlouis Pétillant (semisparkling), likewise served at 50°F (10°C) as an aperitif and a good accompaniment to sweetbreads and rabbit.

BOURGUEIL
A.C.

Red and a small quantity of rosé, which is made in much the same way as the rosés of Touraine.
Grape varieties
Cabernet Franc, possibly supplemented by max. 10% Cabernet Sauvignon.
Production zone
Communes or part of communes of Bourgueil, Saint-Nicolas-de-Bourgueil, Restigné, Ingrandes-de-Touraine, Saint-Patrice, Benais, La Chapelle-sur-Loire, Chouzé-sur-Loire.
Characteristics
Deep color according to soil, predominantly carmine, with a touch of garnet. The bouquet, of vegetables, fruit, and flowers, sometimes animal and, in older wines, mineral, is very well developed. Characteristic aromas are very strong and persistent. The wine is full, light, velvety, and lively with a good measure of astringency and an excellent aptitude for ageing.
Serving temperature and suggested accompaniments
Serve at 57°F (14°C) with soups, vegetable dishes, roast pork, cheese, etc.

SAINT-NICOLAS-DE-BOURGUEIL
A.C.

Red and a very small quantity of rosé, vinified in the same manner as the rosés of Touraine.
Grape varieties
Cabernet Franc, possibly supplemented by max. 10% Cabernet Sauvignon.
Production zone
Part of the commune of Saint-Nicholas-de-Bourgueil.
Characteristics
Light color with a dominant redcurrant-garnet nuance. The bouquet, according to *crus*, is vegetable, animal, mineral, fruity, and floral, and well developed. Characteristic aromas are very strong and persistent. The wine is supple, velvety, well blended, and lively, with a good measure of typical astringency and an excellent ageing capacity.
Serving temperature and suggested accompaniments
Serve at 57°F (14°C) to go with sweetbreads, cheese, roast chicken, etc.

CHINON
A.C.

Principally red; small quantities of white and rosé, vinified in the same manner as those of Touraine.
Grape varieties
Cabernet Franc, possibly supplemented by max. 10% Cabernet Sauvignon.
Production zone
Communes or part of communes of Avoine, Beaumont-en-Véron, Savigny-en-Véron, Chinon, Huismes, Ligré, Rivière, Cravant, Panzoult, La Roche-Clermault, l'Ile-Bouchard, Anché, Sazilly, Tavant, Crouzilles, Theneuil, Avon-les-Roches, Marçay, Saint-Benoit-la-Forêt.
Characteristics
Light to deep color, with dominant nuances of carmine, garnet or redcurrant according to soil and age. Very well developed vegetable, animal, mineral, fruity bouquet. Characteristic aromas very strong and persistent. The wine is supple, velvety, well blended, lively, typically astringent, with an excellent capacity for ageing.
Serving temperature and suggested accompaniments
Serve at 57°F (14°C) with rabbit, pork, roast poultry, kidneys, cheese, etc.

VINS DU HAUT-POITOU
V.D.Q.S. White, Red, and Rosé

Grape varieties
White: Sauvignon, Chardonnay, Chenin (max. 20%), Pineau Blanc.
Red and rosé: Pinot Noir, Gamay, Merlot, Cot, Cabernets, Chaudenay (max. 20%), Grolleau (max. 20%).
Production zone
Vienne: 45 communes.

Characteristics
Light color, the reds with a predominantly carmine-redcurrant nuance, the whites slightly straw-yellow. Well developed vegetable, fruity, floral bouquet. Balanced, fresh taste. Strong characteristic aromas. The wines are supple, light, and lively, with little astringency and not much aptitude for ageing.
Serving temperature and suggested accompaniments
The white, served at 50°F (10°C), goes well with snails or broiled eel. The red, served at 55°F (13°C), may be accompanied by veal, duck or hare.

CHEVERNY
V.D.Q.S. White, Red, and Rosé

Grape varieties
White: Pineau Blanc, Arbois, Chardonnay, Romorantin, Sauvignon.
Red: Gamay, Cabernets, Pinot Noir, Cot, Gamay Chaudenay (max. 15%).
Rosé: same varieties with addition of Pineau d'Aunis and Pinot Gris.
Production zone
23 communes of Loir-et-Cher.
Characteristics
Light color, the reds with a predominantly carmine-redcurrant nuance, the whites slightly straw-yellow to greenish-yellow; the rosés clear pink. Well developed vegetable, fruity, floral bouquet. Balanced, fresh taste. Strong characteristic aromas. The wines are supple, light, and lively, with little astringency and not much aptitude for ageing.
Serving temperature and suggested accompaniments
Serve reds at 55°F (13°C) with broiled blood sausages and shallots; whites and rosés should be served at 50°F (10°C), the latter with pig's trotters or goat's cheese.

COTEAUX-DU-VENDOMOIS
V.D.Q.S. Red, White, and Rosé

Grape varieties
White: Chenin, Chardonnay (max. 20%).
Rosé: Pineau d'Aunis, Gamay (max. 30%).
Red: Gamay, Pinot Noir, Cabernets, Pineau d'Aunis (min. 30%).
Production zone
35 communes of Loir-et-Cher.
Characteristics
Light color, the reds with predominately carmine-redcurrant nuance, the whites fairly pale yellow, the rosés clear pink. Well developed bouquet of fruit and flowers. Balanced, fresh taste. Strong characteristic aromas. The wines are supple, light, and lively, with little astringency and fair ageing capacity.
Serving temperature and suggested accompaniments
Serve whites at 50°F (10°C) and reds at 55°F (13°C). The whites go well with cooked meats, the rosés with game, the reds with broiled veal.

VINS DE L'ORLÉANAIS
V.D.Q.S. White, Red, and Rosé

Grape varieties
White: Auvernat Blanc, Auvernat Gris.
Red and rosé: Pinot Noir, Pinot Meunier.
Production zone
Following communes or part of communes: right bank of Loire: Saint-Denis-de-l'Hôtel, Bou, Combieux, Mardié, Saint-Jean-de-Braye, Semoy, Orléans, Fleury-les-Aubrais, Saran, Saint-Jean-de-la-Ruelle, La Chapelle-Saint-Mesmin, Ingré, Chaingy, Saint-Ay, Meung-sur-Loire, Baule, Messas, Beaugency, Tavers, Chécy; left bank of Loire: Olivet, Saint-Hilaire-Sain-Mesmin, Mareau-aux-Prés, Mézières-les-Cléry, Cléry-Saint-André.
Characteristics
Light color, the reds mainly carmine-redcurrant, the whites slightly straw-yellow; the rosés are light, clean pink. Well developed vegetable, fruity, floral bouquet. Strong characteristic aromas. The wines are supple, light, and lively, with little astringency and fair ageing properties.
Serving temperature and suggested accompaniments
Serve whites at 50°F (10°C) and reds at 55°F (13°C). The former go well with snails or fried fish, the reds with game pâté.

VALENÇAY
V.D.Q.S. White, Red, and Rosé

Grape varieties
White: min. 60% Arbois, Chardonnay, Sauvignon, supplemented by Pineau Blanc and Romorantin.
Red and rosé: min. 75% Cabernets, Cot, Gamay, Pinot Noir, Chardonnay, supplemented by Gascon, Pineau d'Aunis, Gamay Chaudenay, Grolleau (max. 19%).
Production zone
Communes or part of communes of Chabris, Faverolles, Fontguenand, Luçay-le-Mâle, Lye, Mentou-sur-Nahon, Parpeçay, Poulaines, Sembleçay, Valençay, Varennes-sur-Fouzon, La Vernelle, Veuil, Villentrois, in Indre; Selles-sur-Cher in Loir-et-Cher.
Characteristics
Light color, the reds mainly carmine-redcurrant, the whites straw-yellow to greenish-yellow, the rosés clean pink. Well developed bouquet of fruit and flowers. Balanced, fresh taste. Strong characteristic aromas. The wines are supple, light, and lively, with little astringency. They do not age well except in particularly sunny years.
Serving temperature and suggested accompaniments
Serve reds at 57°F (14°C) and whites and rosés at 50°F (10°C). The white goes well with dry Valençay goat's cheese or broiled eel; the red with the same type of cheese, potato *galette* or broiled white meat; the rosé with mushroom omelet.

SANCERRE
A.C. White

Grape varieties
Sauvignon.
Production zone
Communes or part of communes of Bannay, Bué, Crézancy, Menetou-Ratel, Menétréol, Montigny, Saint-Satur, Sainte-Gemme, Sancerre, Sury-en-Vaux, Thauvenay, Veaugues, Verdigny, Vinon.
Characteristics
Light color, straw-yellow, green. Well developed bouquet of vegetables and fruit. Strong and persistent characteristic aromas. The wine is full-bodied and fresh, slightly astringent with good ageing properties.

Serving temperature and suggested accompaniments
Serve at 50°F (10°C) with goat's cheese, oyster or crab consommé, or baked sausages.

SANCERRE
A.C. Red and Rosé

Grape varieties
Pinot Noir.
Production zone
Communes or part of communes of Bannay, Bué, Crézancy, Menetou-Ratel, Menétréol, Montigny, Saint-Satur, Sainte-Gemme, Sancerre, Saury-en-Vaux, Thauvenay, Veaugues, Verdigny, Vinon.
Characteristics
Medium color, the reds with mainly carmine-garnet nuances, the rosés clear pink. Well-developed vegetable, animal, fruity bouquet. Strong characteristic aromas. The wines are supple, velvety, and fresh, slightly astringent with good ageing capacity.
Serving temperature and suggested accompaniments
Serve rosés at 54°F (12°C), reds at 57°F (14°C). The former go well with pâté *en croûte* and the latter with roast quail.

REUILLY
A.C. White, Red, and Rosé

Grape varieties
White: Sauvignon.
Red and rosé: Pinot Noir and Pinot Gris.
Production zone
Communes or part of communes of Reuilly, Diou, Cerbois, Lury-sur-Arnon, Preuilly, Chéry, Lazenay.
Characteristics
Light color, the reds mainly carmine-redcurrant, the whites straw-yellow, the rosés clear pink. Well developed vegetable, fruity bouquet. Very strong characteristic aromas. The wines are supple, light, and velvety, slightly astringent with good ageing properties.
Serving temperature and suggested accompaniments
Serve whites and rosés at 52°F (11°C), reds at 57°F (14°C). The whites go well with goat's cheese, eel or scallops, the rosés with mushroom omelet, the reds with chicken in aspic.

QUINCY
A.C. White

Grape varieties
Sauvignon.
Production zone
Communes or part of communes of Quincy, Brinay.
Characteristics
Light straw-yellow color. Well developed vegetable, mineral, fruity bouquet. Strong characteristic aromas. The wine is supple, delicate, and lively, slightly astringent, and ages well.
Serving temperature and suggested accompaniments
Serve at 50°F (10°C) to go with oysters, asparagus or braised lettuce.

POUILLY-SUR-LOIRE
A.C. White

Grape varieties
Chasselas and Sauvignon.
Production zone
Communes or part of communes of Pouilly-sur-Loire, Saint-Andelain, Tracy-sur-Loire, Saint-Laurent, Saint-Martin-sur-Nohain, Garchy, Mesve-sur-Loire.
Characteristics
Light pale yellow color. Well developed vegetable, fruity bouquet. Balanced, fresh taste. Strong characteristic aromas. The wine is supple, soft, and lively, slightly astringent. It has little capacity for ageing.
Serving temperature and suggested accompaniments
Serve at 52°F (10°C). It can go with oysters, shrimp, and fish terrines.

POUILLY FUMÉ
A.C. White

Grape varieties
Sauvignon.
Production zone
Identical to area for Pouilly-sur-Loire.
Characteristics
Medium straw-yellow color. Well developed vegetable, mineral, fruity bouquet. Characteristic aromas strong and persistent. The wine is full, delicate, and fresh, slightly astringent, with very good ageing properties.
Serving temperature and suggested accompaniments
Serve at 52°F (11°C). This wine goes well with chicken or a hot freshwater-fish terrine.

MENETOU-SALON
A.C. White, Red, and Rosé

Grape varieties
White: Sauvignon.
Red and rosé: Pinot Noir.
Production zone
Communes or part of communes of Aubinges, Menetou-Salon, Morogues, Parassy, Pigny, Quantilly, Saint-Céols, Soulangis, Vignoux-sous-les-Aix, Humbligny.
Characteristics
Light color, the reds mainly carmine-redcurrant, the whites slightly straw-yellow, the rosés clear pink. Well developed vegetable, fruity bouquet. Strong characteristic aromas. The red wines are supple, fresh, and velvety, the whites light and delicate; they posses little astringency and age well.
Serving temperature and suggested accompaniments
Serve whites and rosés at 52°F (11°C) and reds at 55°F (13°C). The whites can go with goat's cheese and fried fish, the rosés with asparagus in vinaigrette, the reds with roast kid.

CHÂTEAUMEILLANT
V.D.Q.S. Red and Gris

Grape varieties
Gamay (max. 85%).
Pinot Gris, Pinot Noir (min. 15%).
Production zone
Communes or part of communes of Châteaumeillant, Reigny, Saint-Maur, Vesdun, Champillet, Feusines, Néret, Urciers.

Characteristics
Light color, the reds with a predominance of redcurrant, the gris pale pink. Well developed vegetable, fruity bouquet. Strong characteristic aromas. The wines are supple, light, and fresh, slightly astringent, with little aptitude for ageing.
Serving temperature and suggested accompaniments
The reds, served at 57°F (14°C), go nicely with rabbit soup or shallots; the gris, served at 54°F (12°C), with lamb.

CÔTES ROANNAISES
V.D.Q.S. Red

Grape varieties
Gamay, Saint-Romain.
Production zone
Communes or part of communes of Saint-Jean-le-Puy, Saint-Maurice sur-Loire, Villemontais, Lentigny, Saint-André-d'Apchon, Saint-Alban-les-Eaux, Renaison, Ambierle, Changy, Bully, Saint-Haon-le-Vieux, Pouilly-les-Nonains, Saint-Cyr-de-Favières, Saint-Haon-le-Châtel, Ouches, Le Crozet, La Pacaudière, Villerest, Cordelle, Commelle-Vernay, Notre-Dame-de-Boisset, Saint-Vincent-de-Boisset, Saint-Nizier-sous-Charlieu, Saint-Pierre-la-Noaille.
Characteristics
Light carmine-redcurrant color. Well developed vegetable, mineral, fruity bouquet. Strong characteristic aromas. The wine is supple, light, lively, slightly astringent, with little ageing capacity.
Serving temperature and suggested accompaniments
Serve at 57°F (14°C) to accompany cooked meats and local cheeses.

CÔTES-D'AUVERGNE
V.D.Q.S. White, Red, and Rosé

Grape varieties
White: Chardonnay.
Red and rosé: Gamay, Pinot Noir.
Production zone
Following communes or parts of communes: Côtes d'Auvergne-Boudes: Boudes, Chalus and Saint-Hérent; Côtes D'Auvergne-Chanturgue: Clermont-Ferrand and Cébazat; Côtes d'Auvergene-Châteaugay: Châteaugay, Cébazat, and Ménétrol; Côte d'Auveregne-Corent: Corent, Les Martres-de-Veyre, La Sauvetat, and Veyre-Monton; Côtes d'Auvergne-Madargues: Riom; Côtes d'Auvergne: 37 communes of the Clermont-Ferrand *arrondissement*, 11 communes of the Riom *arrondissement*, and 5 communes of the Issoire *arrondissement*.
Characteristics
Light color, the reds with a predominantly carmine-redcurrant brick-red nuance, the whites straw-yellow. Well developed vegetable, mineral, fruity bouquet. Strong characteristic aromas. The wines are supple, well blended, light, and fresh, slightly astringent, with little ageing aptitude.
Serving temperature and suggested accompaniments
Serve reds at 57°F (14°C), rosés at 57°F (12°C) and whites at 52°F (11°C). The reds go well with beef or cabbage, the whites with broiled pork or ham, and the rosés with ham omelet or tripe.

CÔTES DU FOREZ
V.D.Q.S. Red and Rosé

Grape varieties
Gamay.
Production zone
Communes or part of communes of Arthun, Bellegarde-en-Forez, Boën-sur-Ligon, Bussy-Albieux, Champdieu, Débats-Rivière-d'Orpra, Ecotay-l'Olme, l'Hôpital-sous-Rochefort, Leigneux, Lézigneux, Marcilly-le-Châtel, Marcou, Moingt, Pralong, Sail-sous-Couzan, Saint-Georges-Haut-Ville, Saint-Laurent-Rochefort, Saint-Sixte, Saint-Thomas-la-Garde, Sainte-Agathe-la-Bouteresse, Trelins.

Characteristics
Light color, the reds with a predominantly carmine-redcurrant, brick-red nuance, the rosés pale pink. Well developed vegetable, fruity bouquet. Strong characteristic aromas. The wines are supple, velvety, fresh, and slightly astringent. They do not age well.
Serving temperature and suggested accompaniments
Serve the reds at 55°F (13°C), the rosés at 52°F (11°C). The former go well with soups, cooked meats, pork with lentils, and cheeses, the rosés with scrambled eggs and onions.

COTEAUX DU GIENNOIS
V.D.Q.S. White and Red

Grape varieties
Red: Pinot Noir, Gamay.
White: Sauvignon, Pinot Blanc de la Loire.
Production zone
Following communes or part of communes: Loiret *département:* Beaulieu, Bonny-sur-Loire, Briare, Châtillon-sur-Loire, Gien, Ousson, Thou; Nièvre *département:* Alligny-Cosne, La Celle-sur-Loire, Cosne-sur-Loire, Cours-lès-Cosne, Myennes, Neuvy-sur-Loire, Pougny, Saint-Loup, Saint-Père.
Characteristics
Light color, the reds with a dominant carmine nuance, the whites straw-yellow. Faint bouquet of vegetables and fruit, weak characteristic aromas. The wines are supple, the reds full-bodied, the whites fresh. They possess little astringency and do not age well.
Serving temperature and suggested accompaniments
Serve reds at 55°F (13°C) and whites at 50°F (10°C). The reds go well with shell beans, cabbage soup or chicken, the whites with braised white meat.

SAINT-POURÇAIN-SUR-SIOULE

V.D.Q.S. White, Red, Rosé, and Gris

Grape varieties
Red: Gamay, Pinot Noir, Gamay Teinturier (max. 10%).
White: Tressalier (max. 50%), Saint-Pierre-Doré (max. 10%), Aligoté, Chardonnay, Sauvignon.
Production zone
Communes or part of communes of Chemilly, Besson, Bresnay, Meillard, Châtel-de-Neuvre, Montenay-sur-Allier, Chontigny, Verneuil-en-Bourbonnais, Saulcet, Bransat, Louchy-Montfand, Saint-Pourçain-sur-Sioule, Cesset, Montord, Chaareil-Cintrat, Fleuriel, Fourilles, Deneuille, Chantelle.
Characteristics
Light color, the reds predominantly brick-red–carmine, the whites straw-yellow, the rosés deep pink, the gris pale pink. Well developed vegetable, fruity bouquet. Strong characteristic aromas. The wines are supple and well blended, the reds lively, the whites and rosés quite soft. They have little astringency and do not age particularly well.
Serving temperature and suggested accompaniments
Serve reds at 57°F (14°C), whites at 52°F (11°C). The reds go well with braised lamb's tongue, cheeses, the whites with chestnut soup, the rosés with pork terrine.

Alsace, the eastern vineyards, and Champagne

This is a very ancient part of France's wine-growing country. It comprises the vineyards of Moselle and Toul, with a small but not negligible production, and of Alsace, mainly with dry white wines, varied and modulated according to the grape varieties used. The choice and distribution of these wines are in keeping with the diversity of the local hill soils (chalky, sandstone, and gneiss).

The continental climate of the plain of Alsace, situated at the foot of the Vosges mountains, allows the vine to ripen admirably and to furnish wines which are noted for their ageing properties. At altitudes of 650–1300 ft (200–400 m), covering an area of c. 30,000 acres (12,000 hectares), the wines of Alsace are elegant, well structured and notable for the characteristic scent of their grapes. But the grower has an additional problem with the climate, and this is reflected in late harvests. For he has to take a gamble with time – a gamble which, when successful, results in a wine which has an additional measure of distinction and refinement, fully worthy of accompanying the finest Alsace cuisine.

Also in this northeastern corner of France is the most famous wine-growing region in the world: Champagne. The sparkling, bubbling wine that bears this name is literally exhilarating as it slips down the throat and leaves its incomparable tingle on the palate. It is the wine for toasts, for special occasions and for happy, glowing memories. The vineyards stretch over a vast area, where huge caves, cut into the chalk, provide cool and quiet storage conditions. The three grapes most characteristic of this soil are the Pinot Meunier, which is the main variety, the Pinot Noir, and the Chardonnay. The rules for making the wine are very precise, in particular those relating to pressure, and the méthode champenoise *is a specialized and highly perfected technique. Champagne goes well with innumerable dishes and adds a touch of refinement to any meal.*

VINS D'ALSACE

A.C. White

Grape varieties
For white wines: Gewürztraminer, Riesling, Pinot Gris (Tokay d'Alsace), Muscat Blanc, Muscat à Petits Grains, Muscat Ottonel, Pinot Blanc, Auxerrois, Pinot Noir vinified *en blanc*, Sylvaner Blanc, Chasselas Blanc and Rosé.
For red and rosé wines: Pinot Noir.
Production zone
This is a vast region, covering 110 communes. Among the most famous are, in the Bas-Rhin: Mutzig, Molsheim, Rosheim, Obernai, Barr, Gertwiller, Mittlebergheim, Andlau, Dambach, Kintzheim: in the Haut-Rhin: Rorschwihr, Bergheim, Ribeauvillé, Hunawihr, Riquewihr, Beblenheim, Mittelwihr, Kientzheim, Sigolsheim, Kaysersberg, Ammerschwihr, Ingersheim, Turckeim, Wintzenheim, Wettolsheim, Eguisheim, Andolsheim, Voegtlinshofen, Obermorschwihr, Hattstatt, Pfaffenheim, Rouffach, Soulzmatt, Gueberschwihr, Orschwihr, Bergholtz.
Principal regions for Sylvaner: regions of Barr (Bas, -Rhin) and Rouffach (Haut-Rhin).
Principal regions for Muscat: communes of Voegtlinshofen, Riquewihr, Ribeauvillé.
Principal regions for Riesling: Riquewihr, Zellenberg, Ribeauvillé, Dambach.
Characteristics
These depend on the grapes from which the wines are produced. Rieslings, the most widely distributed in the Alsace region, are bright greenish-yellow in color, possess a very fruity nose and have a mellow taste with a perfect balance between acidity and strength. They linger pleasantly in the mouth, particularly when they are some years old.
Sylvaner is a little less green in tone; it is equally dry, with a lighter aroma than Riesling.
Gewürztraminer is the most highly scented wine of the Alsace region. It ages wonderully well, one of the vintage wines, soft to mellow, according to the year.
Chasselas is a very smooth wine, quite fresh and fruity, simple in character.
Muscat also has a relatively light structure but its aromatic quality is distinctive and it lingers nicely in the mouth.
The Pinot Gris or Tokay d'Alsace has a

more racy, spicy scent, with a full-bodied and lingering taste, very typical of the region.
Serving temperature and suggested accompaniments
Serve at 50°F (10°C). The recommended dishes have to be determined by the type of wine concerned. Chasselas, a simple wine drunk mainly in summer, is served locally with frogs' legs, provided there is not too much garlic in the dish. Sylvaner goes well with the game terrines and with *choucroute*. Pinot Blanc is also an elegant wine which can accompany fish, such as poached turbot, soups or a sausage salad. Riesling, if very young, can be served with seafood and, of course, the region's traditional *choucroute*, but if it is a *cru* and already some years old, it goes marvelously with fish dishes, especially when they include poached oysters. Muscat is very good with cardoons or with desserts (e.g. Kougelhopf, Savoy cake). Gewürztraminer is traditionally drunk with Munster cheese, but is also an excellent accompaniment to cakes (apple strudel, cherry tart, Kougelhopf). Tokay d'Alsace should be served with game, pheasant and goose, and, prepared in various ways, pâté de foie gras.

ALSACE GRAND CRU
A.C. White

Grape varieties
Riesling, Gewürztraminer, Pinot Gris, Muscat.
Production zone
Part of the Alsace *appellation*.
Characteristics
These wines age particularly well and are among the finest wines in Alsace, possessing the original features mentioned above.
Suggested accompaniments
The same as already mentioned but with somewhat richer and fancier dishes.

CRÉMANT D'ALSACE
A.C. White

Grape varieties
Riesling, Pinot Blanc, Pinot Noir, Pinot Gris, Auxerrois, Chardonnay.
Production zone
Entire region of Alsace.
Characteristics
These are fruity, fairly soft, sparkling wines, with a slight touch of acidity.
Suggested accompaniments
They are best served as an aperitif.

CÔTES-DE-TOUL
V.D.Q.S. White, Red, and Gris

Grape varieties
Red: Pinot Noir, Pinot Meunier.
White: Aubin Blanc, Aligoté.
Gris: Pinot Noir, Pinot Meunier, Gamay Noir à jus blanc (in proportion of 85%), plus 15% white varieties mentioned above.
Production zone
Communes or part of communes of Lucey, Bruley, Pagney-derrière-Barine, Ecrouves, Domgermain, Charmes-la-Côte, Mont-le-Vignoble, Blend-les-Toul, Bulligny.
Characteristics
The gris is the most famous wine of this region. It is dry, with marked acidity but not unpleasantly so. The bouquet is well developed.
Serving temperature and suggested accompaniments
These are simple wines, to serve cool with eel, pike, pig's trotters or entrées such as *quiche lorraine*.

VINS DE MOSELLE
V.D.Q.S. White and sometimes Rosé and Red

Grape varieties
Gamay (30%), Auxerrois Blanc, Auxerrois Gris, Meunier Blanc, Meunier Gris, Pinot Noir, Pinot Blanc, Elbling (20%), Sylvaner, Riesling, Gewürztraminer.
Production zone
Communes or part of communes of Lorry-Mardigny, Vezon, Fey, Ancy-sur-Moselle, Dornot, Novéant, Marange-Silvange, Plappeville, Lessy, Contz-les-Bains, Sierck, Vic-sur-Seille, Laquenexy.
Serving temperature and suggested accompaniments
These wines should be served cool with local cooked meats, particularly pork.

CHAMPAGNE
A.C.

Grape varieties
Different grapes are used, according to zone, i.e., Côte des Blancs: Pinot Chardonnay; Vallée de la Marne: Pinot Meunier, Pinot Noir; Montagne de Reims: Pinot Noir, Pinot Meunier.
Making the wine
Champagne is made by the *méthode champenoise*. This is based on the preparation of *curvées*, wines of the first growth. The wine undergoes two successive fermentations, the second of which is called *prise de mousse*. Placed on racks, shaken and disgorged, the wine is then topped up with its *liqueur d'expédition*.
The dosage for the driest champagne, *brut*, is less than 15 g sugar per liter; the extra dry contains 12–20 g, the *sec* 17–36 g, the *demi-sec* 35–50 g, the *moelleux* more than 50 g.
Production zone
Marne *département;* Aisne *département;* and, in the Aube *département*, the communes of Cunfin, Trannes, Précy-Saint-Martin.
In each of these production zones, there is a scale of values for the *crus* of the grapes. Some communes are rated 100%, and they have the right to the denomination *grand cru*. The communes classified at 90–100% are entitled to the denomination *premier cru*.
The following, for example, are some of the leading communes, according to zones:
Zone of Vallée de la Marne: Ay (100%), Mareuil-sur-Ay (98%), Diz y-Magenta (95%), Avenay (93%), Champillon (93%), Mutigny (93%), Cumières (90%), Hautvillers (90%).
Zone of Côte d'Epernay: Chouilly (90% black grapes, 93% white grapes), Pierry (90%), Epernay (90%), Moussy (90%), Vinay (86%), Saint-Martin-d'Ablois (86%).
Zone of Côte d'Ambonnay: Ambonnay (100%), Bouzy (100%), Louvois (100%), Tours-sur-Marne (100% black grapes, 90% white grapes), Tauxières-Mutry (93%).
Zone of Côte Blanche: Avize (100%), Cramant (100%), Oger (98%), Diz y (99%), Le Mesnil-sur-Oger (90%), Grauves (90% black, 93% white), Cuis (90% black, 93% white), Monthelon (80%), Chavot-Cour-

court (87% black, 88% white), Mancy (86% black, 90% white), Brugny-Vaudancourt (86%).
Zone of Côte de Vertus: Vertus (93%), Bergères-lès-Vertus (90% black, 93% white).
Zone of Haute Montagne de Reims: Sillery (100%), Puisieulx (100%), Beaumount-sur-Vsele (100%), Verzenay (100% black, 86% white), Mailly-Champagne (100% black, 86% white), Verzy (99% black, 86% white), Rilly-la-Montagne (94%), Montbre (94%), Ludes (94% black, 86% white), Chigney-lès-Roses (94% black, 86% white), Trépail (90%), Villers-Marmery (90%), Villers-Allerand (90%).
Each region nevertheless possesses individual characteristics. The wines of the communes of Ay and Mareuil, for example, are fine and aristocratic, with body. Those of the regions of Ambonnay, Bouzy, and Louvois are more vigorous, rich and well rounded. The wines of the Côte des Blancs, i.e. Avize, Cramant, Oiry, Le Mesnil-sur-Oger and Grauves, are more delicate, very fresh, more or less vinous according to communes. In the Reims region, at Sillery, Beaumont-sur-Vesle, Verzenay, and Mailly-Champagne, for example, the wines have good vinosity and a strong bouquet.
It is obvious, therefore, that one cannot expect to find a single wine in Champagne, but a number of different types delineated by their origin.

Serving temperature and suggested accompaniments

Champagne is drunk the world over, notably for special, celebratory occasions. It should be served at fairly low temperatures, around 46°F (8°C). Vintage champagnes can be served at around 50°F (10°C).
Ideally, champagne should be drunk prior to the meal, as an aperitif. However, several champagnes, preferably vintage, can be served throughout a meal to accompany various dishes. The rare *blanc de noir* champagne, made solely from Pinot Noir, goes very well with ham and poultry; *blanc de blanc* champagne, exclusively from white Chardonnay, can be served with fish such as salmon, with sweetbreads and with desserts, provided the wines are sufficiently sweet and mature.

COTEAUX CHAMPENOIS
A.C. White, Rosé

Grape varieties

Pinot Noir, Pinot Meunier, Chardonnay.

Production zone

Identical to the area for the Champagne *appellation*.

Characteristics

These are very young, dry wines; some are rosés. They are fairly light and distinctively fruity, the taste lingering in the mouth.

Serving temperature and suggested accompaniments

These wines are served cool, around 50°F (10°C). They can accompany a variety of dishes.

COTEAUX CHAMPENOIS
A.C. Red

Grape varieties

Pinot Noir.

Production zone

There is a small production of these wines in the communes of Bouzy and Mareuil-sur-Ay.

Characteristics

The wines are light in color, mainly garnet-redcurrant. They smell very fruity, predominantly of strawberry and raspberry, age moderately well and linger normally in the mouth.

Suggested accompaniments

These wines go well with pork sausage and leek tart.

ROSÉ DE RICEYS
A.C. Rosé

Grape varieties

Pinot Noir.

Production zone

Commune of Riceys.

Characteristics and uses

These dry, crisp wines are for drinking very young; they are deep pink in color and smell very fruity. They should be served at 48°F (9°C) and are good with onion tart.

The central-eastern vineyards

The wines grouped together in this area of French vineyards include those of Franche-Comté, of Savoy and the Ain, and, not least, those of Burgundy, the last subdivided into five regions:

– Basse Bourgogne, represented primarily by Chablis;

– Côte-d'Or, where the connoisseur can choose between two côtes, *de Nuits and de Beaune;*

– Côte Chalonnaise, transitional zone with the Mâconnais;

– Mâconnais;

– Beaujolais, with a range of delightful wines known all over the world, particularly the vin nouveau.

These vineyards, with very rare exceptions, produce wines derived from single varieties of grape. The reds are made from Pinot Noir or Gamay, the whites from Chardonnay. It is fascinating to discover these wines and compare their different qualities according to the climatic and soil conditions to be found in this lovely area.

As in all traditional vine-growing regions, it has taken centuries of long observation and experience to bring these wines to their present pitch of refinement and excellence. In Burgundy, a fairly homogenous continental climate but with a wide variety of soils, there is only one grape, the Pinot Noir. The variety is ideally suited to the environment, and the region boasts a long list of crus, *some of which cover an area of not much more than a hectare. Moreover, within the same* appellation, *we find small parishes known as* climats, *each of which has its characteristic wine and which give the Côte-d'Or its originality, proving the true importance of the place in moulding the product.*

This richness and variety are reflected in the local cuisine, so that a meal in Burgundy, complete with the warmth of the ambiance, is an experience to be savored and remembered.

CÔTES-DU-JURA
A.C. White

Grape varieties
Savagnin, Chardonnay.
Production zone
Communes or part of communes of Villers-Farlay, Salins, Arbois, Poligny, Sellières, Voiteur, Bletterans, Conliège, Lons-le-Saunier, Beaufort, Saint-Amour, Saint-Julien.
Characteristics
Deep, straw-yellow to amber color. Well developed mineral, floral bouquet, and strong characteristic aromas. The wine is full, fresh, and pleasantly astringent. It has good ageing properties.
Serving temperature and suggested accompaniments
Serve at 50°F (10°C) with egg dishes and cold meats. There are also sparkling wines in this *appellation*, which are quite distinctive and may be served as an aperitif.

CÔTES-DU-JURA-VINS JAUNES
A.C. White

Grape varieties
Savagnin.
Production zone
Identical to the area for the Côtes-du-Jura *appellation*.
Characteristics
Deep amber-yellow color, well developed animal, mineral, floral bouquet. Characteristic aromas very strong and persistent. The wine is full, well blended, with a typical measure of astringency. It ages excellently.
Serving temperature and suggested accompaniments
Serve at 54°F (12°C) to accompany chicken.

CÔTES-DU-JURA-VIN DE PAILLE
A.C. White

Grape varieties
Identical to that of the Côtes-du-Jura *appellation*.
Characteristics
Deep golden-amber color. Very well developed vegetable, mineral, floral bouquet. Balanced taste with predominance of sugar, the wines containing a minimum of 18.5° of sugar and alcohol, of which the alcohol is minimum 14.5°. The wine is full-bodied and well blended, slightly astringent. It ages excellently.
Serving temperature and suggested accompaniments
Serve at 50°F (10°C). It goes well with pears in wine.

CÔTES-DU-JURA
A.C. Red and Rosé

Grape varieties
Poulsard, Trousseau, Gros Noirien. The white varieties for the rosé are Savagnin, Chardonnay, and Pinot Blanc, which can be macerated with the red varieties. The term "rosé" implies a vinification *en rouge* but made from white and red grapes.
Production zone
Identical to the area for white Côtes-du-Jura.
Characteristics
Light carmine color. Well developed mineral, fruity, flowery bouquet, with strong and persistent characteristic aromas.
Serving temperature and suggested accompaniments
Serve at 57°F (14°C) with quiche.

ARBOIS
A.C. Red and Rosé

Grape varieties
Poulsard, Trousseau, Gros Noirien. For rosés, red, and white varieties used for the *appellation:* Savagnin, Chardonnay, Pinot Blanc.
Production zone
Part of the canton of Arbois. The name of the commune of Pupillin may perhaps be added to the wines from this zone.
Characteristics
Light carmine-redcurrant color. The vegetable, fruity, flowery bouquet is well developed, as are the characteristic aromas. The wine is supple, velvety, with typical astringency. It ages well.
Serving temperature and suggested accompaniments
Serve at 57°F (14°C). Goes well with herring or hare.

ARBOIS
A.C. White

Grape varieties
Savagnin, Chardonnay, Pinot Blanc.
Production zone
Part of canton of Arbois. The wines from the commune of Pupillin may be sold under this name.
Characteristics
Deep straw-yellow color. Well developed vegetable, mineral, fruity bouquet. Strong characteristic aromas. The wine is full, well blended, quite fresh, and with little astringency. It has good ageing properties.
Serving temperature and suggested accompaniments
Serve at 50°F (10°C). The wine goes nicely with asparagus or sausage. There is a sparkling wine under this *appellation*, made by the *méthode champenoise*.

ARBOIS-VIN-JAUNE
A.C. White

Grape varieties
Savagnin.
Production zone
Identical to the area of the Arbois *appellation*.
Characteristics
Deep amber-yellow color. Well developed vegetable, mineral, flowery bouquet. Very strong and persistent characteristic aromas. The wine is full, well blended, with typical astringency. It has excellent ageing properties.
Serving temperature and suggested accompaniments
Serve at 54°F (12°C) with sweetbreads or lobster.

ARBOIS-VIN DE PAILLE
A.C. White

Grape varieties
Savagnin.
Production zone
Identical to the area of the Arbois *appellation*.
Characteristics
Similar to those of Côtes-du-Jura-Vin de Paille.
Serving temperature and suggested accompaniments
Serve at 50°F (10°C). Goes well with *foie gras* or walnut pie.

CHÂTEAU-CHALON
A.C. White

Grape varieties
Savagnin.
Production zone
Communes or part of communes of Château-Chalon, Ménétru, Nevy, Domblans.
Characteristics
Similar to the Vins Jaunes du Jura or d'Arbois.
Serving temperature and suggested accompaniments
Serve at 50°F (10°C) with hare.

L'ETOILE
A.C. White

Grape varieties
Similar to those for Vins Jaunes du Jura and d'Arbois.
Production zone
Communes or part of communes of L'Etoile, Plainoiseau, Saint-Didier (*département* of Jura).
Serving temperature and suggested accompaniments
Serve at 50°F (10°C). Goes marvelously with mushrooms in cheese sauce.
There is a sparkling wine of this *appellation*, made by the *méthode champenoise* from Chardonnay, Poulsard, and Savagnin grapes.

CRÉPY
A.C. White

Grape varieties
Chasselas Roux, Chasselas Vert.
Production zone
Communes or part of communes of *département* of Haute-Savoie: Ballaison, Douvaine, Loisin.
Characteristics
Light straw-yellow color. Well developed vegetable, mineral, fruity bouquet. Balanced, dry taste. Strong and persistent characteristic aromas. The wine is supple, well blended, fresh, and slightly astringent. It has good ageing properties.
Serving temperature and suggested accompaniments
Serve at 50°F (10°C). Goes well with trout *à la meunière*, fondue, salmon, and perch.

SEYSSEL
A.C. White

Grape varieties
Roussette.
Production zone
Communes or part of communes of Seyssel (Haute-Savoie), Seyssel dans l'Ain, Corbonod.
Characteristics
Light straw-yellow color. Well developed vegetable, fruity, flowery bouquet. Balanced, dry taste. Strong characteristic aromas. The wine is supple, well blended, fresh, and delicate, slightly astringent, with good ageing capacity.
Serving temperature and suggested accompaniments
Serve at 50°F (10°C). It goes nicely with fondue.
There is a sparkling Seyssel made from Roussette, Chasselas, and Molette grapes according to the *méthode champenoise*, very popular in the mountain villages. It is served at 50°F (10°C).

VIN DE SAVOIE – ROUSSETTE DE SAVOIE
A.C. White

Grape varieties
Different varieties are used: Aligoté, Roussette, Jacquère, Chardonnay, Malvoisie, and Mondeuse; also, in the Ain: Molette and Chasselas; in Haute-Savoie: Molette, Gringet, and Chasselas; in Isère: Marsanne and Verdesse. For the *crus*, varieties are more restricted according to zones.
Production zone
29 communes in Savoie, 26 in Haute-Savoie, 2 in Isère, and 2 in Ain. The Savoie and Roussette wines may be supplemented by the names of the following *crus:*

Vins de Savoie:
- Abymes: Apremont (part), Chapareillan, Les Marches (part), and Myans.
- Apremont: Apremont (part), Les Marches (part), and Saint-Badolph.
- Arbin: Arbin.
- Ayze: Ayze, Bonneville, and Marignier.
- Charpignat: Le Bourget-du-Lac.
- Chautagne: Chindrieux, Motz, Ruffieux, and Serrières-en-Chautagne.
- Chignin: Chignin.
- Chignin-Bergeron or Bergeron: Chignin, Francin, and Montmélian.
- Cruet: Cruet.
- Marignan: Sciez.
- Montmélian: Francin and Montmélian.
- Ripaille: Thonon-les-Bains.
- Saint-Jean-de-la-Porte.
- Saint-Jeoire-Prieuré: Saint-Jeoire-Prieuré.
- Sainte-Marie-d'Allois: Sainte-Marie-d'Allois.

Roussette de Savoie:
- Frangy: Bassy, Challonges, Chaumont, Chessenaz, Clarafond, Desingy, Franclens, Frangy, Musièges, Usinens, and Vanzy.
- Marestal or Marestal-Altesse: Jongieux and Lucey.
- Monterminod: Saint-Alban-Leysse.
- Monthoux: Saint-Jean-de-Chevelu.

Characteristics
Deep straw-yellow color. Well developed vegetable, fruity, flowery bouquet. Balanced, dry taste. Very strong and persistent characteristic aromas. The wine is supple, full-bodied, velvety, fresh, and slightly astringent. It has good ageing properties.
Serving temperature and suggested accompaniments
Serve at 50°F (10°C). It goes perfectly with perch *à la meunière*, goat's cheese, *gratin dauphinois* or veal.

VIN DE SAVOIE
A.C. Red and Rosé

Grape varieties
Gamay, Mondeuse, Pinot Noir. In Savoie: Cabernets, Persan. In Isère: Persan, Etraire de la Dui, Servanin, Joubertin. Additionally, a maximum of 20% of white varieties. For the *crus*, varieties are more restricted.
Production zone
Identical to the area of the white Vin de Savoie *appellation*.
Characteristics
Light color, reds carmine-redcurrant to brick-red, rosés coppery. The rosés have a well developed mineral, fruity, floral bouquet; balanced taste, dry in case of the rosés and clairets. Strong characteristic aromas. The wines are supple, quite fresh, velvety, with typical astringency. They have good ageing properties.
Serving temperature and suggested accompaniments
The rosés, served at 52°F (11°C), go well with terrines, the reds, served at 57°F (14°C), with hare and *gratin savoyard*.

GIVRY
A.C. White and Red

Grape varieties
Red: Pinot Noirien, Pinot Beurot, Pinot Liébault.
White: Pinot Blanc, Pinot Chardonnay.
Production zone
Territory of the commune of Givry.
Characteristics
Medium color, the reds mainly carmine, the whites straw-yellow. Well developed fruity, floral bouquet. The whites are of the dry type. Strong characteristic aromas. The red wines are supple, velvety, soft, and slightly astringent. The whites are well blended. Both types possess good ageing properties.
Serving temperature and suggested accompaniments
Serve whites at 50°F (10°C) as an aperitif, the reds at 57°F (14°C) with lamb.

MERCUREY
A.C. Red

Grape varieties
Pinot Noirien, Pinot Liébault, Pinot Beurot.
Production zone
Commune of Mercurey and part of communes of Saint-Martin-sous-Montaigu, Bourgneuf-Val-d'Or.
Characteristics
Medium carmine color. Well developed fruity, floral bouquet. Very strong and persistent characteristic aromas. The wine is full, light, and slightly astringent, with very good ageing capacity.
Serving temperature and suggested accompaniments
Serve at 57°F (14°C). A good foil for duck with cherries and meat in sauce.

MERCUREY
A.C. White

Grape varieties
Pinot Chardonnay.
Production zone
Identical to area for red Mercurey *appellation*.
Characteristics
Light straw-yellow color. Well developed vegetable, fruity bouquet. Balanced, dry taste. Strong and persistent characteristic aromas. The wine is full, well blended, soft, and slightly astringent. It has very good ageing properties.

MONTAGNY
A.C. White

Grape varieties
Pinot Chardonnay.
Production zone
Communes or part of communes of Montagny, Buxy, Saint-Vallerin, Jully-lès-Buxy, corresponding to a total area of 755 acres (306 hectares).
Characteristics
Medium pale to straw-yellow color. Well developed fruity, flowery bouquet. Balanced, dry taste. Strong and persistent characteristic aromas. The wine is full and well blended, with good ageing properties.
Serving temperature and suggested accompaniments
Serve at 50°F (10°C). Goes nicely with fried fish or shellfish.

RULLY
A.C. Red

Grape varieties
Pinots Noirien, Liébault and Beurot, with possible supplement of max. 15% white grapes.
Production zone
Communes or parts of communes of Rully, Chagny.
Characteristics
Medium carmine color. Well developed bouquet of fruit and flowers. Strong and persistent characteristic aromas. The wine is supple, full-bodied, well blended, and slightly astringent, with good ageing properties.
Serving temperature and suggested accompaniments
Serve at 55°F (13°C) with veal escalopes.

RULLY
A.C. White

Grape varieties
Pinot Chardonnay.
Production zone
Identical to area for red Rully.
Characteristics
Light pale to straw-yellow color. Well developed vegetable, fruity bouquet. Balanced, dry taste. Strong characteristic aromas. The wine is supple, soft, and quite lively. It has good ageing properties.

Serving temperature and suggested accompaniments
Serve at 50°F (10°C) with cheese quiche or fish.

MÂCON, MÂCON SUPÉRIEUR AND MÂCON-VILLAGES (PINOT CHARDONNAY MÂCON)
A.C. White

Grape varieties
Pinot Blanc, Chardonnay.
Production zone
Arrondissement of Mâcon and, for the denominated communes: Azé, Berzé-la-Ville, Berzé-le-Chatel, Bissy-la-Mâconnaise, Burgy, Bussières, Chaintres, Chânes, La Chapelle-de-Guinchay, Chardonnay, Charnay-lès-Mâcon, Chasselas, Chevagny-lès-Chevrières, Clessé, Crêches-sur- Sâone, Cruzille, Davayé, Fuissé, Grévilly, Hurigny, Igé, Leynes, Loché, Lugny, Milly-Lamartine, Montbellet, Péronne, Pierreclos, Prissé, Pruzilly, La Roche-Vineuse, Romanèche-Thorins, Saint-Amour-Bellevue, Saint-Gengoux-de-Scissé, Saint-Symphorien-d'Ancelles, Saint-Vérand, Sologny, Solutré-Pouilly, Vergisson, Verzé, Vinzelles, Viré, Uchizy.
Characteristics
Light straw-yellow to amber color. Well developed vegetable, mineral bouquet. Balanced, dry taste. Strong characteristic aromas. The wine is supple, light, and fresh, with little astringency. It has good ageing properties.
Serving temperature and suggested accompaniments
Serve at 50°F (10°C) with mussel soup, ravioli or trout.

MÂCON AND MÂCON SUPÉRIEUR
A.C. Red (Rosé)

Grape varieties
Principal varieties: Gamay, Pinot Noir, Pinot Gris; supplementary varieties: white grapes (max. 15%).
Production zone
Arrondissement of Mâcon and communes or part of communes of Boyer, Bresse-sur-Grosne, Champagny-sous-Uxelles, Champlieu, Etrigny, Jugy, Laives, Maney, Montceaux-Ragny, Nanton, Sennecey-le-Grand, Vers.
Characteristics
Medium color, mainly carmine, slightly garnet. The bouquet of vegetables and fruit is well developed, as are the characteristic aromas. The wine is supple, velvety, slightly astringent, and ages reasonably well.
Serving temperature and suggested accompaniments
Serve at 57°F (14°C) with veal, sausages or a chicken *waterzoï*.

POUILLY-FUISSÉ
A.C. White

Grape varieties
Chardonnay.
Production zone
Communes or part of communes of Fuissé, Solutré, Pouilly, Vergisson, Chaintré.
Characteristics
Light straw-yellow color. Well developed vegetable, fruity bouquet. Balanced, dry taste. Strong and persistent characteristic aromas. The wine is full-bodied, fresh, and delicate. It has good ageing properties.
Serving temperature and suggested accompaniments
Serve at 50°F (10°C) with scallops, snails or pike.

POUILLY-LOCHÉ
A.C. White

Production zone
Commune of Loché.
Grape varieties and characteristics
Identical to those of Pouilly-Fuissé.
Serving temperature and suggested accompaniments
Serve at 50°F (10°C) with mussels.

POUILLY-VINZELLES
A.C. White

Production zone
Communes or part of communes of Vinzelles, Loché.
Varieties and characteristics
The same as for Pouilly-Fuissé.
Serving temperature and suggested accompaniments
Serve at 50°F (10°C) with lobster.

SAINT-VÉRAN
A.C. White

Grape varieties
Chardonny.
Production zone
Communes or part of communes of Chânes, Chasselas, Davayé, Leynes, Prisse, Saint-Amour, Saint-Vérand, Solutré (*département* of Saône-et-Loire).
Characteristics
Light straw-yellow color. Well developed fruity, floral bouquet; balanced, dry taste. Strong characteristic aromas. The wine is supple, full-bodied, and lively. It ages reasonably well.
Serving temperature and suggested accompaniments
Serve at 48°F (9°C). Goes well with *gratinée lyonnaise*, herring, crab.

CHABLIS
A.C. White

Grape varieties
Pinot Chardonnay.
Production zone
Communes or part of communes of Chablis, Fyé, Poinchy.
Characteristics
Light greenish straw-yellow color. Well developed mineral, fruity, floral bouquet; balanced, dry taste. Strong, persistent characteristic aromas. The wine is full, light, and well balanced. It has good ageing properties.
Serving temperature and suggested accompaniments
Serve at 50°F (10°C) with lobster, pike or veal kidneys.

There is also a *premier cru* Chablis *appellation*, produced on some 30 *climats*, and a *grand cru*, made on seven *climats*. Both age wonderfully well and go splendidly with fish and white meat.

PETIT CHABLIS
A.C. White

Grape varieties
Pinot Chardonnay.
Production zone
Communes or part of communes of Chablis, Beines, Béru, La Chapelle-Vaupelteigne, Chemilly-sur-Serein, Chichée, Courgis, Fleys, Fontenay, Fyé, Lignorelles, Ligny-le-Châtel, Maligny, Milly, Poilly-sur-Serein, Poinchy, Préhy, Rameau, Villy, Viviers.
Characteristics
Light pale yellow color, well developed fruity bouquet, balanced, dry taste. Strong characteristic aromas. The wine is supple, soft, and lively. It ages quite well.
Serving temperature and suggested accompaniments
Serve at 48°F (9°C) with fried fish.

BEAUJOLAIS
A.C. Red

Grape varieties
Gamay Noir, Pinot Noir, Pinot Gris and possibly supplements of white grape varieties (max. 15%).
Production zone
Département of the Rhône: *arrondissement* of Villefranche, canton of Arbresle and communes of Bully, Denicé, Nuelles, Sarcey, Saint-Germain-sur-l'Arbresle. *Département* of Saône-et-Loire: canton of La Chapelle-de-Guinchay.
Characteristics
Light to deep color, mainly carmine. Well developed fruity bouquet. Very strong characteristic aromas. The wine is supple, full-bodied, light, quite lively, slightly astringent. It ages normally, except, of course, for the *primeurs*.
Serving temperature and suggested accompaniments
Serve at 55°F (13°C). The wine goes well with sausages, boiled beef, chicken, etc. There are also Beaujolais Rosés, dry and clean in color.

BEAUJOLAIS
A.C. White

Grape varieties
Pinot Chardonnay, Aligoté.
Production zone
Identical to area for red Beaujolais *appellation*.
Characteristics
Light straw-yellow color, well developed bouquet of fruit and flowers, balanced, dry taste. Strong characteristic aromas. The wine is supple, soft, and quite lively. It ages normally.
Serving temperature and suggested accompaniments
Serve at 50°F (10°C) with baked sausages.

BEAUJOLAIS-VILLAGES
A.C. Red and Rosé

Grape varieties
Gamay Noir à jus blanc, Pinot Noir, Pinot Gris.
Production zone
29 communes of the Rhône and 8 communes of Saône-et-Loire.
The following communes have the right to mention their name: *département* of the Rhône: Juliénas, Jullié, Emeringes, Chenas, Fleurie, Chiroubles, Lancié, Villié-Morgon, Lantigné, Beaujeu, Regnié-Durette, Cercié, Quincié, Saint-Lager, Odenas, Charentay, Saint-Etienne-la-Varenne, Vaux, Le Perréon, Saint-Etienne-des-Ouillières, Blacé, Salles-Arbuissonnas, Saint-Juliens, Montmelas, Rivolet, Denicé, Les Ardillats, Marchampt, Vauxremard.
Département of Saône-et-Loire: Leynes, Saint-Amour-Bellevue, La Chapelle-de-Guinchay, Romanèche-Thorins, Pruzilly, Chânes, Saint-Vérand, Saint-Symphorien-d'Ancelles.
Characteristics
Light to fairly deep color, ranging from cherry-red to violet-red. The wine has a markedly fruity bouquet, balanced taste and strong aromas. Well constituted, vigorous, and easy to drink, it ages well, except, of course, for Beaujolais-Villages *primeur*.
Serving temperature and suggested accompaniments
Serve *primeur* at 55°F (10°C), otherwise at 54°F (12°C) to go with hot or cold cooked meats, roast red or white meat or cheese.

BROUILLY
A.C. Red

Grape varieties
Gamay Noir à jus blanc and, in proportion of max. 15%, white varieties: Pinot Chardonnay, Aligoté, Melon.
Production zone
Part of communes of Odenas, Saint-Léger, Quincié, Cercié, Charentay, Saint-Etienne-la-Varenne.
Characteristics
Medium color, mainly garnet-redcurrant. Well developed vegetable, fruity, flowery bouquet. Strong and persistent characteristic aromas. The wine is full and velvety, with a slight and very typical astringency. It ages well.
Serving temperature and suggested accompaniments
Serve at 55°F (13°C) with braised steak.

CHENAS
A.C. Red

Grape varieties
Gamay Noir à jus blanc.
Production zone
Communes or part of communes of Chenas, La Chapelle-de-Guinchay.
Characteristics
Medium carmine color, well developed fruity bouquet, and characteristic aromas. The wine is full, well blended, slightly astringent, and ages well.
Serving temperature and suggested accompaniments
Serve at 55°F (13°C). It goes nicely with steak, chicken or braised ox tongue.

CHIROUBLES
A.C. Red

Grape varieties
Gamay Noir à jus blanc.
Production zone
Commune of Chiroubles.
Characteristics
Fairly deep carmine color, well developed fruity bouquet. Strong characteristic aromas. The wine is supple, full, slightly astringent, and ages well.
Serving temperature and suggested accompaniments
Serve at 55°F (13°C) with tongue.

CÔTE-DE-BROUILLY
A.C. Red

Grape varieties
Gamay Noir, Pinot Noir, Pinot Gris and max. 15% of local white varieties such as Pinot Blanc and Chardonnay.
Production zone
Communes or part of communes of Odenas, Saint-Léger, Cercié, Quincié.
Serving temperature and suggested accompaniments
Serve at 55°F (13°C) with rabbit, chicken or beef.

FLEURIE
A.C. Red

Grape varieties
Gamay, and, max. 15% local white varieties.
Production zone
Part of commune of Fleurie.
Serving temperature and suggested accompaniments
Serve at 55°F (13°C) with chicken or sausage.

JULIÉNAS
A.C. Red

Grape varieties
Gamay. It is possible to add, in proportion of max. 15%, of local white varieties.
Production zone
Communes or part of communes of Juliénas, Emeringes, Jullié, Pruzilly.
Characteristics
Similar to those of other Beaujolais *crus*.
Serving temperature and suggested accompaniments
Serve at 55 °F (13°C) with pheasant or steak.

MORGON
A.C. Red

Grape varieties
Gamay. It is possible to add, in proportion of max. 15%, local white varieties.
Production zone
Part of commune of Villié-Morgon.
Characteristics
Similar to those of other Beaujolais *crus.*
Serving temperature and suggested accompaniments
Serve at 55°F (13°C) with veal shoulder.

MOULIN-À-VENT
A.C. Red

Grape varieties
Gamay. It is possible to add, in proportion of max. 15%, local white varieties.
Production zone
Communes or part of communes of Chenas, Romanèche-Thorins.
Characteristics
Similar to those of other Beaujolais *crus*.
Serving temperature and suggested accompaniments
Serve at 55°F (13°C) with marinated lamb leg.

SAINT-AMOUR
A.C. Red

Grape varieties
Gamay. It is possible to add, in proportion of max. 15%, local white varieties.
Production zone
Part of commune of Saint-Amour.
Characteristics
Similar to those of other Beaujolais *crus.*
Serving temperature and suggested accompaniments
Serve at 55°F (13°C) with chicken or beef.

RÉGNIÉ
A.C. Red

Since 1988, the tenth Beaujolais *cru*.
Grape varieties
Gamay Noir à jus blanc exclusively.
Production zone
Communes of Régnié-Durette and Lantigné.
Characteristics
Similar to those of Brouilly.
Serving temperature and suggested accompaniments
Serve at 55°F (13°C) with local cooked meats.

BOURGOGNE
A.C. Red

Grape varieties
Pinots Noirien, Liébault and Beurot. In the Yonne there is also César and Tressot. In all cases, it is possible to supplement these with max. 15% of local white varieties.
Production zone
Départements of Côte d'Or, Saône-et-Loire, Yonne.
Arrondissement of Villefranche-sur-Saône, in the Rhône *département*.
The following *appellations* may be linked with that of Bourgogne, according to the production zones: Hautes-Côtes-de-Beaune: communes of Baubigny, Bouze-lès-Beaune, Cirey-lès-Nolay, Cormot, Echevronne, Fussey, La Rochepot, Magny-lès-Villers, Mavilly-Mandelot, Meloisey, Nantoux, Nolay, Vauchignon in Côte-d'Or *département.*
In the Saône-et-Loire *département*, part of communes of Cheilly-lès-Maranges, Dezize-lès-Maranges, Sampigny-lès-Maranges, Changé, Créot, Epertully, Paris-l-Hôpital.
Hautes-Côtes-de-Nuits: *département* of Côte-d'Or, communes or part of communes of Arcenant, Bévy, Chaux,

Chevannes, Collonges-lès-Bévy, Concoeur-et-Corboin, Curtil-Vergy, L'Etang-Vergy, Magny-les-Villers, Marey-lès-Fussey, Messanges, Meuilley, Reuille-Vergy, Segrois, Villars-Fontaine, Villers-la-Faye.
Marsannay-la-Côte (red and rosé wines) is part of the Bourgogne Clairet or Rosè *appellations*: communes of Marsannay-la-Côte and Couchey (Côte-d'Or).
Irancy (red and rosé wines): communes of Irancy (Yonne).
Particular mention should be made of the wines originating in the Saône-et-Loire and the *arrondissement* of Villefranche-sur-Saône, which may bear the Bourgogne *appellation*; they are made in similar conditions to the various communal or local *appellations* of Brouilly, Chenas, Chiroubles, Côte-de-Brouilly, Fleurie, Juliénas, Morgon, Moulin-à-Vent, Saint-Amour, and Régnié.
Characteristics
Medium carmine color. The fruity bouquet is well developed, as are the characteristic aromas. The wine is supple, velvety, and slightly astringent, with good ageing properties.
Serving temperature and suggested accompaniments
Serve at 57°F (14°C) with beef fillet, eggs, etc.
The vins rosés or clairets of Marsannay and Irancy have a lovely color and are dry, light, and very fruity. They should be served cool at 52°F (11°C) with sausages and egg dishes.

BOURGOGNE
A.C. White

Grape varieties
Pinot Blanc, Chardonnay.
Production zone
Identical to area for red Bourgogne *appellation*.
Characteristics
Light page to straw-yellow color. Well developed vegetable, fruity bouquet. Balanced, dry taste. Strong characteristic aromas. The wine is supple and well balanced. It has good ageing properties.
Serving temperature and suggested accompaniments
Serve at 50°F (10°C). Goes well with pig's trotters.

BOURGOGNE ORDINAIRE (or GRAND ORDINAIRE)
A.C. Red

Grape varieties
Pinot, Gamay and in Yonne *département* César and Tressot. It is possible to add, in proportion of max. 15%, local white varieties.
Production zone
Identical to that of red Bourgogne.
Characteristics
Light carmine in color. The fruity bouquet is well developed, as are the characteristic aromas. The wine is supple, well blended, and slightly astringent.
Serving temperature and suggested accompaniments
Serve at 55°F (13°C) with broiled pig's trotters.
There are also dry Bourgognes rosés and clairets. Served chilled, they are very supple and pleasant, good with terrines or chicken.

BOURGOGNE ORDINAIRE (or GRAND ORDINAIRE)
A.C. White

Grape varieties
Pinot Blanc, Aligoté, Melon and, in Yonne *département*, Sacy.
Production zone
Identical to area of red Bourgogne *appellation*.
Characteristics
Light pale yellow color. Well developed vegetable, fruity bouquet, balanced, dry taste. Normal characteristic aromas. The wine is light and supple.
Serving temperature and suggested accompaniments
Serve at 50°F (10°C). It goes well with savory fritters.

BOURGOGNE ALIGOTÉ
A.C. White

Grape varieties
Aligoté, with or without Chardonnay.
Production zone
Identical to area of red Bourgogne *appellation*.
Characteristics
Light straw-yellow color. Well developed vegetable, fruity bouquet, balanced, dry taste. Strong characteristic aromas. The wine is supple, well blended, and slightly astringent. It has good ageing properties.
Serving temperature and suggested accompaniments
Serve at 50°F (10°C) with ham, or as an aperitif with *cassis* (the famous *kir*).
There is also a Bourgogne Aligoté Bouzeron *appellation*.

BOURGOGNE PASSE-TOUT-GRAINS
A.C. Red

Grape varieties
Pinot Noirien, Pinot Liébault: min. one-third Gamay; also, if necessary, max. 15% of local white varieties.
Production zone
Identical to area of red Bourgogne *appellation*.
Characteristics
Light, mainly carmine color. The fruity bouquet is well developed, as are the characteristic aromas. The wine is supple, full-bodied, slightly astringent, with normal ageing properties.
Serving temperature and suggested accompaniments
Serve at 55°F (13°C). Goes well with tripe, sausage or *boeuf bourguignon*.
There are also dry, fruity rosés under the Passe-Tout-Grains *appellation*.

CRÉMANT-DE-BOURGOGNE
A.C. White

Grape varieties
Pinot Noir, Pinot Gris, Pinot Blanc, Chardonnay, Aligoté, Melon, Sacy, Gamay (max. 15%).
Production zone
Identical to area of Bourgogne *appellation*.
Characteristics
Light greenish-pale yellow color. Well developed vegetable, fruity, flowery bouquet. Strong characteristic aromas. The

wine is supple, velvety, light, and slightly astringent, with normal ageing properties.
Serving temperature and suggested accompaniments
Serve at 50°F (10°C) as an aperitif.
There is also a Bourgogne Mousseux (sparkling).

□

APPELLATIONS COMMUNALES DE LA CÔTE-DE-NUITS

CÔTE-DE-NUITS-VILLAGES
A.C. Red

Grape varieties
Pinots Noirien, Beurot and Liébault, possibly supplemented, in proportion of max. 15%, by local white varieties.
Production zone
Communes or part of communes of Brochon, Comblanchien, Corgoloin, Fixin, Prissey (*département* of Côte-d'Or).
Characteristics
Medium ruby color. Well developed vegetable, fruity, floral bouquet. Strong and persistent characteristic aromas. The wine is supple, velvety, well blended, and slightly astringent. It has good ageing properties.
Serving temperature and suggested accompaniments
Serve at 57°F (14°C) with coq au vin or venison.
There is also a very small production of white Côte-de-Nuits.

CHAMBOLLE-MUSIGNY
A.C. Red

Grape varieties
Pinots Noirien, Beurot, and Liébault.
Production zone
Part of commune of Chambolle-Musigny (56 *climats*).
Characteristics
Light to deep, mainly ruby, color. Well developed mineral, fruity, floral bouquet. Very strong and persistent characteristic aromas. The wine is velvety, well blended, and slightly astringent.
Serving temperature and suggested accompaniments
Serve at 57°F (14°C) with cheese or omelet.

FIXIN
A.C. Red

Grape varieties
Pinots Noirien, Beurot, Liébault.
Production zone
Part of commune of Fixin.
Characteristics
Light to deep, mainly carmine, color. Well developed vegetable, animal, mineral bouquet. Strong and persistent characteristic aromas.
Serving temperature and suggested accompaniments
Serve at 57°F (14°C) with *coq au vin* or game.

GEVREY-CHAMBERTIN
A.C. Red

Grape varieties
Pinots Noirien, Beurot, Liébault.
Production zone
Part of commune of Gevrey-Chambertin (11 *climats*).
Characteristics
Light to deep color, with ruby nuances. Well developed animal, fruity, floral bouquet. Strong and persistent characteristic aromas. The wine is full, velvety, quite soft, and slightly astringent. It has good ageing properties.
Serving temperature and suggested accompaniments
Serve at 57°F (14°C). It goes well with game, lamb or duck.

MOREY-SAINT-DENIS
A.C. Red

Grape varieties
Pinots Noirien, Beurot, Liébault.
Production zone
Part of commune of Morey-Saint-Denis.
Characteristics
Fairly deep color, with ruby nuance and touch of garnet. Well developed animal, mineral, fruity, floral bouquet. Strong and persistent characteristic aromas. The wine is full, soft, and gently astringent. It has very good ageing properties.
Serving temperature and suggested accompaniments
Serve at 57°F (14°C) with red meat or variety meats.

MOREY-SAINT-DENIS
A.C. White

Grape varieties
Pinot Blanc, Chardonnay.
Production zone
Part of commune of Morey-Saint-Denis.
Characteristics
Quite deep straw-yellow color. Very well developed vegetable, fruity, floral bouquet. Balanced, dry taste. Strong and persistent characteristic aromas. The wine is full, rich, and delicate. It has good ageing properties.
Serving temperature and suggested accompaniments
Serve at 50°F (10°C). Goes well with fish roe.

NUITS-SAINT-GEORGES (NUITS)
A.C. Red

Grape varieties
Pinots Noirien, Beurot, Liébault.
Production zone
Part of communes of Nuits-Saint-Georges, Prémeaux.
Characteristics
Fairly deep color, mainly carmine with a touch of redcurrant. Well developed animal, mineral, fruity, floral bouquet. Very strong and persistent characteristic aromas. The wine is full bodied, soft, and velvety, slightly astringent. It has good ageing properties.
Serving temperature and suggested accompaniments
Serve at 57°F (14°C) with meat, game or poultry.

NUITS-SAINT-GEORGES
A.C. White

Grape varieties
Chardonnay, Pinot Blanc.
Production zone
Identical to area of red Nuits-Saint-Georges *appellation*.
Characteristics
Light straw-yellow color. The fruity, flowery bouquet is well developed, the taste balanced and dry. Strong and persistent characteristic aromas. The wine is full, well balanced, and delicate. It has good ageing properties.
Serving temperature and suggested accompaniments
Serve at 50°F (10°C). Goes well with sole fillets.

VOSNE ROMANÉE
A.C. Red

Grape varieties
Pinots Noirien, Beurot, Liébault.
Production zone
Part of communes of Vosney-Romanée (45 *climats*), Flagey-Echezeaux (19 *climats*).
Characteristics
Fairly deep ruby color. Well developed mineral, fruity, floral bouquet. Strong and persistent characteristic aromas. The wine is full, well blended, delicate with a typical gentle astringency. It has very good ageing properties.
Serving temperature and suggested accompaniments
Serve at 57°F (14°C) with poultry, broiled meat or cheese.

VOUGEOT
A.C. Red

Grape varieties
Pinot Noirien, Beurot, Liébault.
Production zone
Part of commune of Vougeot (5 *climats*).
Characteristics
Fairly deep garnet-redcurrant color. Well developed animal, mineral, fruity, floral bouquet. Strong and persistent characteristic aromas. The wine is full-bodied with a supple, typical astringency. It ages very well.
Serving temperature and suggested accompaniments
Serve at 57°F (14°C) with venison.

VOUGEOT
A.C. White

Grape varieties
Pinot Blanc, Chardonnay.
Production zone
Identical to area of red Vougeot *appellation*.
Characteristics
Deep straw-yellow color. The vegetable, floral bouquet is well developed, the taste balanced and dry. Strong and persistent characteristic aromas. It ages very well.
Serving temperature and suggested accompaniments
Serve at 50°F (10°C) with fish.

□

GRAND CRUS
DE LA CÔTE-DE-NUITS

LA TÂCHE
A.C. Red

Grape varieties
Pinot Noirien, Beurot, Liébault.
Production zone
Part of commune of Vosne-Romanée.
Characteristics
Fairly deep carmine-garnet color. The animal, mineral, floral, spicy bouquet is very strong, as are the characteristic aromas. The wine is full-bodied and velvety, with a good, very typical astringency. It ages very well.
Serving temperature and suggested accompaniments
Serve at 57°F (14°C) with *boeuf bourguignon*.

ROMANÉE-SAINT-VIVANT
A.C. Red

Grape varieties
Pinots Noirien, Beurot and Liébault.
Production zone
Part of commune of Vosne-Romanée.
Characteristics
Fairly deep carmine-garnet color. Well developed animal, fruity, floral bouquet. Strong and persistent characteristic aromas. The wine is velvety, well balanced, soft, and slightly astringent. It ages very well.
Serving temperature and suggested accompaniments
Serve at 57°F (14°C) with game.

ROMANÉE-CONTI-
A.C. Red

Grape varieties
Pinots Noirien, Beurot and Liébault.
Production zone
Part of commune of Vosne-Romanée.
Characteristics
Fairly deep carmine-garnet color. Well developed animal, mineral, fruity, floral bouquet. Strong and persistent characteristic aromas. The wine is full-bodied, well blended, and slightly astringent. It ages very well.
Serving temperature and suggested accompaniments
Serve at 57°F (14°C) with hare.

LA ROMANÉE
A.C. Red

Grape varieties
Pinots Noirien, Beurot and Liébault.
Production zone
Part of commune of Vosne-Romanée.
Characteristics
Fairly deep carmine-garnet color. Well developed animal, mineral, floral bouquet. Strong and persistent characteristic aromas. The wine is full, velvety, and slightly astringent. It ages very well.
Serving temperature and suggested accompaniments
Serve at 57°F (14°C) with steak.

RICHEBOURG
A.C. Red

Grape varieties
Pinots Noirien, Beurot and Liébault.
Production zone
Part of commune of Vosne-Romanée.
Characteristics
Fairly deep carmine-garnet color. Well developed vegetable, animal, fruity, floral bouquet. Strong and persistent characteristic aromas. The wine is full, velvety, soft, and slightly astringent. It ages very well.
Serving temperature and suggested accompaniments
Serve at 57°F (14°C) with game.

MUSIGNY
A.C. Red

Grape varieties
Pinots Noirien, Beurot and Liébault.
Production zone
Part of commune of Chambolle with *climats* of Les Musigny, Les Petits-Musigny and La Combe-d'Orveau.
Characteristics
Fairly deep ruby color. Well developed vegetable, animal, floral bouquet. Strong and persistent characteristic aromas. The wine is full, well balanced, soft, and slightly astringent. It ages very well.
Serving temperature and suggested accompaniments
Serve at 57°F (14°C) with poultry.
There is a small production of white Musigny. The wines are dry, soft, and elegant. The grape variety is Chardonnay.

CHAMBERTIN
A.C. Red

Grape varieties
Pinots Noirien, Beurot and Liébault.
Production zone
Part of commune of Gevrey-Chambertin.
Characteristics
Fairly deep ruby-garnet color. Very well developed animal, mineral, fruity, floral bouquet. Strong and persistent characteristic aromas. The wine is full-bodied and well blended, gently astringent. It ages very well.
Serving temperature and suggested accompaniments
Serve at 57°F (14°C) with *coq au vin* or hare.

CHAMBERTIN-CLOS-DE-BÈZE
A.C. Red

Grape varieties
As for Chambertin.
Production zone
Identical to that of Chambertin.
Characteristics
Fairly deep carmine-garnet color. Well developed animal, mineral, fruity, floral bouquet. The wine is full-bodied, velvety, well blended, and pleasantly astringent. It ages very well.
Serving temperature and suggested accompaniments
Serve at 57°F (14°C) with veal.

CHAPELLE-CHAMBERTIN
A.C. Red

Grape varieties
As for Chambertin.
Production zone
Part of commune of Gevrey-Chambertin.
Characteristics
Fairly deep carmine-garnet color. Well developed animal, mineral, fruity, floral bouquet. Strong and persistent characteristic aromas. The wine is full, velvety, and pleasantly astringent. It ages very well.
Serving temperature and suggested accompaniments
Serve at 57°F (14°C) with duck.

CHARMES-CHAMBERTIN and MAZOYÈRES-CHAMBERTIN
A.C. Red

Grape varieties
As for Chambertin.
Production zone
Part of commune of Gevrey-Chambertin.
Characteristics
Fairly deep color with ruby nuance. Very well developed vegetable, animal, floral bouquet. Strong and persistent characteristic aromas. The wine is velvety, well blended, soft, and pleasantly astringent. It ages very well.
Serving temperature and suggested accompaniments
Serve at 57°F (14°C) with quail and red meat.

GRIOTTES-CHAMBERTIN
A.C. Red

Grape varieties
As for Chambertin.
Production zone
Part of commune of Gevrey-Chambertin.
Characteristics
Fairly deep color, mainly carmine with touch of garnet. Well developed animal, fruity, floral bouquet. Strong and persistent characteristic aromas. The wine is full-bodied, soft, and slightly astringent. It has good ageing properties.
Serving temperature and suggested accompaniments
Serve at 57°F (14°C) with ham.

LATRICIÈRES-CHAMBERTIN
A.C. Red

Grape varieties
As for Chambertin.
Production zone
Part of commune of Gevrey-Chambertin.
Characteristics
Fairly deep carmine-redcurrant color. Well developed animal, mineral, fruity, floral bouquet. Strong and persistent characteristic aromas. The wine is full-bodied, velvety, soft, and slightly astringent. It ages very well.
Serving temperature and suggested accompaniments
Serve at 57°F (14°C) with lamb.

MAZIS-CHAMBERTIN
A.C. Red

Grape varieties
As for Chambertin.
Production zone
Part of commune of Gevrey-Chambertin.
Characteristics
Fairly deep carmine-redcurrant color. Well developed animal, mineral, fruity, floral bouquet. Strong and persistent characteristic aromas. The wine is full-bodied, velvety, soft, and slightly astringent. It ages very well.
Serving temperature and suggested accompaniments
Serve at 57°F (14°C) to go with beef fillet.

RUCHOTTES-CHAMBERTIN
A.C. Red

Grape varieties
As for Chambertin.
Production zone
Part of commune of Gevrey-Chambertin.
Characteristics
Medium carmine-garnet color. Very well developed animal, fruity, floral bouquet. Strong and persistent characteristic aromas. The wine is full-bodied, velvety and slightly astringent, with excellent ageing capacity.
Serving temperature and suggested accompaniments
Serve at 57°F (14°C) with veal or game.

CLOS-DE-LA-ROCHE
A.C. Red

Grape varieties
Pinots Noirien, Beurot and Liébault.
Production zone
Part of commune of Morey-Saint-Denis.
Characteristics
Fairly deep carmine-garnet color. Well developed animal, mineral, fruity, floral bouquet. Strong and persistent characteristic aromas. The wine is full, velvety, and pleasantly astringent. It ages very well.
Serving temperature and suggested accompaniments
Serve at 57°F (14°C) with game or beef fillet.

CLOS-SAINT-DENIS
A.C. Red

Grape varieties
Pinots Noirien, Beurot and Liébault.
Production zone
Part of commune of Morey-Saint-Denis.
Characteristics
Lovely carmine-redcurrant color, very well developed vegetable, animal, floral bouquet. Strong and persistent characteristic aromas. The wine is velvety, well blended with a pleasantly soft astringency. It ages very well.
Serving temperature and suggested accompaniments
Serve at 57°F (14°C) with beef sirloin.

BONNES-MARES
A.C. Red

Grape varieties
Pinots Noirien, Beurot and Liébault.
Production zone
Part of communes of Morey-Saint-Denis and Chambolle-Musigny.
Characteristics
Deep carmine-garnet color. Very well developed vegetable, animal, mineral, floral bouquet. Strong and persistent characteristic aromas. The wine is full-bodied and fairly astringent. It ages very well.
Serving temperature and suggested accompaniments
Serve at 57°F (14°C) with goose or hare.

CLOS-DE-TART
A.C. Red

Grape varieties
Pinots Noirien, Beurot and Liébault.
Production zone
Part of commune of Morey-Saint-Denis.
Characteristics
Fairly deep carmine-garnet color. Well developed vegetable, animal, mineral bouquet. Strong and persistent characteristic aromas. The wine is full-bodied, soft, and fairly astringent. It ages very well.
Serving temperature and suggested accompaniments
Serve at 57°F (14°C). It goes very well with game.

CLOS-DE-VOUGEOT
A.C. Red

Grape varieties
Pinots Noirien, Beurot and Liébault.
Production zone
Part of commune of Vougeot.
Characteristics
Fairly deep ruby-carmine color. Well developed animal, mineral, fruity, floral bouquet. Strong and persistent characteristic aromas. The wine is full-bodied, velvety, and softly astringent. It ages very well.
Serving temperature and suggested accompaniments
Serve at 57°F (14°C) with duck.

ECHEZEAUX
A.C. Red

Grape varieties
Pinots Noirien, Beurot and Liébault.
Production zone
Part of commune of Vosney-Romanée.
Characteristics
Fairly deep carmine-garnet color. Well developed vegetable, animal, fruity bouquet, with touch of flowers. Strong and persistent characteristic aromas. The wine is full-bodied, velvety, and softly astringent. It ages very well.
Serving temperature and suggested accompaniments
Serve at 57°F (14°C) with lamb or pheasant.

GRANDS-ECHEZEAUX
A.C. Red

Grape varieties
Pinots Noirien, Beurot and Liébault.
Production zone
Part of commune of Vosne-Romanée.
Characteristics
Fairly deep carmine-garnet color. Well developed animal, mineral, fruity, floral bouquet. Strong and persistent characteristic aromas. The wine is full, well blended, with typical astringency. It ages very well.
Serving temperature and suggested accompaniments
Serve at 57°F (14°C) with veal or pork.

□

APPELLATIONS COMMUNALES
DE LA CÔTE DE BEAUNE

ALOXE-CORTON
A.C. Red

Grape varieties
Pinots Noirien, Beurot and Liébault.
Production zone
Part of communes of Aloxe-Corton, Pernand-Vergelesses, Ladoix-Serrigny.
Characteristics
Fairly deep carmine-garnet color. Well developed vegetable, animal, mineral, fruity bouquet. Strong and persistent characteristic aromas. The wine is full-bodied and slightly astringent. It ages very well.
Serving temperature and suggested accompaniments
Serve at 57°F (14°C). It goes well with wild boar and poultry.
There is a small production of white Aloxe-Corton wine, made with Chardonnay. It is rich, dry, and distinguished.

AUXEY-DURESSES
A.C. Red

Grape varieties
Pinots Noirien, Beurot, and Liébault.
Production zone
Part of commune of Auxey-Duresses.
Characteristics
Fairly deep carmine-garnet color. Well developed animal, mineral, fruity, flowery bouquet. Strong and persistent characteristic aromas. The wine is full-bodied and gently astringent. It ages very well.
Serving temperature and suggested accompaniments
Serve at 57°F (14°C) to accompany wild boar cutlets.

BEAUNE
A.C. Red

Grape varieties
Pinots Noirien, Beurot and Liébault.
Production zone
Commune of Beaune.
Characteristics
Fairly deep purple color. Well developed vegetable, animal, mineral, fruity bouquet. Strong and persistent characteristic aromas. Supple and full-bodied, slightly astringent, the wine ages very well.
Serving temperature and suggested accompaniments
Serve at 57°F (14°C) with game or cheese. There is also a small production of white Beaune, a well structured wine made from Chardonnay and Pinot Blanc.

BLAGNY
A.C. Red

Grape varieties
Pinots Noirien, Beurot and Liébault.
Production zone
Part of communes of Meursault and Puligny-Montrachert.
Characteristics
Light to deep carmine color. Well developed vegetable, animal, mineral, bouquet. Strong and persistent characteristic aromas. The wine is full, velvety, and slightly astringent. It ages very well.
Serving temperature and suggested accompaniments
Serve at 57°F (14°C) with venison.

CHASSAGNE-MONTRACHET
A.C. Red

Grape varieties
Pinots Noirien, Beurot, and Liébault.
Production zone
Part of communes of Chassagne-Montrachet and Remigny.
Characteristics
Fairly deep carmine-garnet color. Well developed vegetable, animal, fruity, floral bouquet. Strong and persistent characteristic aromas. The wine is full, well blended, and softly astringent. It ages very well.
Serving temperature and suggested accompaniments
Serve at 57°F (14°C)with roast turkey.

CHASSAGNE-MONTRACHET
A.C. White

Grape varieties
Chardonnay, Pinot Blanc.
Production zone
Part of communes of Chassagne-Montrachet and Remigny.
Characteristics
Lovely straw-yellow color. Well developed vegetable, mineral, fruity, floral bouquet. Balanced, dry taste. Strong and persistent characteristic aromas. The wine is full-bodied and delicate. It ages very well.
Serving temperature and suggested accompaniments
Serve at 50°F (10°C) with trout or salmon.

CHEILLY-LÈS-MARANGES
A.C. Red

Grape varieties
Pinots Noirien, Beurot and Liébault.
Production zone
Part of commune of Cheilly-lès-Maranges.
Characteristics
Fairly deep garnet-redcurrant color. Well developed vegetable, animal, mineral bouquet. Strong and persistent characteristic aromas. The wine is full, well blended, and slightly astringent. It ages very well.
Serving temperature and suggested accompaniments
Serve at 55°F (13°C) with steak or beef.

CHOREY-LÈS-BEAUNE
A.C. Red

Grape varieties
Pinots Noirien, Beurot and Liébault.
Production zone
Part of commune of Chorey-lès-Beaune.
Characteristics
Fairly deep carmine-redcurrant color. Well developed vegetable, animal, mineral bouquet. Strong and persistent characteristic aromas. The wine is full, velvety, and slightly astringent. It ages very well.

Serving temperature and suggested accompaniments
Serve at 57°F (14°C) with venison.
There is also a small production of the very elegant white Chorey-lès-Beaune, made from Chardonnay and Pinot Blanc.

LADOIX
A.C. Red

Grape varieties
Pinots Noirien, Beurot and Liébault.
Production zone
Part of commune of Ladoix-Serrigny.
Characteristics
Fairly deep carmine color, with a vegetable, animal, mineral bouquet. Strong and persistent characteristic aromas. The wine is full, velvety, and slightly astringent. It has very good ageing properties.
Serving temperature and suggested accompaniments
Serve at 57°F (14°C). It goes well with venison or hare terrine.
There is a small production of white Ladoix, a very aromatic wine which ages well.

DEZIZE-LÈS-MARANGES
A.C. White

Grape varieties
Pinots Noirien, Beurot and Liébault.
Production zone
Part of commune of Dezize-lès-Maranges.
Characteristics
Fairly deep straw-yellow color, with a vegetable, fruity, bouquet. It is dry, full, and lively, with a good ageing capacity.
Serving temperature and suggested accompaniments
Serve at 50°F (10°C) with scallops.

MEURSAULT
A.C. White

Grape varieties
Chardonnay, Pinot Blanc.
Production zone
Part of commune of Meursault.
Characteristics
Deep straw-yellow color. Very well developed vegetable, animal, mineral, fruity bouquet; balanced, dry taste. Strong and persistent characteristic aromas. The wine is soft, full-bodied, and slightly astringent. It has excellent ageing properties.
Serving temperature and suggested accompaniments
Serve at 50°F (10°C) with sweetbreads or crayfish.

MEURSAULT
A.C. Red

Grape varieties
Pinots Noirien, Beurot and Liébault.
Production zone
Part of commune of Meursault.
Characteristics
Fairly deep carmine color. Well developed vegetable, animal, mineral bouquet. Strong and persistent characteristic aromas. The wine is full, velvety, and slightly astringent. It ages very well.
Serving temperature and suggested accompaniments
Serve at 57°F (14°C) with hare terrine.

MONTHÉLIE
A.C. Red

Grape varieties
Pinots Noirien, Beurot and Liébault.
Production zone
Part of commune of Monthélie.
Characteristics
Fairly deep garnet-redcurrant color. Well developed vegetable, animal, mineral bouquet. Strong and persistent characteristic aromas. The wine is full, velvety, and slightly astringent. It ages very well.
Serving temperature and suggested accompaniments
Serve at 57°F (14°C). The wine goes nicely with duck or beef.
There is also a small production of the very pleasant white Monthélie.

PERNAND-VERGELESSES
A.C. Red

Grape varieties
Pinots Noirien, Beurot and Liébault.
Production zone
Part of commune of Pernand-Vergelesses.
Characteristics
Fairly deep carmine color. Well developed vegetable, animal, fruity bouquet. Strong and persistent characteristic aromas. The wine is full, well blended, slightly astringent, and has excellent ageing properties.
Serving temperature and suggested accompaniments
Serve at 57°F (14°C) with pigeon pâté.

PERNAND-VERGELESSES
A.C. White

Grape varieties
Chardonnay, Pinot Blanc.
Production zone
Part of commune of Pernand-Vergelesses.
Characteristics
A lovely straw-yellow color, the wine has a well developed mineral, fruity, flowery bouquet and a balanced, dry taste. Strong and persistent characteristic aromas. It is full, light, and delicate, with good ageing capacity.
Serving temperature and suggested accompaniments
Serve at 50°F (10°C) with crayfish.

PULIGNY-MONTRACHET
A.C. White

Grape varieties
Chardonnay, Pinot Blanc.
Production zone
Part of commune of Puligny-Montrachet.
Characteristics
Deep straw-yellow color, well developed vegetable, fruity, floral bouquet, balanced, dry taste. Strong and persistent characteristic aromas. The wine is full and well blended. It ages very well.
Serving temperature and suggested accompaniments
Serve at 50°F (10°C) with fish.

PULIGNY-MONTRACHET
A.C. Red

Grape varieties
Pinots Noirien, Beurot and Liébault.
Production zone
Part of commune of Puligny-Montrachet.
Characteristics
Light to deep carmine color. Well developed vegetable, animal, mineral, fruity bouquet. Strong and persistent characteristic aromas. The wine is full, velvety, and softly astringent. It ages very well.
Serving temperature and suggested accompaniments
Serve at 57°F (14°C) with lamb shoulder.

SAINT-AUBIN
A.C. Red

Grape varieties
Pinots Noirien, Beurot and Liébault.
Production zone
Part of commune of Saint-Aubin.
Characteristics
Fairly deep garnet-redcurrant color. Well developed vegetable, animal, mineral bouquet. Strong and persistent characteristic aromas. The wine is full, velvety, and slightly astringent. It ages very well.
Serving temperature and suggested accompaniments
Serve at 57°F (14°C) with rabbit.

SAINT-AUBIN
A.C. White

Grape varieties
Chardonnay, Pinot Blanc.
Production zone
Part of commune of Saint-Aubin.
Characteristics
Deep straw-yellow color, well-developed vegetable and mineral bouquet. Dry, full and well rounded, with little astringency, the wine ages very well.
Serving temperature and suggested accompaniments
Serve at 50°F (10°C) with fish.

SAINT-ROMAIN
A.C. Red

Grape varieties
Pinots Noirien, Beurot and Liébault.
Production zone
Part of commune of Saint-Romain.
Characteristics
Fairly deep carmine color. Well developed vegetable, animal, mineral bouquet. Strong and persistent characteristic aromas. The wine is full, velvety, and slightly astringent, with good ageing properties.
Serving temperature and suggested accompaniments
Serve at 57°F (14°C) with veal cutlets.

SAINT-ROMAIN
A.C. White

Grape varieties
Chardonnay and Pinot Blanc.
Production zone
Part of commune of Saint-Romain.
Characteristics
Quite deep color, with a straw-yellow to golden nuance. Well developed fruity bouquet with touches of animal. Dry, full, and firm, the wine ages well.
Serving temperature and suggested accompaniments
Serve at 50°F (10°C) with eggs, crayfish, etc.

SAMPIGNY-LÈS-MARANGES
A.C. Red

Grape varieties
Pinots Noirien, Beurot and Liébault.
Production zone
Part of commune of Sampigny-lès-Maranges.
Characteristics
Fairly deep carmine-redcurrant color. Well developed animal, mineral, fruity bouquet. Strong and persistent characteristic aromas. The wine is full, well blended, and slightly astringent. It ages very well.
Serving temperature and suggested accompaniments
Serve at 57°F (14°C) with lamb.

SANTENAY
A.C. Red

Grape varieties
Pinots Noirien, Beurot and Liébault.
Production zone
Part of commune of Santenay and Remigny.
Characteristics
Lovely carmine-redcurrant color. Well developed animal, mineral, fruity, floral bouquet. Strong and persistent characteristic aromas. The wine is full-bodied, velvety, with supple astringency. It has good ageing properties.
Serving temperature and suggested accompaniments
Serve at 57°F (14°C) with lamb.
There is also a small production of white Santenay, a fine wine which ages very well.

SAVIGNY-LÈS-BEAUNE
A.C. Red

Grape varieties
Pinots Noirien, Beurot and Liébault.
Production zone
Part of commune of Savigny-lès-Beaune.
Characteristics
Light to deep ruby-redcurrant color. Well developed animal, mineral, fruity, flowery bouquet. Strong and persistent characteristic aromas. The wine is vel-

vety, well blended, and slightly astringent. It ages very well.
Serving temperature and suggested accompaniments
Serve at 57°F (14°C) with chicken.
There is also a white Savigny, a well structured, elegant wine.

VOLNAY (VOLNAY-SANTENOTS)
A.C. Red

Grape varieties
Pinots Noirien, Beurot and Liébault.
Production zone
Part of communes of Volnay and Meursault.
Characteristics
A lovely carmine-redcurrant color, the wine has a well developed animal, fruity, floral bouquet. Strong and persistent characteristic aromas. It is velvety, well blended, softly astringent, and has very good ageing properties.
Serving temperature and suggested accompaniments
Serve at 57°F (14°C) with game or poultry.

POMMARD
A.C. Red

Grape varieties
Pinots Noirien, Beurot and Liébault.
Production zone
Commune of Pommard (57 *climats*).
Characteristics
Lovely garnet-redcurrant color, well developed animal, mineral, fruity, flowery bouquet. Strong and persistent characteristic aromas. The wine is full, velvety, and soft, with a gently, typical astringency. It has excellent ageing properties.
Serving temperature and suggested accompaniments
Serve at 57°F (14°C) with game.

□

GRAND CRUS
DE LA CÔTE DE BEAUNE

CORTON
A.C. Red

Grape varieties
Pinots Noirien, Beurot and Liébault.
Production zone
Part of communes of Aloxe-Corton, Ladoix-Serrigny, Pernand-Vergelesses.
Characteristics
Deep carmine-garnet color. Very well developed vegetable, animal, mineral, fruity, floral bouquet. Strong and persistent characteristic aromas. The wine is full-bodied, rich, and well blended, with a typically soft astringency. It has excellent ageing properties.
Serving temperature and suggested accompaniments
Serve at 57°F (14°C) with hare.

CORTON
A.C. White

Grape varieties
Chardonnay.
Production zone
Identical to area for red Corton.
Characteristics
Lovely straw-yellow color. Well developed vegetable, animal, mineral, fruity, floral bouquet; balanced, dry taste. Strong and persistent characteristic aromas. The wine is full-bodied and well blended. It has excellent ageing properties.
Serving temperature and suggested accompaniments
Serve at 54°F (14°C) with lobster.

CORTON-CHARLEMAGNE
A.C. White

Grape varieties
Chardonnay.
Production zone
Part of communes of Aloxe-Corton, Ladoix-Serrigny, Pernand Vergelesses.
Characteristics
Deep straw-yellow to golden color. Well developed mineral, fruity, floral bouquet; balanced, dry taste. Strong and persistent characteristic aromas. The wine is full-bodied and delicate. It has excellent ageing properties.
Serving temperature and suggested accompaniments
Serve at 54°F (12°C) with lobster or *foie gras*.

BÂTARD-MONTRACHET
A.C. White

Grape varieties
Chardonnay.
Production zone
Part of commune of Chassagne-Montrachet.
Characteristics
Lovely golden straw-yellow color. Well developed animal, mineral, fruity, flowery bouquet; balanced dry taste. Strong and persistent characteristic aromas. The wine is rich and full-bodied, with excellent ageing properties.
Serving temperature and suggested accompaniments
Serve at 54°F (12°C) with fish or seafood.

MONTRACHET
A.C. White

Grape varieties
Chardonnay.
Production zone
Part of communes of Puligny-Montrachet and Chassagne-Montrachet.
Characteristics
Deep golden straw-yellow color. Well developed vegetable, mineral, fruity, flowery bouquet; balanced dry taste. Strong and persistent characteristic aromas. The wine is soft, full-bodied, and well blended, with excellent ageing properties.
Serving temperature and suggested accompaniments
Serve at 54°F (12°C) with lobster or ham.

CHEVALIER-MONTRACHET
A.C. White

Grape varieties
Chardonnay.
Production zone
Part of commune of Puligny-Montrachet.
Characteristics
Lovely straw-yellow color. Well developed mineral, fruity, flowery bouquet; balanced dry taste. Strong and persistent characteristic aromas. The wine is full and well blended. It has excellent ageing properties.
Serving temperature and suggested accompaniments
Serve at 54°F (12°C) with eggs or fish.

BIENVENUES-BÂTARD-MONTRACHET
A.C. White

Grape varieties
Chardonnay.
Production zone
Part of commune of Puligny-Montrachet.
Characteristics
Lovely straw-yellow color. Well developed mineral, fruity, flowery bouquet. Strong and persistent characteristic aromas. The wine is full, rich, well blended, and lively. It has excellent ageing properties.
Serving temperature and suggested accompaniments
Serve at 54°F (12°C) with crayfish, etc.

CROITS-BÂTARD-MONTRACHET
A.C. White

Grape varieties
Chardonnay.
Production zone
Part of commune of Chassagne-Montrachet.
Characteristics
Lovely golden straw-yellow color. Well developed mineral, fruity, flowery bouquet. The taste is well balanced and dry. Strong and persistent characteristic aromas. The wine is soft and full-bodied, ageing extremely well.
Serving temperature and suggested accompaniments
Serve at 54°F (12°C) with fish.

COTEAUX DU LYONNAIS
A.C. Red

Grape varieties
Gamay (min. 85%), Chardonnay, Aligoté.
Production zone
59 communes.
Characteristics
Light carmine-redcurrant color. Normal fruity, floral bouquet. Strong characteristic aromas. The wine is supple, light, well blended, and slightly astringent. It does not age particularly well.
Serving temperature and suggested accompaniments
Serve at 57°F (14°C). It goes nicely with tripe dishes.
There is also a dry, fruity white wine of this *appellation*, made with Chardonnay and Aligoté.

VINS DE BUGEY
V.D.Q.S. White, Red, and Rosé

Grape varieties
Red and Rosé: Gamay, Pinot Noir, Poulsard, Mondeuse and (max. 20%) local white varieties.
White: Chardonnay, Altesse, Aligoté, Mondeuse Blanche, Jacquère, Pinot Gris. Only Altesse and Chardonnay varieties are used for the Roussette-de-Bugey *appellation*.
Production zone
65 communes of the Ain.
The names of the following *crus* may be added to the *appellation*:
Vins du Bugey: Virieu-le-Grand, Montagnieu, Manicle, Machuraz, Cerdon.
The Roussette-du-Bugey *appellation* may likewise be completed by that of a *cru*:
Anglefort, Abrignieu, Channay, Lagnieu, Montagnieu, Virieu-le-Grand.
Characteristics
The color of the reds is medium carmine-redcurrant, the whites slightly straw-yellow, the rosés quite deep pink. The fruity, flowery bouquet is well developed, the taste balanced, the whites and rosés being dry. Strong characteristic aromas. The red wines are supple and velvety, with little astringency; the whites are light and soft. Both types age reasonably well.
Serving temperature and suggested accompaniments
Serve the reds at 57°F (14°C), the whites at 50°F (10°C). The former go well with veal, the latter with cheese.

SAUVIGNON DE SAINT-BRIS
V.D.Q.S. White

Grape varieties
Sauvignon.
Production zone
Communes or part of communes of Saint-Bris-le-Vineux, Chitry, Irancy, Vincelottes.
Characteristics
Light greenish-straw-yellow color. Well developed vegetable, fruity bouquet; balanced dry taste. Strong characteristic aromas. The wine is light, soft and lively. It ages reasonably well.
Serving temperature and suggested accompaniments
Serve at 50°F (10°C) as an aperitif. The wine also goes well with fish and pastry.

The Mediterranean vineyards

This extensive zone is under the influence of the Mediterranean climate. It includes the vineyards of the Côtes-du-Rhône, Provence, Corsica, Languedoc, and Roussillon.

The stamp of the Mediterranean is already noticeable in the northern and southern areas of the Côtes-du-Rhône appellation, *the originality of these wines being expressed in a warmth derived from the sun combined with their natural fruity, floral qualities.*

The wine makers of this region have to be particularly scrupulous in choosing those grape varieties which are best suited to local soils and climatic conditions. The vineyards range from the Hermitages, with a single variety, the Syrah, to the white stone soil of Châteauneuf-du-Pape, where up to thirteen varieties are used, showing the paramount importance of human skill and artistry in producing this celebrated wine.

Along the seacoast, the wines of Provence, so much appreciated by holiday-makers, include numerous unassuming reds of great originality. All the wines of the Rhône valley and from the eastern Mediterranean region are a splendid match for the delicacies of the local cuisine with its subtle flavors often derived from the deliciously scented aromatic plants which grow so profusely here.

The red wines of Corsica seem to have a more northerly character, typified by the use of the Malvoisie grape, an excellent accompaniment to a varied and highly colorful style of cooking.

If northeastern France is notable especially for its white wines, the southeast is renowned almost exclusively for its producion of red wine, and this applies likewise to the vineyards of Languedoc-Roussillon, situated farther west in the départements *of the Pyrénées-Orientales, Hérault and Gard.*

The entire region constitutes one of the biggest wine-producing areas in the world in terms of acreage of planted vines. It is responsible for 75–80% of all France's red table wines, roughly 13% of all French V.D.Q.S. and 10% of all appellations contrôlées, *not to mention great dessert wines such as Banyuls and Muscat.*

It is a pity that these soft, aromatic and well structured wines are not drunk more often with dessert courses, for just as the fall of a curtain at the end of a play sometimes leaves the audience hungry for more, a meal can similarly be left hanging in mid air, and these delicious wines provide the perfect climax to a convivial dinner.

CÔTES-DU-RHÔNE
A.C. Red

Grape varieties
Carignan (max. 30%), Grenache, Clairette, Syrah, Mourvèdre, Picpoul, Terret Noir, Picardan, Cinsaut, Roussanne, Marsanne, Bourboulenc, Viognier.
Supplementary varieties (in proportion of 30%) are Counoise, Muscardin, Vaccarèse, Pinot Fin de Bourgogne, Mauzac, Pascal Blanc, Ugni Blanc, Calitor, Gamay, Camarèse.
Production zone
Ardèche (32 communes), Drôme (31 communes), Gard (45 communes), Loire (5 communes), Rhône (3 communes), Vauclause (48 communes).
Characteristics
Deep carmine color, well developed fruity bouquet, balanced taste without excessive acidity, minimum alcohol content 11°. Strong characteristic aromas. The wine is full-bodied with a typically good measure of astringency. It ages well.
Serving temperature and suggested accompaniments
Serve at 57°F (14°C). The young wines go well with a hotpot, the maturer wines with various cuts of beef.

CÔTES-DU-RHÔNE
A.C. White

Grape varieties
The normal white varieties for this zone.
Production zone
Communes or part of communes of the red Côtes-du-Rhône *appellation*.

CÔTES-DU-RHÔNE VILLAGES
A.C. Red

Grape varieties
Grenache Noir (max. 65%), Syrah, Mourvèdre and Cinsaut (min. proportion of 25%) and max. 10% of other varieties for A.C. Côtes-du-Rhône.
Production zone
Following communes or part of communes: Drôme *département*: Rochegude, Saint-Maurice-sur-Eygues, Vinsobres, Rousset-les-Vignes, Saint-Pantaléon-les-Vignes; Vaucluse *département*: Beaumes-de-Venise, Cairanne, Rasteau, Roaix, Séguret, Vacqueyras, Valréas, Viscan, Sablet; Gard *département*: Chusclan, Laudun, Saint-Gervais.
Characteristics
Deep carmine-garnet color. Well developed animal, fruity bouquet, balanced taste, min. alcohol content 12°. Strong characteristic aromas. The wine is full-bodied, well blended, with a typical good measure of astringency. It ages well.
Serving temperature and suggested accompaniments
Serve young wines at 57°F (14°C), older wines at 61°F (16°C). The former go nicely with braised beef, the latter with wild boar.

CÔTES-DU-RHÔNE VILLAGES
A.C. Rosé

Grape varieties
Grenache Noir (max. 60%), Camarèse and Cinsaut (min. 15%), Carignan (max. 15%) and max. 10% of other varieties used for red Côtes-du-Rhône-Villages.
Production zone
Communes or part of communes of area for red Côtes-du-Rhône-Villages *appellation*.
Characteristics
Medium clear pink color, well developed fruity, flowery bouquet, balanced taste without preponderance of sugar, min. alcohol content 12°. The wine is full, without much astringency. It has normal ageing properties.
Serving temperature and suggested accompaniments
Serve at 50°F (10°C) with various meat and vegetable dishes, particularly stuffed eggplants.

CÔTES-DU-RHÔNE VILLAGES
A.C. White

Grape varieties
Clairette, Roussanne, Bourboulenc (max. 80%) with max. 10% of Grenache Blanc and max. 15% of other regional white varieties.
Production zone
Communes or part of communes of the red Côtes-du-Rhône-Villages *appellation*.
Characteristics
Light straw-yellow color, normal vegetable, fruity bouquet, balanced taste, strong characteristic aromas. The wine is fairly full-bodied, soft, and slightly astringent. It ages well.
Serving temperature and suggested accompaniments
Serve at 50°F (10°C) with fish, tripe, etc.

CHÂTEAUNEUF-DU-PAPE
A.C. Red

Grape varieties
Grenache, Syrah, Mourvèdre, Picpoul, Terret Noir, Counoise, Muscardin, Vaccarèse, Picardan, Cinsaut, Clairette, Roussanne, Bourboulenc.
Production zone
Communes or part of communes of Châteauneuf-du-Pape, Bédarrides, Courthézon, Orange, Sorgues (Vauclause).
Characteristics
Deep color, mainly garnet. Very well developed vegetable, animal, mineral, fruity bouquet. Balanced taste without any dominant element, min. alcohol content 12.5°. Strong and persistent characteristic aromas. The wine is full, well blended, soft, and with a typical good measure of astringency. It has excellent ageing properties.
Serving temperature and suggested accompaniments
Serve at 59°F (15°C). It goes marvelously with red meat, venison, and vegetable dishes.

CHÂTEAUNEUF-DU-PAPE
A.C. White

Grape varieties
White varieties of the *appellation*.
Production zone
Communes or part of communes in the area of the Châteauneuf-du-Pape *appellation*.
Characteristics
Fairly deep straw-yellow to golden color; very complex and individual bouquet, perfectly balanced taste. Very strong and persistent characteristic aromas. The wine is full-bodied, well blended, delicate, and slightly astringent. It has excellent ageing properties.
Serving temperature and suggested accompaniments
Serve at 50°F (10°C) with salmon, marrow, truffles, etc.

COTEAUX-DU-TRICASTIN
A.C. Red

Grape varieties
Syrah, Picpoul Noir, Carignan (max. 20%) and max. 20% of following white varieties: Grenache Blanc, Clairette, Picpoul, Bourboulenc, and Ugni Blanc (max. 30%) which are also used to make a very limited amount of white wines of this *appellation*.
Production zone
Communes or part of communes of the Drôme *département*: Allan, La Baume-de-Transit, Béconne, Chamaret, Chantemerle-lès-Grignan, Châteauneuf-du-Rhône, Clansayes, Colonzelle, Donzère, La Garde-Adhémar, Les Granges-Gontardes, Malataverne, Montségur-sur-Lauzon, Réauville, La Roche-Saint-Secret, Roussas, Salles-sous-Bois, Saint-Paul-Trois-Château, Saint-Restitut, Solerieux, Valaurie.
Characteristics
Fairly deep garnet-carmine color. Well developed vegetable, animal, fruity bouquet; balanced taste, with min. alcohol content of 11°. Strong characteristic aromas. The wine is full with a good measure of typical astringency. It ages well.
Serving temperature and suggested accompaniments
Serve at 57°F (14°C) with roasts.

CÔTE-RÔTIE
A.C. Red

Grape varieties
Syrah (max. 80%), Viognier.
Production zone
Communes or part of communes of Rhône *département*: Ampuis, Saint-Cyr-sur-le-Rhône, Tupin-et-Semons.
Characteristics
Fairly deep garnet-redcurrant color. Very well developed vegetable, animal, mineral, fruity bouquet. Strong and persistent characteristic aromas. The wine is full, velvety, and typically astringent. It ages well.
Serving temperature and suggested accompaniments
Serve at 59°F (15°C) with roast meat or duck.

GIGONDAS
A.C. Red

Grape varieties
Grenache Noir (max. 65%) and min. 25% of Syrah, Mourvèdre and Cinsaut; also max. 25% of all other A.C. Cotes-du-Rhône varieties, except for Carignan.
Production zone
Communes or part of commune of Gigondas.
Characteristics
Deep carmine-garnet color. Well developed vegetable, animal, fruity bouquet. Strong characteristic aromas. The wine is full and rich, pleasantly astringent. It has excellent ageing properties.
Serving temperature and suggested accompaniments
Serve at 59°F (15°C) with meat or venison.

GIGONDAS
A.C. Rosé

Grape varieties
Grenache Noir (max. 60%), Cinsaut (min. 15%), and 25% of all other varieties used for A.C. Côtes-du-Rhône, except for Carignan.
Production zone
Commune of Gigondas.

Characteristics
Medium clear pink color, well developed vegetable, fruit bouquet, balanced taste without preponderance of sugar. Strong characteristic aromas. The wine is supple, full, soft, and slightly astringent. It ages well.
Serving temperature and suggested accompaniments
Serve at 50°F (10°C) with tomatoes and cheese dishes.

LIRAC
A.C. Red

Grape varieties
Principally (60%) Cinsaut, Mourvèdre and Grenache, which alone should represent min. 40%; supplementary varieties are Bouboulenc, Calitor, Clairette, Maccabéo, Picpoul, Syrah, Carignan (max. 10%).
Production zone
Communes or part communes of Lirac, Saint-Laurent-des-Arbres, Roquemaure, Saint-Geniès-de-Comolas.
Characteristics
Medium carmine-garnet color, well developed vegetable, fruity bouquet, balanced taste with min. alcohol content of 11.5°. Strong characteristic aromas. The wine is full, velvety, light, and typically astringent. It ages well.
Serving temperature and suggested accompaniments
Serve at 59°F (15°C) with rabbit or beef.

LIRAC
A.C. Rosé

Grape varieties
Identical to those for area of red Lirac.
Production zone
The same as the red Lirac *appellation*.
Characteristics
Medium clear pink color, well developed fruity bouquet, balanced taste without too much acidity. Strong characteristic aromas. The wine is supple, quite full-bodied, with little astringency. It has normal ageing properties.
Serving temperature and suggested accompaniments
Serve at 52°F (11°C). It goes extremely well with scrambled eggs or chicken.

LIRAC
A.C. White

Grape varieties
Clairette (min. 30%), Bourboulenc, Ugni Blanc, Maccabéo, Grenache, Picpoul and Calitor (max. 25% for last two).
Production zone
Identical to that of red Lirac *appellation*.
Characteristics
Medium straw-yellow color, faint fruity, floral bouquet, balanced taste with min. alcohol content of 11.5°. Strong characteristic aromas. The wine is quite full and soft. It has normal ageing properties.
Serving temperature and suggested accompaniments
Serve at 50°F (10°C) with eggs or fish.

TAVEL
A.C. Rosé

Grape varieties
Grenache, Cinsaut (min. 15%), Clairette Blanche, Clairette Rose, Picpoul, Calitor, Bourboulenc, Mourvèdre, Syrah, Carignan (max. 10%).
Production zone
Commune of Tavel.
Characteristics
Medium clear pink with brick-red nuance. Well developed animal, fruity, flowery bouquet, balanced taste with min. alcohol content of 11°. Very strong characteristic aromas. The wine is full, well blended, soft, with typical astringency. It has excellent ageing capacity.
Serving temperature and suggested accompaniments
Serve at 54°F (12°C) with fish dishes.

CORNAS
A.C. Red

Grape varieties
Syrah.
Production zone
Commune of Cornas.
Characteristics
Deep carmine-garnet color. Well developed vegetable, animal, mineral, fruity bouquet. Strong and persistent characteristic aromas. The wine is full, well blended, and typically astringent. It ages well.
Serving temperature and suggested accompaniments
Serve at 59°F (15°C) with duck or roast meat.

SAINT-JOSEPH
A.C. Red

Grape varieties
Syrah.
Production zone
Following communes or part of communes of Ardèche *département*: Andance, Ardoix, Arras-sur-Rhône, Champagne, Charnas, Châteaubourg, Félines, Glun, Guilherand, Lemps, Limony, Mauves, Ozon, Peyraud, Saint-Désirat, Saint-Etienne-de-Valoux, Saint-Jean-de-Muzols, Sarras, Sécheras, Serrières, Talencieux, Tournon, Vion. Loire *département*: Chavanay, Maleval, Saint-Pierre-de-Boeuf.
Characteristics
Fairly deep carmine-garnet color. Well developed vegetable, animal, fruity bouquet. Strong and persistent characteristic aromas. The wine is full, well blended, and typically astringent. It ages well.
Serving temperature and suggested accompaniments
Serve at 59°F (15°C) with braised beef.

SAINT-JOSEPH
A.C. White

Grape varieties
Marsanne, Roussanne.
Production zone
Identical to area of red Saint-Joseph *appellation*.
Characteristics
Medium straw-yellow color. Well developed vegetable, fruity, floral bouquet. Strong and persistent characteristic aromas. The wine is quite full, well blended, soft, and slightly astringent. It ages very well.
Serving temperature and suggested accompaniments
Serve at 50°F (10°C) with fish.

HERMITAGE (or ERMITAGE)
A.C. Red

Grape varieties
Syrah, supplemented by max. 15% Roussanne and Marsanne.
Production zone
Communes or part of communes of Tain l'Hermitage and Crozes Hermitage.
Characteristics
Deep carmine-garnet color. Well developed animal, mineral, fruity, floral bouquet. Very strong and persistent characteristic aromas. The wine is full-bodied, well blended, soft, with a pleasantly typical astringency and good ageing qualities.
Serving temperature and suggested accompaniments
Serve at 57°F (14°C) with game.

HERMITAGE (or ERMITAGE)
A.C. White

Grape varieties
Roussanne, Marsanne.
Production zone
Identical to area of red Hermitage *appellation*.
Characteristics
Medium straw-yellow to golden color. Well developed mineral, fruity, floral bouquet. Very strong and persistent characteristic aromas. The wine is full, well blended, soft, and slightly astringent. It has excellent ageing properties.
Serving temperature and suggested accompaniments
Serve at 52°F (11°C) with poultry.

CROZES-HERMITAGE
A.C. Red and White

Grape varieties
Red: Syrah.
White: Roussanne and Marsanne.
Production zone
Crozes-Hermitage, Tain l'Hermitage, and 9 other surrounding communes.
Characteristics
Similar to those of Hermitage *appellation*, but rather less powerful and with inferior ageing qualities.
Serving temperature and suggested accompaniments
Serve reds at 57°F (14°C) with red meat or roast duck, the whites at 52°F (11°C) with fish.

CÔTES-DU-VENTOUX
A.C. Red

Grape varieties
Grenache, Syrah, Cinsaut, Mourvèdre, Carignan (max. 30%), and overall max. 20% of Picpoul Noir, Counoise, Clairette, Bourboulenc, Grenache Blanc, Rousanne, Ugni Blanc, Picpoul Blanc, Pascal Blanc.
Characteristics
52 communes or part of communes situated to the east of the area of the Côtes-du-Rhône *appellation*.
Characteristics
Medium, mainly carmine, color. Well developed vegetable, fruity bouquet, balanced taste with min. 11° alcohol content. Strong characteristic aromas. The wine is supple and full, with a good measure of typical astringency. It has normal ageing properties.
Serving temperature and suggested accompaniments
Serve at 57°F (14°C). It goes well with beef and cooked meats.

CÔTES-DU-VENTOUX
A.C. White

Grape varieties
Clairette, Bourboulenc and, in overall proportion of max. 30%, the following secondary varieties: Grenache Blanc, Roussanne, Ugni Blanc, Picpoul Blanc, Pascal Blanc.
Production zone
Identical to area of red Côtes-du-Ventoux *appellation*.
Characteristics
Light straw-yellow color. Well developed vegetable, fruity, floral bouquet. Strong characteristic aromas. The wine is full, well blended, and slightly astringent. It ages well.
Serving temperature and suggested accompaniments
Serve at 52°F (11°C) with cheese omelet.

CONDRIEU
A.C. White

Grape varieties
Viognier.
Production zone
Communes or part of communes of Limony (Ardèche), Chavanay, Malleval, Saint-Michel-sur-Rhône, Saint-Pierre-de-Boeuf, Vérin (Loire), Condrieu (Rhône).
Characteristics
Medium straw-yellow to golden color. Well developed vegetable, fruity, floral bouquet. Strong and persistent characteristic aromas. The wine is full, rich, soft, and slightly astringent. It has excellent ageing properties.
Serving temperature and suggested accompaniments
Serve at 54°F (12°C). It goes nicely with lobster or artichoke hearts.

CHÂTEAU-GRILLET
A.C. White

Grape varieties
Viognier.
Production zone
Communes or part of communes of Saint-Michel-sur-Rhône, Vérin.
Characteristics
Quite deep straw-yellow to golden color, very well developed vegetable, mineral, flowery bouquet, balanced taste with min. 11° alcohol content. Very strong and persistent characteristic aromas. The wine is full, velvety, soft, and slightly astringent. It has excellent ageing qualities.
Serving temperature and suggested accompaniments
Serve at 54°F (12°C) to accompany crayfish, caviar, pike, etc.

CHÂTILLON-EN-DIOIS
A.C. Red

Grape varieties
Gamay (min. 75%), supplemented by Syrah and Pinot Noir.
Production zone
Following communes or part of communes in Drôme *département*: Châtillon-en-Diois, Aix-en-Diois, Barnave, Jansac, Laval d'Aix, Luc-en-Diois, Menglon, Molières-Glandaz, Montlaur-en-Diois, Montmaur-en-Diois, Poyols, Recoubeau, Saint-Roman.
Characteristics
Light, mainly carmine, color, well developed fruit bouquet and strong characteristic aromas. The wine is supple and light, with little astringency. It has reasonable ageing properties.
Serving temperature and suggested accompaniments
Serve at 55°F (13°C) with calves' liver.

CHÂTILLON-EN-DIOIS
A.C. White

Grape varieties
Aligoté, Chardonnay.
Production zone
Identical to area of red Châtillon-en-Diois *appellation*.
Characteristics
Light greenish to straw-yellow color. Strong fruity, floral bouquet, and characteristic aromas. The wine is supple, well blended, and lively. It has normal ageing properties.
Serving temperature and suggested accompaniments
Serve at 50°F (10°C) with baked sausages.

SAINT-PÉRAY
A.C. White

Grape varieties
Roussane, Marsanne.
Production zone
Saint-Péray, Toulaud (Ardèche).
Characteristics
Medium straw-yellow color, well developed fruity, flowery bouquet, balanced, fresh taste. Strong and persistent characteristic aromas. The wine is supple, well blended, and slightly astringent. It ages well.
Serving temperature and suggested accompaniments
Serve at 50°F (10°C) with fish or omelets.

SAINT-PÉRAY MOUSSEUX
A.C. White

White Saint-Péray, made by the *méthode champenoise*, is available as a very fresh and agreeable sparkling wine, excellent as an aperitif.

CLAIRETTE DE DIE
A.C. White

Grape varieties
Clairette, Muscat à petits grains.
Production zone
31 communes around Die.
Characteristics
Light straw-yellow to golden color for the wines containing more Muscat. The characteristic fruity, floral bouquet is well developed, the taste is balanced, with a typical sparkle. Very strong and persistent characteristic aromas. The wine is supple, well blended, soft, and fresh, slightly astringent. It ages normally.
Serving temperature and suggested accompaniments
Serve at 48°F (9°C) as an aperitif or with a variety of desserts.

PALETTE
A.C. Red

Grape varieties
Mourvèdre (min. 10%), Grenache, Cinsaut, supplemented, to a proportion of max. 50%, by the following varieties: Manusquin, Durif, Muscat, Noir, Carignan, Syrah, Castets, Brun-Fourcat, Terret Gris, Petit-Brun, Tibourenc, Cabernet Savignon, plus max. 15% of local white varieties.
Production zone
Communes or part of communes of Meyreuil, Le Tholonet, Aix-en-Provence.
Characteristics
Medium carmine-garnet color. Normally developed fruity bouquet. Strong characteristic aromas. The wine is supple and well blended with good typical astringency. It has normal ageing qualities.
Serving temperature and suggested accompaniments
Serve at 57°F (14°C) with a calves' liver.

PALETTE
A.C. White

Grape varieties
Clairette (min. 35%), supplemented, in proportion of max. 45%, by Ugni Blanc, Ugni Rose, Grenache Blanc, Muscats Blancs, Picpoul, Pascal, Aragnan, Colombard (local "Tokay"), Terret Bourret (max., 20%).
Production zone
Identical to area of red Palette *appellation*.
Characteristics
Light pale to straw-yellow color, well developed vegetable, floral bouquet. Strong characteristic aromas. The wine is supple, well blended, soft, and sometimes fresh. It ages reasonably well.
Serving temperature and suggested accompaniments
Serve at 50°F (10°C) with scrambled eggs or red mullet.

BANDOL
A.C. Red

Grape varieties
Mourvèdre (min. 50%), Grenache and Consaut, these three varieties representing min. 80% of the whole. Secondary varieties: Calitor, Carignan, Syrah, Tibouren and max. 20% of white varieties used for white Bandol.
Production zone
Communes or part commune of Bandol, Sanary, La Cadière-d'Azur, Le Castellet.
Characteristics
Fairly deep carmine-garnet color. Well developed animal, mineral, fruity bouquet; balanced taste, with min. 11° alcohol content. Very strong and persistent characteristic aromas. The wine is full and well blended, with a typical,

distinctive astringency. It has excellent ageing properties.
Serving temperature and suggested accompaniments
Serve at 57°F (14°C) with duck or cabbage.

BANDOL
A.C. White

Grape varieties
Bourboulenc, Clairette, Ugni Blanc (60%). Secondary variety: Sauvignon (max. 40%).
Production zone
Identical to the area of the red Bandol *appellation*.
Characteristics
Medium straw-yellow color. Well developed vegetable, fruity, floral bouquet, balanced, dry taste. Strong characteristic aromas. The wine is supple, well blended, and quite soft. It ages well.
Serving temperature and suggested accompaniments
Serve at 52°F (11°C) with red mullet or brill.

CASSIS
A.C. Red

Grape varieties
Grenache, Carignan, Mourvèdre, Cinsaut, Barbaroux, Terrets (max. 5%).
Production zone
Commune of Cassis.
Characteristics
Deep carmine-garnet color, well developed vegetable, animal, fruity bouquet, balanced taste, with min. 11° alcohol content. Strong characteristic aromas. The wine is full, well blended, pleasantly astringent, with good ageing properties.
Serving temperature and suggested accompaniments
Serve at 57°F (14°C) with roast mutton.

CASSIS
A.C. White

Grape varieties
Ugni Blanc, Sauvignon, Doucillon, Clairette, Marsanne, Pascal Blanc.
Production zone
Identical to area of red Cassis *appellation*.
Characteristics
Fairly deep straw-yellow to amber-yellow color. Well developed mineral, fruity bouquet, balanced taste, with min. 11° alcohol content. Strong and persistent characteristic aromas. The wine is full, soft, and slightly astringent. It ages well.
Serving temperature and suggested accompaniments
Serve at 50°F (10°C) with *bouillabaisse* or sea-bass.

CÔTES-DE-PROVENCE
A.C. Red

Grape varieties
Principal varieties, representing 70%: Cinsaut, Grenache, Mourvèdre, Tibouren, Carignan (max. 40%). Secondary varieties: Cabernet Sauvignon, Calitor, Syrah.
Production zone
15 communes of Bouches-du-Rhône, 69 communes of Var, and Villars-sur-Var, in the Alpes Maritimes.
Characteristics
Fairly deep carmine-garnet color. Well developed vegetable, fruity, floral bouquet. Strong characteristic aromas. The wine is full, well blended, pleasantly astringent, and with good ageing properties.
Serving temperature and suggested accompaniments
Serve at 57°F (14°C) with meat and vegetable dishes.

CÔTES-DE-PROVENCE
A.C. Rosé

Grape varieties
Principal varieties, representing 70%: Cinsaut, Grenache, Mourvèdre, Tibouren, Carignan (max. 40%). Secondary varieties: Cabernet Sauvignon, Calitor, Syrah, Barbaroux.
Production zone
Identical to the area of the red Côtes-de-Provence *appellation*.
Characteristics
Medium redcurrant to brick-red color. Well developed fruity, flowery bouquet, balanced, dry taste. Strong characteristic aromas. The wine is smooth, soft, and slightly astringent. It ages well.
Serving temperature and suggested accompaniments
Serve at 54°F (12°C) with salads, artichokes, *bouillabaisse*, pork, etc.

CÔTES-DE-PROVENCE
A.C. White

Grape varieties
Clairette, Sémillon, Ugni Blanc.
Production zone
Identical to area of the red Côtes-de-Provence.
Characteristics
Light straw-yellow color, sometimes with greenish tints. Well developed vegetable, mineral, fruity, floral bouquet, balanced, dry taste (under 3 g sugar per liter), strong characteristic aromas. The wine is soft and supple, slightly astringent, and has good ageing qualities.
Serving temperature and suggested accompaniments
Serve at 50°F (10°C) with zucchini, lamb or fish.

COTEAUX VAROIS
V.D.Q.S Red and Rosé

Grape varieties
Carignan, Cinsaut, Grenache, Mourvèdre, Syrah. Secondary varieties: Tibouren, Cabernet Sauvignon.
Production zone
Brignoles and 27 adjoining communes.
Characteristics
Medium to deep color, well developed vegetable, fruity, floral bouquet, strong characteristic aromas. The reds are full-bodied and supple, slightly astringent; the rosés are light and soft, with little astringency. They age reasonably well.

Serving temperature and suggested accompaniments
Serve the wines cool, the reds with poultry or vegetables, the rosés with anchovies or soup.

BELLET
A.C. Red

Grape varieties
Braquet, Folle Noire, Cinsaut, supplemented (max. 40%) by Grenache Noir and local white varieties.
Production zone
Part of commune of Nice.
Characteristics
Fairly deep carmine-garnet color. Well developed animal, fruity, floral bouquet. Strong characteristic aromas. The wine is supple, smooth, and soft, with a good and typical measure of astringency. It ages well.
Serving temperature and suggested accompaniments
Serve at 57°F (14°C) with veal.

BELLET
A.C. White

Grape varieties
Rolle, Roussanne, Mayorquin. Secondary varieties (40%): Clairette, Bourboulenc, Chardonnay, Pignerol, Muscat à petit grain.
Production zone
Identical to area for red Bellet.
Characteristics
Light straw-yellow to golden color. Well developed mineral, fruity, floral bouquet; balanced dry taste. Very strong and persistent characteristic aromas. The wine is full, well blended, slightly astringent, and has good ageing properties.
Serving temperature and suggested accompaniments
Serve at 52°F (11°C) with lobster or ravioli.

VIN DE CORSE
Followed or not by local *appellation*: Patrimonio, Ajaccio, Sartène, Calvi, Cap-Corse, Figari Porto-Vecchio.
A.C. Red or Rosé

Grape varieties
Patrimonio zone: principal variety Nielluccio (min. 60% for reds and 40% for rosés), supplemented by Sciacarello, Grenache Noir, Vermentino, Ugni Blanc. Ajaccio zone: principal varieties Sciacarello (min. 40% for reds and 50% for rosés), Nielluccio, Barbarossa, Vermentino, supplemented by Grenache Noir, Cinsaut, Carignan (max. 10% for reds and 20% for rosés). Sartène, Calvi, Cap-Corse, Figari and Porto-Vecchio zones: principal varieties Nielluccio (min. 30%), Grenache Noir, supplemented (min. 50%) by Cinsaut, Mourvèdre, Barbarossa, Syrah, Carignan (max. 20%), Vermentino (max. 20%).
Production zone
67 communes or part of communes of Corisca.
Characteristics
Deep color, mainly carmine for reds. Well developed vegetable, mineral, fruity bouquet, the taste of the rosés balanced and dry. Strong characteristic aromas. The rosés are supple, the reds full-bodied, with good, typical astringency. They age well.
Serving temperature and suggested accompaniments
Serve rosés at 52°F (11°C) with broiled fish, the reds at 57°F (14°C) with mullet, rabbit, goat's cheese, etc.

CORSE
A.C. White

Grape varieties
Patrimonio: Vermentino (min. 60%), Ugni Blanc.
Ajaccio: Vermentino (min. 80%), Ugni Blanc.
Other zones: Vermentino (min. 75%), Ugni Blanc and Codivarta for Cap-Corse zone.
Production zone
Identical to *appellation* area for red Vin de Corse.
Characteristics
Fairly deep color, predominantly straw-yellow. Well developed vegetable, fruity, floral bouquet. Strong characteristic aromas. The wine is supple, well-blended and slightly astringent. It ages well.
Serving temperature and suggested accompaniments
Serve at 52°F (11°C) with broiled lobster, soups, and casseroles.

COTEAUX-D'AIX-EN PROVENCE and COTEAUX-DES-BAUX-DE-PROVENCE
A.C. Red and Rosé

Grape varieties
Cinsaut, Grenache, Mourvèdre, Syrah, Counoise, Cabernet Sauvignon (max. 60%), Carignan (max. 30%), Tibouren (max. 30%).
Production zone
Coteaux d'Aix-en-Provence: 48 communes of Bouches-du-Rhône and 2 communes of Var.
Coteaux d'Aix-en-Provence, Coteaux des Baux-de-Provence: communes of Baux-de-Provence, Fontvieille, Maussanne-les-Alpilles, Mouriès, Le Paradou, Saint-Étienne-du-Grès, Saint-Rémy-de-Provence.
Characteristics
Fairly deep color, the reds mainly carmine-garnet, the rosés clear pink. Well developed vegetable, animal, fruity bouquet. Strong characteristic aromas. The wines are supple, the reds full-bodied, the rosés light and soft. The reds are pleasantly astringent. Both types age well.
Serving temperature and suggested accompaniments
Serve rosés at 50°F (10°C). They go well with fennel salad, *aïoli, bouillabaisse* or bourride; *serve reds at 57°F (14°C) with broiled red meats.*

COTEAUX-DE-PIERREVERT
V.D.Q.S. White, Red, and Rosé

Grape varieties
Reds and rosés: Carignan, Cinsaut, Grenache, Mourvèdre, Oeillade, Petite Syrah, Terret Noir.

Whites: Clairette, Marsanne, Picpoul, Roussanne, Ugni Blanc.
Production zone
42 communes of Alpes-de-Haute-Provence.
Characteristics
Fairly deep color, the reds with a mainly carmine nuance, the rosés clear pink, the whites straw-yellow. Well developed vegetable, fruity, floral bouquet. Reasonably strong characteristic aromas. The whites and rosés are supple, the reds quite full, with normal ageing properties.
Serving temperature and suggested accompaniments
Serve whites and rosés at 50°F (10°C) with mixed salad or *pissaladière*; reds at 57°F (14°C) with braised veal.

CÔTES-DU-LUBERON
A.C. White, Red, and Rosé

Grape varieties
Reds and rosés: Grenache, Syrah, Mourvèdre, Cinsaut, Counoise, Carignan (max. 50%). Supplementary varieties (max 30%): Pinot Fin, Gamay, and local white grapes.
Whites: Clairette, Bourboulenc. Supplementary varieties: Grenache Blanc, Pascal Blanc, Roussanne, Ugni Blanc.
Production zone
31 communes of Vaucluse.
Characteristics
The color of the rosés is light, clear pink, that of the reds deep, mainly carmine-redcurrant, that of the whites straw-yellow. The fruity, floral bouquet is well developed, the taste of the whites and rosés balanced and dry, the characteristic aromas normal. The wines are supple and light, the rosés and whites quite soft, the reds typically astringent. They all age reasonably well.
Serving temperature and suggested accompaniments
Serve whites and rosés at 50°F (10°C) with artichokes, the reds at 57°F (14°C) with lamb shoulder.

CÔTES-DU-VIVARAIS
V.D.Q.S White, Red, and Rosé

Grape varieties
Reds and rosés: Cinsaut, Grenache, Mourvèdre, Picpoul, Syrah and (max. 40%) Aubun, Carignan (25% for *appellation* followed by name of *cru*).
Whites: Bourboulenc, Clairette, Grenache, Maccabeu, Mauzac, Picpoul, Ugni Blanc.
Production zone
Following communes or part of communes:
Côtes-du-Vivarais *appellation*:
Ardèche *département*: Bidon, Gras, Larnas, Labastide-de-Virac, Orgnac-l'Aven, Saint-Montan and Saint-Remèze, Vinezac, Lagorce.
Gard *département*: Saint-Privat-de-Champclos, Barjac, Le Garn, Montclus.
Côtes-du-Vivarais *appellation* followed by name of *cru*:
Orgnac: land bounded by communes of Orgnac, Bariac, Labastide-de-Virac, Le Garn, Monclus and Saint-Privat-de-Champclos.
Saint-Montan: land bounded by communes of Saint-Montan and Larnas.
Saint-Remèze: land bounded by communes of Saint-Remèze, Gras and Bidon.
Characteristics
Medium color, the reds mainly carmine, the rosés clear pink, the whites straw-yellow. Well developed fruity, flowery bouquet, balanced taste, the whites and rosés dry. Strong characteristic aromas. The wines are supple, well blended, and soft, the reds pleasantly astringent. They age normally.
Serving temperature and suggested accompaniments
Serve whites and rosés at 50°F (10°C) with cooked meats, the reds at 57°F (14°C) with broiled meats.

MUSCAT DE BEAUMES-DE-VENISE
Natural sweet wine
A.C. White

Grape varieties
Muscat à petit grain.
Production zone
Communes or part of communes of Beaumes-de-Venise and Aubignan (Vaucluse).
Characteristics
Light straw-yellow color; characteristic, very well developed bouquet of fruit and flowers; balanced taste with predominance of sugar. Very strong and persistent characteristic aromas. The wine is rich, fresh, and full-bodied, with good ageing qualities.
Serving temperature and suggested accompaniments
Serve at 50°F (10°C). It goes marvelously with pastries, puddings, and desserts of all kinds.

RASTEAU
Natural sweet wine
A.C. White, Red, and Rosé

Grape varieties
Grenache Noir, Gris or Blanc (90%). Supplementary varieties (10%) as authorized for Côtes-du-Rhône *appellation*.
Production zone
Communes or part of communes of Rasteau, Cairanne, Sablet (Vaucluse).
Characteristics
Deep color, the reds predominantly carmine, brick-red, the whites pale amber-yellow. Well developed vegetable, animal, mineral, floral bouquet, balanced taste with preponderance of sugar. Very strong and persistent characteristic aromas. The wines are full, well blended, and typically astringent. They possess excellent ageing properties.
Serving temperature and suggested accompaniments
Serve at 52°F (11°C) with a variety of cakes, pastries, and desserts.

COLLIOURE
A.C. Red

Grape varieties
Grenache Noir and, in proportion of between 25% and 40%, the following supplementary varieties: Carignan, Mourvèdre, Syrah, Cinsaut.
Production zone
Communes or part of communes of Banyuls, Cerbère, Collioure, Port-Vendres.

Characteristics
Deep color, mainly garnet to violet-red. Well developed fruity, floral bouquet. Strong characteristic aromas. The wine is full, well blended, and rich, with typical astringency. It ages well.
Serving temperature and suggested accompaniments
Serve at 57°F (14°C) with veal, game, etc.

FITOU
A.C. Red

Grape varieties
Principal varieties (min. 90%): Grenache, Lladoner Pelut, Carignan (max. 75%); supplementary varieties: Cinsaut, Maccabéo, Terret, Syrah.
Production zone
Communes or part of communes of Fitou, Coscatel, Caves-de-Treille, Lapalme, Leucate, Paziols, Treilles, Tuchan, Villeneuve-des-Corbières.
Characteristics
Deep color predominantly ruby-garnet. Well developed vegetable, mineral, fruity bouquet. Strong characteristic aromas. The wine is full-bodied with pleasantly typical astringency. It ages well.
Serving temperature and suggested accompaniments
Serve at 59°F (15°C) with poultry or meat.

CÔTES-DU-ROUSSILLON
A.C. Red and Rosé

Grape varieties
Principal varieties (70%): Cinsaut, Grenache, Lladoner Pelut, Carignan (max. 70%); supplementary varieties: Mourvèdre, Syrah, Maccabéo (max. 10%).
Production zone
118 communes.
Characteristics
Quite deep color, mainly carmine. Well developed vegetable, mineral, fruity bouquet. Strong characteristic aromas. The wine is full-bodied and typically astringent. It ages well.
Serving temperature and suggested accompaniments
Serve at 57°F (14°C) with artichokes and tuna.
The rosés are quite bright color, dry in taste. Serve them cool, at 52°F (11°C) with veal.
There is also a dry white wine, made principally from Maccabéo. Served cool at 50°F (10°C), it goes nicely with seafood.

CÔTES-DU-ROUSSILLON-VILLAGES (VILLAGES CARAMANY-VILLAGES LATOUR-DE-FRANCE)
A.C. Red

Grape varieties
Identical to those for Côtes-du-Roussillon *appellation*.
Production zone
Communes or part of communes of Baixas, Bélesta, Calce, Caramany, Cases-de-Pène, Cassagnes, Corneilla-la-Rivière, Espira-de-l'Agly, Estagel, Lansac, Latour-de-France, Lesquerde, Maury, Montner, Opoul, Perpignan, Peyrestortes, Planèzes, Rasiguères, Rivesaltes, Saint-Estève, Saint-Paul-de-Fenouillet, Salses, Tautevel, Vingrau.
Characteristics
Quite deep color, predominantly garnet-ruby. Well developed vegetable, mineral, fruity bouquet. Strong characteristic aromas. The wine is full and well blended, typically astringent, with good ageing properties.
Serving temperature and suggested accompaniments
Serve at 57°F (14°C) with meat.

CLAIRETTE DE BELLEGARDE
A.C. White

Grape varieties
Clairette.
Production zone
Part of commune of Bellegarde.
Characteristics
Light straw-yellow color. Well developed mineral, vegetable, fruity, flowery bouquet; balanced, dry taste. Strong characteristic aromas. The wine is full and light, with little astringency. It ages well.
Serving temperature and suggested accompaniments
Serve at 50°F (10°C) with fish and seafood.

CLAIRETTE DU LANGUEDOC
A.C. White

Grape varieties
Clairette.
Production zone
Following communes or part of communes in the *département* or Hérault: Adissan, Aspiran, Le Bosc, Cabrières, Ceyras, Fontès, Lieuran-Cabrières, Nizas, Paulhan, Peret, Saint-André-de-Sangonis.
Characteristics
Fairly deep straw-yellow to amber color. Well developed vegetable, mineral, fruity, floral bouquet; balanced, dry taste. Strong and persistent characteristic aromas. The wine is full, smooth, and soft, with slight astringency. It ages well.
Serving temperature and suggested accompaniments
Serve at 52°F (11°C) with duck or fish.
There is a Clairette du Languedoc liqueur wine, with 17° alcohol content and containing not more than 40 g sugar per liter. This should be served cool, at 48°F (9°C), as an aperitif.

CABRIÈRES
A.C. Red and Rosé

Grape varieties
Reds: Carignan Noir, Cinsaut Noir, Grenache Noir, Lladoner Pelut Noir, Mourvèdre, Syrah.
Rosés: Carignan Noir, Cinsaut Noir, Grenache Noir.
Production zone
Commune of Cabrières (Hérault).
Characteristics
Fairly deep carmine-pink color. Well developed fruity, floral bouquet; balanced, dry taste. Strong characteristic aromas. The wine is full and soft, slightly astringent, with normal ageing properties.

Serving temperature and suggested accompaniments
Serve at 52°F (11°C) with sweetbreads, etc.

COTEAUX-DU-LANGUEDOC

Accompanied or not by *appellations:* Cabrières, Coteaux-de-la-Méjanelle, Coteaux-de-Saint-Christol, Coteaux-de-Vérargues, Faugères, La Clape, Montpeyroux, Pic-Saint-Loup, Quatourze, Saint-Chinian, Saint-Drézery, Saint-Georges-d'Orques, Saint-Saturnin
A.C. Red and Rosé

Grape varieties
Carignan (max. 50%), Cinsaut, Counoise, Grenache Noir, Grenache Rouge, Syrah, Mourvèdre, Carignan Blanc, Clairette, Listan, Maccabéo, Muscats, Picpouls, Plant Droit, Roussanne, Terret Gris, Ugni Blanc.
Production zone
For the Coteaux-du-Languedoc *appellation*, 100 or so communes or Hérault, 5 communes of Aude and 2 communes of Gard.
Characteristics
Medium color, mainly carmine, with touch of garnet. Fairly strong vegetable, fruity bouquet and characteristic aromas. The wine is full, light, and well blended, with a pleasantly typical astringency and normal ageing properties.
Serving temperature and suggested accompaniments
Serve at 57°F (14°C) with stews and pâtes.

COTEAUX-DE-SAINT-CHRISTOL

A.C. Red and Rosé

Grape varieties
Carignan (30%–50%–), Cinsaut (15%–30%), Grenache (10%–25%), Aramon (max. 20%).
Production zone
Part of commune of Saint-Christol.
Characteristics
Similar to those of other wines of this zone.
Serving temperature and suggested accompaniments
Serve at 57°F (14°C) with broiled meats, etc.

COTEAUX-DE-VÉRARGUES

A.C. Red and Rosé

Grape varieties
Carignan (30%–50%), Cinsaut (15%–30%), Grenache (10%–25%), Aramon (max. 15%).
Production zone
Communes or part of communes of Beaulieu, Boisseron, Lunel, Lunel-Viel, Restinclières, Saint-Geniès-des-Mourgues, Saint-Seriès, Saturargues, Vérargues.
Characteristics
Similar to those of other wines of this zone.
Serving temperature and suggested accompaniments
Serve at 57°F (14°C) with meat.

FAUGÈRES

A.C. Red

Grape varieties
Grenache Noir, Carignan Noir, Cinsaut Noir, Mourvèdre, Syrah.
Production zone
Communes or part of communes of Cabrerolles, Caussiniojouls, Faugères, Fos, Laurens, Roquessels, Autignac.
Characteristics
Deep color, mainly garnet to violet-red. Well developed vegetable, animal, fruity bouquet and strong characteristic aromas. The wine is full and well blended, with a good measure of typical astringency. It ages well.
Serving temperature and suggested accompaniments
Serve at 57°F (14°C) with veal and other meats.

LA CLAPE

A.C. White, Red, and Rosé

Grape varieties
Red and rosé: either Carignan on its own, or two thirds Carignan supplemented by Terret, Grenache, Picpoul, and Malvoisie. White: Clairette, Terret, Grenache, Picpoul, Malvoisie.
Production zone
Communes or part of communes of Narbonne, Armissan, Fleury d'Aude, Salles-d'Aude, Vinassan.
Characteristics
The color is deep, mainly carmine for the reds and straw-yellow for the whites. The mineral, fruity, floral bouquet is well developed, especially for the whites, which are dry. Strong and persistent characteristic aromas. The wines are full, soft, and well blended, the reds pleasantly astringent. The reds age normally, the whites excellently.
Serving temperature and suggested accompaniments
Serve reds at 57°F (14°C) with broiled dishes, and whites at 52°F (11°C) with fish, soups, or cheese dishes.

QUATOURZE

A.C. White, Red, and Rosé

Production zone
Part of commune of Narbonne (Quatourze).
Characteristics
Similar to those of other wines of this zone.
Serving temperature and suggested accompaniments
Serve at 57°F (14°C) with paella.

SAINT-CHINIAN

A.C. Red

Grape varieties
Grenache, Carignan, Cinsaut.
Production zone
Communes or part of communes of Assignan, Babeau-Bouldoux, Berlou, Causses-et-Veyran, Cazedarnes, Cébazan, Cessenon, Cruzy, Pierrerue, Prades-sur-Vernazobre, Quarante, Roquebrun, Saint-Chinian, Saint-Nazaire-de-Ladarez, Villepassans, Creissan, Murviel-lès-Béziers, Puisserguier.
Characteristics
Deep color, mainly garnet to violet red. Well developed vegetable, animal, mineral bouquet. Strong characteristic aromas. The wine is full-bodied and gently astringent. It ages well.
Serving temperature and suggested accompaniments
Serve at 57°F (14°C) with chicken.

SAINT-DRÉZERY
A.C. Red

Grape varieties
Carignan, Cinsaut, Grenache, Aramon (max. 15%).
Production zone
Commune of Saint-Drézery.
Characteristics
Similar to those of other wines of this zone.
Serving temperature and suggested accompaniments
Serve at 57°F (14°C) with beef.

SAINT-GEORGES-D'ORQUES
A.C. Red

Grape varieties
Cinsaut (min. 33%), Carignan (max. 50%), Grenache (10%–40%), Aspiran Noir and various others (max. 5%).
Production zone
Communes or part of communes of Saint-Georges-d'Orques, Murviel-lès-Montpellier, Juvignac, Lavérune, Pignan.
Characteristics
Similar to those of other wines of this zone.
Serving temperature and suggested accompaniments
Serve at 57°F (14°C) with steak.

SAINT-SATURNIN (and MONTPEYROUX)
A.C. Red and Rosé

Grape varieties
Carignan (max. 50%), Grenache, Syrah, Mourvèdre, Cinsaut.
Production zone
Saint-Saturnin *appellation:* Saint-Saturnin, Jonquières, Saint-Guiraud, Arboras. Montpeyroux *appellation:* Montpeyroux.
Characteristics
Similar to those of other wines of this zone.
Serving temperature and suggested accompaniments
Serve at 57°F (14°C) with beef.

PIC-SAINT-LOUP
A.C. White, Red, and Rosé

Grape varieties
White: Clairette, Grenache Blanc, Maccabéo.
Red and rosé: Carignan, Oeillade, Alicante.
Production zone
Communes or part of communes of Claret, Cazevieille, Corconne, Fontanes, Lauret, Saint-Jean-de-Cuculles, Saint-Mathieu-de-Tréviers, Sauteyrargues, Valflaunès, Les Matelles, Le Triadou, Sainte-Croix-de-Quintillargues, Saint-Gély-du-Fesc.
Characteristics
Similar to those of other wines of this zone.
Serving temperature and suggested accompaniments
Serve whites at 52°F (11°C) with fish, reds at 57°F (14°C) with hotpot.

COSTIÈRES-DU-GARD
A.C. White, Red, and Rosé

Grape varieties
Red: Terret Noir, Carignan (max. 50%), Aspiran, Cinsaut, Mourvèdre, Grenache, Syrah, Oeillade, Counoise.
White: Clairette, Grenache Blanc, Maccabéo, Malvoisie, Marsanne, Muscat Blanc, Picpoul, Roussanne, Terret, Ugni Blanc.
Production zone
Gard *département:* Aubord, Beauvoisin, Beaucaire, Bellegarde, Bernis, bezouce, Bouillargues, Le Cailar, Caissargues, Comps, Garons, Générac, Jonquières, Lédenon, Manduel, Milhaud, Meynes, Nîmes, Redessan, Saint-Gilles, Sernhac, Uchaud, Vauvert, Vestric.
Hérault *département:* Mauguio, Montpellier.
Characteristics
Fairly deep color, the reds mainly carmine-redcurrant, the whites pale yellow, the rosés light pink. The vegetable, fruity bouquet is well developed, the taste is balanced, the whites and rosés being dry. Strong characteristic aromas. The wines are supple and quite full, depending on their origins, the reds slightly astringent. They age normally.
Serving temperature and suggested accompaniments
Serve the wines cool, the reds with poultry or broiled meat, the rosés with cold meats and asparagus, the whites with fish.

COTEAUX-DE-LA-MÉJANELLE
A.C. White, Red, and Rosé

Grape varieties
Similar to those of Costières-du-Gard.
Production zone
Following communes or part of communes in Hérault *département:* Mauguio, Montpellier, Castelnau-le-Lez, Saint-Aunès.

CÔTES-DU-CABARDÈS-ET-DE-L'ORBIEL (CABARDÈS)
V.D.Q.S. Red and Rosé

Grape varieties
Carignan (30%), Cinsaut, Cot, Counoise, Fer, Grenache Noir, Mourvèdre, Picpoul Noir, Syrah, Terret, Cabernet Sauvignon.
Production zone
Following communes or part of communes in Aude *département:* Aragon, Conques-sur-Orbiel, Fournes-Cabardès, Fraisse-Cabardès, Villanière, Villardonnel, Villedubert, Villegailhenc, Villemoustaussou.
Characteristics
Similar to those of other wines of this zone.
Serving temperature and suggested accompaniments
Serve reds at 57°F (14°C) with pork cutlets, the rosés at 52°F (11°C) with eggplants.

CÔTES-DE-LA-MALEPÈRE
V.D.Q.S. Red and Rosé

Grape varieties
Reds: principal varieties (max. 60%): Merlot, Cot, Cinsaut. Supplementary varieties: Cabernet Sauvignon, Cabernet

Franc, Grenache, Lladoner Pelut, Syrah.
Rosés: Principal varieties: Cinsaut, Lladoner Pelut, Grenache. Supplementary varieties: Merlot, Cabernets, Syrah.
Production zone
31 communes.
Characteristics
Similar to those of other wines of this zone.
Serving temperature and suggested accompaniments
Serve reds at 57°F (14°C) with veal, rosés at 50°F (10°C) with omelets.

MINERVOIS

A.C. White, Red, and Rosé

Grape varieties
Reds (in proportion of 90%): Carignan, Grenache, Terret, Picpoul, Cinsaut, Aspiran, Alicante, Lladoner Pelut, Mourvèdre, Syrah.
Whites: Grenache Blanc, Malvoisie, Maccabéo, Muscat, Picpoul, Clairette, Teret Blanc, Listan.
The rosé wines are made from all these varieties.
Production zone
61 communes (45 in Aude and 16 in Hérault).
Characteristics
Quite deep carmine-garnet color. Well developed vegetable, mineral, fruity bouquet. Strong characteristic aromas. The wine is smooth and full-bodied, with good typical astringency. It ages well.
Serving temperature and suggested accompaniments
Serve reds at 57°F (14°C) with snails, eggplants, and veal, rosés at 50°F (10°C) with onion dishes.

PICPOUL DE PINET

A.C. White

Grape varieties
Picpoul (max. 70%), Terret Blanc (max. 25%), Clairette (max. 5%).
Production zone
Communes or part of communes of Pinet, Mèze, Florensac, Castelnau-de-Guers, Montagnac, Pomerols.
Characteristics
Fairly deep color, straw-yellow to amber. Well developed vegetable, fruity, floral bouquet; balanced, dry taste. Strong characteristic aromas. The wine is supple, rich, and light, with little astringency, and ages well.
Serving temperature and suggested accompaniments
Serve at 50°F (10°C) with *bouillabaisse* and other fish soups.

CORBIÈRES

A.C. White, Red, and Rosé

Grape varieties
Reds (max. 90%): Carignan, Grenache, Teret, Picpoul, Cinsaut, Lladnoner Pelut, Mourvèdre, Syrah.
Whites: Grenache Blanc, Malvoisie, Maccabéo, Muscat, Picpoul, Clairette, Terret Blanc.
Rosés: all the above-mentioned varieties.
Production zone
92 communes.
Characteristics
The color is fairly deep, predominantly violet-red, garnet, and redcurrant. Well developed vegetable, mineral, fruity bouquet. Strong characteristic aromas. The wine is full and velvety, with good typical astringency. It ages well.
Serving temperature and suggested accompaniments
Serve at 57°F (14°C) with mutton and other meat dishes.
The rosés are dry but full and agreeable. They should be served cool at 50°F (10°C) with tripe or cooked meats. The whites, too, are to be served cool as an aperitif or with seafood.

BANYULS

A.C. Red – natural sweet wine

Grape varieties
Grenaches Gris, Noir and Blanc, Maccabéo, Toiurbat, Muscat Blanc à petits grains, Muscat Romain, Muscat d'Alexandrie, of which min. 50% is Grenache Noir, and min. 10% of the following supplementary varieties: Carignan, Syrah, Cinsaut.
Production zone
Banyuls, Cerbère, Port-Vendres, Collioure.
Characteristics
Deep garnet color. Very well developed floral bouquet, with touch of mineral; balanced taste, with preponderance of sugar. Very strong and persistent characteristic aromas. The wine is full-bodied, well blended, with a pleasantly typical astringency. It has very good ageing properties.
Serving temperature and suggested accompaniments
Serve at 57°F (14°C) with crayfish or walnut pie.

BANYULS

A.C. White – natural sweet wine

Grape varieties
Identical to those of the red Banyuls *appellation*.
Production zone
The same as for red Banyuls.
Characteristics
Deep amber-yellow color. Very well developed fruity, floral bouquet; balanced taste, with preponderance of sugar. Strong and persistent characteristic aromas. The wine is full, well blended, and slightly astringent. It ages very well.
Serving temperature and suggested accompaniments
Served at 54°F (12°C), the wine goes very nicely with blue cheeses and cakes.

BANYULS-RANCIO

A.C. White, Red and Rosé – natural sweet wine

Grape varieties
Same production conditions as for Banyuls. Because of their age, however, and their having been matured in wood, they have a distinctive flavor and a marvelous aroma.

BANYULS GRAND CRU

A.C. Red – natural sweet wine

Grape varieties
Identical to those used for Banyuls, but there should be a minimum proportion of 75% Grenache Noir.
Production zone
Identical to that of Banyuls.
Characteristics
Deep color, predominantly garnet, brick-red, amber. Well developed mineral, fruity, floral bouquet; balanced taste, with preponderance of sugar, less pronounced for the dry wines which contain less than 54 g sugar per liter. Very strong and persistent characteristic aromas. The wine is full-bodied, well blended, with good typical astringency. It has excellent ageing qualities.
Serving temperature and suggested accompaniments
Considering its special quality, this wine should be served at 57°F (14°C) at the end of the meal, to accompany cigars, if required.

FRONTIGNAN (or MUSCAT DE FRONTIGNAN, VIN DE FRONTIGNAN)

A.C. White – natural sweet wine

Grape varieties
Muscat Doré de Frontignan.
Production zone
Communes or part of communes of Frontignan, Vic-la-Gardiole.
Characteristics
Deep amber-yellow color, very well developed fruity, floral bouquet, balanced taste with preponderance of sugar. Very strong and persistent characteristic aromas. The wine is rich and full-bodied, with good ageing properties.
Serving temperature and suggested accompaniments
Serve at 54°F (12°C) with various cakes and desserts.

FRONTIGNAN (or MUSCAT DE FRONTIGNAN, VIN DE FRONTIGNAN)

A.C. White – liqueur wine

Grape varieties
Muscat Doré de Frontignan.
Production zone
Identical to that of Frontignan.
Characteristics
Light straw-yellow to amber color, well developed fruity, floral bouquet, balanced taste with preponderance of sugar. Strong characteristic aromas. The wine is full, with good ageing qualities.
Serving temperature and suggested accompaniments
Serve at 57°F (14°C) with desserts.

MAURY

A.C. Red – natural sweet wine

Grape varieties
Grenache Noir (min. 50%), Grenache Gris, Grenache Blanc, Muscat à petits grains, Muscat d'Alexandrie, Maccabéo, Toubat; supplementary varieties (10%): Carignan, Cinsaut, Syrah, Listan.
Production zone
Communes or part of communes of Maury, Tautavel, Saint-Paul-de-Fenouillet, Rasiguères, Lesquerde.
Characteristics
Deep garnet-amber color. Well developed mineral, fruity bouquet, balanced taste with preponderance of sugar. Strong and persistent characteristic aromas. The wine is full, well blended, and smooth, with typical astringency. It ages well.
Serving temperature and suggested accompaniments
Serve at 55°F (13°C) with cherry tart, cakes, and other desserts.

MAURY

A.C. White or Rosé – natural sweet wine

Production conditions are identical to those for red Maury.

MUSCAT DE MIREVAL

A.C. White – natural sweet wine

Grape varieties
Muscat à petits grains.
Production zone
Communes or part of communes of Mireval, Vic-la-Gardiole.
Characteristics
Light amber-yellow color, well developed fruity, floral bouquet, balanced taste with preponderance of sugar. Strong, persistent characteristic aromas. The wine is full and well blended, with good ageing qualities.
Serving temperature and suggested accompaniments
Serve at 50°F (10°C) with a sweet omelet.

MUSCAT DE LUNEL

A.C. White – natural sweet wine

Grape varieties
Muscat à petits grains.
Production zone
Communes or part of communes of Lunel, Lunel-Viel, Vérargues, Saturargues.
Characteristics
Medium amber-yellow color, well developed fruity, flowery bouquet, balanced taste with predominance of sugar. Strong and persistent characteristic aromas. The wine is full and well blended. It ages well.
Serving temperature and suggested accompaniments
Serve at 50°F (10°C) with various desserts.

MUSCAT DE RIVESALTES

A.C. White – natural sweet wine

Grape varieties
Muscat à petits grains, Muscat d'Alexandrie.
Production zone
Communes or part of communes of the Rivesaltes, Banyuls, and Maury *appellation* areas.
Characteristics
Medium amber-yellow color, well developed fruity, flowery bouquet, balanced taste with preponderance of sugar. Very strong and persistent characteristic aromas. The wine is full, well blended, and slightly astringent. It ages well.

Serving temperature and suggested accompaniments
Serve at 50°F (10°C) with crêpes and other desserts.

MUSCAT DE SAINT-JEAN-DE-MINERVOIS

A.C. White – natural sweet wine

Grape varieties
Muscat Doré de Frontignan.
Production zone
Commune of Saint-Jean-de-Minervois.
Characteristics
Medium golden-yellow color, with touch of amber. Very well developed fruity, floral bouquet, balanced taste with preponderance of sugar. Strong and persistent characteristic aromas. The wine is full-bodied, rich, and slightly astringent. It ages well.
Serving temperature and suggested accompaniments
Serve at 50°F (10°C) with fruit tarts, cakes, etc.

RIVESALTES

A.C. White, Red, and Rosé – natural sweet wine

Grape varieties
Muscat Blanc à petits grains, Muscat d'Alexandrie, Grenache Gris, Grenache Noir, Grenache Blanc, Maccabéo, Tourbat and max. 10% of Carignan, Cinsault, Syrah, Listan.
Production zone
86 communes of Pyrénées-Orientales and 9 communes of Aude.
Characteristics
Light to medium color, the reds garnet to brick-red, the whites golden-yellow, slightly amber. Well developed vegetable, mineral, fruity bouquet; balanced taste with preponderance of sugar. Strong characteristic aromas. The wines are full and smooth with a good measure of typical astringency. They have good ageing properties.
Serving temperature and suggested accompaniments
Serve at 50°F (10°C) with various cakes and desserts.

Village of Itterswiller (Alsace).

Bain-marie. Receptacle containing boiling water in which a smaller receptacle (such as a heatproof dish) is placed to cook gently or reheat by indirect heat.

Bard. To wrap a lean cut of meat with leaves or thin slices of barding fat, usually pork back fat taken from the layer next to the skin, tied in place with trussing thread or fine kitchen string. The meat is basted by the pork fat which melts very slowly as it is roasted or cooked over high heat.

Béchamel sauce. To serve 6: 3 tbsp butter; 1/2 cup all-purpose flour; 1 cup cold milk mixed with 1 cup cold water; 1/2 tsp fine salt; freshly ground white pepper to taste. Melt the butter gently over low heat in a saucepan then stir in the flour, making sure there are no lumps and the mixture is smooth. Continue stirring until the mixture bubbles and froths. Do not allow to color. Gradually stir in three quarters of the milk and water mixture; increase the heat, stirring continuously as the sauce slowly heats to boiling point. When it has started to thicken, add the remaining milk and water and stir well. Add the salt and pepper and continue stirring as the sauce returns to a boil and cook until it has become velvety and has thickened to the desired consistency.

Beurre manié. Paste made of equal amounts of butter and all-purpose flour used to thicken liquids. A small quantity of solid butter at room temperatures is kneaded or beaten as flour is added; the resulting *beurre manié* can be chilled or added at room temperature to a hot liquid that is to be thickened and stirred continuously. As the solid butter is stirred into the hot liquid it melts, the flour is gradually released, and the liquid thickens without the formation of lumps.

Blanch. To plunge raw food (vegetables, meat etc.) into boiling water for a brief period varying from a few seconds to several minutes. This may be done for a variety of reasons, e.g. to tenderize; to eliminate unpleasant smells or excessively strong tastes; to seal; to loosen skin prior to peeling (as in tomatoes or peaches). The food is then drained and refreshed by rinsing under running cold water or plunging it into cold water.

Bouquet garni. Can be bought ready-made in the form of little cheesecloth bags with a long string attached for easy removal containing a mixture of herbs (most commonly bay leaf, thyme, and parsley) but it is much better and cheaper to make your own. Tie the bay leaf and/or sprigs of fresh herbs as specified for the various recipes and depending on what is in season, into a little bundle with thread or place them in the center of a small piece of cheesecloth and gather up the edges to enclose the contents and tie this little bag securely. The term *bouquet garni* can also mean any small bundle or bag of ingredients added to flavour the dish as it cooks and may include such items as celery etc. The *bouquet garni* is always removed before the dish is served.

Broth. This is most frequently made with beef, veal or chicken (fish broth or *fumet* is dealt with as a separate entry). These broths come under the general heading of *fonds de cuisine* in French cookery, the basic flavored liquids used in all sorts of dishes and sauces etc. Make your own broth whenever possible as this makes all the difference to the finished dish. For a light chicken or veal broth, roughly equal proportions of fresh, raw bones and meat are placed in a saucepan with enough cold water to come 1–1 1/2 in above them and heated gently to simmering point (do not allow to go beyond the gentlest boil). Keep removing the scum that collects on the surface as it forms until no more rises. Then add flavorings that may vary but usually include carrots, onions, celery, and a bouquet garni of 1 bay leaf, some parsley sprigs, a sprig of fresh thyme tied in a cheesecloth bag, and a little salt. Bring the liquid up to a very gentle simmer, and leave partly covered (so that the steam can escape) to barely bubble for at least 1 hour, and preferably much longer. Strain the broth into a wide bowl and leave to cool. Chill in the refrigerator so that the surface fat solidifies and is easy to remove. Broth can be successfully deep-frozen. Do not keep broth in the refrigerator for more than 2–3 days to prevent harmful bacteria multiplying.

For a dark, full-flavored beef or veal broth brown the bones, meat, and vegetables in a roasting pan in a very hot oven for about 30 minutes, turning frequently so that they will brown evenly but not burn. Drain off the fat and deglaze (*q.v.*) the roasting pan with about 1 cup water. Follow the method given above, with the bouquet garni being simmered with the other ingredients.

Chimney. A small hole cut in a pie crust, at the highest point of the pastry lid, or at its center, to enable steam to escape as the pie filling cooks. A cylinder of foil can be placed in the hole to keep the airway free. Ceramic pie chimneys are also used for the purpose and to provide extra support for the pie lid and stop it sinking; they are positioned in the center of the pie dish before the pastry lid is placed over its contents.

Chinois. A conical sieve. A useful utensil when straining liquids as they are directed in a thin stream into the waiting receptacle below.

Choux pastry dough. To serve 8: 6 tbsp (scant 1/2 cup or 3/4 stick) butter; 1 1/4 cups water; 3 tbsp superfine sugar; 1 tsp fine salt; 1 3/4 cups all-purpose flour; 8 eggs. Place the water, butter, salt, and sugar in a medium-sized heavy-bottomed saucepan. Bring to a boil and when the mixture bubbles up toward the top of the pan, add all the flour at once and immediately stir vigorously into the liquid and continue stirring fast over low heat to make the dough smooth. When it comes away cleanly from the sides of the pan, remove from the heat and break the first egg into it; beat the egg very thoroughly into the dough, then add the next one and so on until all the eggs have been added. Blending each egg in well is important. At this stage the dough should be very smooth and glossy, supple yet holding its shape. Leave to stand for 15 minutes before using.

Cep (*Boletus edulis*). These mushrooms are often called by their French name of *cèpes* or their Italian name, *porcini*. Their old English name is Penny Bun mushrooms which describes their appearance when fresh: rounded, and a rich, baked brown. They grow wild and are gathered as a free, delicious food; they fetch a good price at local markets and in greengrocers in towns and cities throughout France and Italy. They are sliced and dried for export, retaining most of their delicious, pronounced flavor and should be soaked in warm water for about 20 minutes then drained before use. Sometimes dried ceps have a little harmless grit left on them. Choose packets of ceps that are pale beige in color and still pliable; if they are dark brown, hard and woody this could mean that they have been stored too long. Most packets have a date stamp showing a sell by date to prevent this happening. They are quite expensive but they expand considerably when soaked and a small packet goes a long way.

Court-bouillon. An aromatic broth used for gentle boiling and poaching. Most frequently used in fish and in vegetable cookery. To make, allow the following ingredients and quantities for each quart of water used: 1/2 cup best-quality white wine vinegar; 1 cup dry white wine; 2 tsp coarse sea salt; 1 sprig parsley; 1 sprig thyme; 1 bay leaf; 1 medium-sized carrot and onion, peeled; 1 clove garlic, peeled. Mix all these ingredients with the water in a large saucepan or fish kettle. Bring to a boil and then simmer for 1 hour. Allow to cool to lukewarm or cold before adding the food to be boiled or poached.

Crème Chantilly. Sweetened whipped cream. To make just over 2 cups *crème Chantilly*, stir 1/4 cup sifted confectioner's icing sugar into 1 cup heavy cream in the bowl in which it is to be beaten and chill for 1 hour in the refrigerator. Chill the balloon whisk or beater. Whip the cream at medium speed in an electric mixer, a hand-held electric beater or a balloon whisk, flavoring it with a little pure vanilla extract to taste, if wished. Once the cream forms soft peaks, slow down the speed to avoid overbeating. Stop as soon as it is stiff and light.

Crème fraîche. The literal translation, "fresh cream" is misleading since the cream is matured by natural ferments and lactic acids until a barely acidulated, faintly nutty flavor develops. *Crème fraîche* is invaluable for adding a velvety smoothness and body to sauces, soups etc.; ordinary cream will tend to thin when heated and boiled and in some cases may curdle whereas *crème fraîche* adds a very agreeable texture and flavor. Some cheese shops and enterprising delicatessens stock *crème fraîche* in summer but it is easy to make your own. One method of making it yourself is to mix 1 cup heavy cream (unpasteurized if possible) very thoroughly with 1 tbsp cultured buttermilk in a small mixing bowl, then cover the bowl with Saran wrap and leave to stand for several hours at room temperature (or leave overnight). After this time the cream will have become much thicker. Refrigerate for several hours to thicken further (still tightly covered). This cream will keep for 2–3 days. If you need a larger quantity, simply double the measurements of cream and buttermilk. Another method is to mix 1 1/4 cups heavy cream with 1 tbsp sour cream in a bowl over hot water and heat very gently to lukewarm (keep below 85°F). Allow to cool slowly in the bowl, loosely covered with aluminum foil or a plate and then leave to stand in a warm room (70–75°F is ideal) for about 8 hours or longer, until it has thickened. Stir, cover with Saran wrap, and refrigerate. It will keep for several days.

Crème patissière (also called **confectioner's cream** or **pastry cream)** To serve 6, you will need: 2 cups milk; 1/2 cup sugar; 1/2 vanilla bean or 1 tsp pure vanilla extract; 3 eggs; 1/4 cup/30 g/1 oz all-purpose/plain flour. Bring the milk slowly to a gentle simmer with the sugar and slit the vanilla bean over a gentle heat; take care it does not boil over (use a heat diffuser pad or ring if wished). Break one egg into a mixing bowl and beat in the flour with a balloon whisk, hand-held electric beater or wooden spoon until no lumps remain. Beat in the remaining eggs one at a time, then continue beating as you add the boiling milk in a thin stream. Strain through a very fine sieve into a saucepan and heat gently while stirring all the time over a low heat until the mixture thickens. Pour into a cold bowl and leave to cool. A skin will form unless you coat the surface with 1 tbsp melted butter, or you may prefer to whisk the pastry cream at frequent intervals as it cools.

Deglaze. To add liquid such as water, broth, wine or liquor to a cooking receptacle after removing the main ingredient, usually meat, that has been browned or roasted in it. The liquid blends with the flavorsome solidified cooking deposits and thickened juices, loosening and dissolving them by scraping and stirring with a wooden spoon.

Fish fumet or **fish broth.** To make 1 quart 2-2¼ lb fresh, raw white (non-oily) fish trimmings; 1 small bunch parsley; 6 small to medium-sized onions, peeled; 10 oz cultivated button mushrooms; juice of 1 lemon; 1 heaping tbsp coarse sea salt; 20 peppercorns; 1 quart dry white wine; 1 quart water. Rinse the fish trimmings well and wash the parsley; wipe the mushrooms with a damp cloth. Place all the ingredients in a large saucepan and bring slowly to a boil. Boil gently for 1½ hours. Strain through a conical sieve (a *chinois*, *q.v.*) into a clean saucepan and reserve. Bring to a boil again, uncovered, and continue cooking to reduce the volume to 1 quart.

Julienne. Vegetables cut into very thin slices; most frequently applied to julienne strips for which vegetables (e.g. carrots, cucumbers etc.) are cut into ⅛ in slices and these are then cut in turn into matchstick strips ⅛ in thick and of varying lengths but often about 1½–2½ in long. A vegetable *julienne* sweated in butter until tender, is often used as a garnish.

Larding. Strips of chilled larding fat (lardons) are inserted into a larding needle and threaded through the flesh of lean meats or fish to baste them and prevent them becoming dry as they cook. This straightforward but time-consuming process also has a decorative effect when the meat or fish is sliced. Pork belly fat or fat bacon is used most often when basting is the main aim as it melts easily but other meats are used sometimes to add flavor and for decorative effect. If you do not have a larding needle or want to lard meat or fish quickly, make incisions in the meat or fish and insert shorter, wider strips of pork belly fat or fat bacon, with or without seasoning and herbs. When added to stews, casseroles and other dishes the lardons are usually thicker and shorter, cut at right angles (slicing across the strips of fat and lean, not lengthwise in the same direction as the strips). Use smoked bacon provided you blanch the strips in plenty of simmering water for about 10 minutes, then drain, refresh by rinsing under running cold water, and dry well. This will come close to the taste of the French *lard de poitrine frais* (fresh, unsalted, and unsmoked bacon).

Luting paste. A thick flour and water paste which is applied to seal the lid onto an earthenware casserole dish and hardens as it heats in a very gentle oven, making sure that no steam or flavors can escape through the join as the contents simmer for a long time, sometimes for many hours (as in slow-cooked tripe and stews).

Moule à manqué. A round, 2-in deep cake pan about 7 in in diameter across the bottom, with sloping sides widening to a diameter of about 9 in from rim to rim. Once baked, the cake is turned out and the shape is reversed, the sides sloping outward from the top.

Mouli-légumes or **vegetable mill.** A medium- or large-sized vegetable mill is not expensive and very useful for puréeing vegetables and soft mixtures, soups, etc. Usually made of stainless steel but also available in plastic with interchangeable steel perforated plates of varying gauges. Often preferable to using a food processor as the texture is more easily controlled and starchy foods are not at risk of being overprocessed.

Pâte sablée. This is a very friable, melting sweet dough, ideal for tarts and sweet flans and for the plain cookies known as *sablés*; it differs somewhat from *pâte sucrée*, another sweet pastry which is often made with a mixture of finely chopped nuts and sugar. Many pastrycooks like to make their pâte sablée with confectioner's sugar when using it to make pie shells. This is a straightforward version, and will yield 14 oz cookies. You will need: 1 egg; ½ cup superfine sugar; 1¾ cups all-purpose flour; ½ cup butter; pinch salt. Mix the egg, salt, and sugar together in a mixing bowl with a wooden spoon; beat until the mixture becomes pale and runny. Sift in the flour and stir well with the wooden spoon. Taking a handful of the mixture at a time, rub it between your hands so that it breaks up into a fine "sandy" looking consistency (in French this process is called *sabler*); alternatively you can use the "*fraisage*" technique described for the basic pie dough. When you have worked through the whole of the mixture in this way, dust a pastry board lightly with flour and turn the mixture onto it. Place the piece of butter on top and gradually work the sandy mixture into it. Knead lightly and when the mixture is homogenous, roll out into a sheet which will vary in thickness from just under ⅛ in to just over ⅛ in, depending on your requirement. Handle carefully as this is not at all elastic and it will break up very easily.

Pie dough (*pâte brisée*). To serve 6: 1¾ cups all purpose flour; generous ½ cup butter at room temperature; ½ cup fl.oz cold water; 1 tsp fine salt. Sift the flour into a mixing bowl. Add the butter, cut into fairly small pieces. Rub the butter roughly into the flour with the tips of your fingers (or "cut in" with a pastry cutting-in utensil), working quickly to avoid warming the butter. Heap this mixture up in a mound, make a well in the center about 4 in in diameter; stir the salt and water until the salt has dissolved and pour into the well. Stir the water and salt into the flour, gradually working outward (use your cupped hand or a wooden spoon) with a spiral motion toward the outer edge of the mound. Knead by crushing a little of the dough at a time under the palm of your hand, smearing it across the working surface (this is known as *fraisage*); shape into a rough ball and knead very lightly until smooth. Do not overwork it. Wrap in a clean cloth or in waxed paper and leave to rest and chill at least 30 minutes in the refrigerator. Alternatively, make the pie dough in an electric mixer with a dough hook or in a food processor, following the method given in the instruction booklet. Or use thawed frozen pie dough pastry.

Poaching. Gentle cooking in a liquid which partly or wholly covers the food to be cooked, without allowing the cooking liquid to boil.

Puff pastry. To serve 6: 4½ cups all-purpose flour; 1½ cups butter; 2 tsp fine salt; 1 cup cold water. Heap the flour up in a mound on a pastry board or slab or in a mixing bowl, make a well in the center, and in it place the salt and half the water. Gradually stir the water into the flour with a wooden spoon. Add the remaining water and knead the pastry; it shouild be the same consistency as butter, firm but easily cut with a knife. Shape into a ball and leave to rest for 10 minutes. Flatten the dough on the pastry board or working surface into a disk just over ½ in thick with the palms of your hands; cut the butter into small pieces on top of each other if necessary to leave a wide margin free round the edges of the dough. Moisten the outermost ¾ in of the surface of the dough and then gather the edges together, bringing them gently up and over the butter to form a sort of gathered purse or bag, starting in the center; it is important that the butter does not break through the pastry. Roll out into a rectangular piece about 3 times as long as it is wide and ⅜ in thick. Fold one third of the length to come halfway up the remaining two thirds of the length (giving you a double thickness on the portion) and then fold the remaining uncovered third over on top, giving a three-layered piece of dough. Turn, or rotate this piece of pastry through 90 degrees, so that you start to roll it out again with the rolling pin parallel to the edges and at right angles to the folds. Each time you repeat this process of rolling out, folding and turning, it counts as one "turn." Repeat the operation, or turn, and leave the pastry to rest for 20 minutes. Carry out 4 more turns, resting the pastry for 20 minutes after the second turn. This sounds complicated but is easily mastered with practice; consult a step-by-step illustrated pastry method if you are in any doubt or buy deep frozen puff pastry and thaw thoroughly before using.

Quatre épices. Literally translated this means "four-spices" and that is just what this powder is. The composition may vary but pepper always predominates. The best way of making your own is to buy the spices from a reputable shop that has a fast turnover so they will be fresh and full of flavor and grind them yourself into a fine powder in an electric coffee grinder. Use 7 parts of white or black peppercorns or dried allspice berries to 1 part each nutmeg, cloves, and cinammon. This mixture will be suitable for the recipes under which it is listed in this book. The composition of *quatre épices* can vary and can include, for example, 4½ oz white peppercorns, ½ oz cloves, 1 oz ginger, and 1¼ oz nutmeg.

Sauteuse. Deep skillets with very long brass or stainless steel handles. The best, made of very heavy-gauge copper lined with tin, are expensive but they conduct heat very efficiently. The most commonly used size is about 12 in in diameter and the shape varies a little: some have straight sides, some curved sides. A *sauteuse* is particularly practical when preparing dishes where the recipe calls for pieces of raw meat (such as chicken, veal, beef etc.) to be shallow fried and sealed where efficient heat conductivity is a great help, and deep enough to accommodate the addition of liquid, whether thickened or not to make a sauce (a good example is blanquette of veal). These pans must not be heated when empty and must never be placed over very high heat as this will cause the tin lining to blister and they will then need re-tinning. The handles become hot, so use a thick oven cloth to hold them. Small versions are also useful. Enameled cast-iron *sauteuses* are also available: these differ in design but are a practical and cheaper alternative.

Seal. To cook raw food (e.g. meat, fish, vegetables) briefly in fat (lard, butter or oil) over high heat, turning the food so that a cooked outer layer forms and seals in all the juices and flavour, usually browning the surface more or less lightly as you do so.

White sauce. To serve 6: 3 tbsp (scant ¼ cup) butter; scant ½ cup all-purpose flour; 1¾–2¼ cups cold water or cold chicken broth; ½ tsp fine salt; freshly ground white pepper to taste. Melt the butter in a saucepan over low heat, add the flour, and stir until smooth. Continue stirring over the heat until the mixture starts to bubble and froth. Add the cold liquid, increase the heat, and keep stirring without interruption as the mixture gradually comes to a boil and thickens. Add the rest of the liquid a little at a time if the sauce is too thick. Season with salt and pepper and continue stirring over the heat until the sauce returns to a boil.

GENERAL INDEX

INDEX BY REGION

INDEX BY REGION

INDEX OF WINES

Picture sources

AFE, Milan (Walter Leonardi) : pages 108, 109a, 109b.
Agenzia Luisa Ricciarini, Milan : pages 38r, 40a, 40b, 72b (V. Rossi), 217.
Agenzia Laura Ronchi, Milan : page 215 (Piero Orlandi).
Centro documentazione Mondadori : pages 106–107 (M. De Biasi).
Christian Délu, Paris : pages 19, 46, 50, 53, 63, 84, 104, 141, 144.
Explorer, Paris : pages 132–133 (P. Lorne), 134 (L.-Y. Loirat), 135a (P. Thomas), 135b (A. Le Toquin), 136 (P. Roy), 137a (A. Perier), 137b (L.-Y. Loirat), 158-159 (Goudouneix), 160 (Goudouneix), 161a (R. Le Bastard), 161b (R. Le Bastard), 162 (R. Le Bastard), 163b (Goudouneix), 180 (F. Jalain).
Maurizio Fraschetti, Rome : pages 68-69, 70, 71a, 71b, 72a, 73a, 73b.
Katia Kissov (photography) and Nathalie Chassériau Banas (organization), Milan : pages 18, 21, 23, 24, 25, 26, 30, 31, 32–33, 35, 42, 43, 49, 51, 54, 57, 59, 61, 62, 65, 66, 75, 76, 78, 79, 82–83, 85, 90, 92–93, 94, 95, 97, 98–99, 101, 102–103, 113, 114–115, 118, 120, 121, 122–123, 127, 128, 131, 139, 142, 143, 146–147, 148, 149, 151, 152, 155, 156, 164, 166, 167, 168, 169, 170, 171, 173, 174, 175, 176–177, 184–185, 186, 187, 189, 199, 200, 202, 203, 206, 207, 209, 210–211, 218, 220, 221, 225, 227, 229, 230–231, 233. Tableware kindly supplied by : *La Porcellana Bianca, Arezzo* and *Nicola Fasano, Milan*)
Albano Marcarini, Milan : pages 110, 111, 182, 212–213.
Antonio Martinelli, Milan : pages 214a, 216a, 216b.
Francesco Mastrapasqua, Milan : page 181l.
Overseas/Amiard : pages 28, 44, 45, 55, 67, 80, 86–87, 88, 105, 112, 117, 124–125, 138, 153, 170, 188, 190–191, 193, 195, 196–197, 222–223, 228, 296.
Overseas/Explorer : pages 10–11 (H. Berthoule), 12–13 (B. and J. Dupont), 14 (P. Roy), 15a (B. and J. Dupont), 15b (P. Cheuva), 16h (Anderson-Fournier), 16b (Anderson-Fournier), 17a (B. and J. Dupont), 17b, 36–37 (C. Delu), 38l, 39a (Weisbecker), 39b (P. Morel), 41 (F. Jalain), 178–179 (F. Jalain), 181r (P. Lorne), 183a (L.Y. Loirat), 183b (F. Jalain), 214b (F. Jalain), 234–235, 293.
Overseas/Studio Adna : pages 22, 34.
Photo Dossier/Sipa Press : page 110b (Rasmussen).
Prima Press, Milan : pages 27, 29, 48, 204–205.
Francine Recoulez, Milan : page 163a.